Bill Carmody
3 Orchard Street
Port Washington, NY 11050
+1 (646) 867-2252
bill@billcarmody.com
https://www.linkedin.com/in/billcarmody/

July 15, 2025

Dear Reader,

Last year, this book was the foundation of 106 coaches collectively **generating $2,078,897 in just 12-weeks**. This is a self-reported number and, of course, some coaches made $0 and a few made several hundred thousand dollars. The top two earners generated $550,000 and $350,000 each. I myself used the contents of this book to generate $350,000 in my first year of coaching and $850,000 in my second year of coaching. So I can personally attest to its value.

More importantly, I just want to take this opportunity to say, *Thank You!* Thank you for trusting me in this journey together. Thank you for being a powerful coach in the world. And thank you for making this investment in yourself and in your coaching business. I know you just want to make the world dance with the beautiful work you do in your coaching practice.

By growing and scaling your coaching business, you are generating the financial abundance necessary to sustain your own mission and life's purpose. You are supporting your clients to achieve their deepest desired outcome. You are generating appointments in Sage ease and flow. Lastly, you are consistently and expertly converting appointments.

I have placed my very heart and soul in this book so that you may unleash your heart and soul into the world. May you find anything and everything that you need to do the same for others. We were all born into this interconnected web of life in order to serve each other. And so today I am here to serve you so that tomorrow you can serve another human being even more powerfully.

In Love & Gratitude,

Bill Carmody
TEDx Speaker, Bestselling Author &
Creator of AskBill.us (your free AI companion)

SAGE BUSINESS DEVELOPMENT:

Applying Mental Fitness to
Build & Scale Your Coaching Business

Bill Carmody

For permission requests, write to the publisher, addressed "Attention: Permissions Coordinator," at the address below.

Publish Your Purpose
141 Weston Street, #155
Hartford, CT, 06141

Publish
Your Purpose

The opinions expressed by the Author are not necessarily those held by Publish Your Purpose.

Ordering Information: Quantity sales and special discounts are available on quantity purchases by corporations, associations, and others. For details, contact the author at bill@trepoint.com.

ISBN: 979-8-88797-108-7 (hardcover)
ISBN: 979-8-88797-112-4 (ebook)

ARC edition, May 2024.

The information contained within this book is strictly for informational purposes. The material may include information, products, or services by third parties. As such, the Author and Publisher do not assume responsibility or liability for any third-party material or opinions. The publisher is not responsible for websites (or their content) that are not owned by the publisher. Readers are advised to do their own due diligence when it comes to making decisions.

Publish Your Purpose is a hybrid publisher of non-fiction books. Our mission is to elevate the voices often excluded from traditional publishing. We intentionally seek out authors and storytellers with diverse backgrounds, life experiences, and unique perspectives to publish books that will make an impact in the world. Do you have a book idea you would like us to consider publishing? Please visit PublishYourPurpose.com for more information.

TABLE OF CONTENTS

FOREWORD
BY SHIRZAD CHAMINE,
CEO OF POSITIVE INTELLIGENCE

"Money is the source of all evil, and those who pursue financial prosperity are greedy."

For the longest time, even as CEO of the largest coach training organization in the world, I felt conflicted about money and wealth. A voice in my head kept saying that my heroes, Martin Luther King Jr. and Gandhi, were never about money – and that as coaches, we should focus solely on giving, not taking.

What changed my mind was witnessing the devastating impact of a conflicted money mindset on some of the greatest coaches we were training. I saw how financial scarcity stifled their ability to have their full positive impact on the world. Many were unable to pursue coaching full-time, losing precious hours to less impactful work just to pay the bills. Their limiting beliefs about money and their self-worth drained their mental and emotional energy, sabotaging their ability to build a sustainable coaching business. It did not serve our planet for coaches to operate from a state of financial scarcity.

This became particularly alarming in recent years, as hate, racism, sexism, and divisiveness have risen across the globe. For years, I hoped political leaders would steer us back to a healthier path – until I realized that many politicians were actually fueling these problems, serving their own agendas for power and wealth. It became clear to me: it won't be politicians who heal and save our planet. It will be us – coaches.

While these politicians come and go, we coaches are here to stay. We are servant leaders. We are givers and healers by nature. This is our calling. This is why we are on this planet. And this is our time to rise, to answer the call, and to steer humanity back to its positive potential. As coaches, we hold the key to healing and saving our planet.

And to do so, each coach needs to fulfill their full potential for positive impact. That means having the maximum number of coaching clients and ensuring that the impact on each client is truly lasting and transformational. Financial prosperity both enables and is enabled by this impact.

Your financial prosperity as a coach is a critical enabler of your full potential for positive change in the world.

Inspired by this insight, I granted our Positive Intelligence app-guided mental fitness training to coaches, helping to maximize their impact. This initiative has grown into the largest movement in coaching history, with over 100,000 coaches participating as of this writing.

A key component of this breakthrough program is the Sage Business Development curriculum, which is illustrated in this book. Its profound effectiveness lies in its synthesis of best business development practices with the research-backed Positive Intelligence Operating System. This integration reflects a vital truth: even the best business development techniques fail when handled by Saboteurs, and they thrive when led by Sage Powers. In other words, mindset and mental fitness are core essentials to achieving breakthrough success in business development.

The sage mind behind Sage Business Development is Bill Carmody, a passionate purpose-driven creative force whom I am privileged to call a friend and colleague. Before we partnered, Bill built and exited a $25 million marketing agency. He then became a coach, making $350K in his first year and $850K in his second. Pained by how many gifted coaches struggled financially, Bill developed the impactful *Millionaire Coaches Marketing Playbook*.

His program helped many participants achieve breakthrough financial outcomes, proving the methods' power. Yet, some participants struggled despite having the same tools. What was the difference, Bill wondered? Mindset. Specifically, Saboteur versus Sage mindset.

In Saboteur mode, business development for a coach is at best a chore, and too often a source of great anxiety, guilt, shame, self-judgment, procrastination and avoidance. You might feel you're not good enough and ready to put yourself out there, or to charge significantly for your services. You might worry about being salesy or pushy as you offer your services. You might feel scared about truly focusing on a niche and instead try to be all things to all people.

You might operate on the old paradigm of no-pain no-gain, forever guilty that you are not working hard enough to build your business. And you might feel conflicted about truly experiencing financial prosperity, based on old stories about money and how worthy you are.

In Sage mode, business development is fueled by ease and flow, guided by empathy for yourself and others, curiosity, creativity, passion, purpose, and clear-headed fearless laser-focused action. You feel you are more than ready to put yourself out there, and to charge significantly for your services. You don't feel pushy or salesy as your focus is never on you. Instead, you joyfully and lovingly deliver lifechanging gifts to people – the gift of them creating the life they want through working with you. And you are at peace about whether they choose to receive that gift. You confidently focus on a niche that enables you to truly differentiate your messaging, outreach, and services for your prospects and clients.

Rather than relying on discipline to push through, the Sage way emphasizes ease and flow. When something feels hard, you get curious about how your Saboteurs are making things hard, so you find your way back to ease and flow. You revel in how your financial prosperity serves you, your loved ones, your clients, and our planet, by enabling your maximum contribution.

Bill's brilliant work on Sage Business Development has been refined through many iterations and tested with great success. Early drafts of this book were used in the WealthBuilder Program, where a single group of 12 coaches generated over $1 million in 12 weeks. Along the way, most participants shattered limiting beliefs about self-worth, the true value of their coaching, and their relationship with money. Many raised their fees significantly – despite initial hesitation.

Given my own conflicted feelings about money and prosperity, I was skeptical of business development experts who preached prosperity for coaches. There was a pivotal moment in my conversations with Bill when I saw clearly that he was the one to partner with. Over a dinner meeting in San Francisco, Bill shared about his own paralyzing fears of financial scarcity and lack of control while growing up. He shared how after he had achieved prosperity as a coach, he felt it as his life's mission to eliminate scarcity for others. This passion was particularly heartfelt towards the generous coaches around the globe who deserved so much more. The tears in his eyes as he spoke about his mission moved me deeply. Here was a servant leader who was so clear about his calling to serve, and best in the world with the skillset required for that calling.

That passionate focus is the source of the inspiring creativity you'll witness throughout this book. Bill's personal writing style will also give you a glimpse of the loving and soulful man behind these ideas.

Sage Business Development synthesizes proven business development practices with research-backed tools for shifting to the Sage mindset required for their success. The results have already been spectacular for those who have applied its principles. I believe you'll experience similar success as you implement the wisdom in these pages.

Here's to your prosperity, so you can have the full positive impact you're meant to have on our beautiful planet.

With love and gratitude,
Shirzad Chamine
San Francisco, California, January 2025

OVERVIEW

I n 2019, I was "done". Having received my Professional Certified Coach (PCC) from the International Coaching Federation (ICF) in 2018, I had spent the last two years building and scaling my own coaching business to the high six figures in revenue. I was on and could see a clear path to generating more than a million dollars in coaching and training revenue in 2020 without any employees working, and from the comfort of my home. What's more, I had worked it out with my clients that I would take the entire month of July off so that I could spend quality time with my kids.

Life was amazing and the only thing that was truly troubling me was that so many of my professional coaching peers were struggling financially. In fact, at that time the latest report from the ICF stated that the medium income for a professional coach was around $50,000 with some coaches making as little as $27,100 and that broke my heart.

That summer, I visited my mom in Santa Rosa, California and on a whim decided to reach out to the very first coach who had made a seismic impact on my life. Shirzad Chamine was New York Times bestselling author of *Positive Intelligence* and had entered my life when I was at odds with my then two business partners. Shirzad had modeled for me what was possible when working with an executive coach. In what felt like no time at all, I went from plotting my escape from my business partners to truly seeing each of them for who they were and what they were trying to accomplish. With Shirzad's help, I had let go my myopic point of view of my business partners and began seeing new possibilities; ones that would help us more than double the growth of our company and remain together for many years longer than I had ever thought possible.

On this trip, I wanted to thank Shirzad for his incredible influence in my life. It was because of him that I decided I wanted to be a coach and now that I was building my own coaching practice, I wanted to take the time to meet him face to face and thank him for the incredible value he had delivered to me, my family and ultimately the seventy-five employees and their families who vicariously benefited from his working with me and my business partners. I was excited to catch up with him and share the incredible turn my life had taken.

When I reached out, Shirzad graciously accepted my invitation to have dinner in San Francisco. And after I had expressed my gratitude, the conversation naturally turned to what Shirzad was working on. At the dinner table, he asked me to take both my thumbs and index fingers and rub them together with such fine attention to detail that I could feel the fingertip ridges on each finger. I did that for about two minutes and then he asked me to check in with myself and see what I was experiencing. I noticed that I was calm ... peaceful ... and fully present. Upon deeper reflection, I noticed that I had slowed down, was breathing deeply and experiencing a sense of relaxation. Any stress I was holding in my shoulders seemed to melt away.

Curious, I asked him what that was. He referred to the experience as a two minute PQ Rep and reminded me that he had written about it in his book which I had read in 2012 when it was first published. "Huh," I thought, "I don't remember doing this from his book." He then invited me to be his guest and try out his six-week Positive Intelligence mental fitness program. I expressed my gratitude once again for his generosity and accepted his offer to try out his program.

Fast forward two months. After taking his program, not only did I feel like a new person, but I immediately began using his work in my coaching practice. I used his free Saboteur Assessment on the Positive Intelligence website with all of my coaching clients and began integrating his work into my coaching practice. As I suspected, his program wasn't just helping me be a better coach, it was helping my clients become what I referred to as "self-cleaning ovens." In other words, as soon as my clients adopted his mental fitness operating system, our work together as coach and client shifted in a very powerful way. Now, instead of bringing up symptoms of problems, my clients were consistently getting to the heart of their struggles and using mental fitness to make different choices in the moment. The impact was swift and transformational.

"Shirzad," I exclaimed, "I feel like I'm stealing your intellectual property! You gifted me your program and it's had a profound impact not just on my life, but the lives of every client I've introduced your program to. Why don't you create a coaching program based on this platform so that I can properly compensate you for all the incredible work you'd developed?"

"I'm glad you see what I see," Shirzad replied. "Why don't you come help me build it?"

"Oh no, I think you misunderstood," I said. "I meant that *you* should build something for coaches. I wasn't pitching you on my work."

And that led to a two-hour conversation about Shirzad's vision. "Can you imagine," he asked, "what the world would be like if every person had this mental fitness operating system? Think about what that impact would be if every person showed up as their best self and had the tools to see, in the moment, how their own negative self-talk is stopping them. And who better to bring this work into the world than coaches?"

Damn it. He was right. But I had vowed never to work for anyone ever again. Besides, hadn't I worked hard enough these past 25 years? Now that I was on a trajectory to create a seven-figure income for myself as a coach, did I really want to step off that path so that I could help Shirzad with his vision? I wasn't ready to let go of what I had started out to do only two years prior. I knew what sacrifices it would take to build a company from a relatively early start-up phase to the kind of business Shirzad was committed to building. This was going to be a very different path than the one I was currently on.

To his credit, Shirzad wasn't trying to disrupt my own plans. Instead, he asked me to take a step back and align to my own life's purpose. He asked me a powerful coaching question: "At the end of your life, what is it that you will be glad that you accomplished?" I closed my eyes and really thought about what he was asking. I don't know how many minutes passed before I finally opened my eyes and told him, "**I am committed to helping coaches become financially free. I deeply desire to have coaches receive their worth so that they may be well compensated for the incredibly noble profession they have chosen.**"

"Great," he replied. And then followed up with another question. "In your current coaching business, how many coaches do you feel you can impact in the remaining time you plan on working?"

Between my 1:1 coaching, group coaching and training, I could envision impacting several hundred over the coming decades, and so I said as much.

To which he continued, "And what if you had my technology platform to work with? How many coaches could you impact at scale?"

My head exploded.

For the first time, I saw clearly that Shirzad was inviting me to have a seismic impact in the coaching industry. After the initial blinding glimpse of the obvious wore off, I saw the truth in the answer. "I believe that together we can **positively impact 100,000 coaches** and forever change their lives through teaching them mental fitness AND business development best practices."

And after saying that out loud, I began to tear up. I couldn't speak anything more as I choked up. Shirzad held the space for me and asked me what was coming up for me.

"It's just that ..." I paused as I could feel the tears roll down my cheeks. I started again, "It's just that I never imagined that I could be the one to do this ... to have that kind of impact in my own life and the lives of so many. Because when we do this ..." I noticed that I was already jumping to this preordained outcome, "...it means we'll impact **millions of lives**! Just do the math. If each coach impacts just 100 clients over their career, that means 10 million people will be impacted by our work. And most coaches will work with many more clients than that over their lifetime."

That was the moment that I decided to change the trajectory of my career. Yes, I knew that I could always rebuild my own coaching and training business. The opportunity to serve 100,000 coaches was just too compelling. How could I not step into this new possibility for myself?

While I'm happy to share more of this story, I'd like to fast forward to 2022. As I write these words, just two years after our initial launch, more than 20,000 coaches have already completed our multimillion-dollar grant program[1] and many thousands of those coaches went on to our advanced PQ Coach[2] training program including my Business Development track.

Among the greatest joys in my life today are all the incredible success stories I hear from our PQ Coach community. Coaches who once struggled to make ends meet, have landed opportunities that range from $20,000 in a single month to an annual six -figure contract with a single client. Nearly every day I hear from coaches who tells me the profound shift they have experienced in their lives and the lives of their clients.

Those who have applied the mental fitness operating system to their business development efforts are not only achieving their own financial freedom, they are doing it with ease and flow. And that brings us to you, my cherished reader. I've written this book for YOU. Perhaps we've already met as part of the PQ Coach membership program or perhaps someone from that program recommended this book to you. Either way, I'm so excited to have you on this journey with me.

This Book Is For Coaches

I am writing this book for coaches and aspiring coaches. You may already have your certification or you may be thinking about becoming a certified professional coach. Wherever you are on your coaching journey, this book will help you. In fact, I'll be so bold as to say that what I'm going to share with you has the power to forever transform you, your clients and the world. That's a big ass claim! How do I back that up? By the thousands of coaches that I'm already working with each and every day. This book was designed to empower you to step into a much bigger game than most coaches believe they can play. If you apply what is shared in this book, you can't help but be transformed and dramatically expand the business end of your coaching business.

---

[1] For more information on our multimillion-dollar grant program, please visit PositiveIntelligence.com/100x

[2] For more information on our PQ Coach membership program, please visit PositiveIntelligence.com/go

This means you'll make a greater impact for yourself, your family and the lives of the clients you choose to serve.

If you are neither a coach nor have any inclination to become a coach, you can still get value out of the pages that follow, but please know that my heart is and forever will be with coaches. Why is that? I believe coaches are some of the most powerful givers in the world today. Coaches, by their very nature, are empathetic and care about making the world better. What else draws someone into a profession whereby they believe that each of their clients have the best answers for their own lives and that they are whole, perfect and complete. At present, coaches tend to join the coaching profession as a way to give. They aren't drawn in thinking that they will become financially free from working in the coaching profession, but this book is designed to eradicate that limiting belief.

Why Listen To What I'm Sharing?

At last count, there are several thousands of coaching schools certified by the ICF. Why should you care what I have to contribute? Prior to joining Positive Intelligence, I built and exited two multimillion-dollar marketing businesses and know what it takes to build a company from the ground up. If you're interested in my full bio, you can read it at the back of this book. For now, let me highlight the most relevant parts I think you'll be interested in.

I have studied several seven-figure coaches. I had an incredible multi-year journey with Tony Robbins, including multiple one-on-one interviews for his movie *Tony Robbins: I'm Not Your Guru* and his books *Money: Master the Game* and *Unshakeable*. I've had the distinct pleasure to meet with Rich Litvin, co-author of the *Prosperous Coach*. Likewise, I've spent quality time with Peter Cook, co-author of *The Thought Leaders Practice*. I've met with and interviewed Kendall Summerhawk and Suzanne Evans, both who command seven-figure coaching practices.

In my own coaching practice, I trained with Peter J. Reding, author of *Positively Brilliant Self-Mastery* and the co-founder of the *Coach for Life Institute* where I received my Professional Certified Coach (PCC) with the ICF. I've also trained with Bettie J Spruill, founder of Ontological Living. During my two-year journey with Tony Robbins, I completed his Leadership Academy and became a Senior Leader as a volunteer role at his events (i.e. the people with the bright orange shirts if you've been to a Tony Robbins event). I studied with the ALTRU Center to become a transformational trainer. And I've shared much of my incredible journey through the more than 350 articles published on Inc.com, Forbes.com and Entrepreneur.com during my tenure as a contributing writer.

But most of all, I've spent the last three years getting to know thousands of coaches who have the same struggles you have (or will) face. I care deeply about the business success of coaches and how they can use Positive Intelligence's mental fitness operating system for themselves and the benefit of their clients.

I'm On My Own Journey Too!

It's important that I also share with you that I'm not "done" by any stretch of the imagination. In fact, I decided to write this book as part of my own quest. Please allow me to explain.

Shirzad saw that one of the biggest downfalls of most founder-led organizations is that when the founder is no longer part of the company, the company struggles and risks imploding. We've all seen this where a powerful leader is no longer part of the company they founded and as a result the company struggles to continue to grow and thrive. Shirzad spent a lot of time thinking about how Positive Intelligence could continue to grow and expand regardless of his individual contributions.

What Shirzad came up with was the concept of Firekeepers. It was the answer to the question, "Who will light the fire of mental fitness when I'm no longer able to do so?" We then shared this vision with our PQ Coach members and received more than 500 applications. As difficult as it was, we whittled these applications down to 44 interviews and selected 15 to launch our inaugural Firekeeper initiative.

I was fortunate to be among the 15 selected and to kick off our work together, each of us was asked to declare a quest. Mine was this book. I needed something that would stretch me over the six months we'd be working together as a group. What would truly agitate each of my Saboteurs – especially my Judge, Controller and Hyper-Achiever – so that I could practice my own Saboteur Intercepts and, as a result, strengthen my connection to each of my five Sage Powers: Empathy, Explore, Innovate, Navigate and Active?

I even pondered if writing this book was an act of my Hyper-Achieve masking as my Sage. After all, I already have a full-time job as the Head of Coaching for Positive Intelligence. Did I really need to add writing a book in addition to be part of the Firekeepers and my role at Positive Intelligence?

The only way to answer that question in Sage was to do my own PQ Reps. I did a 30-minute PQ Gym session so that I could go deep into my own Sage wisdom and listen. There, I heard clearly that what I had to share was important and would take all that I had worked on in the past thirty years to a new level. Yes, this effort would challenge and stretch me. Having written two other books, I had no illusions of what it would take to write this one. But all I had to do is envision you, my reader, to know that this effort was worth any and all challenges that I would face along this journey to completion.

I say this with all humility: "I am on my own journey, too." I am not "the expert" nor do I claim to have all the answers. I acknowledge that I have made some epic mistakes in business and in life and rather than labeling them "failures" I choose to see each of them as "lessons" and ultimately beautiful gifts of knowledge, power and inspiration.

And that is what I offer you in this book. I will share the best practices that I have both learned from the millionaire coaches I've had the pleasure of interviewing and have subsequently put into my own practice with incredible results. I have further tested these best practices with thousands of our PQ Coach members and continued to refine them based on both the success and lessons they have shared back with me.

What I can say for certain is that when you choose to travel this path of working on the business end of your coaching business, you will meet each of your Saboteurs along the way. In these moments, you will have a choice: "Better or Bitter." Do you choose to become *better* as you strengthen your Sage powers, or will you choose to become *bitter* as you allow your Judge and Accomplice Saboteurs to beat you up emotionally when you're feeling down?

When you fully embrace that this **IS** a choice and it's **YOUR** choice to make, you will have already begun your path towards Sage Mastery.

Be | Do | Have

Sage Mastery is being, not doing or having. Who you become when working on the business end of your coaching business is far more valuable than what you do or even what you have as a result.

Most of us have this backwards. When I talk to coaches, the conversation usually goes something like this:

> Me: *What do you want?*
> Coach: To have a successful, million-dollar coaching practice.
> Me: *Why do you want this?*
> Coach: So that I can have the life I want.
> Me: *Who must you become in order to have the life you want?*
> Coach: [Silent reflection]. I'm not sure.

Given enough time to allow silent reflection, the answer usually emerges. The focus shifts from *having* the life this coach wants to *doing* whatever is necessary to have this life, and eventually *being* the fully expressed best version of him or herself in order to have it all.

And so yes, this book will lay out the daily practices and *doingness* exercises that are necessary for building, growing and having the coaching business you're after. That's what you came for and I'm committed to having you have it. Just don't forget, the real work isn't the *having* or the *doing*, it's the *being* that will ensure your success.

This is your invitation to begin (or continue) your journey towards Sage Mastery Sage Mastery is your ultimate expression of your true self. It is not your ego (which is often driven by your Saboteurs), it is your spirit that connects you to everything. Your spirit is infinite and so is the power that aligns with the infinite.

When you hear the words, "All I need is within me now," it's your Sage being called forward. Your Sage is ever present and sometimes is drowned out by your Saboteurs. This journey will help strengthen your Sage Powers and weaken your Saboteurs. That's the real gift of this work. You will become the best version of yourself as you invite your Sage forward and allow your Saboteurs to take a back seat.

And yes, the measurable outcome is a highly successful coaching business that will enable you to become financially free. The less tangible, albeit more noticeable shift will be your way of being. Who you become in this journey will create a noticeable shift that others will comment on. The people closest to you will notice it first, then friends and even acquaintances. The more you live this work, the more your Sage will become ever-present. You'll notice your own energy increase, your focus and productivity will be the highest it's ever been and your emotional state will be positive and happy most of the time.

That is the high bar we are establishing right up front. This is the mountain we choose to climb together or not at all. "Do, or do not, there is no try," says Master Yoda of Star Wars. When we decide to do something, we're all in. The word "try" is a Saboteur qualifier that minimizes the effort and sows seeds of doubt. There's not "try" in the work we begin together. Which is why I'm giving you an out right up front. If you're ready to grow your Sage and fully express yourself, then let's get to it. If not, then I thank you for taking the time to read up to this point. Feel free to give this book to another coach you know who is ready to take themselves on. No judgment here either way. Remember, you are always at choice.

Purpose of This Book

The purpose of this book is to share with you the foundational principles necessary in building your coaching business. While it's true that these are the same core principles to building any business, all the applications will be from the perspective of being a coach and building your coaching business.

And, the fabulous twist here is doing all of this work while being in Sage. How do you know you're in Sage (and not being driven by your Saboteurs)? You'll know because all of this work will be accomplished in ease and flow. The minute any of this feels difficult or overwhelming, we're going to pull back and check in to see which Saboteur voice may be messing with you. As Shirzad is fond of saying, "The way of the Sage is ease and flow." When you're not experiencing ease and flow, it's best to stop. Rather than forcing your way through something that's difficult, we're going to continue to do our PQ Reps and enroll our Sage to help us.

While it's true that I believe every coach would benefit from being part of Positive Intelligence's PQ Coach membership, I won't be selling you on that idea beyond mentioning it here. There are no hidden agendas in this book.

Prerequisite Reading of *Positive Intelligence*

What is important to know is that this book has a prerequisite. I'm going to assume that you've already read Shirzad Chamine's book, *Positive Intelligence.* While that is not a requirement for understanding the business development principles I'll be digging into with you in this book, it is a prerequisite for accomplishing all of the desired outcomes while remaining in Sage. If you're not familiar with the mental fitness operating system, you are highly encouraged to familiarize yourself with it before proceeding. While you are free to proceed with the rest of the content without having read that book, know that I'm assuming you have and that I'm not going to be spending a lot of time repeating what has already been published in this NY Times bestseller.

With that, if you're ready to being our journey together, I invite you to open your heart and your mind as we discover how best to build and scale your own successful and highly profitable coaching business – all (or mostly) from the comfort of your home doing what you already love to do. Let's begin!

CHAPTER ONE

Your Journey of Self-Actualization & Application to Business Development

W elcome! I'm excited to share part of the ultimate journey of humanity with you. As each of us discovers why we are here, we begin our journey towards self-actualization. While there are many activities in our lives, when we zoom out to see the entirety of our life, it's our journey toward self-actualization that truly matters. Everything that's not actively moving you toward self-actualization becomes a distraction – either a temporary one or something that takes you further from your desired outcome.

Can building your coaching business really bring your closer to self-actualization?

Yes, and so much more than most people realize. Think about what your journey towards self-actualization is really about. "Self-actualization is the complete realization of one's potential, and the full development of one's abilities and appreciation for life."[3] Said another way, self-actualization is your journey toward Sage Mastery – your ability to remain your Sage self in even the most challenging situations and life conditions.

How does one master their Sage self? You don't do it inside your comfort zone. Instead, you stretch yourself by getting out of your comfort zone while remaining in ease and flow. Therein lies both the challenge and opportunity. How does one get out of their comfort zone while remaining Sage?

Your Saboteurs would have you believe in the false premise of, "No pain, no gain." They want you to believe the lie that only through hardship, struggle and suffering will you be able to shift, change and evolve. That's because your brain was not designed to make you happy – it was designed to keep you safe. Your brain is this incredibly

---

[3]   https://www.simplypsychology.org/self-actualization.html

powerful tool that processes immense volumes of information is designed to look for dangers – real or perceived – and keep you out of harm's way. Short-term pleasures and immediate comfort feel good in the moment, but they rarely lead to sustainable growth and prosperity.

"According to Abraham Maslow ... self-actualized people have an acceptance of who they are despite their faults and limitations, and experience the drive to be creative in all aspects of their lives. While self-actualizers hail from a variety of backgrounds and a diversity of occupations, they share notable characteristics in common, such as the ability to cultivate deep and loving relationships with others.[4]

Coaches already have the foundational building blocks for self-actualization. Many, however, are limited by their inability to receive. Coaches tend to be incredible givers. And yet, a coach's resistance or inability to open up to receive prevents the very duality that leads to self-actualization. Ease and flow is about accepting whatever is present and in the moment and then deciding what Sage action(s) to take.

Business development, for most coaches anyway, stirs up all your Saboteurs that prevent you from being your Sage self. Rather than avoiding deep-seated fears that show up in precisely the most inopportune moments, your journey towards self-actualization and Sage Mastery is about allowing these fears to show up in predictable, yet containable and productive ways that allow you to learn, grow and blossom into the very Sage you were born to be.

Mastering the Three x Four Matrix

In Shirzad Chamine's book, *Positive Intelligence*, he presented the three elements to mental fitness: (1) Weaken Your Saboteurs, (2) Strengthen Your Sage and (3) Build Your Self-Command (PQ Brain) Muscles. In order to master business development there are four foundations: (1) Niche and Ideal Clients, (2) Irresistible Offer, (3) Generating Appointments and (4) Converting Appointments. When you put this three x four matrix together, it looks like this:

	Weaken Saboteurs	Strengthen Sage	Build Self Command
Niche / Ideal Clients			
Irresistible Offer			
Generating Appointments			
Converting Appointments			

---

[4] https://www.simplypsychology.org/self-actualization.html

Your journey towards self-actualization and mastery of your Sage is one of discovery as you apply each of the three elements of mental fitness to each of the four foundations of business development. Sounds simple enough, right? And yet, there's so much to unpack in each of these areas.

This book will show you how each of your Saboteurs stop you from having the coaching business of your dreams – the one you know you're capable of having, but for some reason appears to be evading you. We'll explore how to apply each Sage Power toward each of the foundations of business development. And we'll hold the Sage Perspective that every problem and challenge you run into can be turned into a gift and opportunity that will support you in your journey towards self-actualization and Sage Mastery. Building your coaching business using the Sage Business Development methods will also support you in building your PQ brain muscles along the way.

It's not enough to understand and implement the four foundations of any coaching business. That's because a Saboteur-driven implementation leads to predictable results. When your Saboteurs are in the driver's seat, it simply doesn't matter how much effort you're putting into your coaching business; these efforts won't be effective. In the chapters that follow, I'll provide specific and concrete examples. For now, it's enough to share that when you are living in fear and in scarcity, no amount of effort will attract love and abundance into your life. Only by intercepting your Saboteurs, strengthening your Sage Powers and maintaining the Sage Perspective will you build and grow the coaching business of your dreams.

Every "Failure" Gets You One Step Closer to Self-Actualization

As part of this journey, we're going to reframe the concept of "failure" into one of "learning." Failure, by definition, is a lack of success. While learning, by definition is "the acquisition of knowledge or skills through experience, study, or by being taught."[5] A lesson is learned through life experience. Rather than seeing a lesson as "failure" if we can reframe as learning, then we can begin to see ourselves as life-long learners.

In that respect, every "failure" gets you one step closer to self-actualization. Rather than seeing a lack of success, when you see clearly the lesson you're learning and how it applies to your Sage Mastery, you can never fail – but you can be in constant learning mode.

That's what life and this journey toward self-actualization is all about. Rather than being stopped by any challenge, we reframe the challenge into a gift and opportunity (i.e. the Sage Perspective) and get really curious about what we're learning as it's happening. Instead of avoiding taking bold action, we seek it out. In fact, the more

---

[5]   https://www.google.com/search?q=learning+defined

actions we take, the more lessons we learn and the faster we grow, expand and strengthen our Sage Powers and Sage Perspective.

That's why business development is and can be your journey toward self-actualization. As you discover what works, what doesn't work and how your ways of being impact your ability to enroll clients into your coaching practice, you are growing your Sage. Rather than being stopped by your Saboteurs, you see what's been in your blind spot all these years. You may still experience the body sensations you previously described as "fear", but now those same sensations trigger excitement and joy as if you were a child discovering a new toy or game.

Imagine what it would be like to seek out and get excited by what you previously referred to as "failure" and now embrace as a learning opportunity. Instead of avoiding the things that felt challenging or risked potential "failure", you began to seek them out … regularly and with a deep sense of curiosity and passion.

This is the journey we begin together.

While we will most certainly pick up and discuss concrete strategies and design tactical execution plans, none of that matters if these strategies and plans are Saboteur-led. We'll spend more time highlighting how your Saboteurs have previously prevented you from having the coaching business of your dreams, then work on intercepting these Saboteurs, strengthening your Sage Powers and holding that Sage Perspective. In that way, your Sage-led strategies and tactical execution plans will have a significantly higher probability of succeeding.

Your learning with each step along the way will strengthen your resolve and remind you of the path you're on; how each "failure" is taking you one step closer to self-actualization. As you discover and connect with more of your Sage, you open up your one-of-a-kind unique self. This is your true self. And your true self is what the world needs right now – especially your niche and ideal customers. They don't need a manufactured duplicate of someone else. They need the fully authentic and vulnerable you as their coach. This includes how they find you, connect with you and are enrolled by you.

The way of the Sage is ease and flow. Business development is no different. Business development calls upon your Sage to ensure that your true self is who is seen by the people who need you the most. And when you embrace that to be extraordinary in business development, you must first step into your Sage, you'll experience the ease and flow like never before. After all, your Sage self is your true self and all I'm asking is for you to be your true self throughout this journey. It's that simple and that challenging. When you are able to be your Sage self the majority of the time, then you will show up differently and attract the very people who need you most. When you do it, you'll be shocked at just how easy all of this is. And your Saboteurs will scream that this can't possibly be the path for the very reason that it's "too easy."

Be Sage To Be Extraordinary in Business Development

The Sage path is an extraordinary path. When your Sage is fully present, so too are you. People crave authenticity now more than ever before. In world obsessed with looking good and a near obsession with carefully curated image projection in every conceivable medium, it's exceedingly rare to see the real person behind all the facades. That's why when we do see a person fully in their Sage, we honor them with our full focus and attention.

I fell in love with Brené Brown from the very first viewing of her very first TED talk[6]. Scratch that. It happened within the first few lines of her very first TED talk. It happened so viscerally that I used the beginning of her TED talk when training companies on storytelling and presentations skills.[7] She tells the story of how she came to call herself a "researcher-storyteller" and if you haven't watched this particular TED talk with over 57 million views, you're in for a treat. She speaks to her audience as if the two of you were long lost friends catching up and having coffee together. Her talk on *The Power of Vulnerability* is epic because she demonstrates her own vulnerability in her talk *about* vulnerability.

Said another way, Brené Brown is truly a Sage on the stage. She embodies the very qualities that your Sage instantly recognizes. I felt drawn to her immediately because I felt her heart. I was compelled to buy her book, *Daring Greatly* and was both inspired and emotionally connected to her groundbreaking work. Her words moved me to tears more than once and I just knew this woman had changed the world and would continue to do so. From her books to her Netflix special, Brené Brown walks the path of her Sage.

And your Saboteurs might be tempted to have you think, "Well, yeah, that's Brené Brown. I'm not nearly as successful as she is and never will be." But if you watched her Netflix special, you know that all that success came *after* she choose the path of vulnerability, after she called upon her own Sage and quieted her Saboteurs.

And this is my deepest desire for you. Yes, I'd love for you to build a seven-figure coaching business and I'll show you everything I've learned about how to do just that. Financial freedom and living in total abundance is amazing and yet, it's a *result* of being Sage. You become as successful as those you admire most *when* you embody your Sage. It's the beingness that matters most – not the doing or even the having.

---

[6]   https://www.ted.com/talks/brene_brown_the_power_of_vulnerability?language=en
[7]   See http://micdropcourse.com/ for details.

Be | Do | Have

Most people have it backwards and this is an important point to clear up from the start. Your Saboteurs have it backwards and focus on "Have | Do | Be." Your Saboteurs incorrectly believe that only when you *have* whatever it is you are after will you then *do* what is necessary and *be* the person you know you're capable of being. Other of your Saboteurs think it's "Do | Be | Have" which is equally incorrect. These Saboteurs believe that it's all about the doing first. That only when you *do* the correct actions will you *have* the outcomes you want and *be* the person you know you're capable of being.

I'm here to tell you that neither of these approaches work. The only one that does is "Be | Do | Have." When you embody your Sage you are focusing on your ways of being. No matter what's going on around you, you are always at choice with who you choose to be. Your beingness matters more than your doingness or whatever you have. The belief that you must have something or do something before focusing on who you are being is a Saboteur lie. We'll get into this more when we unpack each of the Saboteurs and how they negatively impact your business development efforts.

For now, what's important to understand is that when you fully embody your Sage beingness, you are unstoppable. (By the way, I refer to my Sage self as "UnstoppaBill"). Your Sage essence is your ultimate beingness. It is your embodiment of pure love. Your Sage essence is free of guilt, shame, anger, fear and other negative emotions. When you are your Sage self, you walk the path towards enlightenment and self-actualization. The longer you are able to stay in Sage, the closer you are toward self-actualization.

And there's no better arena to practice calling upon your Sage than in building your coaching business. To have a thriving coaching business, you'll need to do the right things (which are shared in this book), but first you must activate your Sage before you can regularly take these vetted, tested and proven steps. Executing the same strategies driven by your Saboteurs produces and equally predictable result. They simply don't work. That's why beingness is so important before focusing on your doingness.

Sage Business Development looks like this:

1. Activate Your Sage (This is who you choose to BE)
2. In Sage, Grow Your Coaching Business via Four Foundations (This is what do DO)
3. Serve Your Clients Powerfully and Experience Abundance (This is what You HAVE)

No matter how much you wish to *have* a thriving coaching business now, it won't matter what you *do*, until you activate and *be* your Sage. Being your Sage means remaining in the most powerful version of yourself by weakening your Saboteurs, strengthening your Sage powers and building your self-command (PQ Brain) muscles.

That's why the first part of this book focuses here. Your Saboteurs will lie to you and tell you that none of this is important and that you should just skip to the next section and get into the four foundations of every coaching business. That would be a big mistake. Let me tell you why.

Tale of Two Groups of Coaches With Vastly Different Results

In my early years of supporting coaches in the business end of their coaching business, I was surprised when I experienced a divide and mixed results in my training course. I had created what I believed to be a "fool-proof" way to building and scaling your coaching business. I ran a few pilots free of charge and then offered a full money back guarantee to kick off my training program. The feedback was consistent. Something akin to, "This is *THE* best marketing and business training program I've ever experienced for coaches."

I would thank them for the compliment and then ask about their results. While some of the coaches had applied what they learned and were on their way to building six and seven-figure coaching businesses, some appeared to be stuck. Same feedback, vastly different results. None of these coaches shared that my program wasn't valuable. They were convinced that I had delivered well above any expectation they could possibly imagine. So why did some appear to be getting the full benefit of the training and others appeared to be stuck at the starting line?

The more I dug into it, the more I discovered the dichotomy of *knowing* what to do versus actually *doing* what needed to be done. Not a single participant was confused about what actions were required to build and grow the kind of coaching business they wanted. Some dove right in and others just stood there not taking action.

I didn't have the language, knowledge or understanding at the time to share what I now understand, as I had not yet completed Shirzad's flagship six -week mental fitness program myself. The group of coaches who were successful and implemented what they learned tapped into their own Sage while the coaches who were stuck allowed their Saboteurs to stop them.

But Bill, That's Not Me! I'm an Active PQ Coach Member!!!!

Right, and that's why I'm sharing this right here and right now. Because when it happened again with some of our very own PQ Coach members, I was shocked. "Really?" I thought. "Seriously?" How is it even possible that members of our own PQ Coach membership program at Positive Intelligence could have access to Shirzad

Chamine's life-changing work combined with my proven business development track and still struggle?

That's when I discovered the same issues exist. A coach can *know* the principles of mental fitness and still not actually live them by *doing* the daily practices that leads to Sage Mastery. Shirzad himself said it best, "Business Development is your black-belt level, Sage Mastery training." It was so blatantly obvious when I stepped back and looked at it. Using another of Shirzad's analogies, if you're regularly lifting a 10-pound weight, you develop 10-pound muscles that can handle 10-pound problems. But when you encounter a 50-pound problem, it's beyond your current 10-pound muscle strength.

That is why developing your own Sage Mastery is so critical to *Sage Business Development*. It is simply not enough to conceptually *understand* the mental fitness operating system and foundations of business development. This book was written so that you can *live* them. As you continue your journey to Sage Mastery and lean into the four foundations of business development, your coaching business will flourish. Understanding both, but practicing only one (or neither) on a daily basis won't produce the results you truly desire – even if you are enrolled in our PQ Coach membership program. That's like having a gym membership, but rarely going to the gym. The membership itself doesn't make you physically fit. Regular workouts do.

That's what the last section of this book is about: integration. What are the daily habits needed to strengthen your Sage Mastery? And what are the daily habits to continue to strengthen and grow each of the four foundations of your coaching business? When you develop your daily habits in each of these areas, you will see the results they produce. Or, as Henry David Thoreau said, "What you *get* by achieving your goals is not as important as what you *become* by achieving your goals."[8]

Darkness & Light

As a coach, you are familiar with the distinctions between dark and light. In our journey towards self-actualization, we can often feel lost and unsure which direction to take. It is in those times that we allow ourselves to be fully present to what's happening all around us. When we are fully present, we can see the action that would take us closer to the light and alternative actions that would move us further away from the light we seek.

It is in these times when we feel lost that some of the most profound breakthroughs can occur for ourselves and those who choose to support through coaching.

---

[8] https://www.themindsetjourney.com/inspirational-quotes/what-you-get-by-achieving-your-goals-is-not-as-important-as-what-you-become-by-achieving-your-goals-henry-david-thoreau/

Uncertainty is part of the mystery of life unfolding. While it may feel more comfortable to "know" or "predict" what happens next. More often than not, we simply don't know for sure. That is the beauty of life. Uncertainty and mystery provide foundations for tremendous growth. Life wouldn't be nearly as interesting if we always knew what was coming and how to respond. Thankfully, that's not our human experience.

And while not knowing precisely what to do at any given moment is part of the life experience, we are never alone or left without guidance. Imagine there is a veil wrapped around your eyes. This veil blinds you to what's all around you. And yet, with your eyes open beneath the veil, you can notice that the darkness is not complete. As you turn your head 365 degrees, there's one direction that always has more light. With each movement towards that light, it becomes easier to see the direction to go. The veil appears to become more translucent allows you to see more than before with each step closer to that light.

Love & Fear

Another way to examine your path towards self-actualization is that every decision in your life is either based in love or fear. Decisions made from love support your journey toward self-actualization. Decisions made from fear move you further away from self-actualization. The problem arises when our decisions appear to be made automatically and without choice. In truth, we are always at choice, although it may not appear that way in the moment.

It is in these moments of decision when it's important that we slow down long enough to see that we are at choice and that one or more of our choices are grounded in love and one or more of our choices are driven by fear. Only when we are clear which choice comes from love are we empowered to continue our journey of self-actualization. Otherwise, fear-based choices prevent us from our continued progress.

Always At Choice (Even When We Feel Lost)

Our day-to-day decision-making reveals where we are in our journey. On any given day, how many of our decisions are grounded in love? Do we even feel that the actions we are taking are choices? There are certainly days when I experience the feeling of powerlessness; that I am a passenger in my life rather than the driver. While that's not true, it certainly feels that way at the time of the experience.

These illusions are powerful and can trap us for a short amount of time or even long stretches of our life. It is our ability to shatter these illusions and break free from our limiting beliefs that empower us to live our best life. The individual decisions matter, but what's more important is our ability to see the choices we are making.

This is especially true when we wake up to the unconscious choices we've made that feeling of being on autopilot.

The moment we see we are operating on automatic, we have the power to get off automatic and see the choices we are making. Before we can make any choice, we must first be aware that there are choices we are making.

Never Not Committed

When we're unsure of the choices we're making, we need to see what we are committed to. Our choices reveal our commitments. Not what we *say* we are committed to, but by our actions what we are *actually* committed to. For example, I may say that I'm "trying to lose weight", but the decision to consume alcohol, snack late at night, and help myself to those sugary treats reveals my actual commitment. Rather than being committed to my health, my actions reveal that I'm committed to short-term pleasure and feeling good.

As we begin this journey together, be willing to explore what is truly stopping you and getting in the way of both your self-actualization and transcendence. As you get clear on the outcomes you're committed to having in your coaching business, notice your current commitments. Often, they are survival skills such as being safe, comfortable, right and in control. When you begin to see what you are committed to (as evidenced by your current actions and current daily habits), you'll see what anchors you have dropped along the way to steady the ship of your life in what was once a turbulent sea. Or perhaps you're still experiencing sizable waves in the ocean of your life. As Jon Kabat-Zinn shared, "You can't stop the waves, but you can learn how to surf."[9]

Learning to Surf the Tidal Waves of Your Life

Developing your Sage Mastery is the equivalent of learning how to surf the gigantic tidal waves in the ocean of your life. You'll never control those waves, but as you become an expert in surfing, you may not want to. That is, once you have the ability to surf the most sizable waves in your life, rather than fearing these waves, you get excited to play and surf them. When you don't know how to surf, big waves are terrifying as they have the power to hold you down in the water and you risk drowning. But when you can surf those waves, you move with incredible speed and feel the rush of the wind as you harness the power of the wave that had terrified you –when you didn't know what to do about it.

---

[9]   https://philosiblog.com/2016/01/21/you-cant-stop-the-waves-but-you-can-learn-how-to-surf/

As you develop your Sage Mastery and apply your learning of the four foundations of any business, these tidal waves will no longer appear as things to avoid at all costs. Instead, you will begin to see them as invitations calling you to your greatness. And to be sure, great surfers don't go from novice to expert without some epic wipeouts. But if you watch carefully, once that surfer's head pops up from the water, they shake it off and get back on their surf board. Some even laugh at the mistake(s) they made as they enjoy the invaluable lesson(s) they were just taught. The bigger the waves, the more focused they become and soon they are riding even the most gigantic tidal waves with ease and flow.

Check in with yourself right now. What are you hearing in your own mind? Excitement or judgment? Is it your Sage calling you forward into this incredible journey? Or do you hear the negative voices of your Saboteurs saying something to the equivalent of, "That will never be me!" If you're already hearing the growing negativity of your Saboteurs, then let's head over to the next chapter together and deeply explore which Saboteurs are stopping you from having the coaching business of your dreams. Since they are already choosing to speak up, let's listen to what they have to say and rather than believe their lies, let's get to the root of their fears which can often stop you from making progress in the areas you are committed to improving.

CHAPTER TWO

How Our Saboteurs Prevent Us From Having The Coaching Businesses We Deserve

Coaching is arguably one of the most noble professions you can choose. A core belief of coaching is that your clients have the best answers for their life. We're not here to give advice, consult, or tell another person how to live their life; instead, as a coach, we hold the space for our clients to look deep within themselves and discover the answer to any challenge or problem they face.

So why is it so difficult for coaches to do the same thing for themselves? As I write this chapter, the ICF's latest report shows that the average coach in North America earns an annual income of $62,500, with a global average of $47,100.[10] For many coaches, this may be an acceptable number either because this is their second (or third) career and/or this is the second income in the household. In other words, if you are not relying on this income exclusively to support yourself and your family, then this represents an acceptable second income stream.

But what if you're the sole breadwinner for yourself and your family? Depending on where you live and the cost of living in your area, you may find it difficult to thrive at this level of income. It most likely isn't building the financial freedom that will allow you to retire comfortably or create wealth for yourself and your family. And because these numbers are averages, that means many coaches are making far less.

Simply put, when I discovered where the coaching industry was financially, I was surprised and dismayed. I experienced my own Saboteurs in this moment. My Judge was judging the situation harshly. "What the hell is wrong with this coaching industry? Who in their right mind would sign up to be a coach with such dismal income levels?

---

[10] https://coachfederation.org/research/global-coaching-study which leads to https://coachingfederation.org/app/uploads/2020/09/FINAL_ICF_GCS2020_ExecutiveSummary.pdf

No wonder the coaching industry is suffering!" It was swift and visceral. I blamed the coaching industry for not doing a better job of paving the way for coaches to earn a decent living. I blamed the coaches who came before me for accepting such low-income numbers. And part of me was just sad and angry that the biggest "givers" in the world weren't receiving the true value of their incredible gifts.

The Sage Perspective

That's when I caught myself and switched to my Sage. I heard Shirzad Chamine's voice in my head that "Every problem can be turned into a gift and opportunity." So what was the gift in such low income numbers? I remained curious and began asking the most successful seven-figure coaches I had access to. First up was Rich Litvin, co-author of *The Prosperous Coach*.[11] I loved his book and wanted to get his take on the state of the coaching industry. Then I spoke with several other seven-figure coaches including Kendall SummerHawk, Peter Cook and Suzanne Evans.

By the time I was done interviewing these bad-ass coaches, I had a really good idea of what the problem most likely was, and so I turned the coaching income problem into each of the three gifts: (1) Gift of Knowledge, (2) Gift of Power, and (3) Gift of Inspiration.

Gift of Knowledge

In order to tap into the gift of knowledge, I needed to answer an important question that Shirzad asks, "What knowledge would I need to gain so that the payoff in the future could be much larger than what this problem is costing me now?"

At the time, I wasn't quite clear on the best answer to this question.

When I tapped into my own Sage Power Empathy, I immediately felt deep empathy for these coaches as well as empathy for their situation. What I learned is that by and large coaches are incredible at what they do and most of them coach because they love being in service to their clients. Most coaches have mastered their ability to give without expectation. Where they struggle is their *ability to receive without resistance*. That was my first gift of knowledge. Knowing that these coaches were incredible givers and struggled with receiving showed me the first reason most coaches don't earn the kind of money they are truly capable of earning.

But I didn't stop there. I stayed curious to see what other insights I could generate. I discovered that most coach training schools spend the bulk of their energy on training coaches how to be great coaches. Duh! But what they tend not to focus on is the business-end of building a coaching business. Fortunately, the International

---

[11]   NOTE: Need to upload my video to http://billcarmody.com/coaches

Coaching Federation (ICF) got that memo and is putting more of an emphasis on business development. That's great for the next generation of coaches in the years to come, but what about the sixty thousand or so coaches who are already out there doing their best to make a living?

It got worse. The more I looked around, what I saw were bottom-feeders preying off coaches who were struggling to make ends meet. This is where I felt physically ill. Everywhere I looked, I saw offers for appointment setting, marketing funnels and various "done for you" services which all promised the world and felt incredibly suspect. The more I explored what was being offered, the more I felt that these services felt a lot like gambling where "the house always wins." In other words, if you don't know what you're doing, there's a big risk of spending what little resources coaches had and not getting the kinds of clients they needed to grow and scale their business.

The more I unpacked, the clearer I became about the problem and how to solve it. Coaches have developed incredible skills from deep listening to asking powerful open-ended questions to being fully present. What was missing was a clear understanding of the core principles of business development and how to grow and scale the business end of their coaching business.

This problem really was a huge gift. The knowledge I uncovered propelled me to see how I could play an important role in the change I deeply desired to see in the coaching industry. Now I began to get excited. And this was only the first of the three gifts. So, I kept going.

Gift of Power

With the gift of power, Shirzad asks us to "See the problem as a weight in a gym, against which muscles can grow. Which mental muscle / power must grow to handle this [problem]? And what is the gift of that power growing?"

For me, I saw my ability to grow all five of my Sage Powers as part of this effort. I saw how (1) having deep **empathy** for coaches and the coaching industry would propel me to (2) **explore** what was preventing coaches from earning substantially more income. This would lead me to (3) **innovate** the kind of education and training needed to connect to my own (4) **navigate** power where I would discover a new-found sense of purpose in my life. And all of this would (5) motivate me to **activate** swiftly and boldly so that I could make a big impact.

Not only would this challenge strengthen each of my five Sage Powers, it would require me to intercept my Saboteurs – especially my Controller and Hyper-Achiever – in order to deliver this education and training content in a powerful and lasting way that would help thousands upon thousands of coaches build the coaching business of their dreams.

So good. And yet, I could sense there was more, so I turned my attention to the third gift.

Gift of Inspiration

This one hardly took any time to see my inspired action. It was more like a blinding glimpse of the obvious. Clearly I was meant to pull together something in order to fill this gap- something that would challenge me to access everything I had learned about marketing and building businesses to support individual coaches with building and growing their coaching business.

It seemed so clear to me that I wanted to check with people I respected to make sure that I wasn't blinded by my own inspiration. I asked the coaches that I went to school with if they would be interested in taking a course with me on applying my last 25 years of building and exiting two multimillion-dollar marketing companies to helping them build their coaching businesses. They looked at me with a bit of shock and awe. Of course! They loved the concept and were happy to be my guinea pigs.

That's all I needed. One-part inspiration, one-part built-in audience and one-part connection to source. I'm not kidding. The moment I put my fingers on the mouse and keyboard, what emerged was organic and surprising to me. It was if I was a bystander watching someone else work. It was an out-of-body experience where I simply observed my fingers type feverishly and my mouse move content around until I found myself in a near trance.

The gift of inspiration kept on giving. The minute I sat down at my computer, I could feel a deep sense of purpose and an energy flow that was tapping into the deepest part of my Sage. I didn't stop to allow my Saboteurs to criticize me. I knew I had a friendly audience who would give me constructive feedback. I'd know what "landed" when I actually presented my material. After all, this was version 1.0 and I just needed to let it out.

As a side note, that's what I'm experiencing right now as I write this to you. While I can't clearly picture you reading this book, I have a sense of our interconnected oneness and that I'm not writing this for me or for Positive Intelligence. I know my Sage is speaking to your Sage and the medium in which I'm able to do this is via the written word. Sure, I'd love to meet you in real life one of these days, but for now I'm inspired to keep going because I trust that what I'm sharing with you will have a seismic impact on your life. That is the true gift of inspiration. It's what wakes me up at 5:00am and won't let me go back to sleep. I'm full of energy and excited to share this journey with you. So let's keep this party going.

Why Creating a Thriving Coaching Business is Essential

Have you taken the time to reflect on how essential *you* are? This is not a rhetorical question. When COVID-19 hit, the concept of an *essential worker* came into our vocabulary. At the time, essential workers started with the medical, police and fire fighter community. Everyone else could stay home, but first responders were desperately needed. Then that included school teachers. Then grocery store staff. Eventually it included supply chains and delivery workers.

But what was hidden beneath all of that? The need for trauma-informed mental health and mental fitness workers. The global pandemic shut much of the world down. It was like musical chairs when the music stopped and we all had to find a seat. Suddenly, for the first time, people were questioning their life choices. "Do I really need to pay this much rent for this tiny apartment? I thought I loved this person, but now that we only have each other, I'm not sure I want to be in this relationship. Is what I'm doing actually a career or just a way to earn a paycheck?" Really important questions were being asked. And most people were making massive life decisions without having a coach to support them processing all of what they were going through, feeling and experiencing.

And yes, the coaching industry did take off during this global pandemic. But with only about 60,000 coaches in the world, and with nearly eight billion people on the planet, the demand was significantly higher than the supply. You may not have been deemed an *essential worker* by the Center for Disease Control (CDC), but your services were in high demand – whether you knew it or not.

Creating a thriving coaching business is essential. It's not just about the money. Clearly, I want you to be financially free and I'm going to do everything in my power to help you get there. But what I'd like you to truly appreciate is just how essential your services are in the world. When you can fully appreciate just how powerful your gifts are, nothing will stop you from reaching out, finding the people who need you most and delivering powerful coaching sessions that will support your clients to be the best versions of themselves.

And what happens when this is the norm rather than the exception? If you dare to dream big, you can see what happens when more people remain in their Sage most of the time; imagine the problems we could solve and the impact each of us could make. Whenever I'm feeling lost or unsure what to do next, I reconnect to this vision and it reminds me the value of all my efforts. When you have something like that in the back of your mind, you become unstoppable. When you don't have a clear vision of why you do what you do and the impact it has in the world, your Saboteur thoughts have the power to stop you. Harsh words and criticisms slowly eat away at your positive energy and what's left are unfounded fears and skepticism.

How Our Saboteurs Prevent Us From Having the Coaching Business We Deserve

Our brains were not designed to make us happy. Our brains were designed to keep us safe. Back in our caveman days, when the bushes rustled, our amygdala triggered our fight, flight or freeze response. That's what kept us alive and our brains got really good at processing threats. But now that same amygdala is processing our false fears and limiting beliefs with the same life-threatening response and this paralyzes us from taking action. We stop ourselves from repeating the daily habits that will lead us to everything we want in our coaching business.

What becomes challenging is to notice the lies of our Saboteurs by labeling them and dismissing them before we begin to believe them. Let's take a look at some of the more common statements and see if you can recognize the lies your Saboteurs are telling you. That way, we can weaken the power these lies have on you. Once we do that, you'll be in a position to activate your Sage and take the actions that will lead to your desired outcome.

How Our Master Saboteur, the Judge, Stops Us

As you are aware from Shirzad's work, the Judge is our top Saboteur. As part of our brain's limbic system, we are constantly judging ourselves, judging others and judging situations. Remember, our brains are not designed to make us happy, they were designed to keep us safe. The more critical we are of ourselves, others around us and the situations we find ourselves in, the more "safe and secure" we feel.

And yet, we don't grow inside our comfort zone.

Think about anything you've learned how to do. As a toddler, you first learned to crawl, then you took a step and fell down. Then you took another step and fell down again. And you repeated this process until you developed your balance and began to walk. Same thing when you learned to ride a bicycle. You started with training wheels. When you wanted to go faster, the training wheels came off and what happened? You wobbled and fell over. You then tried again and wobbled some more. Perhaps one of your parents gave you a good push and you found that momentum to keep peddling. Eventually, you mastered riding a bike.

But if it were up to your Judge, you'd never take any risks. Inherently, according to our Judge, taking risks are dangerous and should be avoided whenever possible. But that same caution stops us from growing and it's so much worse than making mistakes and learning from them. When it comes to your coaching business, your Judge is a lot more prevalent than you may realize. Let's take a look at each of the three areas where your Judge lives.

Judgment of Self

When we step into being our own worst critic, we say things to ourselves that we would never say out loud to another person. Our self-judgments are brutal because they arise from (and are grounded in) our fears and self-doubts. Notice the power of these judgments by connecting to our fears.

- "They don't want to talk with me." (Fear of rejection)
- "I'm not that interesting." (Fear of being unworthy)
- "It doesn't matter what I do or how hard I try, I'll never get this!" (Self-Doubt)
- "No matter what I do, I'll never generate enough income doing what I love." (Scarcity)
- "I suck at this. I must be a terrible because nobody wants to hire me." (Shame. Guilt.)

And of course, we're only scratching the surface. As the Judge is the master Saboteur, this voice tends to be dominant in our minds. Those self-judgments and microaggressions are ever present. "Why did I do that?" "So dumb!" "How could you make that mistake ... again!" Until we can clearly hear that this voice is the voice of our Judge, we won't have the energy to get back up when we experience being knocked down or off course.

Take a moment and think about the self-judgment you experience the most. What question do you continue to ask yourself over and over again? It's likely rooted in a fear or false belief.

The Self-Judgment I Hear Most Often is: _____

_____

For me, I would constantly ask myself, "Why am I not successful?" Notice that this question assumed facts not in evidence. The question was rooted in a false belief that I wasn't already successful. At the time that this question was looping in my head, I had already built my second multimillion-dollar company, had a blissful marriage, two amazing children, was financially free, and I could go on and on. If that's not "success," then what is? And yet, my self-judgments were all around my own scarcity fears; that I wasn't enough and I would never be enough.

"What's wrong with me?" was another favorite on the self-judgment Top 40 play list. Again, notice the false assumption that there was, in fact, something wrong with me. My fear was that there was something wrong and that I couldn't diagnose it and so I needed to judge myself for anything that wasn't "normal." My Judge would use the slightest mistake as evidence of my brokenness. "Are you kidding me? Shouldn't you be better than this by now? What the hell is wrong with you?"

And, of course, there's an immediate desire to "normalize" all this critical self-loathing and so my Judge wouldn't stop there. I'd immediately need to become critical of others and blame them as well as any situation I found myself in. What a crazy downward cycle. First, I blame and criticize myself, then I look for others to do that to and then when that wasn't enough, I could always find some situation to blame.

Judgment of Others

The lies went something like this, "Yes, I'm broken and clearly not very good, but it's really [Insert Person's Name Here]'s fault. They're really to blame." I'd look for all the evidence to justify my mistakes and shortcomings. In my mind, I'd villainize someone and just keep piling up the evidence as to why I was right. The anger and the occasional rage felt like letting off some steam. I could temporarily release my negative emotions by directing them at someone else – even if that judgment of the other person was only in my head.

Ever have a looping argument in your head? Sometimes that judgment of others shows up in an argument that's never even taken place. My judge was preparing for the big fight. To do so, I'd play both sides against each other. What would I say? How would (s)he respond? Then what would I say next? I could easily spend 15 minutes or more lost in my head preparing for an argument that never happened and most likely would never happen. Even if I did confront the person, it never went down the way I predicted in my head.

Sound familiar? Now let's see how judging others prevent us from having the coaching business we deserve. See if any of these internal thoughts sound familiar:

- "There's no way they can afford my coaching services, I shouldn't even offer them."
- "This person is clearly holding back; I can't coach a person who isn't willing to share what's really going on."
- "He just lost his job, sure he could use my help, but there's no way he'll hire me now that he has no income."
- "It's clear she's about to get divorced, money will probably be tight for a while. It wouldn't be fair to charge her for my coaching."
- "We just met tonight. There's no way I'm going to offer him/her a discovery session."
- "She's such a good friend of mine, I shouldn't convolute our relationship by enrolling her into my coaching practice."

We have thoughts like these all the time. Our judgment of others prevents us from being fully present to the person in front of us. What's worse, judging a potential prospect often blinds us to a possibility we simply can't see. Our judgment of another person blinds us. When I decide that a person can't afford me, I rob them of making that choice. When I decide it's too soon to offer up a discovery call, I create an artificial barrier to enrolling a perfectly qualified prospect. When I allow a person's circumstances to influence my decision to offer up my coaching, I'm denying that same person the very support that could turn things around – and quickly.

Judgment of Situations

And the judgment just keeps on going. Why stop at judging yourself and your potential prospect when you can have a triple play by judging the situation too?

- "His divorce is all consuming. He has neither the time nor the money to invest in coaching."
- "Her company won't pay for coaching." (Often coupled with, "...and she can't afford to pay me directly.")
- "He just lost his job and wasn't in a good financial place to start with."
- "Her sister recommended me, but she's just out of college and hasn't found that first foothold in the job market yet."
- "Normally, he'd be a perfect client for me, but his dad just passed away and he's going through hell. Now is not the time."
- "This just isn't a good time to bring up what I do as a coach."

In truth, we're barely scratching the surface here. The circumstances are infinite. And, if we allowed these situations to stop us, we'd never enroll clients. Do you see how judging situations prevent us from having the coaching business we deserve? Our Judge is scanning for every reason to prevent us from putting ourselves out there.

In truth, these are all just circumstances. By their very nature, situations and circumstances are temporary. And yet, many of these situations could be the very reason the person you're talking to *needs* you as their coach.

When it comes to relationships, if you're catching someone *before* they get divorced, you may be in a position to help them turn their relationship around and save both your client and their spouse 50% of the combined accumulated wealth let alone all the heartache and emotional pain that comes with a divorce. If you're catching them after having just gotten divorced, they are looking to move past the pain of what just happened and make sense of what's next in their life.

For someone who just lost their job, sure they may be watching their expenses, but what's the value of landing an even better job they truly enjoy and receiving higher compensation? What's the value of having a coach help them to land on their feet and see a possible gift to their future career aspirations in what would otherwise feel like a detrimental blow?

When we take the time to stop and consider the flip side of any potentially "bad" situation or circumstance, we can begin to see a new possibility; one that was previously hidden from us by our Judge. And, if this were all that we had to do, then we could elevate our Sage Perspective to see past the lies of our Judge. Unfortunately, our Judge has other plans in mind and seeks our Accomplice Saboteurs so that, together, they can overpower our Sage and keep us from taking the consistent actions that are necessary to have the coaching business we deserve.

How Our Accomplice Saboteurs Gang Up With Our Judge in Business Development

Having read the book *Positive Intelligence*, you're familiar with your top Accomplice Saboteurs. If you're not clear on which are currently your top Accomplice Saboteurs, head over to PositiveIntelligence.com and take the Saboteur Assessment for a refresher. For most coaches, the results of your Saboteur Assessment either solidify what you suspected or shed new light on the repeating patterns you are familiar with in your life. Rather than repeating what you know, this section will connect how each of your Accomplice Saboteurs negatively impact your ability to grow and scale your coaching business.

Several times as part of the PQ Coach membership program, Shirzad has shared that your path to Sage mastery comes from your ability to face your Saboteurs when building and growing your coaching business. Here's the outline of how each of your Accomplice Saboteurs likely show up in precisely the wrong moments as you look to build your coaching business.

Avoider

Your Avoider Saboteur has you focus on the positive and pleasant aspects of your coaching business in an extreme way. Rather than facing the difficult and unpleasant tasks that are necessary for growth, your Avoider Saboteur convinces you that not dealing with tasks and any potential conflicts associated with your efforts is the best strategy.

Your Sage knows that avoiding the difficult and unpleasant tasks don't make them go away. If anything, the act of avoiding the very tasks necessary for growing your coaching business exacerbates them to a point where they seem insurmountable. The paradox is that the more you avoid the difficult and unpleasant aspects of your coaching business, the more difficult and unpleasant they become in your mind. All this builds anxiety about what has been avoided or procrastinated.

Negative Impacts on Your Coaching Business

The Avoider Saboteur typically shows up most closely associated with any aspect of new client enrollment such as generating appointments on your calendar and converting any appointments into paying clients. For most coaches, the concept of "putting yourself out there" and "asking for business" goes against their natural *giving* tendencies. People who enter the coaching industry tend to be incredible givers, but don't realize their ability to give is hindered by their inability to receive.

One of my early mentors, Chad Cooper, explained it to me this way. When you resist the opportunities to receive, you constrict your capacity to give. Imagine your garden hose. For most coaches, they have the spicket turned all the way on and the water is full blast coming out of their garden hose. But, if they received without resistance, that garden hose would become a fire hose or even a larger water pipe. The more we open up to receive, the higher our capacity to give becomes. Receiving doesn't negate your desire to give; it empowers your ability to give more.

The Avoider Saboteur, however, convinces us that all this new client enrollment is just too unpleasant. The justification lie we hear from our Avoider Saboteur is that, "If I let this go, it will take care of itself." It doesn't. Sure, in any business you're bound to get *some* organic referrals, but not enough to build the kind of coaching business you deserve.

And, yes, other parts of your coaching business are also impacted by your Avoider Saboteur. If you're nervous about speaking publicly, for example, your Avoider Saboteur will stop you from raising your hand when conference organizers hold their call for speakers. You'll ignore opportunities to speak about your coaching business on a podcast. These are just a few of many examples you can think of where your Avoider Saboteur stops you from taking bold action. Rather than leaning into the abundance all around you, which your Sage would have you do, your Avoider Saboteur convinces you not to take action and instead settle for the perceived scarcity you are most likely currently experiencing.

Original Strengths Distorted By Your Avoider Saboteur

To be clear, your Avoider Saboteur tapped some of your innate Sage strengths and took them too far so that these original strengths became weaknesses and ultimately a detriment of your coaching business. Your Sage strength naturally seeks peace and harmony both internally with yourself and externally with others. That peace and harmony taken to the extreme result in inaction. At your core, you're flexible and adaptable, but taken too far, that flexibility turns into a deep focus on what's easy and avoidance of anything that challenges you or stretches your abilities, because that feels uncomfortable.

The way of the Sage is "ease and flow" and this is the part we will keep while also tapping into Sage Power Activate. This is the work to reduce the resistance of the Avoider Saboteur and instead tap into your Sage Power Activate – especially in the new client enrollment activities that will lead you to having the coaching business you deserve. While we all have aspects of avoidance in our work, if your Avoider Saboteur is one of your top two Accomplice Saboteurs, then this book will show you what actions to take consistently to have a powerful transformation and breakthrough in your coaching business.

Antidote to Your Avoider Saboteur

Please spend more of your time with the chapters on Generating Appointments and Converting Appointments. This is where your Avoider Saboteur is likely most prevalent in your coaching business. The things you've already done and created are wonderful and are likely "good enough" to support the actions you're currently not taking in your coaching business. Rather than updating your website (again) or posting event more on social media or falling into the trap you tend to find yourself spending an inordinate amount of time on, your journey here will be to schedule and honor your commitment to generating and converting appointments on a consistent basis.

When you replace Sage Power Activate instead of procrastinating and avoiding the things you don't enjoy doing, your coaching business will take off. Not only will we show you the plans necessary in order to take these actions, we'll have you spend more time doing PQ Reps and activating your Sage PQ brain to ensure you follow through with your committed actions.

It will also support you to have an accountability buddy or group to ensure you're taking the actions you typically avoid. If your accountability team knows what you typically avoid and support you to follow through with the actions you're currently not taking, it won't be long before you see a dramatic increase in your coaching business and can celebrate the new-found growth you so richly deserve. That's what you can anticipate in the chapters ahead. Woo Hoo!

Controller

The Controller Saboteur will do its best to convince you that having your Controller in charge isn't a problem! In fact, your Controller will point to all the "success" you've already achieved and argue that, "Without the Controller, you can't get much done."

It's a very tempting lie to want to believe. If that were the only lie, your Sage might be able to overcome this limiting belief. But wait, there's more! Your Controller also wants to make sure you believe other lies, including:

- "You need to push people, otherwise they won't take action."
- "If I don't control everything, then I will be controlled and I can't live with that."
- "Besides, I'm attempting to accomplish all of this for all of our sakes."

Your Controller projects strength and tends to be out front pushing yourself and other people beyond their comfort zone. Your Controller comes alive when doing "the impossible" and "beating the odds," and can be very intimidating to others. Often, other people will follow along so as not to be damaged or on the receiving end of the strong energy and momentum moving in a particular direction – even if that direction isn't optimal. Short-term results fuel the Controller as evidence that being in Control is the "only way" things get done and is surprised that others get hurt as a result of the Controller's actions.

Negative Impacts on Your Coaching Business

The Controller Saboteur is often a powerful enroller when it comes to getting prospects to "say yes." When a potential client feels lost or confused, the sheer confidence of the Controller, while often off-putting, can result in a temporary decision to agree to whatever coaching service is being offered. That is, until the strong energy of the Controller is no longer dominating the decision-making process and immediately the prospect regrets his or her decision and ultimately changes his or her mind.

The Controller Saboteur uses the initial "Yes" as fuel to justify the dominant approach in both generating and converting appointments. Controllers generally don't have a problem with momentum. Instead the negative impact comes later when prospects who initially agreed to be coached realize they were "sold" or "pressured" into saying yes, when it wasn't quite right for them. Think short-term gain, long-term problem. The more momentum the Controller experiences, the lie of needing the Controller is justified and reinforced. That is, until, all those steps forward are reversed and what you are left with is a revolving door of clients who change their minds, drop out and find any excuse to terminate the relationship.

Not to be deterred, the Controller, in turn, doubles down and argues that these individuals were either not "ready" to be coached or they were not the right niche after all. Clearly, the efforts being made are "working" as evidenced by the initial traction. What is confusing to the Controller Saboteur is how the coaching business appears to take a few steps forward, and then even more steps backwards with no long-term, sustainable momentum.

Original Strengths Distorted By Your Controller Saboteur

Before they were abused by your Saboteur, the original Sage strengths that get manipulated and twisted by the Controller include confidence, being decisive, determined and having a persistent bias towards action. The strength is the willingness to challenge yourself and to challenge others. Deep down, you're able to do the right thing even if it's unpopular. Your Sage sees possibilities and is willing to take action both for yourself and with others toward a desired outcome.

When it comes to the five Sage Powers, coaches with a strong Controller Saboteur tend to over-calibrate towards the Activate Power. The Sage perspective that every problem can be turned into a gift or opportunity is often lost on the Controller Saboteur as no time is given to truly examining the problem itself. Nor does the Controller tap into all five Sage Powers (i.e. Empathy, Explore, Innovate, Navigate, and Activate). Worst, the Controller Saboteur tends to jump in solo without tapping into the wisdom of others before taking that swift action.

The distortion comes with thinking that whatever problem exists can be solved with swift action. "You're either with me, or against me." Another favorite is, "Lead, follow or get out of my way!" Rather than taking the time to examine the best solution for the problem ahead, the Controller is convinced he knows best, so let's "jump off the proverbial cliff and build the plane on the way down." This against all odds philosophy can create breakthroughs, but when things don't work out as planned, it can create all kinds of damage and destruction.

Antidote to Your Controller Saboteur

Measure twice, and cut once instead of cutting all the time. The antidote for the Controller Saboteur is to deploy the principle of "slowing down to speed up," which feels paradoxical to the Controller Saboteur who is used to diving in and figuring it all out on the fly. There's no issue with taking action, but rather than always tapping into the one Sage Power you're comfortable with, begin working on the power of the other four.

When you consider that not only are there five Sage Powers, but there's an order to these five sage powers. Before diving into solve any particular problem, the antidote to your Controller Saboteur is to begin using these five Sage Powers *in order*. In the next chapter we'll dive into how to leverage all five Sage Powers in your coaching business. For now, if your Controller Saboteur is your top one keeping you from having the coaching business you deserve, your path towards mastery will be to ease up on Sage Power Activate, and begin developing the other four Sage Powers so that they are at the same level of strength as your Activate Power.

Your Controller Saboteur has "no time for empathy" and this is one major blind spot for coaches with strong Controller Saboteurs. There's no empathy for yourself and how hard you work, little to no empathy for the very real struggles your prospects and clients are facing, little concern or empathy for the situations we all find ourselves in. By jumping straight into action without experiencing the empathy needed first, we're disconnected from the present moment and therefore miss the treasure trove of what's really happening right in front of us. We're so busy putting our blinders on, we fail to see the big picture and that leads to swift action without all the information available to us. No chance we're taking the right actions if we haven't even paused to look around and see what's going on. Then, beyond that, we haven't taken the time to put ourselves in the shoes of others to really feel their experience with deep empathy.

This is the path. Rather than lose or weaken your Sage Power Activate, the journey is to spend time strengthening the other four Sage Powers so that they are equally strong. Your Controller has convinced you that you only need one power to be successful. Imagine how much easier it would be to build the coaching business you deserve using not one, but all five Sage Powers. When your other Sage Powers are as strong as your Sage Power Activate, you'll be unstoppable, and your Sage will be in the driver's seat with ease and flow.

Hyper-Achiever

The Hyper-Achiever does its best to make you dependent on constant performance and achievement for self-respect and self-validation. When it comes to your coaching business, your Hyper-Achiever Saboteur will convince you that wherever you are in your journey, you should be further along than you are. If you're just starting out, your Hyper-Achiever Saboteur will make you feel small and unworthy because you don't already have a thriving coaching business with tons of clients.

What's worse, even when you *do* manage to enroll your first clients, rather than celebrate your wins, your Hyper-Achiever Saboteur will compare your "meager progress" to titans of industry. A common question being, "Why am I not successful?" The Hyper-Achiever Saboteur is highly focused on external success. This leads to unsustainable workaholic tendencies at the expense of deeper emotional or relationship needs. Your Hyper-Achiever is only concerned with your latest win and continued growth at the expense of any possible joy, happiness or fulfillment along your journey.

Imagine playing a sport where every time you scored a goal, the goal posts were moved out even further. What began as an easily winnable game becomes increasingly difficult with no end in sight. Every achievement resets the goal and the result is feeling further and further behind despite all your incredible progress. It's an unwinnable game and even if you do overcome all of these growing obstacles, your Hyper-Achiever Saboteur robs you of any pleasure associated with your continued achievement.

Negative Impacts on Your Coaching Business

At first, it's actually difficult to spot the negative impacts on your coaching business because from the outside looking in, you appear to be doing well. Your Hyper-Achiever Saboteur convinces you that this constant drive is what's needed to succeed. Especially in the United States where social status tends to be intimately linked to your entrepreneurial growth, the initial drive is seen as a "good thing" to be celebrated.

Look around at the books on being successful at business. You need only read the titles to get a sense of what society celebrates. Daymond John, a New York Times bestselling author and star of ABC's *Shark Tank* published *Rise and Grind: Outperform, Outwork and Outhustle Your Way to a More Successful and Rewarding Life*. How did this book do? Along with his previous two books, he's sold hundreds of thousands of copies[12]. The key message is that there are no short cuts to success. Keep grinding it out if you want to succeed. This is very much the message telegraphed by your Hyper-Achiever Saboteur. What very few entrepreneurs like to admit, however, is that this is a clear path to burn out.

I broke the unspoken rule of entrepreneurs (namely, that we should all struggle in silence) in my TEDx talk on *The Power of Audience-Centered Storytelling*[13]. During that talk, I shared that I had already achieved financial freedom, built and exited two multi-million dollar companies, was recognized by Inc 5,000 as one of the fastest growing companies in America two years in a row, had a blissful marriage, two amazing children and the list kept going. Yet, at the top of my game when I should have been happiest, I felt numb and empty inside. What I didn't share in the TEDx talk was that I was seriously considering suicide.

That's the real damage of your Hyper-Achiever Saboteur. When all the joy and happiness in life is gone, what remains is darkness and despair. My friends, my family, and everyone around me assumed I must be thrilled by all my success. The truth was, I was ready to end it all. I never want you to have to experience this. This was one of my driving forces as to why I joined Shirzad in helping to bring mental fitness to the world and to coaches specifically. Please stay with me. As the saying goes, it's always darkest before dawn. I am excited to share the turnarounds that I experienced and how I got my joy and happiness back using the mental fitness operating system and applying it to everything. Those five Sage Powers are a game changer.

---

[12]   http://prhinternationalsales.com/book/?isbn=9780804189958 (see Author link)
[13]   https://youtu.be/-YlkVH5opcU

Original Strengths Distorted By Your Hyper-Achiever Saboteur

At the foundational level, the core Sage strengths are that you're driven, pragmatic, adaptable, goal-oriented and self-directed. This is another example of Sage Power Activate combined with a strong dose of the Explore and Innovate powers. Being driven is wonderful. When you combine drive with being adaptable, it means that you have an insatiable curiosity and willingness to overcome any obstacle that stands between you and your goal. That's amazing! And we don't want to lose these incredible Sage strengths. At your core, you are capable of growing yourself and supporting the growth of those around you in order to achieve full potential. You're no stranger to achievement and meaningful growth.

Said another way, you were born to shine bright. Deep down, you connect to a sense of purpose that you were put on this earth to create something world-changing. You already know how capable you are and whatever you put your mind to gets done. Period. That's such an incredible super power – as long as this strength does not become "all consuming" and at the cost of any joy and happiness you have along the way.

Antidote to Your Hyper-Achiever Saboteur

Peace and happiness need not be fleeting and short-lived as the Hyper-Achiever would have you believe. Rather than moving from one achievement to the next, the antidote to your Hyper-Achiever Saboteur is to stop and celebrate your many accomplishments. This will allow you to build self-acceptance rather than continuing looking externally for validation and the next achievement. The key is to step out of the performance vortex and shift the lopsided focus from external achievement to connecting with your internal feelings.

We need not abandon the path of meaningful growth and achievement. The difference is that with each new phase of growth the shift will be on connecting with your emotions associated with your accomplishments rather than seeking external validation and jumping into the next challenge to be overcome.

Deep empathy for yourself will begin to shift the focus from "out there" to "in here." The more PQ Reps you do – especially on feeling your emotions – the easier it will become to savor your wins rather than the constant drive towards success and additional goals to achieve. It's fine to be driven, adaptable and goal-oriented, as long as these strengths are not taken to the extreme where you struggle to experience joy and happiness in your life. Your Sage Mastery journey will be about self-acceptance and regaining connection to your deeper feelings and your ability to connect deeply with others. As you become more heart-centered, you will experience the joy of achievement, rather than the constant drive to do more.

Hyper-Rationale

Your Hyper-Rationale Saboteur insists that logic and the rational mind are where it's at and that feelings are generally distracting and irrelevant. Knowledge, understanding and insights are valued above all else. This leads to an intense and active mind, sometimes coming across as intellectually arrogant or secretive. Your Hyper-Rationale Saboteur leads to feeling different, alone, and not understood. Feelings are distracting and irrelevant except for the passion that shows up in ideas, problem-solving and breakthrough thinking. Due to analyzing rather than experiencing feelings, there are inherent limits on the depth and flexibility of relationships in work and in life.

Your Hyper-Rationale Saboteur is frustrated by the wasteful intrusion of people's messy emotions and needs. Can't they see if they were more rational, they would be more productive, smarter and get more work done? Feelings are distracting and irrelevant. Any problem in a relationship can be solved logically with intense and exclusive focus on rational processing. Why do other people spend so much time on their feelings? It's simply not productive, effective, or worth the time and energy. Acting on these thought distortions leads to others perceiving you as cold, distant and intellectually arrogant. But that's generally okay because your Hyper-Rationale Saboteur is already skeptical or even cynical of these intellectually inferior people. Besides, your Hyper-Rationale Saboteur is perfectly content to watch all the craziness around you and analyze from a distance. Logic, after all, will win the day. That is, once these people come to their senses.

Negative Impacts on Your Coaching Business

Right off the bat your Hyper-Rationale Saboteur leads you down a path towards isolation, disconnection and establishes a negative perception that you're generally cold, distant and intellectually arrogant. No one wants to feel intimidated by someone who is so analytically intense, so skeptical and regularly cynical.

Not only are you starting off with negative brand perception due to your Hyper-Rationale Saboteur's perceived superiority and intellectual arrogance, when your coaching business isn't growing and scaling, logic appears to have left the building. All your problem-solving skills appear to evade you because from a purely rational space all of your efforts should be working, but they simply are not. The more your Hyper-Rationale Saboteur leans into the rational processing of every aspect of your coaching business, the more frustrated you become.

As your self-worth is attached to mastering knowledge and competence, the problem is further exacerbated by "doubling down" on logic. "Think!" your Hyper-Rationale Saboteur demands, "You just need more time to process what's happening and solve this problem through deeper insights and objective analysis."

But your Hyper-Rationale Saboteur won't allow you to see how feelings and emotions play a critical role in your relationship building and enrollment of clients. To your Hyper-Rationale Saboteur, emotions have nothing to do with this, so why spend time even considering this possibility? Despite how observant and perceptive you are, your Hyper-Rationale Saboteur refuses to even consider the possibility that emotions have anything to do with it. This, in turn, anchors the problem inside an expanding blind spot. The fact that this problem eludes you only elevates frustration, self-judgment and self-criticism and the problems continue to grow.

Original Strengths Distorted By Your Hyper-Rationale Saboteur

By your nature, you're capable of deep insight and understanding through objective analysis. You can be very observant and perceptive. You have honed the power of great mental concentration. Your drive towards great expertise in areas of knowledge are impressive. For many, this leads towards deep exploration and innovation. People easily recognize how smart you are and are impressed by the way you think through problems.

The good news is that you don't need to lose your incredible skills as a rational thinker, your passion for ideas or objective analysis. The distortion by your Hyper-Rationale Saboteur is when you're out of balance because you've all but rid yourself of your emotions.

Antidote to Your Hyper-Rationale Saboteur

Allow yourself to feel your emotions. Rather than escaping into the neat and orderly rational mind, allow yourself to "get messy" by letting go of logic as your default. Begin with empathy for yourself. If you find this challenging, start by connecting with your passion. Think of a recent idea that you felt passionate about. Rather than blowing past that passion in order to create a step-by-step plan to execute on the idea, give yourself permission to connect with the passion you're feeling. By staying with this emotion of excitement, you can open up your feelings towards yourself, others and situations all around you.

Did you know you have not one, but three brains? In addition to your cranium, you also have a heart-brain and a gut-brain. Begin tuning into your heart-brain by paying attention to the available information that has previously been tuned out. Rather than thinking through every problem, begin to listen for the cues being sent to you via your heart-brain. Similarly, you can tune into your gut-brain and receive a wealth of new insights. As you being to use all three of your brains, you'll notice when you're out of alignment.

Sometimes, your heart-brain will alert you to something that your cranium would prefer to ignore – simply because these feelings can't be rationalized. When you are experiencing this internal conflict, check in with your gut-brain. Often, that's as easy as putting your dominant hand on your gut and just asking the question you're grappling with.

All of these are simply tools to add another layer that's been missing. Coming back into balance requires an openness to feel your feelings and listen to them before reacting. The more you can tune into your feelings, the better equipped you'll be to tune into the feelings of those around you and open up a whole new world of possibilities.

Hyper-Vigilant

Your Hyper-Vigilant Saboteur produces a continuous and intense anxiety about all the dangers around you. There is a near obsession with what could go wrong in any given situation. Hyper-Vigilant is vigilance that can never rest. "When is the other shoe going to drop?" your Hyper-Vigilant Saboteur keeps asking. It really does feel like danger is everywhere. An over-active amygdala (the part of your brain that produces the fight, flight or freeze response) feels jammed up in the "on" position. That intense anxiety creates that false sensation that everything is important and if you're not constantly looking over your shoulder, something truly terrible will happen.

That heightened alert system is exhausting. It takes so much energy to remain stressed out about everything all the time. Often the fear of making a mistake leads to inaction. It's less about making the mistake and more about everyone jumping down your throat. Your Hyper-Vigilant Saboteur makes you suspicious of the motives of the very people you wish to trust. And wherever you operate, there's an intense desire to know what the rules are even if you choose not to always follow them.

The risk of failure is ever present and it causes anxiety. This leads to skepticism and even a cynical way of viewing the world. Simply put, this is an extremely hard way to live. The constant anxiety burns a great deal of vital energy that could otherwise be put to great use. Your Hyper-Vigilant Saboteur also has you lose credibility due to the perception that you're "crying wolf."

Negative Impacts on Your Coaching Business

While there are many negative impacts on your coaching business, the fear of not getting clients and having your coaching business fail utterly weighs heavy on the minds of most Hyper-Vigilant Saboteur thoughts. Beyond the actual possibility of failure is the real fear underneath. Deep down, there's a growing belief in the lie that you're not good enough and/or that you're not worthy of having a hugely successful coaching practice.

Instead of seeing a rejection of your coaching offer, your Hyper-Vigilant Saboteur does its best to convince you that it's you that is being rejected. The lie is that you're no good and of course no one wants to work with you. Every rejection hits you to the core of your being and a continued outreach resulting in stirring up these deep, dark fears is a non-starter. This inaction becomes a self-fulfilling prophecy. By not doing the work of generating appointments and vulnerably offering your coaching services, there's no chance for someone to hire you. The fear of failure of your coaching business is realized through self-infliction.

Running a business has inherent risks. Rather than working to mitigate these risks (or tolerating them), your Hyper-Vigilant Saboteur has you "do nothing" because inaction feels safe. But as Seth Godin reminds us in his bestselling book, *Purple Cow*, "Being risky is safe. Being safe is risky." The irony is that the more chances you take in your coaching business, the safer you actually are as you have more opportunities to succeed.

Original Strengths Distorted By Your Hyper-Vigilant Saboteur

At the core of vigilance is your sensitivity and awareness of true risks and dangers to yourself, others and situations, often seen as a guardian of families, communities and institutions. You are loyal, reliable, dependable and hardworking. You are capable of perseverance and consistent work towards objectives. Many people admire your uncanny ability of instituting and preserving systems and structures to impose order and stability.

People around you are clear on how hard you work and can appreciate how you create order and stability. You're seen as the protector. There is comfort in knowing that you're looking out for everyone's best interest – even if there seem to be a lot of false alarms. No one questions your intentions to keep everyone safe and secure.

Antidote to Your Hyper-Vigilant Saboteur

Vigilance is prudent. Hyper-Vigilance is exhausting. The journey towards Sage Mastery is about letting go and being okay with all the uncertainty that life brings, or, as Tony Robbins likes to say, "The quality of your life is determined by the amount of uncertainty you can comfortably live with." Sage discernment is distinct from Saboteur judgment. Your ability to distinguish real threats versus all the myriad possible, but unlikely threats will allow you to let go and be okay with all the low-probability risk that is everywhere you look.

Taking more chances and being okay with failure will open up new possibilities in your life. As Michael Jordon, arguably one of the best basketball players of all time shared:

"I've missed more than 9,000 shots in my career. I've lost almost 300 games. 26 times I've been trusted to take the game winning shot and missed. I've failed over and over and over again in my life. And that is why I succeed."

Did you feel that? Whenever I read this quote, something deep inside of me resonates. I believe this is our Sage telling us to take our shot. Said differently, "You miss 100% of the shots you don't take." Your Hyper-Vigilant Saboteur would prefer you never take a shot because you might miss. And yet, if you're going to fail, might as well give it everything you got. Sure, mistake will be made, but by giving it your best, the likelihood of failing is, paradoxically, minimized. Your best efforts will ensure your success. So go ahead and make mistakes. "It's not about how many times you fall down. It's about the number of times you get back up that matters."

Pleaser

Your Pleaser Saboteur indirectly tries to gain acceptance and affection by helping, pleasing, rescuing or flattering others. This would seem like a strength of building your coaching business. After all, as a servant leader, your deep empathy creates that initial spark that opens up the opportunity to establish and then grow a relationship. Left unchecked, however, your Pleaser Saboteur will have you so focused on your prospect and clients that you lose sight of your own needs and become resentful as a result.

Putting others needs ahead of your own may seem like the right thing to do until you realize your own needs are not being met. In the airline industry, they remind you to put your own oxygen mask on first before helping others. Your Pleaser Saboteur would have you skip that step to "save time" and instead focus on the needs of everyone else around you. The result is predictable. Without putting your own oxygen mask on first, you are unable to sustain the genuine support you wish to deliver to other people.

The unspoken survival function your Pleaser Saboteur has convinced you is that you must give love and affection in order to get any back. Rather than simply being worthy, there's a growing part of you that believes you must earn love and affection. Your Pleaser Saboteur has you give and give until there's nothing left. Your inability to open up to receive restricts your ability to give at the levels you truly desire. The predictable result is that you feel empty inside having depleted your ability to give more – especially when you are surprised that all those people you've helped haven't returned the favor to you. That resentment is based on this implied, yet unspoken, law of reciprocity which rarely manifests in the ways you anticipate.

Negative Impacts on Your Coaching Business

Your Pleaser Saboteur stops you from asking for the sale and in the more extreme examples, you won't even positioning what you do as part of your coaching business. Your Pleaser Saboteur can have you feel uncomfortable in the spotlight, preferring to deflect compliments and acknowledgements onto other people your Pleaser Saboteur believes deserve attention more than you do. Rather than being seen, your Pleaser Saboteur will have you play small so as not to "ruffle any feathers." The underlying belief is that "the nail that sticks out, gets hammered," so why would you accept recognition, elevation or praise when it's so much more comfortable working from behind the scenes.

Left unchecked, your Pleaser Saboteur can even have you coach people in real time without their knowledge or consent – all in the name of being in service to whomever needs you. This leads to awkward experiences for the people you choose to support as they are not clear on what's happening or how the conversation has shifted into coaching.

Think about it this way. If you were at a social event and were speaking with a doctor, you might tell that doctor of a problem you're experiencing. Rather than diagnosing you right there on the spot, this doctor will give you their business card and ask that you make an appointment to dig into the issue. Your Pleaser Saboteur doesn't like this approach and would rather dive right in and help the person in front of you right here and right now. Even if that person has a powerful breakthrough, they won't understand that this is your profession and that you are interested in enrolling them as a client. Instead, the person will thank you, move on and not think twice about what you did for them. Your Pleaser Saboteur is perplexed by this as it doesn't appear to follow the rules or reciprocity which leads to resentment and burnout.

Even if you do take time to generate an appointment and conduct a proper discovery call, your Pleaser Saboteur will stop you from making your offer at the end of the session. The justification by your Pleaser Saboteur is that you help others selflessly and don't expect anything in return. Your Pleaser Saboteur further believes that the world would be a better place if everyone did the same. Unfortunately, that's not how life or businesses work. Without following the enrollment process, these discovery calls do not result in converting prospects into new clients. Despite how much effort you give to your coaching business, you experience an energy drain based on all the outward facing efforts you make without much progress or growth in your coaching business.

Original Strengths Distorted By Your Pleaser Saboteur

Your empathy for others is second to none. You are loving and extremely giving. You are tuned into the feelings and needs of those around you. You're emotionally self-aware and have the potential for high emotional intelligence.

These are all important Sage qualities that are then distorted by your Pleaser Saboteur. By believing that expressing your own needs directly feels selfish, you hold back from asking for what you need. Instead, your Pleaser Saboteur has you worry that insisting on your own needs may drive others away. This leads to being resentful for being taken for granted, but even then you notice you have difficulty expressing what you are feeling.

Antidote to Your Pleaser Saboteur

Begin with empathy for yourself and your situation. While your empathy for others is already very strong, self-empathy tends to be weak. Rather than constantly putting the needs of others ahead of your own, practice putting your own oxygen mask on first. Your ability to give more is restricted by your inability to receive. The true antidote to your Pleaser Saboteur will be to refocus your energy on opening up to receive. As you receive without resistance, you'll also notice you will give without expectation.

While your Pleaser Saboteur has high expectations for what you get in return for what you give, your Sage gives without expectation and receives without resistance. That balance allows for sustainable growth. To move closer to this desired outcome, begin with having empathy for yourself and the situation you find yourself in. Then explore new possibilities where you can receive without resistance. Allow yourself to see the ultimate outcome you're focused on and how opening up to receive will support your ability to sustain your growth and build a thriving and sustainable coaching business for years to come. Then take action toward allowing yourself to receive. This could start off small by allowing someone else to pick up the dinner check, bring something to a party or drive you to an event. Eventually, you'll want to apply this learning toward generating appointments on your calendar and converting these appointments which we'll spend some time going over in the chapters that follow.

Restless

Your Restless Saboteur has you constantly in search of greater excitement in the next activity rather than being fully present in the moment. To the untrained eye, your Restless Saboteur perpetuates constant busyness. And yet, with your Restless Saboteur in charge, you rarely are at peace. Nor are you content with the current activity you're working on. The desire not to miss out on anything has you shifting from one thing to the next without a feeling of accomplishment or completion. Your Restless Saboteur has you convinced that life is too short and must be lived fully. Not wanting to miss anything means you shift focus regularly and multi-task constantly – all of this despite the evidence that this approach is not generally effective or productive in the long run.

Your Restless Saboteur has you impatient with whatever is happening now and instead wondering "What's next?" The fear of missing out on other more worthwhile experiences has you worried that prolonged focus on any unpleasant feeling will grow and become overwhelming. The belief that the next thing has got to be more exciting has you always on the lookout for something better. For your Restless Saboteur, the proverbial grass is always greener elsewhere and that leads to lack of fulfillment with whatever you're doing. Besides, no one seems to be able to keep up with you, so why bother.

That constant seeking of new stimulation keeps you "busy" juggling many different tasks and plans. Juggling so many balls in the air leads to being easily distracted and too scattered. Comfort and safety are regularly exchanged for excitement and variety.

Negative Impacts on Your Coaching Business

Being on the constant lookout for excitement and variety has you trying new things constantly. While many tasks are started, the problem arrives when no one strategy is committed to long enough to be effective. Rather than choosing one ideal customer, your Restless Saboteur has you constantly trying to coach different niches. Before you've given your offer enough time to work, it's changed to something else. Despite having a passion for one way to generate appointments on your calendar, tactics are always changing ensuring that your coaching business never has a chance to truly flourish.

There are so many ways your Restless sabotages your coaching business and nearly all of them come down to a lack of follow through. When you chase three rabbits you won't catch even one of them. Rather than building a plan and following through, your Restless Saboteur has you reading the latest articles, enrolling in the latest training course, investing in the latest marketing technology and none of these investments seem to pay off. It's confusing to both you and to many of the people closest to you because you seem to be a Jack of All Trades and extremely busy all the time. But being busy doesn't mean you're effective, does it? In the long-run your Restless Saboteur will have you expend more and more energy, but only a little bit on way too many things and your inability to produce your desired results will invite your Judge to tag team by lying to you and do its best to convince you that you're not cut out for this work.

Original Strengths Distorted By Your Restless Saboteur

Your high energy and vitality means you're up for just about anything. When everyone else is burned out, you somehow have even more to give. You're open, curious and spontaneous. Your enthusiasm is contagious and you maintain a deep appreciation of all that life has to offer. You are capable of great productivity and creativity. You bring energy to whatever you focus on and have an uncanny way of engaging others in co-creation with you. You are capable of a great breadth of activity and pursuits. Others have recognized your many diverse talents and skillsets.

All of these strengths have become distorted by your Restless Saboteur simply by taking them to the extreme. Imagine what you could create with that same level of high energy and vitality when you choose to really focus your efforts. Your natural curiosity means you don't stay stuck for very long and instead bring your unique creativity to solve any problem that stands between you and your desired outcome.

Antidote to Your Restless Saboteur

Pigheaded stubbornness, or what Jim Collins refers to as the hedgehog strategy in his bestselling book, *Good to Great*. While a fox has many different strategies, the hedgehog has only one – but what the hedgehog does is extremely effective. We want to keep all your incredible strengths and direct them towards one incredibly focused path. Pigheaded stubbornness means you're not distracted by the latest research, insights, technology, training, certification or peer recommendations. Your Sage path to incredible business development success will come from evaluating as many options as you deem prudent, but then narrowing your focus to as few activities as possible – ideally just one that you stick with despite how "boring" your Restless Saboteur tries to convince you it is.

While you're free to have as much excitement *outside* your coaching business, your path towards Sage Mastery is about discovering the ease and flow that comes with doing what you love and doing the same things consistently rather than getting distracted by the unlimited alternative paths and spreading yourself too thin. After having deep empathy for yourself, you'll have the opportunity to explore many options, but then land on the single path that keeps you focused and ensures your effectiveness over time. Rather than abandoning proven strategies with tried and true formulas, sticking to one and giving it the time it needs to succeed will keep you grounded and ensure the outcomes you desire.

Stickler

The lies of your Stickler Saboteur have you believe that perfection achievable and strict order and organization are the only way to live. If you can't do it perfectly, don't do it at all. Your Stickler Saboteur is quick to point out the lax standards of everyone around you. This leads to a limiting belief that you need to be more organized and methodical than others, so that things get done. Mistakes are avoidable, rather than inevitable, your Stickler Saboteur would have you believe and there's a right way to do things and a wrong way. Your Stickler Saboteur is confident that you know the right way and anyone who has a different approach is wrong.

This leads to a constant frustration and disappointment with yourself and others for not living up to ideal standards. And this further leads to anxiety that others will mess up the order and balance you've worked so hard to create. Your Stickler Saboteur is convinced that your suppressed anger and frustrations are totally justified and that your sarcasm and self-righteous overtones are for the other person's own good and learning.

In order to maintain these ridiculously high standards, your Stickler Saboteur has you believe that it's up to you to fix whatever mess you encounter; it's a personal obligation. After all, perfection makes you feel good about yourself. Perfection is good as there is usually a clear right and clear wrong way of doing things. The feeling that you know how things should be done compels you to do the right thing – no matter what the cost to yourself or others.

Negative Impacts on Your Coaching Business

Your Sage knows that perfection is an illusion. While perfection may be something to strive for, believing that it's not only possible to achieve, but that perfection is the gold standard to hold yourself to inevitably sets you up for disappointment and a feeling of failure. This stance that there's a right way to do things causes rigidity and reduces flexibility in dealing with the inevitable ebb and flow of any business – especially your coaching business.

Your Stickler Saboteur has you looking down on the very prospects you'd like to enroll into your coaching practice and then is surprised when these clearly inferior people have the audacity not to hire you. Despite your Stickler Saboteur's self-righteous vibe, some prospects are drawn to your high ideals, unbelievable standards and self-discipline. But these early wins are often short lived as clients are frustrated by their inability to live into your impossibly high standards and the level of discipline you appear to model and unwittingly impose on your clients.

When generating appointments, your Stickler inadvertently sabotages your efforts through your appearance of self-righteousness. The content generated feels out of touch and unattainable so it doesn't land or resonate with the very people you are looking to attract into your coaching business. Rather than attracting clients into your coaching business, you appear to be driving people away. When clients do get on your calendar, they can feel intimidated and have difficulty relating with you.

This sometimes leads to a prospect saying yes and then immediately having buyer's remorse so you end up chasing them down only to find them ghosting you so that they don't have to re-engage with you.

Original Strengths Distorted By Your Stickler Saboteur

At your core, you're incredibly self-disciplined and principled. You maintain high standards and ideals. Your superpower is bringing organization and order to anything that is steeped in ambiguity and chaos. Your capable of leading yourself and others to live and work based on clear guiding principles. You are direct and discerning with an uncanny ability to see and communicate things as they are. When someone wants something done right, they will seek you out to lead it and give you a high degree of trust and latitude to get it done.

These strengths are distorted by your Stickler Saboteur by taking them too far. Rather than acknowledging that perfection is an illusion, you place an unreasonable burden on yourself and those around you to actually BE perfect. This sets you and those around you up for failure and is ultimately the thing that stops you from achieving your desired outcomes.

Antidote to Your Stickler Saboteur

Relax. Chill out. See the goal of perfection and acknowledge to yourself and others that while we may strive toward that goal, we will never get there. Rather than being self-righteous, seek humility in that which you choose to take on. By celebrating your own imperfections and failures as important lessons in your life's journey, you can drop the sarcastic overtones and let go of your suppressed anger and frustrations. This is how you begin to truly enjoy the journey and let go of the drive and constant compulsion to reach perfection.

During my transformational training with ALTRU Center, I was given a poem that illustrated the key differences between perfection and excellence.

> *Perfection is being right.*
> *Excellence is willing to be wrong.*
> *Perfection brings on fear*
> *Excellence encourages risk.*
>
> *Perfection leads to anger and frustration.*
> *Excellence generates power.*
> *Perfection is being in control.*
> *Excellence is being spontaneous.*

Perfection is judgment.
        Excellence is acceptance.
Perfection is talking.
        Excellence is giving.

Perfection is doubt.
        Excellence is letting it flow.
Perfection is the destination.
        Excellence is the journey.

Experience EXCELLENCE in your life![14]

These distinctions really helped me in my own journey of transformation. I saw how I was holding perfection at the expense of excellence. I now see how to keep all those original strengths before they were distorted by my Stickler Saboteur. And thanks to having clarity here, I am able to experience excellence in my life.

Victim

Your Victim Saboteur has you stay emotional and temperamental as a way to gain attention and affection. Think martyr with an extreme focus on internal feelings, particularly painful ones. Tend to brood over negative feelings for a long time. Even when around people you're close to, your Victim Saboteur has you feeling alone and lonely. There can also be feelings of melancholy and abandonment as well as envy and critical negative comparisons to others.

"No one understands me," your Victim Saboteur will have you believe. Your Victim Saboteur will have you asking yourself, "Why do terrible things always happen to me?" These feelings have you living into the false belief that you are uniquely disadvantaged or flawed. Feelings, left unchecked, can inaccurately define who you are and lead to a deep desire to have someone rescue you from this terrible mess. Self-pity leads to helplessness all in the hopes to get some of the love and attention that you deserve. The justification and lie of your Victim Saboteur is that sadness is a noble and sophisticated thing that shows exceptional depth, insight and sensitivity.

Meanwhile, others feel frustrated, helpless or guilty that they can't put more than a temporary Band-Aid on the Victim's pain. The strategy of your Victim Saboteur backfires as the mood swings end up pushing people away. Rather than experiencing the spice of life, your Victim Saboteur has you wasting your vitality through focusing on internal processing and brooding.

---

[14]   ALTRU Center, Inc. Poem on Excellence used with permission.

Negative Impacts on Your Coaching Business

To quote your Victim Saboteur, "Why even try? What's the point since I'm going to fail anyway?" That feeling of helplessness spills over into all your perceived "wasted" efforts. You end up half-heartedly trying things because you feel you're supposed to, but your Victim Saboteur has you convinced that you are uniquely disadvantaged or flawed. This false belief manifests in unintentional or inadvertent sabotaging of your efforts to build and scale your coaching business. Like the arsonist who feels a compulsion to start fires, your Victim Saboteur creates a self-fulfilling prophecy by blinding you to the very actions that would deliver you the coaching business you desire. The struggle is real, but with the Victim Saboteur's hands on the steering wheel of your coaching business, much of the struggle is self-inflicted.

Sharing the pain you experience from your Victim Saboteur can help you appear vulnerable and brave which, in turn, emboldens your Victim Saboteur and the downward cycle continues. While others may pity you for all the circumstances you find yourself in, they don't see you as the kind of expert coach they are willing to invest their hard-earned dollars with. The attention your Victim Saboteur receives is confusing because it doesn't result in business growth. Instead, the attention feels good temporarily and then leads to a reinforcement of the lies of your Victim Saboteur that somehow you are uniquely disadvantaged or flawed. What your Victim Saboteur takes great pains to have you avoid seeing clearly is that this continued suffering is usually self-inflicted and often the result of a choice.

Original Strengths Distorted By Your Victim Saboteur

At your core, you have a unique ability to feel your own emotions deeply and clearly. Your sensitivity goes way beyond tuning into yourself. Your superpower is your ability to perceive nuanced emotions in yourself and in others. Some go as far as to refer to you as empathic due to your uncanny ability to sense what's going on long before it's spoken out loud. You are incredibly introspective and capable of deep and courageous introspection and self-discovery. This carries into a deep appreciation of your own unique qualities and the uniqueness of others.

You are perceptive of nuanced inner workings of the mind and are capable of using these nuances to connect with others, teach, inspire and heal. Inside of you is a desire to help others heal. While not the only reason, this desire to help others heal is one of the reasons you choose to become a coach in the first place. You've seen the power of coaching and the healing power it has on those who are in pain and experience suffering.

Antidote to Your Victim Saboteur

Choose gratitude. It is not possible to simultaneously be grateful and to also suffer. When you experience your Victim Saboteur leading you down the path of suffering, choose the Sage Perspective that every "bad thing" can be turned into a gift and opportunity. In the next chapter we'll go into more detail on how the Sage Perspective applies to your coaching business. For now, it's important to understand that your Sage knows that are always at choice.

While pain is inevitable, suffering is not. Suffering is about keeping your hand held firmly on that hot stove. If you saw a child holding their hand on the hot stove while complaining bitterly about the pain they were experiencing, you have them take their hand off that hot stove. You can see that clearly. What's more difficult to acknowledge is how your Victim Saboteur has you doing that more often than you care to admit. Your Victim Saboteur blinds you to this as a way of self-protection, and yet not being aware of these self-sabotage choices leads to repeating the same pattern.

Choose love. Choose gratitude. As you open up your willingness to see and acknowledge your part in where you find yourself today, you will be free. Free to make a different choice. Free to release yourself from the suffering you experience.

A Note on Trauma

This in no way excuses, minimizes or diminishes the very real and actual trauma you may have experienced. With the help of a trained therapist, there's real work to be done to let go of past traumatic events. With gratitude and the Sage Perspective, you are empowered to let go and end the cycle of the re-traumatization that occurs whenever you revisit the past traumas in your mind. The lie of your Victim Saboteur is that, "Terrible things always happen to me" and that "I am uniquely disadvantaged or flawed." That's the kind of thinking that traps the real you – your Sage self – from letting to and making a new choice. That's the work and while you may not have anticipated facing this work in the journey of building your coaching business, you can be that this one distinction will change everything for you and ensure you have the impact in the world that you know you're capable of having. That's the light you see and what's possible.

Check In

How are you feeling right now? That was a lot to take in. Even if you only focused on your own top Accomplice Saboteurs, this can be energy draining. No one enjoys staring their Saboteurs in the face or examining the patterns that have prevented you from having the coaching business of your dreams. This can be challenging work.

Before we dive right into the next chapter, I encourage you to take some time and reflect. I find journaling can be extremely helpful – especially when you're feeling heightened emotions.

At this point in your journey, your Saboteurs would love to convince you that you're not cut out for this work. That perhaps it's time to let go of your dreams of having a thriving coaching business and forget about continuing your own journey toward self-actualization. Please don't allow your Saboteurs to win here.

Your Sage knows the truth.

The truth is that the world needs you more than you could possibly realize. The human species is an interconnected web of life. If the global pandemic has taught me anything, it's that we're all in this together. In the town where I live, there was a simple lawn sign that one of my neighbors put it. It simply read, "We grow through what we go through." That about summed it up for me. In your own journey of self-actualization, the obstacles are not there to stop you. If you believe, as I do, that every challenge you face was designed to help you become who you are today, then you can shift your perspective. Rather than feeling defeated by the challenges you face, I invite you to remain curious and trust that you can handle whatever shows up in your path toward self-actualization.

As a coach, isn't it cool how the challenges your clients bring into a coaching session are often a mirror reflection of similar challenge you also face? Is this a coincidence? Or is this a reminder that we're all in this together?

In South Africa, they use the word ubuntu. One source puts it this way, "The presence of ubuntu is still widely referenced in South Africa, more than two decades after the end of apartheid. It's a compact term from the Nguni languages of Zulu and Xhosa that carries a fairly broad English definition of "a quality that includes the essential human virtues of compassion and humanity."[15] When I first learned of the word in my transformational training work, it was simply defined as, "I am, because we are."

This is our journey of shared humanity. It manifests itself everywhere, and especially in the areas of your life that are most important to you. You are a coach because you care about people. Your journey to self-actualization is a journey of overcoming your Saboteurs and shifting to the Sage Perspective as you strengthen each of your Sage Powers. This is the focus of the next chapter. Knowing your Saboteurs is an important first step. Your ability to weaken their power over you comes from building and strengthening your Sage muscles. No where will you find a better playground and well-defined sandbox where you can weaken your Saboteurs and strengthen your Sage than in the building and growing of your coaching business.

---

[15] https://theculturetrip.com/africa/south-africa/articles/understanding-the-meaning-of-ubuntu-a-proudly-south-african-philosophy/

Remember to Take Action

As a reminder, this book is not intended as an intellectual exercise. Yes, you will come away with some really important insights, but as Gothe says, "To know and not to act is not to know."[16] Filling up your cerebral cortex with a ton of information won't help you build the coaching business you desire. Nor will insights lead you toward self-actualization. The real game here is to apply what you're learning and that comes in the form of action.

For this chapter, here are the following recommended actions to take.

1. **Buy a Five-Year Journal** if you don't have one already. Unlike a traditional journal, each page has only space for a few lines per day, but you're writing these lines on the same page for each day of the year – five years in a row. What that does is allow you to summarize your daily progress and see patterns as you read where you've been on this same day the years before. This is a daily habit that can lead to powerful and regular insights as you continue your journey toward Sage Mastery.

2. **Begin Your Daily 20 Minute PQ Gym Sessions.** In order to keep working on weakening your Saboteurs and strengthening your Sage Powers, really lean into the daily habit of starting your day with a longer PQ Gym session. This will support activating your PQ Brain first thing in the morning and reduce your chances of being and/or staying hijacked by your Saboteurs.

3. **Identify Your Accountability Buddy, Triad or Pod.** We'll get into this toward the end of the book, but for now be thinking about who you'd love to travel on this journey toward self-actualization, Sage Mastery and building your thriving coaching business with. You are far more likely to succeed when you travel with one or more individuals who want what you're after. If you need help with this part, we'll dive deeper into finding, selecting and setting up your systems of accountability as part of this journey.

Lastly, keep going! One of the most challenging lessons I've had to incorporate into my life is finishing what I start – especially when I find it challenging, uncomfortable or experience resistance in my body. We don't grow inside our comfort zone. This is your invitation to remain curious while to step outside your comfort zone in order to grow into what you want most. From the end-game of self-actualization to what's immediately right in front of you, your ability to stay disciplined and focused will lead to outcomes you desire.

---

[16] Pull exact quote and reference from "Trust & Inspire" book

Thank you for beginning this journey with me. I am honored and privileged to be here with you as you raise your own bar, take on your Saboteurs, strengthen your Sage Powers and continue your journey towards self–actualization. It's not only an epic ride, it's the only game worth playing full out and for the rest of your life. The rewards are greater than you can imagine and the people you choose to support in your coaching business will be forever changed by your commitments, efforts and application of this work. I can't wait for you to experience all of this.

CHAPTER THREE

Leveraging The Sage Perspective and Your Five Sage Powers In Your Coaching Business

I n the pages that follow, we're going to go deep into the core principles of building any successful business. I have built and successfully exited two multimillion-dollar marketing agencies before joining Positive Intelligence.

In my very first year of hanging my shingle as a coach, I generated over $350,000 of income. By the time I joined Positive Intelligence, that number grew to over $800,000 and there was no question in my mind my next year would have been a million-dollar year. If you know me personally, you also know that I don't say that to brag, but rather to share context of what's possible when you apply what I have learned to building and growing your own coaching practice. I'm going to share these very principles that I used to build each of my businesses.

And yet, if you are not already mentally fit, none of this information will matter to you. Why? Because your Saboteurs will prevent you from ever reaching the promised land. When the voices in your head fill you with negative emotions such as anxiety, shame and self-doubt, you're doomed. That is, unless you have already created the daily habits around quieting those negative voices and tapping into your five Sage Powers.

In this chapter, we're going to explore each of these five Sage Powers and how they directly apply to building and growing your coaching business. As a reminder, I'm assuming you've already read Shirzad Chamine's NY Times bestselling book, *Positive Intelligence*. Ideally, you've also already taken part in Positive Intelligence's multimillion-dollar coaching grant (see PositiveIntelligence.com/100x) and are part of the PQ Coach membership (see PositiveIntelligence.com/go) and practicing your focus of the day and regular PQ Reps.

If you are, then you're right where you need to be as you gear up to leverage the Sage Perspective and each of your five Sage Powers in building and growing your coaching business.

How The Sage Perspective Changes Everything In Your Coaching Business

As a quick reminder, the Sage Perspective holds that *everything* can be turned into a gift and opportunity. When it comes to building and scaling your coaching business, the way you know you're holding the Sage Perspective is your sense of ease and flow in all that you do. Take a moment and picture in your mind the most challenging and difficult parts of building your coaching business. For some it's generating new clients. For others it's the back-end administrative tasks such as invoicing, payments, agreements and bookkeeping. What is it for you? Take a moment here and connect with any aspect of your coaching business that feels hard and battery draining

What is it that makes this aspect of your coaching business so challenging? When you begin to breakdown the individual tasks, you'll discover that you can handle all of it. So what makes it difficult? Usually, it's the (Saboteur) feelings we attach to the thing we enjoy the least. If generating new clients feels difficult, ask yourself how hold the Sage Perspective would help you here. What knowledge would you need to make this aspect of your coaching business easy? What Sage Power would you need more of? What inspiration would you need to connect with in order to let go of any negative thoughts or feelings you have associated with this aspect of your coaching business?

As we continue to explore each of the five Sage Powers, set your intention up front. Consider any aspect of your coaching business you wish to work on and improve. When you activate your PQ Brain using PQ Reps, you can intercept those Saboteur thoughts and hold the Sage Perspective instead. Knowing that *everything* can be turned into a gift and opportunity, become curious about what may be hidden in your blind spot. Rather than feeling frustrated or defeated by a particular aspect of your coaching business, use the Sage Perspective to turn this "hard" or "difficult" aspect of your coaching business into an incredible gift.

When I was at a Tony Robbins *Unleash the Power Within* event, he reinforced a key insight that usually before you can have a breakthrough, most people have a breakdown. If you can begin to see that any breakdown can be turned into a breakthrough, you can remain curious about what's causing the breakdown and how a fresh Sage Perspective can turn that breakdown into a breakthrough. What's truly exciting and inspirational is knowing that the very things you currently hold as challenging can ultimately illuminate the path of the Sage. Reimagine those "hard" or "difficult" aspects of your coaching business showing you the path that will lead you to your ultimate desired outcome.

Can you see it? Do you have a sense of what's possible here? The Sage Perspective has the power to change *everything* in your coaching business. Rather than "grinding it out" and "pushing through" all these difficult aspects, isn't it inspiring to know there's a far easier and sustainable way? The way of the Sage is ease and flow. Why would this be any different in your coaching business? It's not. Your Saboteurs would have you *believe* that this is true, but they are lying to you. Only when you believe the lies of your Saboteurs will you struggle. Believing the lies of your Saboteurs will box you into your own limiting beliefs and stop you from having the coaching business you deserve.

Remember, to have the coaching business of your dreams, you must first work on your being, not your doing. Your Saboteurs would have you believe success is all about the doing. Sure, that's part of it, but if you're taking actions hijacked by your Saboteurs, I assure you it won't go well. Be your Sage self, hold the Sage Perspective and then every action you take will lead you to more ease and flow.

As Shirzad has shared with us over and over again, you can't control the wind or the waves of the ocean, but you can choose to surf. That's the feeling of ease and flow. Even the most turbulent wave can be handled in ease and flow when you learn to hold the Sage Perspective and surf. I love that vision and go back to it whenever I experience resistance, struggle or difficult challenges I don't feel I can handle. It helps me remember that this is just a Saboteur lie that I'm currently believing. The minute I stop believing it, I get up on my proverbial surf board and have the ride of my life. You may not be a surfer in real life, but you can mentally jump on your surf board anytime you see a big wave headed your way.

Soon, as you continue to ride these big waves, you'll shift from dreading them to seeking them out. The more turbulent the ocean, the bigger the waves and the more fun they are to ride. Holding the Sage Perspective is the key to becoming that surfer. No longer is the wave preventing you from having the coaching business you want, it's actually propelling you towards your desired outcome. You need only to shift from fear of that wave to deep gratitude, appreciation and love that this very wave is headed directly to where you want to go. You need only pop up on your surf board and let it carry you there. That's what Sage Mastery feels like and that's what we're going to be working on together.

In truth, it takes just as much effort to run a $40,000 a year coaching business as it does to run a million dollar one. Imagine expending *less* effort than you are today and generating a level of abundance you never before thought possible. That's the game we're playing. It's what we're up to when we hold the Sage Perspective. And the money is simply a biproduct of your journey towards self-actualization and making a seismic contribution to the world. If you're willing to hold that vision, let's play! No longer does any aspect of your coaching business need to be difficult. From here on out, we're going to tap into your innate abilities and strengthen your Sage Powers so that you can live into all of this every moment of every day.

The Five Sage Powers

Did you ever notice that the five Sage Powers are always displayed in this order: Empathy, Explore, Innovate, Navigate, and Activate? Shirzad is a huge fan of architecture and as such he's painstakingly built the sequential roadmap to unlocking your very best in any seemingly difficult situation. We're going to follow his architecture in this book as there's a tremendous amount of deep reflection and strategic thinking in not just what each Sage Power is, but the order in which each is accessed and leveraged.

Begin with Empathy

The first Sage Power is Empathy. As a quick refresher, there are three parts to Empathy: (1) Empathy for Yourself, (2) Empathy for Others and (3) Empathy for Situations. Here's the secret: When you master empathy, you're already so far ahead of most coaches who struggle to build their businesses. Mastering empathy takes the wind out of the sails of your top Saboteurs. And, when applied to generating customers, it ensures you never become a dreaded high-pressure Used Car Salesman when enrolling your coaching clients.

Here's how it applies to building and growing your coaching business.

Empathy for Yourself

It's best to begin with you. If you don't have empathy for yourself, then you're going to beat yourself up for every little mistake you make and every rejection you receive. This is a sure-fire way to ensure you avoid the business end of your coaching business like the plague.

Empathy for yourself in the context of building your coaching business begins with recognizing a few important insights. If you've never built a business for yourself before, then then is a great place to start. Have empathy for not knowing precisely what to do nor having the previous experience to draw on in order to build and scale your coaching business.

Remember the childhood picture exercise? Perhaps it's a good time to reconnect with your childhood picture if it's been some time since you've done so. See the powerful being that you are who deserves all of your love and affection. Building any business takes a tremendous amount of discipline and resilience. By connecting with your inner child, that innocence can support you along your journey.

Even if you have built businesses before, if this is the first coaching business you've ever built, have empathy for yourself in not knowing precisely what of your past experience applies here. Understand that just because something worked well in a previous business doesn't guarantee that it will work in this new context of building a coaching business.

Having empathy for yourself is the most important first step to connecting with your Sage self. When you are in Sage, you have the power of blameless discernment. Rather than judging yourself for the imperfect human being that you are, your blameless discernment will illuminate the path forward that will support you for years to come. In the immediate term this blameless discernment will reveal the next best step to take so that you don't allow your Saboteurs to verbally attack you and "kick you when you're down."

Go Back to Practicing Empathy For Yourself

In the flagship six-week program that you completed (seven weeks when you were part of the Coaching Grant program), you practiced a week of empathy in Week Five. As part of your PQ Coach membership, you have the ability to change your Daily Focus in the PQ App so that you can repeat your week of Empathy practice. By doing this, you're strengthening Sage Power Empathy as you work towards building more empathy toward yourself.

While part of you is itching to dive into direct applications of building your coaching business, by not being in Sage, you'll end up spending a lot of extra effort; more energy applied to produce the same or worse results.

Steven R. Covey in his bestselling book, *The Seven Habits of Highly Effective People* used a powerful analogy that has stuck with me throughout my career. He shared that if you and he were both lumberjacks and had the same amount of time to chop down a tree, he's spend the bulk of his time sharpening his axe. While taking the axe given to you and wildly swinging away at the tree feels like the right thing to do, a dull blade will not produce the desired results. That's why the 7th Habit is "Sharpen the Saw."

> "Sharpen the Saw means **preserving and enhancing the greatest asset you have—you**. It means having a balanced program for self-renewal in the four areas of your life: physical, social/emotional, mental, and spiritual."[17]

In the context of building and growing your coaching business, this means putting your own oxygen mask on first before attempting to help others. Without having empathy for yourself, you have a much higher probability for burnout. If what you're committed to having is a sustainable six or seven-figure coaching practice, then the greatest asset your coaching business has is *you*. In your work towards self-actualization, there's nothing more important than preserving and enhancing the greatest asset you have ... your Sage self.

---

[17]   https://www.franklincovey.com/habit-7/

It's all integrated. As you build and grow the powers of your Sage, your ability to build and grow your coaching practice will follow as a natural result. This will allow you to remain in ease and flow and minimize the chance of burnout before your reach your goals.

Increase Your Early Morning PQ Reps to At Least 20 Minutes

We'll talk more about this later, but if you're looking for a daily action that will produce immediate and noticeable results, increase your PQ Gym sessions to at least 20 minutes in the morning. What this does is charges up your PQ Brain at the start of your day. By making this a regular practice, will help keep your Sage present no matter what else you choose to do. Imagine if every day you began your day in Sage – what would that simple change do for you in the months and years that come?

I'm speaking from experience here. When Shirzad first asked me to take this on, I resisted. After all, I was already doing the Focus of the day, wasn't that enough? Wasn't the whole point of the PQ App to do two minutes about every three hours during my work day? Ease and flow, right?

Knowing what I was up to and seeing that this was an important step in building my own Sage Mastery, I (somewhat reluctantly) agreed. It took some practice and dedication in order to incorporate 20–30 minutes of PQ Reps in the morning, but after about two weeks, I began to really notice shifts in myself. I had an accountability pod (I was one of three) and since we all agreed to do this together, we shared what we were experiencing. I wasn't alone. Each of us experienced important shifts in ourselves due to incorporating this new daily habit.

Even before finishing this book, I urge you to being this practice now so that you can experience these benefits for yourself. If you have a pod you're working with, speak with them about what you're up to and see if they are willing to do it with you. It really is supportive to have others who are on this journey with you.

Empathy for Others

Once you have practiced empathy for yourself, seek to generate empathy for others – especially your prospects, current clients and those people in your network who can introduce you to your niche (which we'll discuss in greater detail in the chapters that follow). This can take many shapes in your coaching business. The really important point to understand is that having empathy for others does not mean sacrificing yourself or your coaching business for them. This is where our Pleaser Saboteur begins to show up. Remember, empathy is a core strength that your Pleaser Saboteur takes too far. Let's explore what this can and should look like from a Sage space.

What If They Can't "Afford" Your Coaching Services?

Practicing empathy for a prospective client that can't afford your coaching services, does not mean you need to lower your rates. Instead, you can practice empathy for another person by helping them see just how powerful and resourceful they are when they choose to be. Remember, your client may not always be the person who pays you for your coaching services. Often the "sponsor" and the "client" are the same person – but not always.

There are *at least* three ways to go here that have a positive (rather than an negative) impact on your coaching business: (1) Your client enrolls their own sponsor, (2) Your client has a breakthrough in investing in themselves, and/or (3) You recommend possible sponsors that cater to your prospect. Let's look at each of these just to get a clear picture of what Sage empathy for others could look like.

Your Client Enrolls Their Own Sponsor

Sage empathy for a potential prospect doesn't mean "pity." Rather than being enrolled into their (Saboteur?) story or limiting belief, what if you focused on their Sage just itching to break free? Sage empathy for others begins by holding them whole, perfect and complete and not by judging their current and temporary circumstances.

Imagine how powerful it would be for your client to acknowledge where they are financially, see how your coaching would support them and to ask for what they need. This could be from their place of employment, a family member, or an organization that caters to their particular challenge (which we'll cover separately).

One of the biggest hang-ups many people have include: (1) Asking for what you need, and (2) Asking for financial support. The moment your prospect reached out to you, the opportunity to begin a coaching relationship was identified. Any person who's willing to take themselves on is really committed to their work with you. They are willing to ask for the support they need and break out of the limiting beliefs in which they have allowed their own Saboteurs to trap them. While this is an ideal next step, it's not the only path forward.

Your Client Has a Breakthrough In Investing In Themselves

Another example of Sage empathy for your potential prospect is challenging the very premise that they can't afford your coaching services. For some, this may be a reality in which case we'll explore another option in a minute. But far more common is the avoidance of making an investment in their own transformation, self-development and self-actualization. What if you held Sage empathy for them, saw them as the innocent childhood version of themselves and helped them connect with their Wiser, Elder Self?

Having your prospects have a breakthrough in investing in themselves begins with empathy for them. When you deeply care about them and the (temporary) circumstances they find themselves in, you can support them in seeing how they view their circumstances. What are they choosing to make more important than investing in themselves right now? Be curious. The more you can remain in your Sage, the more likely they can see what's possible. And, when they see it too, they will shatter their own limiting beliefs and step into the life of their own design; one made from their own Sage and not driven by their Saboteurs.

You Recommend Possible Sponsors that Cater to Your Prospect

And sometimes, money really is a big problem in their life and they truly can't afford what you're offering them. When you have activated your Sage empathy for them, you will see that fact clearly. They simply don't have the financial wherewithal to invest in your coaching services. This is where you can support them in getting the support they need.

Let's say, for example, that you choose to work with children in foster care. And let's say you know that from ages 18 to 24, there's a big black hole in the support a foster child receives. This is because they are technically an adult and it's time for them to go to college or begin their working life.

It breaks your heart that they have "aged out" of the foster care system and aren't receiving financial or other support that would set them up for the rest of their lives. Now you could build such a successful coaching business that you choose to take on these youth free of charge. Or, you can find the non-profit associations which see what you see and align with them. There are financial grants from generous contributors that exist to support whatever group of people you want to work with.

Rather than struggle financially yourself for the foreseeable future, consider who also is committed to helping the very people you wish to take on as your clients. That combines the empathy for yourself, empathy for your prospective client and, what's next, empathy for situations.

Empathy for Situations

Beyond having empathy for yourself and empathy for others, how much empathy are you generating for the situations you find yourself and your clients in at present? Empathy for situations in the context of growing and building your coaching business means reframing the way your Saboteurs define it. Judgment of situations translates to, "Why is *THIS* happening *TO* Me?" Your Sage asks a set of different questions, such as:

- What might my Saboteurs stop me from seeing in this situation?
- What else could this situation mean?
- What if this situation was happening FOR me instead of TO me?
- At the end of my life looking back, how will I likely see the situation I'm in presently?
- How might I turn this "bad" situation into a gift and opportunity? (Sage Perspective)

Even if I can't see the gift right now, am I willing to hold the possibility that there's more going on than I may be able to see right now as it's happening? Empathy for situations is a powerful shift because it helps you not be so hard on yourself and others. Unless you are in immediate danger requiring immediate action, most of our stress is self-inflicted.

As William Shakespeare said in *Julius Caesar*, ""A coward dies a thousand times before his death, but the valiant taste of death but once. It seems to me most strange that men should fear, seeing that death, a necessary end, will come when it will come."[18] I loved this quote from the time I first read it in my High School. It had me question all of my fears. Are they really necessary? Sure, there is value in being alert to real and present dangers, but most of my fear shows up on low-probability items. Could it happen? Sure. Is it statistically likely to happen? Not really. And when it does happen, the situation I feared the most was never as bad in reality as my Saboteurs made it out to be.

That's the power of empathy for situations. When you can empathize for the current situation you find yourself in, you can stop making the very real situation so much bigger than it actually is. Let's take your coaching business for a moment. If you're the primary revenue generator for yourself and your family, that can generate a lot of pressure. How much of that pressure is real versus imagined? Is it possible that you'll never generate any clients fail your business entirely? Yes, while that's a low probability (especially now that you're reading this book), it cannot be ruled out 100% as a possibility.

I'll tell you this, however, whatever you focus on, expands. Often our Saboteurs generate the very fears that become self-fulfilling prophecies. In an extreme example, if you were to sit and worry about not getting clients instead of taking the necessary actions to actually generate clients, you increase that probability of having your coaching business fail. The opposite is also true. When you feel that fear, but take action anyway, you dramatically increase your odds of success and radically reduce your odds of failure. That's the power of empathy for situations.

---

[18]   https://www.goodreads.com/quotes/192269-a-coward-dies-a-thousand-times-before-his-death-but

There is a natural progression here from empathy for situations toward the Sage Perspective. When you hold the Sage Perspective, you see that everything can be turned into a gift and opportunity. The opportunity, then, is to live into this Sage Perspective as soon as possible, rather than allowing your Saboteurs to use the situation as fuel for your Judge and Accomplice Saboteurs.

Applying Empathy for Situations for Your Clients & Prospects

Having empathy for your clients is wonderful. And when you extend that empathy to the situations your clients find themselves in, you begin to see beyond the person and expand your vision toward their environment. Empathy for your client's situations allows you to look past what they see and expand your vision to the complete picture of what's going on – even if your client is judging the situation as "bad."

The same holds true for your prospective clients. When we dive into Niche development, this is going to be so incredibly important. That's because what your prospects actually buy isn't coaching … it's the solution to the problem they believe they have that's stopping them from what they want. Applying empathy for situations with your prospects means you're seeing clearly the situation your prospects find themselves in … and why they might want to hire you as their coach.

Explore Power

When it comes to your coaching business, your Sage Power Explore can illuminate what's currently hiding out in your blind spot. The only person we can't coach is ourselves. And yet, Sage Power Explore is the next best thing as it has you become a fascinated anthropologist as you take a look at what's working, what's not working and what you could add in order to grow and scale your coaching business.

Explore power shifts our focus from things *I Know That I Know* to things *I Know That I Do NOT Know* and all the way into the domain of things *I Don't Even Know That I Don't Know*. These are the three circles of knowledge and our Saboteurs would have us spend the bulk of our time in the domain of things I know that I know. Why? Because that's where our Saboteurs feel safe and secure. While we may "know" that we don't grow while inside our comfort zone, are we activating Sage Power Explore regularly to actually get outside of our comfort zone?

I see Sage Power Explore as the foundation of discovery. Before we can change the trajectory of our coaching business, we must first have the power to see things as they are … not as our Saboteurs would have us believe. Sage Power Explore is about getting really clear on what's happening in our coaching business. Only once we are clear on what's really happening, we can then investigate why it's happening without attachment to being right about the way we think things should be happening.

There's no point in wishing things were different than the way they are. Wishing and hoping isn't a strategy. Instead, wishing and hoping invites our Saboteurs to come in and judge us for not being further along in our journey. Sage Power Explore is about getting curious as to what it is that we may not be seeing clearly. This power to explore activates our PQ Brain and allows us to ponder, without judgment, what's really going on. It also allows us to see clearly what's working well so that we can reinforce our efforts here while paying attention to what's not working so well and what can be done about it.

Before diving right into Sage Power Explore, I invite you to do a few PQ Reps to ensure you're truly in your PQ Brain with your Sage fully activated and present. The worst lie I've discovered about my own Saboteurs is when they pretend to be my Sage and abuse these powers. If I'm ever not sure I'm in Sage, then I do as many PQ Reps as necessary to ensure I'm in Sage before proceeding. That can be as little as two minutes or as long as 20 minutes.

What's Working?

With your PQ Brain fully activated, we invite our inner Sage to illuminate what's working. Our Saboteurs would have us skip this step altogether and instead dive right into the next step of exploring what's not working. Your Sage knows better. Whatever we focus on, expands. Rather than focusing on what's not working, it's extremely important to first explore what is working so that you can double down and not lose what is working in your pursuit to grow and expand your coaching business.

Take a moment and write down what is working in your coaching business. Make sure you write down *at least* 10 things that are currently working in your coaching business. Be listening for those Saboteurs lies that prevent you from seeing clearly what is already working.

1. _____
2. _____
3. _____
4. _____
5. _____
6. _____
7. _____
8. _____
9. _____
10. _____

If you need more space, please grab your notebook, journal or a clean sheet of paper to keep this list going. Once you began writing down what is already working, notice if this process began to snowball for you (meaning it became easier and easier) or if you experienced resistance as part of the exercise. If it was really hard for you, I suggest doing a longer PQ Gym session such as 20 minutes and repeat the exercise.

Doing this, or any work, while hijacked by your Saboteurs produces predictable results. Rather than focusing on the assignment, our Saboteurs will have us looping the lies in our heads. Lies such as:

- "Nothing's working in my coaching business, that's why I'm reading this book!!!"
- "If I knew what was working, I'd be doing it already."
- "This is such a waste of time, I should skip this chapter and this stupid exercise."
- "I can only think of three things that are working. That's good enough."
- "I get Bill's point, but I don't need to do this. What's next?"

No, I'm not in your head, it's just that we all have similar thoughts – even if we're not consciously aware of them while we're having them. Sometimes reading them out loud helps us recognize the whisper of our Saboteurs. The whisper of our Saboteurs can be the deadliest because we don't experience ourselves as being hijacked and may not even be fully aware of the constant chatter our Saboteurs are spewing in the back of our minds. If we're not careful, we can begin to believe the lies of our Saboteurs – especially the lies we are barely hearing below the surface of our minds.

And, if after doing a long PQ Gym session you're still struggling with this exercise, let's look at a few examples to kick off your exploration of what's working in your coaching business. Feel free to use any or all of these to help get you started and explore areas you may have overlooked.

- I have my own coaching business – it's not just an idea, it's a bona fide business
- I continue to build and grow my own mental fitness
- I have at least one client and/or have had clients in the past
- I have successfully completed my coach training
- I am a certified coach or I'm in the process of becoming a certified coach
- I regularly work to improve my own skills as a coach and get better every week
- I have claimed my role as a coach and regularly introduce myself as a coach
- I have accountability partners I regularly work with to improve my skills
- I hired my own coach and regularly meet with them to grow and expand
- I am a PQ Coach member and tap into the resources available to me

And yes, I could keep going here. The point was to get you started if you were experiencing a bit of "blank page" anxiety. Notice what else showed up for you as you reviewed this list. What new discoveries came up for you in areas of your coaching business that are already working for you? Rather than charging ahead in this book, I encourage you to take a brief time out and write these additional insights down to reinforce what's already working in your coaching business. We can revisit these again when you're looking for inspiration.

What's NOT Working?

Notice which Saboteurs show up immediately when you ask yourself "What's not working?" And then what is your Saboteur focused on? For example, your Judge might be judging you for not having figured all of this stuff out already. Or your Stickler may tell you that nothing is working because you're not ready. Or perhaps your Avoider is telling you that there's simply too much to think about so better focus on something else entirely.

Before you list out what's not working, please do some PQ Reps to get out of any Saboteur thoughts and switch to Sage discernment (instead of negative judgment on yourself or your situation). Sage discernment will have you see clearly what's not working without any of the judgmental overtones delivered by our Saboteurs. This is a really important practice whenever you want to improve any aspect of your coaching business. Rather than diving right into what's not working, pause and do PQ Reps first to ensure your Sage PQ Brain is activated. This will help you separate "fact" from "interpretation."

For example, "I'm not generating enough appointments" may be true, but notice how your Saboteurs interpret this fact. It might go something like, "I SUCK at getting clients. I don't know how to ask for money, so I give away my coaching services like an IDIOT!"

Your Saboteurs may be a bit sneakier than that, but if you listen for the undertone of judgment, it's likely there. Yours might sound more like, "I'm just not cut out for generating business." Or, "I'm overwhelmed by just how much I don't know and how much I still need to do." The non-verbal implication being that you don't get it, you'll never get it so you should just stop trying. Those are the lies of your Saboteurs and if you begin to believe them, you'll trap yourself into limiting beliefs that will prevent you from having the coaching business you deserve. So let's try this with some Sage discernment.

Take a moment and write down what is *not* working in your coaching business. Make sure you write down *no more than* five things that are currently *not* working in your coaching business. Any more than that and we won't be able to focus on what's really important and needs your attention. Continue listening for those Saboteurs lies that prevent you from seeing clearly what is already working versus what's truly not working for you right now.

1. _____
2. _____
3. _____
4. _____
5. _____

If you need more space, you certainly can write down everything in a free-flowing exercise to truly "release" any of the negative energy you're experiencing in your coaching business. But then begin to chunk them. In truth, there are only 4 areas to pay attention to and they are:

1. I'm not clear on my niche and ideal customer ... yet.
2. I have not created my irresistible offer ... yet.
3. I'm not generating enough appointments on my calendar .. yet.
4. I'm not converting enough appointments ... yet.

These are the four foundations of any coaching business. If you're writing down things like "My website needs updating" and "My social media presence is lacking," these may be true, but should not be the priority. You'll see why in the next section of "What Could I Add?" You're going to want to filter out all the things that can (and eventually will) be better so that you can focus on what *really* matters the most.

Also, did you catch the "...yet" I added to each of the four foundations? That comes from NY Times bestselling author, Neil Pasricha, in his book, *You are Awesome: How to Navigate Change, Wrestle with Failure, and Live an Intentional Life.* One of the key principles he shares in this book is the power of "...yet" added to anything that you choose to be awesome at doing. In his own words:

> *"Everything you do, every path you take, every diagnosis you get, every wall you hit, every setback, ever failure, every rejection. All of these experiences are part of the unfished sentence of your life story. Sometimes the best think you can do is learn to add that dot-dot-dot ... and keep going."*[19]

---

[19] Pasricha, Neil. *You Are Awesome: How to Navigate Change, Wrestle with Failure, and Live and Intentional Life*. Simon & Schuster. ©2019, page 11.

By adding "...yet" you are acknowledging where you are in this moment. Not from a place of "bad" or "wrong" as your Saboteurs would have you believe, but rather from a place of Sage discernment. Here's where I am now and I acknowledge I get to learn and grow in this area of my coaching business. That encompasses "ease and flow" into your journey towards Sage Mastery and self-actualization.

None of this is hard. Yes, sometimes the learning (which some label "failure") can be jarring. When you are able to shift your perspective from Saboteur to Sage and see that everything can be turned into a gift and opportunity, you begin to realize the truth. Life is happening *for* me, not *to* me. When you begin to see the world through this lens, you welcome the opportunities to grow, expand and improve.

What Could I Add?

Here again, this question can be answered from both the Saboteur and Sage perspective. The knee jerk Saboteur response is, "EVERYTHING!!!!" With individual flavors of Saboteur responses ranging from the Avoider, "None of this feels good. Maybe if I let it go, it will take care of itself." To the Stickler, "I'm nowhere near where I need to be!" To the Victim, "Doesn't matter, I'm just going to fail anyway."

Adding to your coaching business requires Sage discernment. Our focus here isn't to include everything that's falling short of your own expectations – at least not right now all at once. Sage discernment will have you tap into Sage Power Explore so that you can clearly see the most important aspects of your coaching business to focus on. What will support us here is what is referred to in business as the *Pareto Principle* also known as the 80/20 rule.

"Vilfredo Pareto, an Italian economist, "discovered" this principle in 1897 when he observed that 80 percent of the land in England (and every country he subsequently studied) was owned by 20 percent of the population. Pareto's theory of predictable imbalance has since been applied to almost every aspect of modern life."[20]

Applied to your coaching business, this means that 20% of your efforts produce 80% of the results. When you're clear on the results you want to see in your coaching business, Sage Power Explore will have you tap into the 20% driving the 80%. Whereas your Saboteurs do the opposite. They would have you obsess on the last 20% that requires 80% of your effort. These are the lies of your Saboteurs – that an 80% result is unacceptable, so let's get after that last 20% by multiplying your effort by a factor of 4. That's right, 400% more effort to get the final 20% of the result you're after. If you're feeling burnt out, this is the place to look.

---

[20]   https://www.aafp.org/fpm/2000/0900/p76.html#:~:text=Vilfredo%20Pareto%2C%20an%20Italian%20economist,every%20aspect%20of%20modern%20life.

Think about it, is your website ever "done"? Hell no. How about posting, liking, sharing, and tagging on social media? What about your email inbox? Asked another way, what are you willing to slow down or let go of entirely to get the real result you're after?

Can you even imagine what it would be like if you never checked your email ever again? Or what if you took a social media detox break? When's the last time you completely unplugged on vacation and didn't pick up your phone? For many of us, this is a real challenge. We've become addicted to our devices. "I'm ON therefor I AM" has become a way of life – mostly driven by our Saboteurs.

So when I ask, "What Could I Add?" I'm asking you to focus on the 20% of the effort that drives 80% of the results you want. You may not believe me yet, but there's only 4 places you need to look and we covered them in the previous section:

1. Get clear on my niche and ideal customer. Who do I choose to serve powerfully?
2. Create my irresistible offer so that my ideal customer can't wait to hire me.
3. Generate appointments on my calendar doing what I truly love doing already.
4. Convert appointments with ease and flow. No selling. Just enrollment of my ideal clients.

While there are many paths that will get you to where you want to go, use these four foundations as your guideposts. Within each of them is the 20% of the effort that will get you to 80% of your desired result – all with "ease and flow" with very little difficulty.

Innovate Power

After you've generated empathy for yourself, your clients (and prospective clients), empathy for your situation and then Explore what's working, not working and what you can add into your coaching business, what's next is Sage Power Innovate. Simply put, your Innovate Power is the one that will open more opportunities and convert more "No for Nows" into a solid "Hell Yes!" And, it's all about being fully present in your Sage in the moment of enrollment.

When Shirzad first talked about the "Yes, and" game as a means to access our Innovate Power, it took me right back to my very first improv class. If you've ever taken an improv class, you know where I'm headed. If not, please consider signing up. Improv lessons did more for me in a few classes than all sorts of sales training courses ever did.

In the world of improv, the only "rule" is that you *must* accept any premise given – no matter how crazy it may sound. So if we were on stage right now, I might ask you,

"Didn't I see you walking a goat wearing a tuxedo down my block yesterday?" You're not allowed to argue as this brings the dance of improv to a screeching halt.

So, instead, you come up with a clever way to turn it right back on me. "Absolutely, Bill. And I was surprised that you weren't standing in solidarity with me and your other neighbors who are standing up for the rights of our local farm animals. You see ..."

Goofy example, I know, but you get the point. In improv you must accept any premise given to you. The crazier, the better and the more hilarious. Masters of improv exhibit no fear. Take a look at Wayne Brady or any of the stars of the hit television show, *Who's Line Is It Anyway?* What impresses me the most about Wayne Brady is his ability to not only improv, but make up songs that rhyme, do entire skits in reverse, come up with incredibly funny applications of props and work with anything his audience tosses his way.

Please notice if your Saboteurs are acting up right now telling you that none of this is important, relevant or something you could ever do. That's your Saboteurs holding you small and doing their best to convince you that you're not cut out for all of this. By now, you know the drill. Do a few PQ Reps and lean in. What I'm about to share with you is gold that can make you incredibly successful and financially free.

Accept Your Prospective Client's Premise

When it comes to building and scaling your coaching business, a great place to start is by accepting whatever premise your prospect gives you. While you can still challenge them if you think they are playing small or are in their Saboteurs, consider what would happen if you just acknowledged them first. As Shirzad likes to remind us, at least 10% of what they believe is true, so begin there. "What I like about what you're sharing is ..." and then align to the 10%.

"AND ..." This is where you get to creatively build on what they are sharing with you.

As Theodore Roosevelt famously said, "No one cares how much you know, until they know how much you care."[21] Accepting your client's premise is about deeply listening to what they are sharing and how they see what they are going through. I studied ontological coaching with Bettie Spruill and one of the many profound quotes I picked up from her was, "You reveal your whole life every time you open your mouth."[22] What she showed me was that the words we choose reveal our filters and biases. As I listen to any client or prospect, their words reveal how they see the world,

---

[21]   https://www.theodorerooseveltcenter.org/Learn-About-TR/TR-Quotes?page=112#:~:text=Nobody%20cares%20how%20much%20you,found%20to%20verify%20the%20attribution.

[22]   https://ontologicalliving.com/about-bettie-j-spruill/

what limiting beliefs are stopping them from having what they truly desire and where to focus our efforts together.

This is the ultimate "Yes, and" game as your Sage Innovate Power will lead you to let go of your Saboteurs and help you be fully present to what's right in front of you. Only by accepting the premise of your prospects will you be able to truly listen to their needs and determine how your work supports these needs – or not. It's perfectly fine to acknowledge that what the person in front of you needs is different than what you are offering. Saying "no" to the wrong opportunities will get you one step closer to saying yes to the right ones.

Contrast This to Rejecting Your Prospective Client's Premise

The opposite to "Yes, and" is "No, but." Remember the last time someone gave you a compliment with "BUT" at the end of it? How did that make you feel? "You look amazing tonight, but ..." Suddenly, the comment is almost meaningless. "You are such a powerful coach, but ..." We are trained to negate anything that comes before the word "but."

And when you feel rejected, you're not in a great place to say yes are you? Our words matter so much more than most of us realize. When we share our observations, we need to be really careful that we're creating foundations that serve both us and our prospects. Rejecting the premise of your clients and prospects has the unfortunate side effect of making them defensive. Force is met with more force. If I feel attacked, my natural response is to attack. That's why it's so important to remain in Sage. Negative energy from our Saboteurs invites more negative energy and it's a vicious cycle that leads nowhere productive or effective.

No matter how crazy the premise of a prospect may sound, use your Sage Innovate Power to look for the 10% of what's true and build from there. Even acknowledging that 10% builds trust between you and the person you're engaging with. They feel heard and validated. That's a much better place to end up with someone you want to have as your client.

Innovate Your Way Forward

The last thing I want to share about Sage Power Innovate is that this is your most important Sage Power to get unstuck. Yes, Empathy is important. And Explore helps you discover what's in your blind spot. But Innovate unlocks your creativity and taps your inner genius. Innovation is what drives us to build, create and try new approaches to well-known and well-defined problems. Every time we come up with a new innovative approach to solving a problem, we're flexing our PQ Brain and it feels amazing.

I associate Sage Power Innovate with breakthroughs and transformations. As Tony Robbins likes to say in his *Unleash the Power Within* seminars, "Breakdowns lead to breakthroughs." It's such a simple and powerful concept. When you're experiencing a breakdown, it's usually Saboteur led. But when you hold the Sage Perspective that everything, including this breakdown, can be turned into a gift and opportunity, Sage Power Innovate kicks in and suddenly you see new possibilities that you were not aware of previously. Breakthroughs happen when we Innovate our way out of a problem by tapping our PQ Brain.

Or, as Albert Einstein said, "We can't solve our problems with the same thinking we used when we created them."[23] Different thinking is generated from Sage Power Innovate. It can come from the "Yes, and" game, or any activity that starts with PQ Reps and calling forth your Sage. To innovate is to see what others may not see, to build upon half-baked ideas so that you come to a clear picture of what the next best step should be.

Besides, innovation is fun!

Sage Power Innovate is about tapping into your inner-child and having the freedom to be creative. Your own child-like innocence will allow you to "let go" of all the stuff you're holding onto (including Saboteur negative thoughts) and embrace the freedom of what's new, different and unproven. Sage Power Innovate is you having the freedom to simply BE. Increase your Sage muscles and you'll also increase your abilities to innovate. And the more you innovate, the more you *want* to innovate.

Navigate Power

In the context of business development, Sage Power Navigate is about being fully aligned with your purpose as a powerful coach and why you want the outcome you are declaring. Why is it that you choose to have the kind of coaching business you are building? That may seem like a reactively simple question, but there is a ton of Sage wisdom there when you choose to spend time connecting with your mission, purpose and why it matters.

What's Your Ultimate Outcome?

As a coach, you truly have a superpower that the world needs. The core principles of mental fitness combined with your skills as a professional coach can create seismic change and result in an incredible positive impact in the world. Do you realize just how powerful you are? This is not a question for your egoic self, but rather your Sage self.

---

[23] https://www.brainyquote.com/quotes/albert_einstein_121993

Mahatma Gandhi is often misquoted as having said, "Be the change you wish to see in the world."[24] What he actually said was:

> "We but mirror the world. All the tendencies present in the outer world are to be found in the world of our body. **If we could change ourselves, the tendencies in the world would also change. As a man changes his own nature, so does the attitude of the world change towards him.** This is the divine mystery supreme. A wonderful thing it is and the source of our happiness. We need not wait to see what others do."[25]

While not as memorable or catchy as the simplified version, "Be the change you wish to see in the world," this accurate and complete version goes to the heart of Sage Power Navigate. This journey of self-actualization is about the change you choose to make for yourself and, in doing so, the impact you choose to have in the world.

Sage Power Navigate is about taking the time to really be clear on your intentions for yourself, the clients you choose to serve as their coach and ultimately the impact these efforts will have in the world. When I ask you to reflect on just how powerful you are, this is what I mean.

So many people go through life on what I would refer to as auto-pilot. They are in a constant state of reaction. The way that they show up and the actions they take appear to require little thought or intention. If asked, they would have you believe that life is happening *to* them, not *for* them. I notice this most in people who self-identify with a high Victim Saboteur, but most of us have "woken up" and discovered we've been asleep in our day-to-day choices in our life.

Simply put, when our Saboteurs are in the driver's seat in our life, we tend to react to external events rather than being clear about our intentions and what we're really up to for ourselves and for our coaching business.

Are You Designing Your Life, Or Managing Your Circumstances?

This was one of the most powerful coaching questions my coach, Chad Cooper, asked me in one of our early coaching sessions. Yes, I know it's a closed question (not an open What, How or Why question), but it woke me up all the same. At the time he asked me this question, I truly felt numb. Later, having discovered Positive Intelligence and having the tools to unpack what was happening, I discovered my Hyper-Achiever Saboteur teamed up with my Controller Saboteur and had switched me to autopilot myself.

---

[24] https://medium.com/illumination-curated/gandhi-didnt-actually-ever-say-be-the-change-you-want-to-see-in-the-world-d65b92cf5db

[25] Ibid.

Rather than designing the life I wanted, I was managing any and all circumstances showing up in front of me. I was driven by fear – specifically financial scarcity – and despite all my external success, I had lost all sense of joy, happiness and purpose. If my life were a movie, I wasn't the main actor – I was playing the role of extra in so many other people's movies. I urge you to reflect on this for yourself. Right now, in this moment, are you the main actor in your own movie? Or do you find you play the role of extra more often than you care to admit?

It's so easy to get swept up in the busyness of life that we forget to take that time out and reflect on what we truly want (and why it's important to us). If you're finding your spending the bulk of your time managing your circumstances, then Sage Power Navigate will support you in designing your life.

Design Your Mission, Purpose & Vision with Sage Power Navigate

Shirzad asks, "At the end of your life looking back, what is truly important?"

When you're unsure of what action to take, do a long PQ Gym session and consult your Wiser Elder Self. Imagine seeking guidance from your Wiser Elder Self. S/he is at the end of life, healthy in mind and body. From that ageless wisdom, what would s/he say is most important in this situation? Trust that you intuitively know your mission, purpose and vision, even if you haven't yet written all of it down.

By consulting our Wiser Elder Self, we can begin to check-in with what we truly want. Perhaps you already know, and that's great. If not, then it's important to take the time to get clear on what you're up to and why it's important enough to dedicate your life to accomplishing it.

Your Sage is keenly aware of your spiritual contract. You were put on this earth to make a seismic impact. The world needs your unique gifts and talents. Only you know what your purpose is in this life. When you take the time to reflect on why you're here and the positive impact you choose to make, you'll begin to lift the Saboteur veil of darkness and begin to see the light calling you forth to live into your mission and purpose.

Take One Step Closer To The Light

All decisions are made from love or fear. Decisions made in love come from our Sage and move us closer towards the light. Decisions made in fear come from our Saboteurs and move us deeper into the shadows. Even if you're not clear on your mission, purpose and vision for your life, you can begin to reveal what's important as you consciously reflect on the most important decisions in front of you and notice if you are driven by fear or love; darkness or light.

When you feel lost and are unsure what to do, Sage Power Navigate supports you by connecting with your Wiser Elder Self and seeking that ageless wisdom; your inner knowing. When's the last time you connected with Wiser Elder Self and asked for guidance? You can do this on your own by yourself, with your coach, your Pod, or your accountability partner. The important step is to shift to your Sage, connect, ask a powerful question and allow your Wiser Elder Self to reveal the next step that takes you closer to the light.

With each step closer to the light, you reveal for yourself more of what you were put on this earth to accomplish by becoming the full expression of your Sage self. Sage Mastery is self-actualization and it happens with each choice made in love, not fear, stepping into the light, not retreating into the shadows.

Consider Orchestrating Your Funeral

Stephen R. Covey in *The Seven Habits of Highly Successful People*, urges us to "Begin with the end in mind." The ultimate "end" as he points out is your death. While we don't want to dwell on our own mortality, Covey recommends a great exercise to examine what you anticipate your funeral to be. Specifically, who is there and what do they say about you. If you're struggling to clearly define your mission, purpose and vision for your life, I found this to be a profound exercise (when done in my Sage PQ Brain).

This exercise is about examining who you want to show up and speak on your behalf when you die. Consider your family, friends, co-workers, community and clients. The more granular and specific you get, notice how clear you become on who matters to you in your life. Then script what they would say about you. What did your life mean to them? What is the loss they are grieving because of who you were in your lifetime and what you choose to do for others?

Grief is a Sage response. Grief honors the life of the person and their positive impact. By imagining your own death, you can look past your own mortality and envision the true and lasting impact you have already had and are committed to living into for the rest of your life.

This is such a powerful exercise and I'm eternally grateful for Stephen R. Covey for pointing me in this direction at such an early age. While I was hesitant to take on this exercise when I first read about it in my 20's, I received so much from it, I've gone back and modified it every decade or so. The more I get clear on what I'm up to, the brighter the light I feel empowered to step into. My Sage compels me to remain clear on what I'm up to, whom I choose to serve and the impact this has already had and will continue to have long after I'm dead and gone.

By writing all of this out, I can see clearly my impact – not from my Hyper-Achiever, but rather Sage discernment. My accomplishments are not trophies on my wall, but rather all the transformational shifts I've made for myself, my clients, my wife, my kids, my parents, my brother, my friends, the youth I serve as a youth group leader, the homeless people whose lives I've made better and even as I write these words, I'm thinking about you who have taken the time to read what I'm writing. That feeling of purpose drives me to keep going and share all that I've learned so that you can have the kind of impact you know you're capable of having in the world.

Activate Power

When it comes to building, growing and scaling your coaching business, swift, laser-focused action beats great ideas every day of the week. Sage Power Activate is about breaking the cycle of paralysis of analysis and instead being willing to make mistakes. Your Saboteurs would much rather pepper your mind with all the risks associated with taking action. Remember, their job is to keep you safe and they believe that safety comes from inaction. Your Sage knows better. And so many titans of industry agree:

"The truth is that falling hurts.
The dare is to keep being brave and feel your way back up."
— Brené Brown

"You don't have to be great to start, but you do have to start to be great."
— Zig Ziglar

"Do the one thing you think you cannot do. Fail at it. Try again. Do better the second time. The only people who never tumble are those who never mount the high wire. This is your moment. Own it."
— Oprah Winfrey

"Take the first step in faith.
You don't have to see the whole staircase, just take the first step."
— Dr. Martin Luther King Jr.

"Nothing will work unless you do."
— Maya Angelou

"Dream big, start small, but most of all, start."
— Simon Sinek

"You are what you do, not what you say you do."
— Carl Jung

"The only impossible journey is the one you never begin."
— Tony Robbins

And I'm just scratching the surface here. Google "Motivational Quotes on Action" and find a consistent theme of taking action over inaction by just about any person in history you admire and respect. Remember, our Saboteurs were designed to keep us safe by having us playing small and minimal risk-taking. If it were up to your Saboteurs, you'd never take risks. In one of my all-time favorite books, *Purple Cow* by Seth Godin, he makes the point that "Being risky is safe. Being safe is risky."

That's the paradox your Saboteurs simply don't understand. The act of having you play small and avoid taking risks will seal your fate and ensure your failure. Whereas the more risks you take, the more you learn and the higher the probability of your success. Those set-backs and failures are your greatest teachers. Don't rob yourself of all the incredible learning that comes from making mistakes – even huge and seemingly disastrous ones.

The Incredible Gift of Failure

Throughout this book, I'll share with you some of the biggest most outlandish failures in my life and then show you how they have allowed me to become the person I am today. I'll choose the biggest ones I can think of as I could write another book on all the spectacular failures in my life and how they were the most incredible gifts I've ever received.

Can you imagine investing $350,000 into something you don't understand and losing 100% of your investment with zero recourse? Oh, and imagine doing that when your wife has just had your second child and you just launched a business that doesn't allow you to make any money for the first six months. New family (babies are expensive!), new company (a different sort of "baby" that needs constant care and feeding), new home (parts of the house still in boxes), an epic market crash (2008 housing crisis), and no family members to bail you out.

Losing money under any circumstances is challenging enough, but can you see how this was a "perfect storm" brewing. I had just exited my first marketing agency. While I had successfully helped my business partners grow a multi-million dollar annual revenue agency, we were no longer seeing eye-to-eye and I knew it was time to get out. Rather than having the epic payday that we all thought we would have, I saw my business partner making decisions that I knew would tank the company and I didn't want to be there when it did.

My wife had just given birth to our second child, and we moved to Port Washington, New York, to be closer to her family. We bought the house in 2005 and paid way more than we were expecting to for a house that was far from our dream home.

As I began my new company, I was thinking about the importance of diversification. Despite having a financial advisor, I hadn't learned to truly listen to the advice and council I received. I met a Texan oil driller and did my first investment of $50,000 with him. It wasn't successful, and he ended up leaving the company I had invested with. He called me because he "felt bad" that I had lost my investment and wanted to bring me a deal that couldn't lose. (And yes, looking back, all the signs of this epic fail were there).

What sold me was this person's seemingly incredible knowledge of the oil and gas industry. The biggest risk, he explained, was not knowing where to drill for oil. Why his deal was different was that this was an opportunity to purchase a working oil field that had successfully produced for years, but was no longer producing enough oil to make the pumping worthwhile. But underneath all that oil was a major field of natural gas. By drilling differently, they could get at the massive lakebed of natural gas – as no one had previously been focused on natural gas.

All the geological reports showed the massive amounts of natural gas nearby indicating that this was an absolute sure bet. And so I began sending money to him to license the mineral rights to the land, equipment, drilling and all the start-up costs on the business. I was his partner in this and therefore had a percentage carry on any gas produced.

It took a solid three years to discover he was wrong. After a full $300,000 invested – each investment feeling like it would make the previous investments pay out – I finally gave up. The state government eventually came in and took over the lease when we stopped drilling and then this guy took off with some crazy story about his girlfriend kidnapping his son. I don't know if that part was true, or he just was scared that all of this went belly up and needed to "go dark" for a while.

When it was all said and done, my Saboteurs were having an absolute field day with me. My Judge told me what an idiot I was and how I put my whole family at risk. My Victim invited me to a massive pity party to sulk over how I'd been manipulated and taken advantage of. My Avoider had been with me for quite some time preventing me from seeing the truth. Rather than getting out earlier, I kept throwing good money after bad. And I'm sure every Saboteur made an appearance during this entire fiasco.

So What Are All The Incredible Gifts of This Epic Failure?

At the time, my Saboteurs blinded me to so many of the gifts. I couldn't see them because I didn't want to own my part in any of this. So much easier to blame the person who enrolled me into this deal. But after the dust settled and I was clear that I'd never see any of this money ever again, my Sage showed up and helped me see the incredible gifts I had just received.

Gifts of Knowledge:

1. Never invest in anything you don't truly understand.
2. Don't be a speculative investor.

3. Don't make these kinds of investments by yourself.

4. Have a team of trusted impartial financial experts to advise you including a fiduciary (Registered Investment Advisor), Certified Public Accountant, and qualified independent individuals who have made similar deals themselves.

5. LISTEN to the advice they give you and don't discount it.

6. When something feels too good to be true, it most likely is.

7. Diversification is great, but alternative investments must be a small part of your investment strategy – can't be more than 50% of what you've got.

8. Vet any partner you choose to do business with. What's their track record? Who are their references? What have they accomplished for other investors?

9. Never invest money in speculative investments if you aren't willing to lose 100%.

10. The wealthy don't take these kinds of risks. They protect their capital from downside risk and focus on not losing their investments (versus the upside potential).

Gifts of Power

All five of my Sage Powers grew as a direct result of this experience. My Empathy Power grew as I learned to have empathy for myself when it comes to investing. I grew my empathy for this precise situation and the imperfect human being that I was going into this investment. I even grew my empathy for the person who enrolled me into this failed investment – seeing that he was also doing the best that he could despite the failure.

My Explore Power revealed what was in my blind spot and truly how much I didn't know about the world of investing. I explored what had me invest in something I truly didn't understand. I explored the entire industry of finance and investing and discovered so much about the hidden fees in my mutual funds, 401K plans, and the conflicts my then financial advisor had who was not a fiduciary (i.e. legally required to put my financial interests above his own).

My Innovate Power grew as I played the "Yes, and" game to reveal how other investors protect themselves from similar situations. I innovated my way forward by revamping my entire investment strategy starting with hiring a fiduciary, reading up on the best books available on investing, and coming up with an entirely new approach to investing and wealth creation.

My Navigate Power had me shift from scarcity to abundance. This was, perhaps, the most important gift of them all. No longer would I continue to life a life with a scarcity mindset. I committed to aligning with my abundant nature realizing the truth. That, "All I need is within me now." As I worked on shifting my scarcity to an abundant mindset, so too did my ability to create wealth shift.

My Activate Power had me make immediate course corrections in who I had on my financial investment team, what my dollar-cost-averaging investment strategy was, and how I would vet any future investment that even slightly appealed to me. I created a system to protect myself from speculative investments and felt free to say "No Thank You" so much more aggressively.

<u>Gift of Inspiration</u>

I was inspired by losing this much money to not only learn these invaluable lessons for myself, but to share with as many people as I could about what I learned. This led me to reading *Money: Master the Game* by Tony Robbins, attending his Wealth Mastery seminar, and then having the incredible opportunity to interview Tony Robbins for his book, *Unshakable: Your Financial Freedom Playbook*.

I was so inspired by this experience, that I changed everything about my investing including learning about asymmetric risk (where you have capital protection on your investments and unlimited upside potential), running any and all investments past my fiduciary and actually attaining total financial freedom.

That's right. The biggest gift of this epic failure is that as a direct result of it, my relationship with money and investing forever changed. I began the daily habits that have ensured my ability to be financially free. I not only created wealth for myself and my family, but through careful estate and tax planning, I've set up financial freedom for my unborn grandchildren. If you would have told my 12-year-old self that not only would I be okay financially, but that I would end up with generational wealth, I wouldn't have believed any part of that.

Only through making this gigantic financial mistake was I able to learn what it takes to be financially free – and then follow through with bold action to make it happen. And that's the point. I would never have taken the actions I've consistently taken if I hadn't first experience an epic failure.

Taking Bold, Swift Action

Thinking and learning are important, but not nearly as important as taking bold, swift action. Indecision is both mentally exhausting and can be the root of many problems showing up in your coaching business. A decision you haven't made yet keeps you from taking action. Over time, this leads to paralysis of analysis and the more you choose not to act, the more stuck you begin to feel and live into.

You're never stuck. You're always at choice – even when you make the "wrong" decision. Think about it. No matter how important the decision is, you are only expected to do your best with the information you have and the life lessons you've already learned. The more challenging a decision feels, the more important that you not allow it to weigh upon you and stop you from your forward momentum. That's precisely the strategy of your Saboteurs – to overwhelm you with possibilities so that you choose to do nothing. In their view, this is always the safest choice – even though it rarely is. "If you choose not to decide, you still have made a choice," as the *Freewill* song lyric goes from the band Rush.

When our amygdala triggers our fight, flight or freeze response, we tend to be more aware of the sensations of fight or flight, and less so on freeze. That proverbial "deer in the headlights" feeling is often more subtle than fight or flight. Not taking action can feel appropriate as our Saboteurs paralyze us with too many thoughts, feelings, emotions and options. And yet, when a car is headed toward the deer at high speeds, that freeze response is so much more dangerous than we realize. Freezing has us experience our own powerlessness. Inaction may feel safe in the moment, but typically it's anything but.

While all of your Saboteurs can play a role here, be on the lookout especially for your Avoider, Victim, Hyper-Vigilant and Hyper-Rationale. When it comes to making important decisions, these Saboteurs often act up. If you're more familiar with your Controller, Hyper-Achiever, and Restless, you may be surprised by these Saboteurs you're less familiar with. They may be less active, but they have the power to show up at precisely the wrong time and prevent you from making decisions in Sage Power Activate.

That's why I love this quote:

"Take the first step in faith.
You don't have to see the whole staircase, just take the first step."
– Dr. Martin Luther King Jr.

The moment you decide to take that first step, you've unstuck yourself and you've activated your Sage. Every step you take toward more love, more light and more of your desired outcomes, you are allowing your Sage to help you on your path towards mastery.

Deeper Application of Sage Power Activate to Coaching Business

In my own experience, of all the Sage Powers, Sage Power Activate is the one most of us need to lean into in order to have the coaching business of our dreams. We can have empathy for ourselves, our clients and our situations. We can explore who we are being and what we are doing in any given situation. We can continue to innovate new and better solutions to any problems we face. We can connect all of this to our mission, purpose and our why. But if we fail to take action, how much does any of the others truly matter?

Action leads us to results and feedback. Even if the result is not what we had intended or is taking us in the opposite direction of what we are committed to, with Sage Power Activate, we have the momentum to correct course and continue. Yes, the other four powers are important and integral to your long-term success as a coach. But until you begin taking action, it's all a thought experiment and you'll have nothing to show for all your strategic thinking and incredible plans.

Only through committed action will you have the results you want – even if that means temporarily having the results you *don't* want. When you begin to see that *all* feedback is a gift, you'll experience a drive inside of you that propels you forward – no matter the consequences. You exchange your fears for love and, as a result, become fearless. When you care more about the mission you're on and people you choose to serve, your own success becomes secondary. You see that your contributions matter regardless of how inexpert you feel.

Even beginner coaches who choose to take bold action immediately see their results. Rather than waiting to some undetermined future state and time when they feel "ready," they acknowledge where they are and begin their journey. And that's why I love:

> *"The only impossible journey is the one you never begin."*
> *– Tony Robbins*

The very act of beginning means that you've chosen to start a journey that will challenge you to embody your Sage and be driven by your mission, purpose and vision. At the beginning of every journey, it can *feel* impossible, but it's not – at least, it's not when you choose to take action.

A white belt on their first day of their martial arts class can see a master ninth degree black belt and think, "that will never be me." Or, they can be curious about just how dedicated that master practitioner has worked at his craft and see the truth. That that *will* be me when I continue to dedicate my life to this martial art.

When you choose to take bold action in your coaching business, you are taking one step closer to what you truly want. Every step you take continues to move you closer and closer to your desired outcome. You don't need to be the smartest or most talented coach the world has ever seen to be one of the most successful and globally-recognized impactful coaches. All that is required of you is to commit to the daily practices necessary to hone your craft while you build and scale your coaching business.

Together, These Five Sage Powers Make You UnstoppaBill

Allow me to introduce you to my Sage self. I call him UnstoppaBill. As we continue this journey together, I want you to know that what I'm sharing was written from a

Sage space. Every morning I complete a minimum of 20 minutes of PQ Reps (and often as many as 30 minutes) before I sit down and begin writing. I picture you in my mind as if we were at a café together having coffee. Even though we may have never met, I feel like I know you because I know the profession you have chosen and what drew you to become a coach.

If money were your only driver, you most likely would be doing something else. Being a coach is a calling. It's the part of you that transcends your physical body and plane of existence when you are fully present and support your client (or even a prospect) in having an incredible breakthrough. There's nothing like it. And I should know. I've flown airplanes, jumped out of an airplane, bungee jumped, ridden motorcycles, raced in a Ferrari, skydived indoors, whitewater rafted, kite-surfed, competitively pole vaulted, jumped from incredible heights into large bodies of water, delivered a TEDx Talk, built and exited two multi-million-dollar companies, am a 5th Degree Black Belt, am an advanced open-water scuba diver and completed a full 140.6-mile Ironman. As thrilling as all of these things were, nothing has given my life more meaning and purpose than coaching.

So, you're either someone I know personally, or someone I just haven't had the opportunity to meet … yet. What I do know is that we share the same passion and are committed to a profession where we get to be servant leaders. Your joy and happiness come from that space of deep gratitude and fulfillment in supporting the people you choose to serve in your coaching practice. You may not love the business end of your coaching business … yet. But stick with me here and by the time we're done, I'm going to show you how you can step into your Sage powers in every aspect of your coaching business – even the ones you don't currently love or enjoy … yet.

As we wrap up this chapter, I want to thank you. I am in deep gratitude for the work you do in the world. I am inspired by your Sage and what you will accomplish in your coaching business, specifically, all the incredible souls you will choose to support and hold high. By helping your clients remember that they are whole, perfect and complete, you are supporting them in reconnecting with their Sage. By arming them with the tools of mental fitness, you are giving them an operating system that will empower them for years to come.

I acknowledge and appreciate you because you are bringing mental fitness to the world. I see the interconnected web of existence of which we are all a part. As the South African phrase Ubuntu goes, *I am, because we are*. "In fact, the word ubuntu is just part of the Zulu phrase "Umuntu ngumuntu ngabantu", which literally means that a person is a person through other people.[26] That is the collective we that I see in you and in all of us. That is what fuels my passion for this work and why my Sage, UnstoppaBill has compelled me to share all of this with you.

---

[26] https://www.theguardian.com/theguardian/2006/sep/29/features11.g2

CHAPTER FOUR

Understanding the Four Foundations of Any Successful Business

As Tony Robbins likes to say in his Business Mastery event, "Success leaves clues." What I love about Tony Robbins is that he studies the most successful people in the world and looks for those clues. The thinking being that if you can understand the blueprint for success, then you can replicate that blueprint for yourself.

This is what we're doing in this chapter. We're going to provide an overview of the four foundations of any successful business. Then, in the chapters that follow, we'll go deep into each foundation and ensure you're clear on how to apply each one to your coaching business. If all we were doing in this book was giving you the blueprint for success, you'd be done.

However, as you probably already know from experience, knowing what to do is never enough. Or, as the great poet Morpheus in the movie *The Matrix* liked to put it, "There is a difference between knowing the path and walking the path." This chapter and the four that follow will make sure you're completely clear on what the path of success looks like. After that, we'll turn our attention from *knowing* the four foundations of any successful business to *applying* the daily habits that will have you live into each one. Doing so will remove any barriers you are currently experiencing in establishing and growing the kind of coaching business you know you're capable of having.

In Ron Friedman's book, *Decoding Greatness: How the Best in the World Reverse Engineer Success*, he shares, "...that progress without difficulty is impossible and that mastery isn't a destination. It's a way of life."[27] Or, as my mentor Bettie Spruill liked to

---

27 Friedman, Ron. *Decoding Greatness: How the Best in the World Reverse Engineer Success*. Simon & Schuster. ©2021, page 168.

share, "Every master was once a disaster." I love that because it speaks to the key that unlocks everything you want in the business end of your coaching business. When you decide to let go and stop obsessing over looking good, being in control, and being right, you begin your journey towards mastery.

Only when you're willing to "fail" which I'll reframe to mean "learn" will you succeed. Not convinced? Let me share my favorite quote from arguably the best athlete of our time, Michael Jordan:

> *"I've missed more than 9,000 shots in my career. I've lost almost 300 games. 26 times I've been trusted to take the game winning shot and missed. I've failed over and over and over again in my life. And that is why I succeed."*

When life passes you the ball, take the shot! Once we've examined each foundation of any successful business, you'll have a choice: (1) Understand these core foundations at an intellectual level (meaning without taking action), or (2) Live into these foundations every day as if your life and the lives of your clients depend on it. That may sound extreme to you, but what most coaches are not thinking about is how their work save lives. When you connect to this truth and accept the enormous power you have been given as a coach, nothing can stop you. Or at least that's what I thought. It turns out your own negative self-talk – those Saboteur voices in your head as we've already discussed in the previous chapter – are the only things that can and will stop you. So I've devoted the rest of the book to ensure that these negative thoughts don't stop you, or, at the very least, what actions to take when it does.

Foundation One: Your Niche and Ideal Customer

Notice right now when you read this. Did you hear it? That voice in your head that said something akin to, "I already know that. Let me skip to the next foundation." That is precisely what we were just talking about. I am assuming you are truly committed to building and scaling your coaching business. For that to happen, I invite you to take a beginner's mind here. As the Zen Buddhists like to remind us, "Empty your cup. You can't add water to a cup that's already full."

For the best understanding and application of this material, I'm inviting you to empty your proverbial cup. Or as master Yoda from the Star Wars movies would tell you, "You must unlearn what you have learned." Forget what you think you know about your niche and ideal customer. Or, at the very least, put it aside for this part of the book. You can always reassess once you're done with this section and compare what is shared here to what you were previously taught.

What Is A Niche?

Your niche is the group of people you choose to focus on. It is how you distinguish someone who is a prospect for your coaching practice and someone who is not.

Let's begin with the end in mind. There are nearly eight billion people on the planet at the time of the writing of this book. How many of these people do you need to have a fabulously successful coaching practice? We'll run the numbers later in the book so you have a precise answer to this question, but for now let's chunk it down. Let's assume you are willing to work full time at 40 billable hours a week and you coach your clients for 45 minutes twice a month. If you did nothing else in your business (which isn't true for most coaches), you could handle a *maximum* of 80 clients.

Realistically, most coaches begin to hit their celling much sooner than that at around 30-40 clients. And in truth, you don't need that many to create a seven-figure coaching practice. In fact, when interviewing Rich Litvin, co-author of the *Prosperous Coach*, I asked him directly, "Is it possible to create a million-dollar annual revenue business with just one-on-one coaching clients?" Without missing a beat, he said, "Of course. You just need 10 clients willing to pay you $100,000 each and you're there!"

That answer rocked my world and shifted my paradigm. It showed me how small I was playing and where my head was at prior to speaking with him. But we can dig into that later when we map your own Money Mindset. For now, can we agree that the total number of clients you need is somewhere between 10 and 80? Rounding up to the approximately eight billion people on this planet, means your 80 clients represents 0.000001% of the global population.

The paradox for most coaches is that they want to serve *everyone*! I get it. You have this incredible super power and you're excited to flex your coaching muscles. And, truth be told, you probably *can* coach just about anyone you choose. But when you chase multiple rabbits, you catch none of them. That's why you need a laser-sharp focus on who you choose to focus on. Without that deep, deep focus on who you choose to serve as a coach, your business simply will not scale to the level you desire.

And this is the paradox. The narrower you focus, the more expansive your coaching business will be. The opposite is also true. The wider your focus, the more challenging your coaching business will be to grow and expand.

Your niche is similar to the law of gravity. It's an invisible force. You may not "see it", but you are certainly impacted by it. Choose to ignore it at your own peril.

Why Does My Niche Matter?

Your niche is your foundation for everything that follows in your coaching business. Having a clear niche well defined and narrowly focused will make your day-to-day decision making immeasurably simpler.

For example, when deciding which podcast you want to be a guest on, your niche will help you decide which are the best podcasts to be on so that you can share your insights with your ideal customers. Or perhaps you've just been invited to a networking event, should you go? Knowing ahead of time if your ideal customers will be in attendance can make that an easy decision to make. Let's say you love spending time on social media. Which platform should you be investing the most time on? Having a clearly defined niche makes this a much easier decision to make.

Without a clearly defined niche, the risk is that you'll invest significant time and feel like you're working hard despite not being able to generate or convert appointments. After a sustained period of investing time and not producing results, your Saboteurs will convince you that you're not good at this and should look for something else to focus on. I believe that this is why so many coaches struggle to become financially free doing what they love.

In the next chapter, we're going to dive deep into how to create a niche that will exponentially simplify where you spend your time to produce the results you want in your coaching business. For now, it's important to understand why your niche is one of the four foundations of any successful business.

Foundation Two: Irresistible Offer

Knowing who you will be reaching out to is the first foundation. How you invite them into your coaching business is the next foundation. It doesn't matter if you're crystal clear on who your ideal customer are if you're unable to attract them into your coaching business. Having an irresistible offer is a game changer and you can only have an irresistible offer once you've clearly defined your niche and ideal customer.

That's because a truly irresistible offer is only "irresistible" if it's uniquely suited for the clients you choose to serve. Mass marketing shows the folly here. The concept of "one size fits all" is a fallacy. Every person is unique in that they have their own wants, needs and are motivated by what's most important to them.

Let's take relationship coaching as an example. How you will attract a single male into your coaching business is different than how you would attract a divorced male. How you attract a couple into your practice is different than how you'd attract an individual. And so on. As we explore the unique needs of your ideal customer, we're going to find the sweet spot that will make your offer irresistible. And what may seem a bit crazy is that your irresistible offer will have little to do with coaching itself.

Your Irresistible Offer is NOT About Your Coaching Abilities

Think about this for a moment. Nobody "buys coaching." What your ideal customer is investing in is the outcome that is a *result* of your coaching. Going back to the relationship example, a single person isn't interested in buying coaching. What he or she wants is to be in a relationship. If your coaching helps shift that person's way of being so that they end up in the relationship of their dreams, you will have created a raving fan- that is, someone who can't shut up about what a great coach you are.

However, before that happens, your ideal client will need to respond to your irresistible offer that speaks about them having what they want most. In this example, that's the relationship of their dreams. For a coach focused on career development, their ideal customer is not interested in coaching either. They want the next promotion or raise or to find a better job suited to their innate talents and abilities.

Notice that in NONE of these examples is the ideal customer seeking "coaching." Instead, they want the outcome of what your coaching delivers. The only way we can create a truly irresistible offer is to know the specific needs of your ideal customer so that we can craft an offer that aligns with what they want most. Only then will your offer be truly irresistible.

Your Ideal Customer Will "Buy" on Emotion, Then Backfill With Logic

Another big mistake coaches make is rationalizing their offer. Let me be clear, logic comes *after* the buying decision is made. Simply put, people buy on emotion and backfill with logic. Let me prove that to you.

When is the precise moment when someone decides to buy a car?

Some people will answer it's when they are doing the research on the best cars. Others will insist that it's when the contract is about to be signed. In reality, it's during the test drive when all or most of your senses are activated and you can "see yourself" owning the car. That's when you've bought the car in your mind. The rest of the transaction is just the details needed to complete the purchase.

It begins with your eyes. You enjoy the look of the car and can imagine yourself driving it. As you enter the car, you can smell that "new car smell." With your hands on the wheel, you can feel the touch of your car. When you turn on the car, you hear the engine "purr." And if you ever test drive a luxury car, you will often be offered a piece of chocolate when you head out to do your test drive. The salesmen actually want all five of your senses activated.

And, at some point during your test drive, you decide in your mind. "This is MY car" or "Meh, not what I wanted after all." This is the point of decision. You must decide in your mind that you are committed to having this car before you take the next series of actions including asking questions and ultimately signing the paperwork.

In the chapter on *Creating Your Irresistible Offer*, we're going to dive deep into how to create an offer that will be irresistible to your ideal clients. This will ensure that the people you choose to coach will not hesitate to reach out to you and engage you as their coach. This will increase the effectiveness of your enrollment efforts and further produce the results you want in your coaching business. For now, it's important to understand why having an irresistible offer is one of the four foundations of any successful business.

Foundation Three: Generating Appointments

Generating appointments is about converting your non-coaching time and efforts into measurable appointments on your calendar. But all appointments are not created equally. The art of generating appointments isn't a "spray and pray." Meaning that having a higher volume of appointments on your calendar in and of itself does not produce the desired results you want. Generating appointments is about connecting with your niche in powerful ways that both weed out those who are not your ideal customers and invites in those you want.

It's important to note that there are many different ways to generate appointments and part of what we'll be exploring together is connecting your passions with your purpose. Right off the bat, think about what you love to do outside of coaching. The list is incredibly long and a great place to see the full abundance you are in when it comes to generating appointments. When you let go of the tyranny of "how" and instead focus on "what" you see as possible, you can begin to have a glimpse of your Sage path to generating appointments – one that remains in ease and flow rather than experiencing "the grind" you may have experienced in the past.

What Do You Already LOVE to Do (Other Than Coaching)?

Before showing you the abundant path and all the ways you can generate appointments, I'm curious – what do you already love to do outside of coaching? Take a moment to write down the activities you thoroughly enjoy without worrying about how they might lead to generating appointments on your calendar. Give yourself permission to be free and capture your passions below. And, before proceeding, be sure you're in Sage. If you have any doubt (or if it's been longer than three hours since you last did your PQ Reps), please do at least five minutes of PQ Reps of your choosing before writing anything down. Then, in ease and flow, capture your passions right here. What do you already LOVE to do?

1. _____

2. _____

3. _____

4. _____

5. _____

6. _____

7. _____

8. _____

9. _____

10. _____

Now take a look at this list you just created. What patterns do you notice emerging? Is there a form of activity that is becoming clear to you? That, given a few hours of free time, this is what you naturally gravitate towards doing.

Here's the next step of the exercise. Go back to what you wrote down and see if you can begin to organize your list into a few categories of your choosing. This process allows you to group together diverse activities into a single category to see what more emerges.

For example, let's say I wrote down:

1. Giving keynote speeches on large stages
2. Hosting webinars where I can share my insights
3. Joining meet-ups and local networking events
4. Writing articles for LinkedIn, Medium, and other publications
5. Reading and authoring books
6. Sharing content on social media
7. Exercising via my karate, biking, running and swimming
8. Spending quality time with friends and family members
9. Listening to and being interviewed on podcasts
10. Speaking at my congregation and sharing my learning with my community

What patterns would you see emerging for me? I've put in bold what I see for myself and if the word wasn't explicit, I added the essence at the end of the sentence to capture the underlying intention of the activity:

1. Giving keynote **speeches** on large stages
2. Hosting webinars where I can share my insights (**Speaking**)
3. Joining meet-ups and local **networking** events
4. **Writing** articles for LinkedIn, Medium, and other publications

5. Reading and authoring books (**Writing**)
6. Sharing content on social media (**Writing** / **Networking**)
7. Exercising via my karate, biking, running and swimming (**Socializing**)
8. Spending quality time with friends and family members (**Socializing**)
9. Listening to and being interviewed on podcasts (**Speaking**)
10. **Speaking** at my congregation and sharing my learning with my community

For me, I'm clear on my extrovert tendencies. Rather than fearing the stage, I love, love, love being the *Sage on the Stage*. At least four of my 10 (40%) of my activities involve speaking. Guess what, that's an obvious place from which to generate appointments. That is, as long as the people I'm speaking to are my niche and represent my ideal clients. Otherwise, can you see how I could spend a lot of unproductive time in the domain of public speaking and struggle to generate appointments with my ideal customers?

What also emerges is how much I enjoy writing. By honing that skill and directing it towards the kinds of content my ideal customers want, do you see how that would generate appointments? Conversely, if I'm just writing to write, do you also see how these activities could result in a ton of unproductive time in the domain of writing and struggle to generate appointments with my ideal customers?

Same goes for socializing and networking. When I am intentional about who I'm socializing with and the networking events I choose to show up in, this could be an incredible way for me to generate appointments. Or, left unchecked, I could expend a tremendous amount of energy socializing and networking without generating any meaningful and relevant appointments on my calendar.

Back to you. What do you notice about your list? Knowing what I just shared with you, feel free to repeat the exercise if you believe you have a better understanding of the desired outcome we're looking to get to in this exercise, and understand that this is just a first pass at all of this.

In the chapter on *Generating Appointments: Do What You Love*, we're going to dive deep into how to tap into your Sage and generate appointments in ease and flow. By doing what you already love to do, the act of generating appointments will simply feel like an extension of your Sage showing up in the spaces you already love. Don't worry if you self-identify as an introvert. There are plenty of opportunities to share your brilliance by tapping into your natural gifts and talents. All of your efforts in the domain of generating appointments will create an abundance of opportunity to enroll clients into your coaching business. For now, it's important to understand how doing more of what you love with the intention of generating appointments is one of the four foundations of any successful business.

Foundation Four: Converting Appointments

Once you have identified your niche and spent time really understanding the needs and desired outcomes of your ideal customer, you then create an irresistible offer and do what you already love doing to generate appointments that compel your ideal customer prospects to want to grab time on your calendar. The last step in the process is to masterfully convert these appointments into paying customers. This is often the place where our Saboteurs tend to show up the most often and with the most energy.

I'm sure you know what I'm talking about. You're having a fabulous discovery call with a prospective client and they are having some incredible breakthroughs from your engagement. Then it comes time to make your offer and your Saboteurs begin their dance in your head. See if any of these thoughts sound familiar:

- "You're having such a good session, why screw it up by turning it into a sales call?"
- "This is my ideal customer! Too bad they can't afford my coaching services."
- "Don't screw this up! You know what you need to do, but you're about to mess this up!"
- "Don't do it! Now is not the time to make an offer. You can send an email instead."
- "Did your voice just crack? What are you, 13 years old going through puberty? Idiot!"
- "What if they don't say yes? How will I afford to keep coaching when no one buys?"
- "Here we go again. I deliver an incredible session and they just take it and leave. Why does this always happen to me?"
- "Make sure you explain EVERYTHING so that they know what they are buying."
- "Asking for money is not what coaching is about. You're doing a good deed. Why screw that up now and cheapen the experience?"
- "Were you not listening? He just lost his job. How can he possibly afford you right now?"
- "Are you nuts? Did you not just hear she's getting a divorce and isn't sure she can afford to pay for her living expenses? Asking her to hire you as her coach is so insensitive!"
- "It's a real shame what's happening. If the circumstances were different, I'm sure (s)he would hire me as their coach. Perhaps another time. Doesn't feel like a good time now to bring up my one-on-one or group coaching offering. Maybe next time."

And of course, this list could fill the whole book if we kept going down the rabbit hole. Bottom line, your Saboteurs are making judgments about your prospective client's: (1) Ability to pay, (2) Interest in hiring you even if they can afford you, (3)

Current circumstances, (4) Your readiness to make an offer, and (5) Your ability to serve them powerfully as their coach. And while these are some of the most common, you may have others that show up consistently.

Don't Sell – Ever!

Converting appointments, like all of the other three foundations, begins with you being in Sage. When you listen to the negative voices of your Saboteurs, you take your focus off your prospective client and for as long as you choose to focus on those negative voices, the coach has left the session – usually at precisely the wrong moment when you are needed the most.

Please hear me that the fourth and final foundation, converting appointments, is *not* about selling. This is *not* about you embodying a used car salesman and "going for the close." If you watched the movie *Glengarry, Glen Ross*, this is the polar opposite of what we're talking about when it comes to converting appointments. By all means, please feel and fully experience the yuckiness of aggressive salespeople. That is so far from what we want. Hold onto that feeling because you never want to do that to anyone ... ever!

I will never ask you to sell in the ways you most likely have experienced being sold. You know what I'm talking about – that pit in your stomach when you realize someone just got you to buy something you probably shouldn't have bought. Or that feeling of buyer remorse where even though you said yes, it was to "get out" of an uncomfortable situation and the minute you left that situation you wished you hadn't said yes. This is all short-term thinking that never works out in the long run, so don't do it.

No One Enjoys Being Sold, But Most People Like to Buy

Now, forget that negative association with selling. We're not doing it, so shake it off. Now think about the last thing you purchased that you flat out LOVED!!! It could be the last vacation you took, new clothes, a really amazing book, a course, a retreat, or even a treat you picked up for yourself on a whim. There was zero pressure to do any of it, right? You felt the urge and you acted on that urge. Then, when you experienced the thing you purchased, you enjoyed it.

People like buying products and services when there's no pressure to do so. Why do you think Amazon.com is so popular? Yes, it's highly convenient to click a button and have stuff arrive on your doorstep in increasingly shorter and shorter time. But once you know what you want and feel you're getting a good price for it, there's a certain satisfaction with clicking the buy button and feeling confident in your purchase decision. You knew what you wanted, you found it, you bought it and you know if you don't love it, you can return it with relatively little hassle. No pressure. No regret. Just find, click and enjoy.

Enrollment Is The Opposite of Selling

Enrollment is to selling what water is to oil. They live in opposite sides of the spectrum. To enroll someone into your coaching practice, you are first tapping into your own Sage discernment. Not every prospect is right for you and your coaching business. If you genuinely (and from a Sage space) feel that the prospective client you're speaking to would not benefit from your coaching, then you thank them for their time and end the session. Even if they want to hire you, if you truly know they are not a good fit, the kindest thing you can do is offer to refer them to someone who would be a better fit.

However, if you've done the first three foundations of any coaching business correctly, then this will be the exception, not a regular occurrence. If it is a regular occurrence, it either means your niche, irresistible offer, or how you're generating appointments are not quite where you need them to be (and you can adjust accordingly).

Enrollment is about supporting your prospective clients to make the decision that's best for them without any attachment to what that decision is. Your Saboteurs live in scarcity while your Sage lives in abundance. As you live into your own abundance, there's no fear that your prospective clients may say "no." You don't take it personally and you are confident that you served them powerfully. If this discovery session is the only interaction you ever have with that person, you feel great knowing the value you delivered without any expectation.

And, when your ideal customer prospect hears your irresistible offer through your ease and flow of generating appointments and feels no pressure to buy from you when in an enrollment conversation, the magic happens. They say yes. Early on, that happens about 1 out of 10 times. As you increase your Sage Mastery, the number of times someone says yes to you out of 10 offers continues to go up. By the time you're done practicing converting appointments from your Sage, this part, like all other aspects of your coaching business, will be done in ease and flow. No judgment. No negative self-talk. Instead, you serve your ideal customer prospects incredibly well and live in total abundance.

No One "Buys" Coaching

Assuming you believe that this ideal customer prospect would be a good fit for your coaching business, then this is about helping them connect to the outcomes they've shared with you in your discovery session. It's really important to understand that no one "wants" or even "buys" coaching. They invest in the outcomes they want in their life. Coaching is simply a means to help them get there – usually in significantly less time and with much less effort than they would on their own.

That said, when you hold your ideal customer prospects as whole, perfect and complete, then you realize the truth. They don't *need* you as their coach. Sure, having you as their coach would support them and all that they are up to, but it's a want, not a need. And what they want is not coaching from you. They want the outcome that your coaching will deliver to them. When you realize this truth, you won't make your offer about you or your coaching. Instead, you'll focus deeply on what your ideal customer prospect wants, needs and is willing to invest in, in order to have the life they truly desire.

This realization will also have you de-couple YOU from your coaching offer. The Saboteur fear of rejection is all about a person rejecting you. When you realize it's not about you, you won't take any "no" personally. Your Saboteurs will lie to you and make up a story about how their "no" means you're not a good coach or some version that you are not enough. It's just their lie in their effort to protect you. You don't need it. And when you hear this lie, you can thank your Saboteurs for their concern and reassure them that you've got this and their support is not needed at this time, thank you very much.

You're Either Enrolling, Or You're Being Enrolled

The last part of enrollment, for now, is to understand that in every moment of every day you are either enrolling or being enrolled. When I'm choosing to drop a few pounds, I'm enrolling myself to eat healthy and exercise regularly. That's my Sage supporting me as I design my life. When, in the middle of my day, I choose not to eat healthy or skip my regular exercise routine, it's my Saboteur enrolling me into a circumstance.

In an enrollment conversation, it's no different. It's either your Sage enrolling you and your ideal customer prospect into the life you both want to have, or your Saboteurs enrolling you and your ideal customer prospect in the present circumstances that prevent having the life you both want to have.

We'll get into this further in the chapter, *Converting Appointments: The Art of the Close*. For now, do you see how mastering this domain of your coaching business will also support your self-actualization and your journey towards Sage Mastery? When you master enrollment in this domain of your life, it will open up your ability to master enrollment in any domain of your life that you choose to focus on. All of your efforts in the domain of converting appointments will create abundance of growth opportunities to support clients into your coaching business. For now, it's important to understand how the power of enrollment, not selling, is one of the four foundations of any successful business.

How the Four Foundations Work Together

In the chapters that follow, we'll go deeper into each of the four foundations of every coaching business and show how accomplishing each in Sage produces the kinds of results you're looking for as you grow and scale. Improvements in one of the four foundations has a positive ripple effect into the others.

For example, you may have a general idea of who your niche and ideal customers are. When you tap into your Sage Explore power, you'll find that there is likely another level to your current understanding including a discovery of some of the pain points and deep desires of your ideal customers. With new insights and revelations, you're then able to apply this learning to creating an even more irresistible offer. That, in turn allows you to generate more appointments and ultimately convert more of those appointments thereby increasing your coaching business.

Or perhaps, as you connect with what you love doing most besides coaching, you discover a powerful way to generate even more appointments. This allows you to better measure your effectiveness when converting appointments and leads you to re-examine your current irresistible offer. Sage Innovate power has you play the "Yes, and ..." game and soon you've upgraded your current irresistible offer to make it even more irresistible than before. The combination of your ability to generate more appointments with an even more irresistible offer means your converting more appointments into paying clients.

These are the small changes that, taken out over time, have an outsized positive impact on your coaching business. As you continue to adjust what you're doing now, you immediately see the positive ripple effects on your coaching business. This, in turn, encourages you to continue to keep an open mind about each of the four foundations and look for never-ending continuous improvement in each foundation.

Another way to envision this is to think of each of the four foundations as a single leg to the platform structure supporting your coaching business. As you work to raise one leg up, you naturally see the opportunities to adjust the other three legs to level-up your coaching business. With improvements to one foundation, you're positively impacting and working on raising the entire foundation of your coaching business. As all four foundations work together, any improvement in one will naturally impact the other three.

What's exciting is that you can actually witness the positive ripple effect in each of the four foundations with each adjustment you make. And, if you're even stuck or challenged by one of the four foundations, you need only turn your attention to the other three for insights and innovation that will support the one you're most interested in improving.

What's also important to remember is that you have all five Sage powers to play with when working on any of the four foundations of your coaching business. Having deep Empathy for yourself, your ideal customers and the situation you're in leads to breakthroughs using the Explore power and, in turn, encourages you to Innovate as you continue to Navigate through to your desired outcome which motivates you to Activate. And the cycle continues to build upon itself as you work on each of the four foundations of your coaching business.

Success begets more success. That is to say, as you first launch your coaching business, it can be discouraging not to see immediate results despite how much initial effort you exert. However, as your efforts begin to take shape, you're turning the flywheel of your coaching business. Those first rotations take substantially more effort as you don't have momentum. After your first few rotations, you build up that momentum and each progressive turn takes less and less effort. This is the paradox, and it's important to truly understand this point.

Initially, it will take a great deal of effort to launch your coaching business. But over time as you continue your progress, it will take less and less effort to generate more and more success. This is why the path of the Sage is truly *ease and flow*. Over time, you begin to trust that your efforts are making the impact you are committed to having. It just took longer to get started in the beginning and, over time, takes less and less effort.

The Only Thing That Can Stop You: Your Saboteurs

There's only one person who can keep you from having the coaching business of your dreams. By now, you are clear that that person is you – the Saboteur-driven version of you. When you connect with your Sage and embody the Sage Perspective – that every challenge can be turned into a gift and opportunity – then you are unstoppable. The trouble is, our Saboteurs have a way of ganging up on us when we lease suspect it. That's why we spent a lot of time in the previous chapter, *How Our Saboteurs Prevent Us From Having The Coaching Business We Deserve* right up front. If you're ever feeling lost, stuck, or ready to throw in the proverbial towel, then go back and read that chapter.

Your Saboteurs are just as predictable as the outcomes they stop you from having in your coaching business. Their fear has the power to hold you back if you allow them to drive you. Your Saboteurs are doing exactly what they were designed to do – keep you safe and prevent you from taking any perceived risks. Your Sage knows better. Your Sage knows that those risks are typically blown out of proportion and much less probable than our Saboteurs make them out to be. To hear your Saboteurs tell it, their fears are forgone conclusions – that the moment you step out of your comfort zone, bad things will happen and you'll lose what little you have worked so hard to accumulate up to now.

Scarcity thinking is your Saboteur's go to, while your Sage lives in abundance.

As Miki Kashtan, a pioneer in Nonviolent Communication (NVC), puts it, "...the entire western order is founded on three fundamental lies: we are separate, what we need is scarce, and we are powerless."[28] While she doesn't use Saboteur language, you can clearly see each of these lies are driven by our Saboteurs. Our Sage will compel us to break through these lies and see the opposite is true: (1) We are all one and part of an inter-connected web of existence, (2) What we need is abundant, and (3) We are powerful beyond measure.

So which is true?

Given the choice, which would you choose to believe and live into? By your actions, which do you believe and choose to live into every moment of every day? As I shared from the very beginning of our journey together, this is your path to self-actualization and transcendence. Every moment of every day, you are at choice. As you notice the choices you make it will become clear what drives your actions – fear or love; darkness or light; scarcity or abundance; powerlessness or power. The choice is yours. The rest are just details and really interesting puzzles you haven't yet solved as you build, grow and scale your coaching business.

---

[28] https://thefearlessheart.org/blog/

CHAPTER FIVE

Defining Your Niche & Ideal Customers

Who do you choose to serve as a coach? In this chapter, we're going to dive deep into that question so that by the time you've completed this chapter, you're either crystal clear on that answer, or, at a minimum, you have lifted the fog around that question and are on the path of discovery. In other words, you're going to know how to discover your niche and ideal customers by taking the actions outlined here.

Do You Remember What A Niche Is & Why It's Important?

Repetition is the mother of skill, so occasionally, I'm going to ask you to recall what was previously shared. This is to ensure you're clear on the material and are ready to go beyond an intellectual understanding and lean into the application. So what's a niche?

Your niche is the group of people you choose to focus on. It is how you distinguish someone who is a prospect for your coaching practice and someone who is not.

And why is it important?

Your niche is your foundation for everything that follows in your coaching business. Having a clear niche well defined and narrowly focused will make your day-to-day decision making immeasurably simpler.

Conceptually, this makes sense, right? But the most common objection to this framework is, "But I have so many different kinds of people that I want to coach!!!" To be clear, explicitly defining your niche does **NOT** prevent you with working with people outside of your niche. It just gives other people an understanding of who you choose to **focus on**. And, you can evolve your niche over time based on what you learn along the way in your coaching practice.

For example, when I first began my coaching practice, my niche was: "World-changing visionaries who are brave enough to build a better future." I was *so* proud of that one. In my mind, it was clear, concise and I knew exactly who I meant. The problem was, when I talked to people in my network, *they* weren't clear who I was talking about. So while I was very pleased with how well my niche sounded, the feedback I received is that the people who had the opportunity to refer me clients didn't know who I was looking to coach.

That's a problem. It failed the cocktail party test.

The Cocktail Party Test

When you're complete with the work outlined in this chapter, you should be able to go to a cocktail party or networking event. When someone inevitably asks, "So, what do you do?" You should be able to deliver your niche statement (without pulling out your phone or piece of paper where it's written down) and the response you're looking for is one of the following:

- "Wow! That sounds interesting. Tell me more."
- "I know precisely who you're talking about."
- "Your timing is uncanny. Not only do I know who you're talking about, s/he's in my network. Give me your contact information so that I can introduce you to each other."

You get the point. What you do NOT want to hear is:

- Silence. A polite head nod and the imaginary scratch of a record far off in the distance.
- An inquisitive look that immediately tells you they have no clue what you mean.
- "Interesting. How about those [insert favorite sports team here]?"

If the person you're speaking to clearly doesn't understand who you're referring to, there are two possible reasons why: (1) They are not connected to anyone you're referring to and don't have the slightest idea of how they would ever come across a person you're describing, or, more likely (2) They have no idea who you are describing.

If you're at a networking event where there really should be prospects that could hire you for your coaching services, your niche needs to pass the cocktail test. If it doesn't you have some work to do.

I've chosen to share this right up front so that you begin with the end in mind. Having a clear target of what you're shooting for means you will be able to concretely measure the effectiveness of your niche statement and know where to go in order to try it out.

What a Niche Statement Really Is

Your niche statement is the equivalent of a headline enticing you to read the full article. Think of it as your headline that invites others to have a conversation with you. The more intriguing a niche statement is, the more people will want to unpack it.

For example, imagine you're a relationship coach. Which of the following headlines would grab your attention and make you want to learn more?

- I empower men to tap into their feminine energy in order to create deeper intimacy.
- I work with couples who are struggling with intimacy issues to take their relationship to the next level.
- I support couples having an incredible sex life.
- I help men get laid.

Now without referencing and re-reading the above niche statements, which one can you remember word for word? Which one grabbed your attention? Which one felt taboo and not something you'd like to build your business around?

For most people, the last one fits the bill for all of those questions. And notice what thoughts you're having right now. If you are a relationship coach, I'm not suggesting that *any* of these niche statements are the best for you. But if you were at a cocktail party and some asked you, "So, what do you do?" And you said that you help men get laid, what do you imagine would happen next?

I promise you, the conversation wouldn't die out. If anything, you're going to get raised eyebrows, funny looks and a lasting impression that will be talked about long after your conversation has ended. And while you don't have to be a sensationalist to have a powerful niche statement, all of this is to show the power of a well-crafted one.

What you may also not be considering is the juxtaposition of what follows. Let's keep playing this scenario out. After you have the full attention of the person you're speaking to, you can tell they are fascinated. A likely response would be something akin to, "I have so many questions!" You've just created a space for which to unpack the essence of what you *actually* do. And that might go something like this:

> *As a relationship coach, I often find that intimacy reveals what's really going on in a relationship. I'm not a therapist, so I'm not here to heal past traumas. Instead, I work with men to help them understand what women really want. They hire me because they want more sex, and while that's the end result, it's not the value I truly create. You might be surprised to hear that women are the ones who refer me the most business. That's because I'm able to help men open up, communicate more effectively and show up differently in the relationship. While the end result is more sex, that's only one metric of a healthy relationship. It just happens to be the one metric men care most about.*

You can see that this coach isn't crass or a pimp. While her niche statement grabbed your attention, it was just a headline. Underneath it was powerful relationship coaching that ensures couples are both getting what they want. With increased and effective communication, the woman feeling loved and cared for the way she wants to feel and experience love, the depth of the relationship grows and the outcome is predictable. And while this relationship coach could have said, "I empower men to tap into their feminine energy in order to create deeper intimacy," you're going to find that "playing it safe" is not effective.

Seth Godin in his book *Purple Cow* said it this way, "Being risky is safe, and being safe is risky." While he was speaking about marketing, the same holds true for your niche statement. The more willing you are to take risks, the faster the payoff you're going to see in your coaching business. Remember, you're not trying to please everyone or even attract hundreds or thousands of clients. You want to speak to and ultimately engage the 10 to 40 or so of your ideal clients with precisely the language they need to hear to want to learn more about you and what you offer.

The Paradox of Growth

Having worked with solopreneurs, successful (and not-so-successful) start-ups, and entrepreneurs of companies from $100,000 in annual revenue to $10 million in annual revenue and more, the problem is the same. When you've chosen to dedicated you time, energy, passion and lifeforce to something, you become convinced that everyone needs what you have to offer. You're proud of what you are up to and you want to tell the world.

Take the popular television show *Shark Tank* where enterprising entrepreneurs pitch their ideas to venture capitalists hoping to receive the funding they believe they need in order to launch and scale their business. How many of those ideas do you judge as crazy, foolish or just not something you'd ever be interested in? How many times have you thought, "I could make something so much better than what this person is pitching!" Did it ever occur to you that you simply may not be the right audience for this concept?

This is the paradox of growth.

There are about eight billion people in the world and you don't need all of them to want what it is that you choose to offer. In fact, you only need about 0.0000005%, or 40 clients, to have a thriving coaching business. Do the math. If you received $500/month times 40 clients, that's $20,000/month times 12 months a year is $240,000 annually. Charge $1,000/month and that brings you to $480,000 annually. And don't worry, we'll dig into your Sage Money Mindset later in the book. For now, all I want you to realize is just how few clients you actually need in order to have a thriving coaching business.

So why is it that most coaches want to help *everyone*? Rather than being discerning about who they choose to focus on, most coaches want to share their newly discovered super power with the world – as in, everyone they have ever met or will meet for the rest of their lives.

The paradox of growth is that **when you narrow your focus, you expand your market**.

To use a fishing analogy, coaches who choose to toss out a wide net don't catch the fish they actually want – and often catch few to no fish at all. A well-crafted niche statement attracts only the fish you wish to catch. Rather than spending all kinds of effort randomly pulling up a giant net and seeing what you've pulled into your boat, your well-crafted niche statement helps you determine what part of this vast ocean you choose to fish in, what bait to use and how to most efficiently use your time to pull in the fish you actually want.

The mistake is thinking that going broad will help you grow quickly. It doesn't work that way. In fact, the opposite is true. The narrower to go, the faster you'll grow.

Is Your Niche Statement a "Prime Number?"

If you remember back to your years of math, there was a simple concept of prime numbers. These are numbers that are only divisible by themselves and no other number. one, two, and three are prime numbers, but four is divisible by two and so it's not a prime number. Five is a prime number, but six can be divided by two and three, so it's not. You get the point. According to the ancient Greek mathematician Euclid, prime numbers are infinite.

In the context of your niche statement, you want to keep narrowing it down until you can't narrow it down any further. Some of the possible ways to get to your prime version of your niche would be to consider all the ways your ideal client sees their identity, including:

- Age
- Gender Identity

- Primary / Romantic Relationship
- Current / Desired Marital Status
- Family / Children
- Profession
- Career Aspirations
- Industry
- Financial Means & Aspirations
- Spiritual / Religious Beliefs
- Race
- Ethnicity
- Political Views
- Citizenship
- Education
- Cause / Volunteer
- Geographical
- Economical
- Legacy

And this is by no means a comprehensive list. When you hear someone say, "I'm a life coach and I work with women," what do you hear? Having worked with thousands of coaches on their niche statement, I can tell you that this niche is overbroad and not helpful to building and scaling your coaching business. What I hear is, I'm a generalist coach who has cut the global population from about eight billion people to about four billion. That's not a niche as you recall you only need about 20 to 40 clients, so this coach has some work to do in order to narrow down.

How about, "I'm a confidence coach and I help people overcome imposter syndrome." Not bad, right? But have we arrived at a prime niche? Nope. Who are the "people?" Imposter syndrome around what? I assume you mean in their career, but imposter syndrome could show up public speaking, dating or negotiating a price on a new car sale.

As we dig into this chapter, you're going to find that despite what you think you know about your niche, there's a Sage version that includes all five powers: Empathy, Explore, Innovate, Navigate and Activate. When you nail that one with a level of specificity that's undeniable, you're going to discover the prime number version of your niche. For now, it's important to see that most niche statements tend to be overbroad and miss out on the very power they are intended to hold.

You'll know you've reached your prime number equivalent when you resonate with your niche at a heart level. That is, when you feel emotionally connected to your PQ Channel – not just the data channel of the actual words you use. Your Sage will light up inside of you when you're on the right track. There will be a feeling of alignment inside of you. Please trust that this is where we're headed as we move forward together in this chapter.

The Discipline of Market Leaders

In any given market, there are the leaders and those who aspire to become market leaders (but are not). What makes the difference between a market leader and those who aspire to be? Discipline (or a lack of discipline). Market leaders have the discipline to choose the customers they want to focus on rather than allowing their circumstances to dictate their actions. Market leaders narrow their focus by doing the 20% of the effort that produces 80% of the result, and that unwavering discipline allows market leaders to dominate. Let's look at each of these to better understand the power as it relates to your niche.

Choose Your Customers

Market leaders choose their customers and they tend to be very choosy indeed. Pick a brand, any brand, and see how it got started. If I asked you to think of the top three brands that immediately come to mind, at least one of them is likely to be Apple, but you might also be thinking Amazon, Google, Microsoft or a host of others. None of these behemoths started out as the "everything to everyone" company. While Microsoft's original vision was, "A computer on every desktop," they choose to focus on businesses because enterprise customers tended to invest in the latest technology innovations.

Meanwhile, Apple decided to give their computers to schools so that early training on computers would happen on their operating system causing early preference. Amazon ships nearly everything to your doorstep, but began with books. Google started out with a high education focus by emphasizing the value of research references. The page rank algorithm used today began by putting a higher value on research that was quoted by multiple sources. And we could keep going. Everyone needs a pair of shoes, but Nike focused on runners and eventually expanded to athletes of all kinds of sports to help fuel its growth.

When you choose your customers, you are making a deliberate choice. The Latin root word of decide is "*decidere* which is a combination of two words: de = 'Off' + caedere = 'Cut'"[29] When you choose your customers, you are intentionally "cutting off" those who are *not* your customers. In that way, you have more opportunity to focus on the customers that matter most to your coaching business.

---

[29]   https://www.meaningfulhq.com/decide-to-cut-off.html

Narrow Your Focus

Even when you choose your customers, it's important to understand that market leaders have the discipline to keep narrowing their focus. The more you can narrow your focus, the more time and attention you can give your most ideal customers.

Just as a thought exercise, imagine I gave you $10,000 to go spend on your marketing efforts. If you were trying to reach 20,000 potential prospects, you'd have 50 cents to spend on each one. You might be able to afford to send them a really nice email and hope that they open it. But what if you only had to focus on 100 potential prospects? Well now you have a budget of $100. Imagine the impact you could make by taking each of them out to a fancy lunch, dinner or even a Broadway Show. If you were competing for attention with the person who sent them an email, who do you think would win the attention of that person?

Think that's not a real example? That actually happened to me on more than one occasion when I was on the receiving end. Besides having multiple dinner invitations from prospective suppliers, I once had a company offer me a high-end Apple product just for taking a meeting with them. This is how Big Pharma used to get the attention of doctors (before all the insurance regulators cracked down). The sellers would take the private doctors out to play golf while sharing their latest drug information and research findings.

Narrowing the focus of your niche allows you to concentrate your efforts. This will become critically important when we turn our attention to generating appointments. You have limited time and money to be investing in your coaching business. The more you narrow your focus, the more value you can create for the few ideal customers you want to attract into your business.

Dominate Your Market

Success begets more success. While choosing a niche makes logical sense, what is less obvious is how sticking with your niche grows your reputation and continues to do so until you are the dominant leader in your market. The more specific you are, the easier it is for people to refer you precisely the ideal customers you seek. This leads to market dominance as your personal brand becomes interwoven with those you choose to serve.

To illustrate this point, who is the biggest advocate of sayings such as, "Start with why" and "People don't buy what you do, they buy why you do it"? If the first person that comes to mind is Simon Sinek, you're not alone.

Or who is the one person you think of when you think of the word vulnerability? While there are many who have illustrated the power of vulnerability, Brené Brown is most closely associated with bringing the power of *Daring Greatly* by being vulnerable.

What's you're one-word association? Or, if that's too challenging at the moment, then how about a few words or short phrase? When it's catchy and easy to remember, it becomes how you are known in the industry. With tens of thousands of professional coaches (and that number appears to be growing exponentially), the more specific you can become, the easier it will be to dominate your market. Think about all the industries that exist out there and how much they need your services. I've worked with judges and lawyers who choose to become coaches and none of them said, "I work with lawyers" as that's still very broad. Instead, a former judge and I played with this approach:

> *As a judge, I've spent years on the bench having all the answers. Lawyers would look to me to make the final call. And yet, what resonated most for me was supporting those very lawyers who were questioning if they had made the right decision to pursue a legal career. Would you like a FREE two hour judgment free coaching session where you can talk out your fears, uncertainties and doubts in a safe and confidential environment?*

Yes, I'm skipping ahead to what we'll be covering in depth in the next chapter, *Creating Your Irresistible Offer*, but for now, can you see clearly what his niche is? He's a former judge who supports newly minted lawyers who are questioning if they made the right decision to pursue a legal career. He's developed workshops, retreats and supports the legal community to ensure those who do pursue a legal career do so by connecting to their own Sage Power Navigate. Alternatively, those who know deep down they pursued a legal career to appease their family members or in search for financial freedom come away with a clear picture of what they actually would prefer doing and end up pursuing their passions free of Saboteur guilt, shame and remorse.

While you may not feel a compulsion to dominate your market, taking the time to consider what would it take to dominate the part of the coaching industry you wish to be a part of will lead you to some powerful Sage discernment about your own unique gifts, talents and abilities – ones that you may currently be taking for granted. Why would you take them for granted? Because they come so naturally to you that your Saboteurs have you convinced that everyone has these same natural gifts and talents. They don't. And your Sage knows that when you lean into that which you already do incredibly well, you can support your ideal customers powerfully. Let's do an exercise to help you define your niche and narrow your focus.

Exercise to Define Your Niche & Narrow Your Focus

In the following pages, you can discover that which may have felt elusive to you when considering which niche to focus on. Please don't allow that Saboteur voice of negativity to prevent you from discovering your niche. If you are already hearing your Saboteur voices piping up, I invite you to stop and do one or more long PQ Gym session(s) before proceeding. Whenever I have an important decision to make or am about to work on something important, I connect with my most resourceful Sage self before proceeding. Doing the following exercises while hijacked by your Saboteurs will produce predictably unhelpful results. It's the same thing that stops most coaches from having the coaching business of their dreams.

At this point, I'm assuming you've given yourself the gift of at least twelve (and ideally 20 to 30) minutes of PQ Reps before proceeding. If not, I highly encourage you to stop and do the work for maximum benefit to yourself and your coaching business.

Step One: Define Your Communities

List five possible groups of people that you know well or are passionately curious about.

If you had a previous career before you choose to become a professional coach, don't be shy to include this community. While your Saboteurs may be screaming for you to leave this chapter of your life behind and never revisit what you've been through in the past, your Sage knows better. As a coach, you are always at choice in terms of who you choose to take on as a client, and how you choose to serve them powerfully.

Do you volunteer with specific non-profit or charitable organizations? Don't be shy about including this option as one of your communities. While your Saboteurs may be highlighting that this community, "can't afford your coaching services," your Sage knows that there is a distinction between your client (i.e. who you coach) and your sponsor (i.e. who pays for the coaching you deliver). While the client and sponsor are often the same person, they don't have to be. If you choose to work with underserved communities, there are grants, government assistance programs and a host of allies that can fund your efforts here, so please include this community in your list below.

Consider all your different interests and passions. Do you practice martial arts? Are you in a running or triathlete club? Do you practice Yoga or other regular group exercise class? Do you participate in a book club? Perhaps you meet regularly at an industry association or work with artists. Keep thinking about what activities you are already part of and causes you care about.

For the purposes of this exercise, you would be well served to include a diverse set of different communities you are either already deeply involved in or are passionately curious about.

1. _____
2. _____
3. _____

4. _____

5. _____

Before moving onto the next step, take a good look at these communities you are either already a part of or are passionately curious about. Be sure they are distinct and not another name for the same group. If you see that two or three are different versions of the same community, that's okay. It means you're very passionate about this particular community and are already leaning in this direction.

For maximum benefit, it's helpful to have five distinct communities for the exercises that follow. That way you can see clearly whom you truly wish to work with as your niche.

Step Two: Define Their Challenges

For each of the five Communities you listed in the first step, we're now going to explore the different problems, fears and desires that each of these different communities share as a group. What you're looking to clearly illustrate is the current situation that an individual member of a specific community is facing as well as their desired outcome. Let's take an example that most coaches can relate to.

Example Community: Coaches Who Wish To Create a Six or Seven-Figure Coaching Business

1. Problem: They are amazing coaches who likely have never built a business before
2. Problem: They are incredible givers, but tend not to be open to receive
3. Problem: They haven't mastered their own Sage money mindset
4. Fear: They won't be successful in the business end of their coaching business
5. Fear: By not creating financial freedom in coaching, they'll have to find work elsewhere
6. Fear: They don't know (or care) enough about business and will be taken advantage of by someone else who does (i.e. Big Corporation, Coaching Conglomerate, etc.)
7. Desire: To have a thriving six or seven-figure coaching business
8. Desire: To deliver incredible value to the people they choose to serve as their coach
9. Desire: To install mental fitness operating systems in their clients so that their clients become self-cleaning ovens and peruse their own self-actualization and transformation
10. Desire: To experience Sage Mastery and transformation by building and scaling their own seven-figure coaching business

Now, while you may not have resonated with *each* of the above statements, chances are high that if you're reading this book, you resonate with at least *some* of them. And that's the point of this part of the exercise. You want to get clear on the distinct challenges of each of your communities so that you can clearly see how powerfully you can serve them. Allow your Sage to play here. Rather than allowing your Saboteurs to stress you out about being "perfect" or having these statements be "exactly correct", allow your Sage to take over and just observe the words flowing from deep inside you.

If that's not happening, try doing a few more PQ Reps to truly connect with your Sage. I promise you that your Sage has all the wisdom you need in this exercise. The minute you quiet your Saboteurs, this wisdom will flow from you in ways you couldn't have anticipated. That's the power of your Sage and it comes from ease and flow. So let's play:

1st Community: _____

    1. _____

    2. _____

    3. _____

    4. _____

    5. _____

2nd Community: _____

    1. _____

    2. _____

    3. _____

    4. _____

    5. _____

3rd Community: _____

    1. _____

    2. _____

    3. _____

    4. _____

    5. _____

4th Community: _____

    1.   _____

    2.   _____

    3.   _____

    4.   _____

    5.   _____

5th Community: _____

    1.   _____

    2.   _____

    3.   _____

    4.   _____

    5.   _____

How was that? Did you surprise yourself at how easily each one flowed once you tapped into your Sage? None of this work is hard when you're in Sage. If you're experiencing difficulty, it's likely one of your Saboteurs messing with you and judging what you allow to come forward. If you are not happy with this first pass, remember that your Sage is happy to have you go again in ease and flow. None of this part should be hard as these are the communities you know, love and are happy to serve. Connect with that essence and try again in Sage.

And, if you're happy with what your Sage already produced, let's go to the next step as we move closer to completing this exercise. Your niche and ideal customers await your own brilliant insights and awakened connection to how you can serve them powerfully. Let's continue our journey forward as you clearly connect with who you choose to serve.

Step Three: Define the Value You Deliver

This is the step where your Saboteurs like to show up with all the unhelpful negative self-talk. To be successful here, it's really important to stay in Sage as you thoughtfully consider the answer to the following question: *What are the unique skill sets you currently have and your community wants and needs?*

If you are drawing a blank here, it helps to connect with your heart brain and gut brain rather than just the brain in your head. Try this. Place your right hand over your heart and ask the question again. But before you do, notice that there will likely be two voices – the positive Sage voice and, immediately following, the negative Saboteur voice doing everything in its power to discredit the first answers that comes to you. Don't listen to that second voice.

For the purposes of this exercise, put your right hand on your heart. Then picture the face of a person in your first community. If you can't think of an exact person, make one up. Imagine what a person from that first community looks like. And then, with your right hand on your heart, ask yourself, *What are the unique skill sets I currently have and my community wants and needs?* Go ahead and write down the first positive answers that came to you. Sometimes your heart speaks in colors and images. It's okay if what you just heard wasn't verbal language in the traditional sense. That's just a different way your Sage voice is speaking to you. Trust that you're doing this right and keep going.

Now move your right hand to your gut – at or just below your belly button. Take a moment to connect with your gut. And, with your right hand on your gut, ask your gut brain, *What are the unique skill sets I currently have and my community wants and needs?* And allow your gut to speak. Here again, trust whatever positive vision, image, or message your gut sends to you and write it down. Notice as you write that even something simple as a color has meaning. Write what that means to you and don't judge it. Just allow your Sage to speak and trust the wisdom that's inside of you.

1st Community: _____

1. _____
2. _____
3. _____
4. _____
5. _____

Repeat this exercise for each of the communities you are considering. It's perfectly fine if at this point in the exercise you're heavily gravitating towards one or two specific communities. As your Sage lives in abundance (and your Saboteurs live in scarcity), lean into the completion of this exercise for each of the communities you were originally thinking about back in Step One. Even if you're already sure these communities are *not* your niche, this part of the exercise will keep you in your creativity and Sage PQ brain. The more you listen to your own intuition and allow your beautiful gifts to emerge, you will discover ways to leverage these gifts for whichever niche you do choose to focus on.

The key here is not to finish prematurely. Allow yourself the creative expression to explore all the incredible value that easily flows from inside of you. Notice all that talent you may have previously taken for granted, and stay alert to your own Saboteur voices judging this exercise and its value to your coaching business. Remember, your Saboteurs are there to keep you small and stop you from growing and expanding. Listening to these negative voices is a sure-fire way to remain stuck rather than blossoming into the world-changing visionary you already are. If it helps, reconnect with your childhood picture as you do this work. What would your five, seven, or nine-year-old self share with you that you may have forgotten? How might you bring childhood joy and happiness into this exercise?

When you connect with your Sage, you're connecting with your most powerful self – that fearless child who was born to make a seismic impact in the world. Let them out to play with you right now. Watch how much more fun you have and creative you feel when you imagine yourself doing these exercises as that fun-loving carefree child.

2nd Community: _____

    1. _____

    2. _____

    3. _____

    4. _____

    5. _____

3rd Community: _____

    1. _____

    2. _____

    3. _____

    4. _____

    5. _____

4th Community: _____

    1. _____

    2. _____

    3. _____

    4. _____

    5. _____

5th Community: _____

    1. _____

    2. _____

    3. _____

    4. _____

    5. _____

Before moving onto step four, please take a moment to reflect on just how awesome you are. Look at all that you have discovered and written down about yourself. This is flowing from inside of you. How cool is that? Look at all the incredible value you can and will deliver to the people who need you the most as their coach. Your skill sets are uniquely yours. These are your natural gifts and talents. They are your embodied beingness even if and when they show up in a form of doingness. Your Sage talents are priceless. Never forget that. Your clients are lucky to have you in their lives. The only voice that disagrees is ... you guessed it, those nasty Saboteurs. Feel free to ignore them and lean into the incredible human being you are.

And if this part was difficult (or you find yourself with less clear value than you'd like), rather than forcing this exercise, go back and do a 30-minute PQ Gym session and reconnect with your Sage. All that difficulty means is that your Saboteurs are doing their absolute best to blind you from your incredible talents. Don't stand for that. You're so much better than your Saboteurs would have you believe. Hopefully, by this point, you're beginning to see what's been holding you back all along. You don't need the latest technology or marketing tactic. YOU are the one you've been waiting for. And, for that matter, your ideal customer prospects have been waiting for you longer than they care to admit.

Step Four: Get Clear on Outcomes

Do you feel it in your body? Do you notice that anticipation of what's next? By now you may be sensing the gold that is being uncovered today and what's next is completely aligned with these feelings. This is the step where we get to pull it all together. Here's the Ven diagram that helps illuminate what you're really up to:

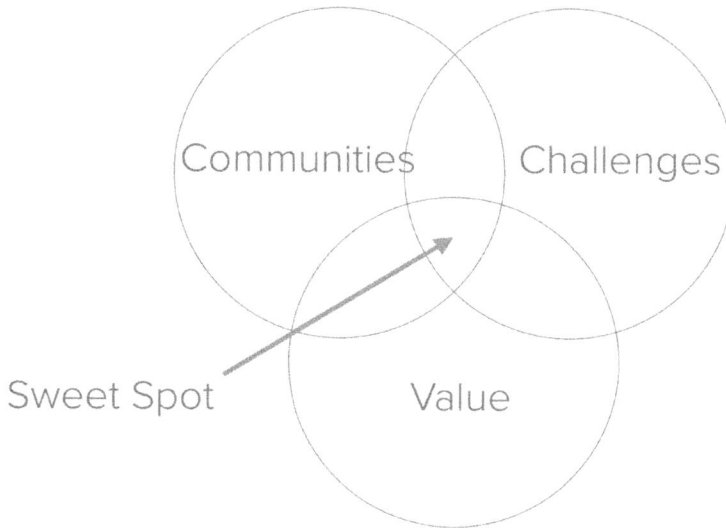

In other words, you've identified five different **Communities** (people who you know well or are passionately curious about), defined their **Challenges** (problems, desires and fears of each Community), and your own unique **Value** (your unique skills which you currently have and they want and need). Where these three overlap is your sweet spot.

Not every Community will share the same Challenges nor desire the incredible Value that you deliver. But when you begin to look at the overlap, you'll begin to see something beautiful emerge. Perhaps more than one Community is seeking the Value you deliver. Or perhaps the Challenges are shared by multiple Communities. The more these three overlap, the easier it will become to see your unique value and how it supports overcoming the Challenges that different Communities have now and for the foreseeable future.

What's next is to get clear on each of your Community's **Current Situation** and **Desired Outcome**. Think of it this way. Every person you meet has a current situation and a future state that they truly desire. Let's look at some of the more common changes that people desire to make in their lives:

	Current Situation	**Desired Outcome**
Wealth	Experiencing Scarcity / Not Enough	Abundance / Total Financial Freedom
Relationships	Single / Divorced / Unhappy Marriage	Blissful Primary Relationship
Career	Stuck / Imposter Syndrome / Under-Valued / Lost / Numb / Confused	Aligned to Mission, Purpose & Legacy

Family	Exhausted / Tense / Poor Communications / Empty Nester	Loving, Supportive Family Unit
Spirituality	Disconnected / Questioning / Lost	Interconnected Oneness & Full Spirit
Happiness	Angry / Frustrated / Disappointed / Empty Inside / Unfulfilled	Regular Belly-Laughs. "I'm so happy, I can't stop smiling."
School	Isolated / Overwhelmed / Misunderstood / Failing	Bright future fueled by a combination of knowledge & wisdom
Health	Overweight / Obese / Low-Energy / Insomniac / Addicted	"I haven't felt this good since …"
Contribution	Desire to "Do Good," but no action	Pillar of any community

And of course, these are extremely generic as a way to get your Sage PQ brain activated and ready for what's next. For step four, I invite you to get really clear on each of your communities and ask yourself two important questions:

1. What is this community's current situation?
2. What is this community's desired outcome?

Let's start with you as an example. As a coach reading this book, how would you describe your current situation? It might go something like any of the following:

- I'm a brand-new coach and I'm just starting to build my coaching business.
- I've been coaching for a few years, but I've struggled to support myself / my family.
- I'm getting by, but I know that I could be doing a lot better in my coaching business.
- I've figure out the foundations of my coaching business, but I'm ready to scale.
- I love my current coaching business, and I know there's another level for me.
- I'm well into my six-figure coaching business, and I'm ready to hit seven figures.

You can already see the desired outcome for yourself as well as each of these coaches outlined above, right? The desired outcome might look something like this:

- As a brand-new coach I'd like to skip the struggle and crush my business now.
- The last few years were much leaner than I'd like. I'm ready to scale my business.
- I'm ready to invest in my coaching business and truly nail it – once and for all.

- I've nailed my coaching business and I'm ready to scale it to the next level.
- As much as I love my current coaching business, I'm ready to switch it up to grow.
- I'm well into my six-figure coaching business, and I'm ready to hit seven figures.

Now it's your turn. For each of your communities, I'd like you to imagine what their current situation is. Be as specific as you can be so that you can then identify their desired outcome. As mentioned previously, it's helpful to complete all five so that you can see patterns emerge. This is you leaning into your Sage Power Explore and Innovate. These will lead you to Sage Power Navigate as you complete this exercise and land on the niche you choose to focus on.

1st Community: _____

Current Situation: _____

Desired Outcome: _____

2nd Community: _____

Current Situation: _____

Desired Outcome: _____

3rd Community: _____

Current Situation: _____

Desired Outcome: _____

4th Community: _____

Current Situation: _____

Desired Outcome: _____

5th Community: _____

Current Situation: _____

Desired Outcome: _____

Now celebrate! That's right, you heard me. Upon completing this part of the exercise, it's time to take your right hand, raise it high in the air (until your arm is straight up), then holding your arm there, bend your elbow and give yourself a nice pat on the back. Seriously! I'm not kidding here. You're doing some excellent work. Please acknowledge your Sage in this process and encourage your Sage by thanking your Sage for all the incredible work you're doing.

Can you believe what you've already created? When you started this process, I suspect your Saboteurs had their doubts, but look what you've done along the way. Nice work! We're nearly done. Here's the last step in the process.

Step Five: Self-Assessment

Take a look at what you've done and the last step is to do a reflection. Some will call this a journal exercise. It's perfectly fine if you prefer to write in your journal vs. in the lines below. What's important is reflect on both the progress you've made and what's emerging in terms of what's next in your niche journey.

Do I Have The Necessary Skills, Knowledge and Internal Belief In Myself to Deliver the Kind of Powerful Transformation My Community Needs?

Yes, because ...

_____

_____

_____

_____

_____

_____

I Will When I ...

_____

_____

_____

_____

_____

It's okay if you filled in both. "Yes, and ..." comes from your Sage Power Innovate. What's important in this last part of the exercise is that you are seeing clearly you do have what your community needs. And/or you are very close to it once you complete a few items that you Sage is discerning are currently in your gap. That is, the gap between what your community needs and what you are currently skilled up to deliver.

Awareness leads to Sage Power Activate as you choose to lean into that which is not currently there; knowing full well that you have what it takes to fill that gap. That's the Sage Perspective. That even the lack of current skill, knowledge or internal belief can be turned into a beautiful gift and opportunity. Remember, everything we're doing together is being done in Sage. The minute you notice your Saboteurs creeping back in, keep doing those PQ Reps so that you can remain Sage throughout these exercises.

After all, remember the end goal here. You're committed to building, growing and scaling your coaching business. The world needs you and especially the communities you choose to serve as your niche. Thank you for the incredible work you've done here. It's going to be the foundation used in all the rest of the foundations of coaching (i.e. Your Irresistible Offer, Generating & Converting Appointments).

Going Deeper & Testing Out Your Niche Statement

Crafting your niche statement can be like peeling an onion when you consider all the possible multiple layers that exist. While a surface niche statement will help you, it will not support your building, growing and scaling your coaching business the same way that a well-crafted and finely tuned niche statement will support you. That's what this next part is all about.

What Your Niche Statement Really Is

As we go deeper into this work together, it's helpful to reflect on what your niche statement really is. At its root level, your niche statement is a headline to the story of your coaching business. When you see your niche statement as a headline, you understand that it's simply an invitation to have a deeper conversation with you and what you're up to in your coaching practice.

Your niche statement does *not* tell the whole story. Instead, your niche makes them curious and wanting to know more. What you'd want to do is be able to share it with someone and after hearing what you have to say, you'd love to hear a response such as:

- That sounds interesting, can you please tell me more?
- Wow, that's awesome. How do you do that?
- Really? I've got someone who I'd like to introduce you to … how can I/they get in touch?

What you're hoping *not* to hear in response is any of the following:

- Silence with a confused look that tells you immediately they are not following you.
- Interesting. [Nodding head while thinking about how to change the subject.]
- How about those [insert local sports team here]. Did you see the game last night?
- What strange weather we've been having, huh?

If this happens, it's only feedback. Remember, all feedback is a gift an opportunity when you hold the Sage Perspective. Rather than getting discouraged by these responses, your Sage gets curious as to what might be confusing about what you've shared and leans into further refinement. So before you start with what you've done thus far, let's see if we can't refine it down to its most basic essence and give you the best possible kickstart in your niche journey.

Simplify Your Niche to, "I help [people] go from [problem] to [promise] by [process]."

What you'd want to do now that you have a good idea of the communities you choose to serve, their current situation, and desired outcomes, is pull it all together. Think of this as the four P's of your niche statement:

People
Who are the people you most want to help and can help?

Problem
What are your people struggling with right now?

Promise
What result will they get when they work with you?

Process
How will your coaching help them get there?

Note that the "process" component is the *lightest* touch and can often be left out entirely. To that end, I encourage you to start with the first three P's as they are the most important:

I help [people] go from [problem] to [promise].

Give it a shot. Take what you've been working on so far and fill in the blanks:

I help _____ go from _____ to _____.

The framework is much more helpful than the precise words. For example, instead of "**help**", you may prefer to use:

- I support
- I work with
- I empower
- I transform
- Etc.

And instead of "go from," you may prefer to use:

- get out of,
- free themselves from,
- break free from,
- who are,
- Etc.

And instead of "to," you may prefer to use:

- get to,
- become,
- experience,
- be,
- Etc.

Some example statements to help get you going could include:

1. I help [mental fitness coaches] break free from [barely making ends meet] to [building seven-figure coaching practices].
2. I help [divorced women] let go of [their scarcity circumstances] so they can [have the relationship of their dreams].
3. I work with [overweight men] to [transform their physical healthy] by [becoming mentally fit] so that they can [reach their health goals].
4. I support [world changing visionaries] who [are brave enough] to [build a better future].
5. I empower [working single moms] to [break free of their scarcity fears] and achieve [total financial freedom].

As you can see, these examples are not attempting to tell the whole story, but rather create a foundation from which the person you're speaking with can understand what you're up to, specifically, as a coach, whom you focus on, what challenges they face and the outcome they truly desire in working with you as their coach.

Now it's time to see if you have reached the core essence of your niche statement (from a place of Sage discernment, of course).

Does Your Niche Pass the Prime Number Test?

I don't remember what grade I was in school when they first introduced the concept of prime numbers. But what I quickly realized was how powerful the concept was. To jog your memory, a prime number is any number that can only be divided by itself and by one. A prime number must be a whole number, not a fraction to qualify. So while one, two, and three are prime numbers, four can be divided by two, so it wouldn't be considered one. five is, but six can be divided by three and two so it's not considered a prime number. What's cool is that prime numbers can get really large. 739, for example is a prime number. And so is 1,549.

What does this have to do with your niche? Well, if you have a solid draft of your niche statement, it's time to test it against the concept of prime numbers. In other words, is your niche statement "prime" or can it be divided down further?

Let's take one of the sample statements I shared earlier such as:

> I help [divorced women] let go of [their scarcity circumstances] so they can [have the relationship of their dreams].

Would you consider this niche prime?

Let's see. In the United States alone, there are approximately 108 million adult females[30] according to the most recent available data. Another source says that "15 percent of adult women in the United States are divorced or separated today, compared with less than one percent in 1920."[31] So 15% of 108 million would be 16.2 million females.

How many of these women would you need to have a thriving coaching practice?

Let's say that you're just starting out as a coach and so you receive only $500/month for 1:1 coaching with your clients. If you had 20 clients, that would be $10,000 per month or $120,000 per year. Or, if you've handled your own money mindset mastery and are receiving $1,000/month, those same 20 clients would deliver $20,000 per month or $240,000 per year. Are we at least in the right ballpark for what you're looking to build?

---

[30] https://www.infoplease.com/us/census/demographic-statistics
[31] https://www.wf-lawyers.com/divorce-statistics-and-facts/

For a seven-figure coaching practice you'd receive $50,000 per client for 20 clients or $100,000 per client for 10 clients. We'll get into that later in the book, but for now I want you to see that you don't need more than 20 of the right clients to have a thriving coaching practice.

So 20 clients out of 16.2 million prospects is 0.000123%. Now your Saboteurs would loudly argue that this is perfect. By having so many prospects (16.2 million) you're sure to build and grow your coaching business quickly, right? Unfortunately, no. While 16.2 million prospects is certainly better than all 108 million females in the US, how might you divide up this number even further?

What if you combined "divorced females" with specific industries or age demographics. For example, what if you knew that, "60 percent of all divorces involve individuals aged 25 to 39."[32] Or, quoting the same statistical sources, that:

Five Professions with highest divorce rates:

- Dancers – 43%
- Bartender s- 38.4%
- Massage Therapists – 38.2%
- Gaming Cage Workers – 34.6%
- Gaming Service Workers – 31.3%

Five Professions with lowest divorce rates:

- Farmers .63%
- Podiatrists – 6.81%
- Clergy – 5.61%
- Optometrists – 4.01%
- Agricultural Engineers – 1.78%

Seeing this data, which would you go for? Would you choose one of the five professions with the *highest* divorce rates or the *lowest*? While you could be successful with either, this is the paradox of growth revealing itself before your eyes. Dancers, with a 43% divorce rate seems like the best option, while Agricultural Engineers with a 1.78% divorce rate seems like the worst option (as so few divorces are happening with this audience).

And yet, I would argue that any of the five professions with the *lowest* divorce rate would help you scale your coaching business faster than those with the *highest* divorce rates. Why? Because these markets are truly underserved. Rather than

---

[32]   https://www.wf-lawyers.com/divorce-statistics-and-facts/

trying to beat out all the other divorce lawyers and industry professionals who see the same information and target the exact same audience demographic, you would be creating a category of one by supporting any of the five professions with the lowest divorce rates.

When we go deeper into the chapter on *Generating Appointments*, you'll see that the more unique your content is, the more relevant it is to the audience you choose to serve. Take Clergy at 5.61% divorce rate. Can you imagine how challenging that must be for someone who is seen, very publicly, as a pillar of their community? Who can a person of the cloth turn to for support when they are likely experiencing a deep sense of guilt, shame and other negative feelings about their divorce? How relieved would they be to know that there's a coach who specializes in their specific challenges?

In other words, I would argue that the following revision meets the prime number test:

> I help [divorced *clergy* women] let go of [their ~~scarcity circumstances~~ feelings of shame and guilt] so they can [have the relationship of their dreams].

Understand that *any* of the narrowing down we just explored would support you having an even more powerful niche statement. There comes a time, however, when you realize you just can't narrow down your niche any further. That's when you've reached your prime number. While your niche isn't required to be a prime number to be effective, it's a great way to evaluate how you might narrow down further to increase your effectiveness in building and scaling your coaching business.

Cocktail Party Test

Similar to the prime number test, the cocktail party test allows you to test out the effectiveness of your niche statement before going to the next foundations of your coaching business such as your irresistible offer, generating and converting appointments. The cocktail party test is when you test out your niche statement with another person (or a small group of three to five people) to gauge their reaction. The most important part of the cocktail party test is that you're saying your niche out loud to another person who either is or knows the ideal client you choose to serve. This serves three important benefits. Specifically, this exercise has you:

1. Say your niche statement out loud to another human being.
2. Notice the difference between what you've been crafting and what you actually said.
3. Receive real-time feedback on your niche statement.

Do NOT read what you wrote. The temptation will be to say your niche statement perfectly. (Thank you, Stickler and Hyper-Achiever Saboteurs, but we've got this). By saying your niche statement out loud, you begin to notice where your heart, gut and brain take shortcuts and simplify what you've been working on. You may also know where you stumble and confuse yourself. How can this be? It's natural when you're practicing to have your Saboteurs show up in precisely the wrong moment and jumble your words and scramble your meaning.

Practicing your niche statement is the best way to refine it and evolve it. As you practice *giving* your niche statement, you'll also be *receiving* real-time feedback that tells you if you're on the right track or if your niche statement still needs work. Does your audience understand who you're talking about? What you do for your niche? The problem your niche has and the outcome they get by hiring you as their coach? Rather than ask these questions directly, you're deeply listening and paying attention to the reaction of the person or small group with whom you're sharing your niche statement. Are they tracking with you or do they seem lost and confused? What questions do they ask? Or do they attempt to change the topic of conversation? How your audience responds can show you if your niche statement is ready for prime time or still needs some adjustments for maximum impact.

Note, this need not be an actual cocktail party. It can be simulated with your fellow coaches, or others who deeply care about what you're up to. Just be sure that if the person you're testing this out with is NOT either a coach nor an actual prospect, their feedback will lack the "real world" context you're going for. While all feedback is a gift, you'd be well served getting the bulk of the feedback you choose to act on from your actual niche or people who know your niche. That way, your continued learning and refinements are likely to be more relevant than a friend, family member or loved one who is already rooting for you to succeed. While they are well-intentioned, they may not be giving you the insights you need to nail your niche.

Add In All Five Sage Powers When Crafting Your Niche Statement

Now that you're becoming clear who your niche and ideal customers are, it's time to tap into each of your five Sage Powers to really elevate and refine whom it is you choose to serve. As far as you've already come, I suspect this next part of the journey will deepen your connection to your Niche statement and ensure that it is as powerful as you want it to be. That is, as you tap into each of your five Sage Powers, you're going to make new discoveries about your niche and these discoveries will help set you up for success for what's next – namely, applying all of these insights to your Irresistible Offer, Generating & Converting Appointments.

Applying Sage Power Empathy to Your Niche Statement

Begin with having empathy for yourself. Take a moment to acknowledge how much work you've already completed. Celebrate your awesome self! No, seriously, it's time to acknowledge yourself here. Your Saboteurs would have you skip to "what's next" and that would be a mistake. Having deep empathy for yourself will lead you to an even better niche statement. That's because having empathy connects you to why you're doing all of this in the first place (see Sage Power Navigate in the pages that follow).

In the context of your niche statement, if you truly wanted to give empathy to yourself, where would you focus your attention? See which of the following statements resonate with you:

- I recognize that I'm a new coach and having this powerful niche statement will expedite my ability to attract new clients into my coaching business.
- I acknowledge that despite how long I've been coaching, I haven't paid all that much attention to my niche and see how this work will pay significant dividends.
- Wow, look at how much I accomplished without having a clearly defined niche!
- I'm excited for the next chapter of my coaching business now that I'm clear on the audience I choose to serve powerfully.
- I thought I knew my niche, but now that I've done this work, I'm seeing how spending more time in this foundation of my business will help me grow and expand.

Whichever it is for you, having empathy for yourself and where you are in your journey will ensure that you keep going. Your niche statement is one of four foundations of your coaching business and the more time you spend refining it and getting crystal clear on it, the faster your business will grow. Have empathy for yourself for having started your coaching business without having nailed your niche. So many of your fellow coaches have allowed their Saboteurs to drive them taking all sorts of ineffective actions because they were not clear on their niche.

And, as you see clearly where you are and how far you've come, have empathy for your situation. Currently, you may not feel like you've completely nailed your niche. That's okay. The point is, you're significantly further along than when you first started exploring your niche. Each time you say your niche statement, you'll discover new ways to refine it. That's part of the process. Have empathy for your situation than your niche can and will evolve. It could potentially change based on the other foundations of your coaching business. The key is to lean into how important having a clearly defined niche will be in growing and scaling your coaching business.

And, lastly, have empathy for this niche you have chosen to serve. By being clear on their challenges, you can tap into your empathy for them. See their desired outcome and the part you play in helping them to achieve this outcome. As you examine each of these areas, your empathy grows for yourself, your situation and your ideal clients. That growing empathy keeps your Sage at the forefront of your coaching business and hold your Saboteurs at bay. It also leads you to Sage Power Explore so that you can continue to refine your niche as you and your coaching business grow and expand.

Applying Sage Power Explore to Your Niche Statement

Once you have connected with Sage Power Empathy for yourself, your ideal customers and your situation, you can now become a fascinated anthropologist as you tap into your Sage Power Explore on your niche statement.

From your Sage perspective, what can you be authentically curious about when it comes to your niche statement? What childlike sense of wonder can you bring to this work? Are you curious about the specific outcomes your ideal customers desire in their lives? Or are the problems they face the thing that pulls you in and has you wanting to look closer and conduct a deeper examination? Or is it the person you have been modeling?

If you were deeply curious, what would you want to know about your ideal customer, their biggest problems and their desired outcome? The more you can tap into your Sage Power Explore, the deeper you can go in thoroughly understanding the needs of the niche you choose to serve powerfully in your coaching practice.

Go deeper and build your ideal customer profile. The following questions will help activate your Sage Power Explore. Use them as guidelines only. Your Sage already knows where to look when it comes to deepening your understanding of your ideal customer. Trust your Sage here and gently explore as many facets of their life as you can. The more you know and understand about your ideal customers, the easier it will be to attract them into your coaching practice.

1. How would you describe their occupation?
2. What are their top saboteurs?
3. What pulls them from their Sage to their Saboteurs?
4. What are their known triggers? (i.e. What sets them off?)
5. Where do they live?
6. How old are they?
7. More likely male or female?
8. What's their education level?
9. What have they already accomplished?
10. What's something they would want you to know about them and what they are up to?

For my visual learners, another fun way to get at this information is to either draw or find a picture of your ideal customer. Back when printed magazines were commonly found around the house, I enjoyed flipping through the pages and cutting out head shots that represent my ideal customers. This was a way to remind me of who I choose to serve. When physical magazines became less common, I turned to LinkedIn for profile pictures of the people I have actually served. I'd print out their picture and have it near my computer screen for inspiration when I would write articles, interview thought leaders or did anything in my coaching business to further attract my ideal customers into my practice.

Sage Power Explore is about getting clear on who, precisely, you choose to serve, their needs and their desired outcomes. The deeper you can connect with these insights, the easier it will be to craft your irresistible offer, generate appointments and then convert those appointments.

Here's another way to go after this. Build a profile that you can refer back to.

Name:	
Occupation:	
Age:	
Living In:	
Gender:	
Education:	
Accomplishments:	
Interests / Hobby:	
Annual Income:	
Get Their News:	
Fears / Concerns:	
Historical Challenges:	
Married?	
Children? #?	
Coaching Need:	
Deep Desire:	
Notable Concerns:	
Tipping Point to Want Coaching:	

In the table above, share a little about your ideal customer. How would you describe what do they do for a living? Consider what they might add to your description if they were sitting next to you while you did this work.

How do they spend their week? What do they do outside of work? Where do they get their news? How much money do they make? How do they feel about their job? What are their concerns in life? What aspects of their life or personality effect how you might approach them?

What about their history? What happened in the past that led them up to this point? How do they feel about what happened in the past? Perhaps a former job, an experience they had, or a trip that they took. What are they currently interested in because of this history?

What is their family and relationship status? Are they married? Divorced? Single? Do they have children? How many? Does anything about their relationships have a bearing on how they might use you as their coach?

What is it about having a rock-solid coach that matters to this person? How does it solve a need, ease a pain, or make them feel good? How does it better their life?

What sorts of thoughts should go through this person's head right before they decide to engage you to be coached? What is the "final straw" that makes them pull the trigger and engage you?

While there are so many different questions you could ask, it's less about knowing everything about your ideal customers and more about painting a clear picture for yourself. This is the proverbial, "walk a mile in their shoes" so that you can really get to know them.

From these insights, I invite you to write-out your Ideal Customer Profile in plain language. It might look something like this:

Meet Connie. Connie is a coach. She is excited to serve her clients, but has struggled to make coaching into the career path she envisioned. She knows she can serve her clients powerfully, but she's unsure how to build a successful coaching practice. She senses that if she had a better command over marketing, she could build a financially lucrative practice and live the legendary life she's always dreamed.

Then take a look and notice what you chose to include and what you left out of this description. Sage Power Explore will have you stay curious. Imagine your childhood self as you continue to look for what's under the next rock. Without any expectations, continue to discover more and more about your niche by asking questions and seeking to learn all you can about them. As you continue your journey and work with different clients from this niche, you can go back and refine this exercise with more concrete insights and interesting antidotes about their life.

Your Saboteurs would have you focus on how much time you're wasting doing all this effort. And your Sage knows that this is about generating a clear focus so that you can save significant time and financial resources as you move into the next foundation of your coaching practice.

Applying Sage Power Innovate to Your Niche Statement

Just when you think you're all tapped out and you've gone as deep as you can in discovery mode with Sage Power Explore, it's time for Sage Power Innovate to take over and help you continue your journey. This is something you can do either by yourself on your own or with your Pod of three to five fellow coaches.

Take one aspect of your niche that you want to work on and deploy the "Yes, and ..." game. As a brief refresher, you're going to look at the 10% of any idea and find the positive aspect you can align with. You need not love the whole idea and in this process the more creative and imaginative you become. Your Saboteurs will keep interrupting you and challenge just how practical these ideas are. Ignore that part for now and focus on the 10% of what you like about the idea and keep going.

A juicy place I like to start is either with the biggest problems my niche has or possible desired outcomes that they want as a result of our coaching work together. So, for example, if I want to really align on the biggest problems my niche has, I want to give myself permission to play here and go to the extremes so that I can illuminate new possibilities for myself. It might look something like this:

<u>Problem:</u> Coaches tend to be great at coaching, but struggle financially.

- What if coaches were hired by the government and never had to worry about money?
- Yes, what I like about that idea is the financial security that would bring. And by not worrying about money, coaches could spend the majority of their time coaching.
- Yes, what I like about coaches spending the majority of their time coaching is that they would continue to get better and better at being a coach. And, by becoming stronger at the delivery of coaching, they would generate powerful referrals and word-of-mouth.
- Yes, what I like about generating powerful referrals is that the coach becomes "pre-vetted" by someone else. And, the referral removes the risk of working with that coach.
- Yes, what I like about removing risk from working with the coach is that the newly introduced prospect would be in a position to build trust in the coach because they were introduced by someone they already trust. And, when

there's deeper trust in the relationship, that will set the new prospective client up for deep and lasting transformation.

- Yes, and ...

Notice that I was playing solo here. While it's great to have your peers to play the "Yes, and ..." game with, you don't need them to activate your Sage Power Innovate. Looking back at what I brainstormed with myself, I see interesting ideas I can play with including:

1. How might I help coaches effectively leverage referrals to grow their business?
2. What might large government contracts do to support the coaching industry?
3. How might coaches spend more time coaching and build and scale their coaching business?
4. What other risk removal strategies might I consider when creating an irresistible offer?
5. Where else could deepening trust early help generate more appointments for coaches?

And I was just getting warmed up. Imagine if you dedicated one hour to this effort. The first 20-30 minutes would be to charge up your PQ Brain by doing a few long PQ Gym sessions and then the next 30 minutes you'd commit to innovating without judging what you were coming up with. By focusing on the 10% of what you like about the "craziest" idea you can think of is that it opens up new possibilities for you. That's what makes Sage Power Innovate so effective. You are giving yourself permission to be creative without having to justify what's coming up. That's the essence of "ease and flow" in a creative process like this.

And sure, having others can help introduce new thinking and different ideas that you might not have considered. Just don't allow your Saboteurs to convince you that you *need* peers to help you with this exercise. You don't. You are more than capable enough to play the "Yes, and ..." game with yourself and produce some really powerful results. You're inviting your Sage to play and your Sage will always answer your call to play. Have fun with this!

Applying Sage Power Navigate to Your Niche Statement

Whenever you're considering a change, it's helpful to align with your Sage Power Navigate. And this is true for your niche as it is for any aspect of your life. At the end of your life looking back, how will you feel about all the hundreds, thousands or millions of lives you've impacted? Sage Power Navigate helps ensure you have completely aligned your coaching business with the desired outcome of your life.

To confirm that this is true for you, go back to your ideal customer. It's helpful to think of just one person rather than all the people who fit your niche. Now envision that person working with you as their coach and accomplishing their desired outcome. Does this connection spark joy for you? Would having this person accomplish their deepest goal support you in reaching your ultimate outcome?

For me, when I imagine you reading this part of the book, I see you as a powerful coach who is excited to support the lives of your clients. My own Sage Power Navigate helps me align to the work you are doing right here and now. I am confident that as you define and refine your niche and get clear on your ideal customers, you will have the power to grow and scale your coaching business helping hundreds if not thousands of people in the world.

It's easy for my Sage to connect with yours. When I decided to join Shirzad Chamine in his mission to bring mental fitness to the world, I knew then (as I know now) that the best path to accomplish this mission in ease and flow is through helping coaches like you create epic coaching businesses that will generate financial freedom.

Every time I'm feeling disconnected to my work or questioning why I'm doing something that I don't particularly enjoy doing, my Sage Power Navigate reconnects me to you and the thousands of incredible coaches just like you who choose to serve their clients powerfully. And, in doing so, I imagine the impact you will be making with your clients and how that ripples into their relationships with their families, friends and work colleagues. It's easy to see how all of my efforts to support you create a seismic shift in the world.

As more and more coaches adopt the principles of mental fitness and have their Sage lean into the business development foundations of their coaching business, the world becomes just a little more alive, conscious, joyful, happy and mentally fit. Our interconnected oneness strengthens as I reach across time and space to support all the incredible efforts you have planned in your coaching business. My own Sage Power Navigate challenges me to show up at my absolute best so that I can make the kind of global impact my Sage knows I'm capable of.

And that's what I invite you to consider right here and right now. By tapping into your own Sage Power Navigate as you apply it to your niche and ideal customers, I'd love for you to project out how your own efforts create positive ripples in the world. When you can envision how your showing up powerfully as a coach enrolls the very clients you choose to serve and positively impacts their lives and the lives of everyone around them, it's easy to see how building and scaling your coaching business is a critical next step in the evolution of humanity.

Small visions can be forgotten and don't even have the power to motivate you. Massive global visions, however, provide the lighthouse for your Sage to navigate and direct all of your efforts toward realizing this expansive vision. That's what being visionary is all about. Having a vision of the world and the ability, as Peter Theil reminds us in his book *Zero to One*, "To see that what others don't see" … or, at least, not at present. As you can envision a better, brighter future and connect all your efforts with your ideal customers accomplishing their desired outcomes, it's easy to get excited about the journey to accomplish this high purpose.

The more you lean into Sage Power Navigate, the more connected you are to your own vision, mission and purpose. You see how each aligns to what you're up to in your coaching business. Otherwise, there are many alternatives to simply making a living. If you're just here for the money, I urge you to reconsider. It's not too late to find a different path towards wealth creation – one that doesn't require every ounce of your soul. I say that because while you can and will become financially free as part of building and scaling your coaching business, money alone will not energize your Sage. Only your vision, mission and purpose can do that.

Take a moment to pause and reflect.

If you are clear on your drive to become a hugely successful coach, then you have your Sage Power Navigate to guide you along your way. If you don't then this is an important discovery to be curious about as you continue your journey. Without alignment with your true purpose, it will be challenging to know who is worth your time and attention. Without connection to purpose, your niche isn't all that important.

Remember, you have a super power as a coach. And your skills transcend any individual customer or niche. You do, in fact, have the power to serve any person. So be choosy here. The more you align your skills and talents with your mission and purpose, the more deeply you will connect with your own Sage Mastery and self-actualization. That is the awesome and hugely compelling principle of Sage Power Navigate. Your niche and ideal customers should inspire you and keep connecting you back to your own high purpose. As you support your ideal customer in their journey, they will inspire you to continue yours. That's the symbiotic relationship between your clients and you as their coach– which leads us to the last of the five Sage Powers: Activate.

Applying Sage Power Activate to Your Niche Statement

Laser focused action comes from your Sage. I have found that when I'm not taking laser focused action, it's because I've lost my way (usually enrolled in some lie concocted by my Saboteurs) and need to go back to the previous Sage Powers … especially Sage Power Navigate. And, when I'm aligned in my purpose, Sage Power Activate comes easy. Why wouldn't I take massive action toward the big vision I hold for myself? It's only when I lose focus that I begin wandering away from my own vision, mission and purpose in life. (Hello, Saboteurs, thank you for all the side quests and surprise circumstances I choose to focus on!)

When it comes to your niche, Sage Power Activate is about being so connected to the needs and desires of your ideal customers that you can't help but show your absolute best in support of serving them. In Saboteur mode, taking action is about knocking items off your "To Do" list. Each action feels hard, difficult and, in extreme cases, it feels like suffering. Saboteur action tends to be energy draining and leads to ineffective and often inefficient results.

In Sage, taking action is about seeing what your niche needs and being of service. Rather than being stopped by your Saboteurs, your Sage connects with the desired outcomes of your niche and identifies all the exciting ways to be of service. Yes, sometimes this means taking action that is uncomfortable, but by remaining in Sage, you're connected to the why of it all rather than the negative emotions your Saboteurs want you to feel instead.

In other words, Sage Power Activate in your niche is about your willingness to be the powerful ally in your ideal customer's journey. That can take many different forms which we'll lean into later in this book … especially in the chapter on *Generating Appointments*. What's important to recognize at this stage is the deeper you are connected to serving your ideal customers at the highest level, your Sage Power Activate kicks in to do whatever it takes to support them. You will surprise yourself at what you can accomplish when you've stopped focusing on yourself (and your Ego) and instead turn your attention to being a servant leader to your niche.

The more value you create for your niche, the more support you will receive from others who are looking to do the same. That's right, you are not alone here. As you take swift, laser-focused action, you will discover others who likewise are here to help your ideal customers. As you contribute more, you are recognized for your leadership. As you align with the needs of your niche, you become known for the service you deliver to them. The gratitude of your niche further enrolls your Sage to go deeper and deliver even more.

This is the Sage contagion effect. Your actions create an echo-chamber effect that reverberate your kindness back to you. The more you give, the more abundance you receive. Yes, that includes money and other resources, but it's the energy exchange of gratitude that transcends everything else. And, as you receive more, you are encouraged to do more. This is your Sage amplification as your activate efforts are graciously received and the desired outcomes of your niche are achieved.

In Jim Collin's book, *Good to Great*, he talks about the flywheel. Specifically, that when you are looking to turn a flywheel, the hardest revolution is the very first one. A flywheel at rest can be very difficult to rotate and takes tremendous effort. But, after a full rotation, the next one becomes easier. The one after that becomes even easier. And this continues until you build so much momentum that the flywheel is spinning so fast it appears to be doing it on its own. At that stage, minimal effort is needed to keep the flywheel turning.

I love this analogy for your coaching business. When it comes to Sage Power Activate, you are going to expend a lot of effort with your initial efforts to support your niche. But the longer you stay at it, the easier it becomes. That's why we spend so much time developing your niche. Getting clear about who you choose to serve brings clarity to all your efforts – not just the *what*, but also *why* you're doing what you choose to do. While it's true that your niche can and will likely evolve as you grow your coaching business, your continued efforts to support the same ideal customers repeatedly will create that spinning flywheel effect.

The way of the Sage is ease and flow. Remember this as you take action on your niche. What you choose to do – especially at the early stages – should feel easy even if it's somewhat uncomfortable. The discomfort comes from stretching yourself in order to be of service. This starts with the next chapter, *Creating Your Irresistible Offer*. That's the next action to take so that you're ready. Early in my career, one of my mentors shared that the concept that luck happens when opportunity meets preparation. We are preparing to be hugely successful when we are intentional about which actions we take (in Sage) and which we let go of (especially when driven by our Saboteurs).

Beware of Your Saboteurs When Looking to Finalize Your Niche Statement

Before we wrap up this chapter, one final word of caution. Your Saboteurs are likely to have a field day with whatever niche statement you've crafted. Your judge will lie to you that it's not good enough and needs substantial work before even thinking about using it. Your Controller wanted this done yesterday and will have you remain at a surface level rather than doing the deep work covered in this chapter. Hyper-Achiever will have you convinced that your niche isn't large enough for you to be successful and that more is better. Restless can't even believe we've "wasted" this much time on the niche. Stickler agrees with your judge that your niche isn't good enough and needs a tremendous amount of work. Pleaser wants someone else to validate the niche statement and focuses externally rather than doing the deep internal work. Hyper-Vigilant reminds you that all these efforts haven't moved your coaching business forward and is creating risk of failure. Avoider just skipped all this effort. If anything, the Avoider would have you do a Google search for niche statements and copy someone else's words. Victim knows this won't work. It may work for others, but certainly not me. And the Hyper-Rational is still wondering of the precise words are being used and what quantitative research method should be used to validate the niche statement.

And of course, this just scratches the surface. Your Saboteurs may be screaming about something else not listed above. The point is not to believe the lies of your Saboteurs. Hear what they have to say, label their thoughts as Saboteur thoughts, then reconnect with your Sage in this work so that you can keep going.

Keep the Sage Perspective As You Test Out Your Niche Statement

And finally, it's a great reminder to keep the Sage Perspective as you begin to test your niche statement. All feedback can be a gift and opportunity if you allow it to be so. Feedback in Sage keeps you curious about what you might have missed or overlooked. The Sage Perspective will have you keep testing out your niche statement with your ideal customers themselves or individuals you are confident are connected to your niche.

Sage discernment ensures that the feedback you listen to resonates deeply and comes from a trustworthy source. A coaching colleague, for example, may have some great questions for you to consider or may offer unsolicited feedback in an attempt to be helpful. Any feelings of negativity will likely be picked up by your Saboteurs and prevent you from hearing the gift or opportunity intended.

Keep asking yourself, "What is the gift or opportunity in this feedback?" Be curious about what may be in your blind spot. And trust your Sage will guide you towards the best outcome for your coaching business.

Perhaps the most important perspective is that whatever you've come up with today will likely evolve (at least somewhat) tomorrow. Trust that you've worked on the 20% of the effort that delivers 80% of the value you need from your niche. While you can refine it further at a future date, for now let's use what you've come up with in order to go to the next step. Your ideal customers have been awaiting your arrival. So when you meet with them, it's best that you've prepared your *Irresistible Offer* so that your Sage invites their Sage to join you in your journey. That's what's next and how you will further grow and strengthen your coaching business.

CHAPTER SIX

Creating Your Irresistible Offer

Now that you are clear on your niche and who your ideal customer is, how do you attract them into your coaching practice? That's what this chapter is all about. By the way, if decided to skip over the last chapter and dive right into what you perceive to be the problem needing the most attention, I've got some bad news for you – there are no shortcuts here.

Your ability to design a truly irresistible offer is predicated on your having done the work of clearly defining your niche and ideal customer. That's because what makes an offer irresistible to one person may only make your offer mildly appealing (if at all) to another person who's not your ideal customer. To make an offer truly irresistible, it's incumbent upon you to have a clear picture of **who you're talking to, what their biggest problems or pain points are, and what outcomes they are committed to having in their life**. Without these ingredients (which we just worked out in the previous chapter), it's not possible to come up with an irresistible offer.

Assuming you've done the work in the previous chapter, let's put together what you have so that you can build, test and refine your irresistible offer.

Building Your Irresistible Offer

It's important to note that you have not one, but two irresistible offer opportunities when growing your coaching business: (1) An irresistible offer to book time with you on your calendar, and (2) An irresistible offer to convert a free discovery call into a paying client. We're going to work backwards here to develop the irresistible offer to convert a discovery call first, and then we'll work on the irresistible offer to get those appointments in the first place.

What Makes an Offer Irresistible?

Not being able to resist an offer is about reflecting back the deepest desires of your ideal customer. The mistake coaches often make is thinking the offer is about coaching. It's *not* about coaching. Coaching is simply a vehicle for accomplishing what your ideal customer truly desires. When you spend too much time talking about coaching, you make it really difficult to persuade your prospective client to hire you.

To be clear nobody "needs" a coach. I stand by that statement. So why did I become a coach if I truly believe that? Because the most successful people I know have *at least* one coach and many have more than one. Coaching is a means to an end. As much as you may love the foundations of coaching and who you have become in your journey to becoming a coach, all of that is secondary to the only thing that matters to your prospective client. Simply put, your ideal prospective customers have two important questions in the back of their minds:

1. Are you the right person who understands me and my challenge?
2. Do I trust that you can help me get what I want?

As Rich Litvin, co-author of *The Prosperous Coach* would tell you, an enthusiastic, "HELL YES!" response to both of these questions is needed in order to get hired as their coach.

If you're not clear on what your prospective client wants, there's no chance of you crafting an irresistible offer. Here five questions to help you evaluate if your offer is irresistible or not:

1. *Would your ideal customer be crazy NOT to take you up on this offer?* If you answered yes, then go to "Why is that?" so that you can be clear on what it is that makes your offer so compelling. If your prospective client is clear on what they want and your offer aligns to what they want most, then you're already on your way. Be thinking about why they should believe you (i.e. "Reasons to believe"). Have you already helped others accomplish what this prospect wants? If so, do you have testimonials? Were they referred to you by someone who accomplished the very thing this prospect wants? Be in the question here so that you're clear on just how compelling your offer is to the person with whom you're speaking.

2. *Will this offer get the attention of your competitors?* This is a simple test you can use. When Google decided to enter the mobile phone industry, they gave their Android operating system away for free. Google didn't need to make money on their software as long as they were able to mine the local search traffic. Think about how terrifying that was for the *then* leading manufactures of

mobile phones: Blackberry, Nokia, Sony Ericson, etc. That offer not only got the attention of Google's competitors, it rocked the mobile phone industry. A free operating system in exchange for the use of Google's mobile web browser and defaulting search to them. That offer took the mobile phone industry by storm. Tom's Shoes rocked their competitors with their "Buy One, Give One" campaign where for every pair of shoes you buy, one is donated to someone in need. Zappos got the attention of Amazon and other online merchants with its "Free return shipping" offer. And I'm sure you can think of many other examples.

3. *Are you truly adding value to your ideal customers (or is it just talk)?* Think of each of the examples referenced in number two above. A free operating system added a ton of value to mobile phone manufacturers. Donating a pair of shoes for each pair you buy makes the purchaser feel good about their decision to buy from Tom's Shoes. Free return shipping decimated the cost of trying on shoes via the mail and got more people to buy more frequently because the risk was removed.

4. *Would your ideal customers rave about your offer or just be happy they got it?* This will quickly shed light on how irresistible your offer is. When LL Bean first launched, they had a lifetime return policy for their clothes. Think about that for a moment. Buy anything from them. Wear it for as long as you wish and at any point if you feel the product didn't stand up to your personal standards, return it. That set the industry standard for what it meant to stand behind your product. Yes, with too many consumers abusing this policy, they eventually had to change it, but what an irresistible offer! If you've visited In-N-Out Burger, their not-so-secret menu was one of the drivers of their success. Ordering off the menu was impressive to those unfamiliar with all the options and made their loyal customers feel special. Think about the last product you couldn't shut up about such as your favorite book, bottle of wine, restaurant, vacation resort, etc. What was it that made is so special?

5. *Does it pass the "Please Don't Tell" test?* In Jonah Berger's book *Contagious: Why Things Catch On* he shares a story about Crif Dogs, a hot dog restaurant in New York City. There you can get any number of hot dog combinations from the most gourmet to the highly unusual. That alone is interesting to anyone who loves hot dogs. But, if you happen to know how to get the code and you enter it at the specified time in the old-fashioned phone booth in the back, you'll open a secret door to one of the hottest bars in New York City – aptly called, *Please Don't Tell*. Why's that? Because a secret like this is the only thing most people truly can't keep.

By now you're getting a sense of what it takes to create a truly irresistible offer. But how do you really know if your offer is irresistible or not? What may be irresistible for one person may only be interesting to another. The good news is that there is a surefire way to know definitively.

How Do I Know My Offer is "Irresistible?"

To answer this question, let's begin with the end in mind on the offer itself. To be clear, you're giving this offer in order to enroll a client into your coaching business, correct? So let's use that as the litmus test. If you want to *know* if your offer is truly irresistible, then build out your measurement of success ahead of time so that you are clear up front on just how irresistible your offer truly is.

The ultimate response, after delivering your Irresistible Offer, would be a passionate "HELL YES!!!" as Rich Litvin so eloquently shared in his co-authored book, *The Prosperous Coach*. And there's one more criterion: You're getting a statistically significant higher number of "Hell Yeses" than the average one in ten close ratios when you're adding up your numbers.

Now stay with me here. Usually when I go into numbers, some coach's eyes begin to glaze over as they distance themselves from the things they don't enjoy doing. If you're noticing that happening with you, do some PQ Reps so that you can stay with me – your metrics will reveal everything you need to know about what's working (and what's not working) in your coaching business. Here's the target formula: **10 Discovery Calls = One New Client.**

What that translates to is if you're a full-time coach and looking to scale your coaching practice, you're going to want to generate as many discovery calls as you can. However, for every ten discovery calls you have, it should result in approximately one new client. We're going to go into detail on this formula and approach in the upcoming chapter on *Generating Appointments*. It's not nearly as scary as the formula may sound. For now, all I'm asking is that you understand the metrics so that we can use this as a barometer to measure how irresistible your offer really is.

If you are able to enroll two out of ten clients, then you are doubling the average. Three out of ten is triple, and so on. As you work on your irresistible offer, you now have a target to shoot for. If you're averaging one client for fifteen or twenty discovery calls, either your irresistible offer isn't that irresistible or you're not following the step-by-step process I've outlined in the *Converting Appointments* chapter.

Step One: Align to the Unique Needs of Your Ideal Customer

Sometimes, it's easier to help someone else with their irresistible offer than it is to craft your own. To that end, let's look at three different scenarios and decide what would be the best irresistible offer knowing the unique needs of a specific niche and ideal customer.

Ideal Customer: An ICF-certified coach who is struggling financially.
What They Need: The ability to create a financially lucrative coaching business.
Why: They want to create impact AND earn an income that supports their family.

What would be a solid irresistible offer if you knew you were talking to this coach and you were convinced that you could support them in building the kind of coaching practice they deeply desire? How about something like this:

I help coaches create the financial freedom they deserve doing what they love.

Or

I help coaches build a six-figure business in as little as six months.

For a truly irresistible offer, I might add, "**...or your money back.**" We'll talk about the pros and cons of risk removal strategies later in this chapter. For now, be thinking about what makes this offer irresistible. And, if there's something you'd change to make it even better, lean into that. These are meant to be examples only. They are not intended to be the "definitive answer" to the problem we're playing with. They are intended to be illustrative options to get your creative juices flowing. Let's try another.

Ideal Customer: C-Suite Executive
What They Need: To be remembered for more than their job title and wealth.
Why: As they begin to round toward retirement, they realize they've traded too much for the position they hold and the financial freedom they have accumulated.

What would be a solid irresistible offer if you knew you were talking to this C-Suite Executive and you were convinced that you could support them in being remembered in the ways they deeply desire? How about something like this:

I empower C-Suite executives to leave the legacy their grandchildren will be proud of.

Or

I help C-Suite executives align to their core principles and live a life of purpose.

Notice that in this case, adding **"...or your money back"** would actually hurt, not help your irresistible offer. For most C-Suite executives, money is not a driving force in their lives, but purpose and legacy are. Introducing a risk-free guarantee to this niche has the potential to inject doubt and prompt questions that may not have been there.

Ideal Customer: Overweight Men
What They Need: To drop the excess pounds and live a healthy life.
Why: They desire to extend their life by optimizing their health and live a healthy lifestyle so that they can enjoy their golden years.

What would be an irresistible offer if you knew you were talking to this overweight man or his significant other? How about something like this:

I help men transform their bodies and become physically fit for life so they can enjoy retirement.

Or

I support men
to release their excess pounds
by becoming physically
and mentally fit
for life.

Remember, these examples are just here to get your creative juices flowing. The first step is simply to get a draft down on paper. You're not looking to complete the exercise in the first step. While you're Saboteurs may urge you towards a "one and done" approach to your irresistible offer, that's not how it works. This is a much more iterative and nuanced process to ensure you're connecting with what's most important to your niche. You'll know you have nailed your irresistible offer when your ideal customers light up. Trust that your Sage already knows the answer you are searching for. This is simply a process to tap into your Sage wisdom and give yourself permission to play.

Step Two: Tap Into Your Sage Powers As You Refine Your Irresistible Offer

When taking this approach, you're going to notice that your Stickler, Hyper-Rationale and other Saboteurs enjoy messing with you during this process. That's because no offer will sound "perfect" no matter how much you revise and work on it. Your Saboteurs will look for what's wrong in whatever you choose to write down. Rather than allowing your Saboteurs to win, let's shift to Sage and see what more emerges from trusting our own inner wisdom.

How Sage Power Empathy Enhances Your Irresistible Offer

To really get the most out of your irresistible offer, begin with empathy. If you're feeling all the negativity of your Judge, it's really difficult to refine your irresistible offer. Rather than listen to the lies of your Saboteurs, begin with empathy for yourself. This is a new concept. You've likely never attempted to create a truly irresistible offer. Do you recall what it was like when you first learned to ride a bike without training wheels? There was a whole lot of wobbling and some falling down before you got it right.

Rather than allowing your Saboteurs to beat you up, tap into self-empathy to see the very point in the journey you're on. This is new. Anytime you attempt something new, you're retraining your brain and muscle memory as you do the work. It's messy by design. You're letting go of previous notions and limiting beliefs as you seek a new approach. Rather than remaining frustrated or experiencing negative emotions, go ahead and laugh at your Saboteurs for being ridiculous. It's perfectly fine to fall over on your proverbial bike as you play with your irresistible offer. In fact, if you never stumbled, it would mean you're not trying all that hard and you're not learning. Embrace the challenges ahead so that you can move right through them.

Next, have empathy for your ideal customers. If you think *this* is hard, imagine what it's like as your ideal customer goes through life not having what they desire most? What must it be like for them as they struggle and haven't yet found you and all the support you're ready to give them? What will it be like when they do realize how much you can help them? Better yet, imagine what it will be like when they forever handle this problem with you as their coach. The more empathy you can have for your ideal customers, the less you will focus on your own struggles as you work to refine your irresistible offer.

And lastly, have empathy for the situation you find yourself in right here and right now as you work on your irresistible offer. You are a perfectly imperfect human journeying towards self-actualization and Sage Mastery. If you already knew these things, you'd already have done them and would already have the coaching business of your dreams. Having empathy for your situation allows you to acknowledge where you are right here in this moment without any attachment to being somewhere else. Enjoy this part of the journey. Once you've completed this process, you will have completely shifted your coaching business. That's something to get excited about rather than frustrated by. Remember, you're already on the path. It's happening, even when you don't see the immediate result.

Move to Sage Power Explore and See What Else Your Ideal Customer Needs

Before attempting to tap into your Sage Power Explore, be sure you're already in Sage. Do more PQ Reps if necessary and connect with your empathy as shared above. There's no such thing as Saboteur Explore since attempting to tap into Explore while hijacked by your Saboteurs will simply leave you cynical, frustrated and disappointed.

From a Sage space, however, you can become fascinated by what you wrote down as your first draft of your irresistible offer. What did I choose to leave out? What might grab the attention of my ideal customer? If I discovered that this statement isn't resonating as much as I thought it would, what part would I consider playing with? Rather than waiting for that feedback, what if I began exploring alternatives to play with now?

In order to deeply Explore your irresistible offer, get curious. Allow yourself to question and ask, "What if ..." For example, what if I was talking to someone who knew my ideal customer? What might they share as a different problem my ideal customer has? What if the problem I've identified is spot on, but my ideal customer has fear about hiring me as their coach? What else might I want to have "at the ready" in case they are interested? What kind of testimonial would I want to have from another ideal customer that would make enrolling new clients easy? What would they say about working with me that my ideal customer would love to hear before hiring me?

Sage Power Explore allows you to be curious about all of this without allowing your Saboteurs to overwhelm you. While your Saboteurs might use these questions as weapons and lies to convince you that you're not ready, your Sage is simply exploring possibilities and seeing what else might support your irresistible offer. That's such an important difference and illuminates which part of your brain is active right now. Does asking these questions excite you and motivate you to learn more? Or do these questions trigger your Saboteurs? By remaining curious, you're going to discover new and interesting ways to engage your ideal customers with your irresistible offer. The more time you spend with possible irresistible offers, you will experience clarity of what matters most to those you choose to serve powerfully as their coach.

Tap Into Sage Power Innovate to Go Even Further with Your Irresistible Offer

I find that there's a natural transition between Explore and Innovate. I often find myself toggling between the two as I play. I have found that I enjoy tapping into my Sage Power Innovate with colleagues, but I've also discovered I can surprise myself with this power when I give myself thinking and imagination time.

If you're interested in trying this for yourself, see what you like about what you've written down (it's always at least 10% right) and play the "Yes, and..." game with yourself. Allow your Sage to play here and release your constraints on having the perfect irresistible offer. When you allow yourself to tap into your inner Sage wisdom, you'll find that your imagination will take you in some fascinatingly creative directions. Give yourself permission to explore even the craziest ideas and see what you like about them. This can lead to new insights and innovative breakthroughs that will serve your ideal customers powerfully.

It might go something like this:

- I help coaches create the financial freedom they deserve while doing what they love.
- What I like about that is creating financial freedom. And, when coaches create financial freedom for themselves, they live a life of purpose and meaning.

- What I like about coaches living a life of purpose and meaning is that they give themselves permission to work with clients that normally couldn't afford them.
- What I like about coaches working with clients that normally couldn't afford them is that they build a reputation in their communities and stand out among all the other coaches who take a more traditional route.
- What I like about coaches who stand out in their communities is that they are recognized leaders whom others turn to for support and model themselves after.
- What I like about others in a community modeling themselves after a coach is ...

And at any time, you can challenge yourself to throw in some truly crazy, nonsensical options just to see what you might do with it.

- What I like about others in a community modeling themselves after a coach is that the mayor or another government official would ask the coach to speak at political events and fundraisers.
- What I like about speaking at any event is the opportunity to deliver powerful messages that align with what that coach is up to in the world and offers a platform to enroll even more clients.

And so on. While the focus here is the irresistible offer, you can see that my Sage is already having me think about the next step of *Generating Appointments*. That's helpful because my Sage is sharing with me opportunities to consider deeper applications of how I might engage my ideal customers with this irresistible offer. Then, when I go back and look at the original statement, "I help coaches create the financial freedom they deserve doing what they love," I can see a depth of meaning that wasn't there previously. I have a vision for myself and my ideal clients as to what financial freedom means in very real terms and even begin to play with the concept of "doing what they love" actually means. This can lead to further refinements and nuances that weren't there previously.

Align Your Irresistible Offer with Sage Power Navigate

All of this brings us to reconsider our mission and purpose in light of these insights. Specifically, are all of the nuances generated thus far in alignment with our Sage Power Navigate? This is an important question to ponder as you tap into an abundance of insights and ideas. Remember, the Latin root of "decide" means "to cut off." Once you generate an abundance of possibilities, use your navigate power to ensure alignment with what you're up to as a coach. Any idea that takes your focus away from your mission and purpose is a distraction, pure and simple.

That's the clarity that Sage Power Navigate consistently brings you. Whenever you feel lost, overwhelmed or confused, lean on your own navigate power to ensure alignment and refocus your efforts. All too often, coaches fall into the trap of relying on others to tell them what to do and how to do it. Please don't allow that to happen to you. Your own Sage knows your truth better than anyone else. As long as you are, in fact, in Sage (and not hijacked by your Saboteurs masking as your Sage), then trust your inner wisdom. Allow Sage Power Navigate to guide you and the important decisions your making – especially about how your irresistible offer will support the needs of your ideal customers.

In the context of refining your irresistible offer, use Sage Power Navigate to help ensure that what you're offering will attract your ideal customer into your coaching business and have them excited to have discovered you. When you are completely aligned with the needs of your customers, your irresistible offer won't just help you attract clients, it will propel you to being the top choice of whom they should be working with. Upon hearing your irresistible offer, your ideal clients should have that, "Where have you been all my life?" sensation. Then, when you deliver on what was promised, you won't just have a satisfied client, you will have a raving fan.

When your ideal customer understands that your mission in life is to solve the very problem that they are struggling with, they get excited that they've found you. When you follow through, they almost can't believe it. For most people, anything that sounds too good to be true usually is. Their skepticism around your irresistible offer comes from years of receiving broken promises and half-truths. When they discover that you are who you say you are and you deliver what you promise, they can't help but sing your praises to others struggling with the same or similar problems. This leads to your systems of referrals (which we'll cover in greater detail in the next chapter, *Generating Appointments*).

See why Sage Power Navigate is such an important step in this process? The more you align to your own mission and purpose, the easier it becomes to enroll your ideal customers and have them become your best and most powerful lead generation engine. By inviting your Sage to keep you aligned with your mission and purpose, Sage Power Navigate will illuminate your best path forward while attracting your ideal clients.

As you allow your Sage to drive the core foundations of your coaching business, you discover the ease and flow available to you. It's your Saboteurs that stop you from having what you want in your coaching business and your Sage that ensures you are fully aligned with your purpose. The more you call on your Sage Power Navigate, the easier it becomes to see immediately ideas that align and those which take you off your path.

See How Your Irresistible Offer Is Already Motivating You Towards Sage Power Activate

Lastly, notice how the other four powers compel you to action. Deep empathy for your ideal customers has you wanting to move mountains for them to ensure they get their desired outcomes. As you explore new areas, ideas and possibilities, notice that drive to immediately take action. Your Sage compels you to act when you have clarity – especially if you've been feeling stuck or unsure of what actions to take. The more you time you spend in explore, the more options you begin to cultivate. Then when you play the "Yes, and ..." game via innovate, you discover the abundance of possibilities; a near endless number of options to choose from. So many, in fact, that it helps to reconnect with your mission and purpose via navigate to ensure the ideas you pursue are in alignment with where your Sage has you focus.

Sage Power Activate is only difficult when you are in Saboteur scarcity and unsure of yourself. Your Sage lives in abundance and knows how powerful you really are. That swift, bold action is a direct result of having clarity on whom you choose to serve as your ideal customers and knowing how you can help them accomplish their desired outcomes. With that level of clarity, of course you're ready to share your irresistible offer with the world. Your Sage discernment sees that clear path of whom you choose to work with, what their biggest needs are and how you are uniquely qualified to help them achieve their desired outcomes.

When you are being driven by your own deep inner wisdom (instead of your Saboteur fears and negativity), you want to act. In the absence of fear, what remains is inner calm, peaceful confidence and a deep sense of purpose and meaning. This doesn't mean you must eliminate all fear in order to act. Quite the contrary. Anytime you get outside your comfort zone, you'll notice your Saboteur fears bubbling up. Sage Mastery comes not from ignoring those fears, but rather feeling those fears and taking action in spite of them. It's only when the fear *stops* you that your Saboteurs win. Having fear isn't a problem, it's part of the growth process. As you take action, you overcome your fears and strengthen your Sage. If you wait until your fear is completely gone, you'll be dead before you take action.

And, each time you overcome your fear through taking action, you shrink your Saboteurs just a little and strengthen your Sage ever so slightly. It's these barely noticeable shifts that, occurring over time, create the seismic breakthroughs you seek. The more action you take, the more you reinforce and strengthen your Sage Powers – even when you make mistakes and "fail" or, as I prefer to say, "learn" what works and what doesn't. Which takes us to the final step in the process- keep working to simplify and continue practicing the delivery of your irresistible offer. No one has the opportunity to say "yes" to an offer they haven't heard. So once you have a workable irresistible offer, it's time to take action and test out what you've created.

Step Three: Simplify & Practice Out Loud to Another Person

You saw that the last Sage Power is Activate. The third and final step is to keep the momentum you created going by practicing out loud to another person. Yes, if it helps you to start practicing in the mirror first, that's totally fine. As long as you don't remain there. As much as your mirror image loves you, you'll never know how powerful and effective your irresistible offer is until you begin practicing out loud to another human being.

Simplify

You'll notice right away when you first go to practice your irresistible offer out loud that you're either tripping over your words or have a compulsion to read what you wrote down. Say hello to your Saboteurs! Don't let them stop you here. Reading your irresistible offer off the printed page can help you memorize your irresistible offer and that is a sure-fire way to prevent your Sage from speaking.

If you're tripping over your words or have that compulsion to read your irresistible offer, then chances are your irresistible offer is too long or too confusing to remember. Less is more here. If you find yourself in this space, then see what you can do to simplify your irresistible offer. One exercise I use in pods of two or three can be helpful here. I will have a triad of three coaches organize into A > B > C where person A is the coach, person B is the client and person C is the observer.

The coach in this exercise (person A) makes their irresistible offer. The, the client (person B) repeats back what they heard. It's at this point that the observer (person C) reminds the coach not to "correct" their client, but rather listen to their client's listening. What did the client hear? What words did they adjust when sharing back your irresistible offer? Then I have the coach refine their irresistible offer and say it again.

In a period of just five minutes or less, the coach has identified where their irresistible offer is falling short. The client has simply mirrored back what they think they heard. And the observer is highlighting what they are experiencing in the exercise which can provide keen insights and support breakthroughs. Then, everyone rotates. Now it's B > C > A, where person B is the coach, person C is the client and person A is the observer.

In as little as 15 minutes, this exercise can sharpen all three participant's irresistible offers. The more you practice, the sharper and more to the point your irresistible offer becomes. Or, said another way, your initial draft offer begins to become truly irresistible. As you refine your irresistible offer, just make sure it's all coming from your Sage and not your Stickler or Hyper-Achiever, for example. Your Saboteurs will want to take charge here and it's your job to stay in Sage during the exercise for maximum impact and effectiveness.

Practice With Your Peers

Do you already see why practicing with your peers is so compelling? Instead of your Saboteurs throwing you a pity party or having you obsess over your irresistible offer, your Sage is calmly considering what's working and what's in the gap. As you play with your irresistible offer, you see opportunities to improve and welcome these opportunities rather than get hijacked by them. It also helps tremendously when you play the role of the client and the observer.

As the client, you're being a generous listener. And while you are being in service, you Sage can't help but learn from the experience and apply what you're learning to your own irresistible offer, albeit often at a subconscious level. Same goes for the role of the observer. As you listen and observe, you are seeing what lands and what needs work for your peers. You simultaneously are thinking about your own irresistible offer and how to apply these learnings.

The more time you spend practicing with your peers, the deeper your learning goes as you experiment and adjust your irresistible offer, As you optimize your irresistible offer, you're also gaining clarity on the best ways to deliver it. Subtle cues about your own voice inflection and body alignment become noticeable. For example, "Did my voice just crack there? That probably means I'm not feeling confident about that part. Why did my voice go up at the end of my irresistible offer? That delivery lacked confidence. Let's try again after I do a few PQ Reps."

And best of all, your peers will notice things that you completely missed. It might be a facial expression that reveals one of your Saboteurs or it could be how you present as nervous as you breath shallowly instead of calmly and deeply. Be open to any and all feedback. And if you're the one giving feedback, notice if what you're sharing you're also doing yourself. Chances are, when you spot it, you got it. The things that you notice in others can give you clues as to what you may (or may not) be doing yourself.

Practice With Your Ideal Customer Prospects

To be clear, practicing with your peers is the equivalent of riding a bike with your training wheels on. Your peers love and adore you. They are safe. Even when they give you feedback, you know it's from a loving space. While this can be a great step toward connecting with your ideal customer prospects, know that you're not complete with your irresistible offer until you've actually practiced it out loud with people who either can hire you directly or know someone who can.

Get outside your comfort zone and practice your irresistible offer on people who can actually hire you as their coach. Otherwise what was the point of all that effort? When you remove those proverbial training wheels, you're going to experience the wobble and maybe even a fall or two. Just keep getting back up on your proverbial bike. Keep testing out your irresistible offer. Your goal isn't to have "the perfect" irresistible offer, but rather to learn what's resonating with your ideal customer prospects (and what's *not* resonating with them).

While it's wonderful to land clients, your early goal here is to test out just how irresistible offer your offer truly is. If it doesn't land in the ways you imagined, remain in Sage and stay curious. You can even ask for feedback. If someone is lost, confused or simply said "no, thank you," see if you can discover what prevented them from saying yes. Ask powerful open-ended questions with the focus to learn rather than "save" or "convert" this prospect (at that's Saboteur scarcity thinking and your Sage lives in abundance).

Ironically, the worst thing that can happen early on is to have to many early wins. As we don't learn from our successes, those easy wins feel great, but don't teach us what we really want to know. So instead of being committed to being right about your irresistible offer, commit to remaining open, curious and in Sage as you deliver it. Allow each "no" to take you one step closer to success as you learn what you can consider improving or changing for maximum effectiveness. Until you practice with your ideal customer prospects, you won't truly know or be able to gauge how irresistible your offer actually is.

Pros & Cons of Money Back Guarantees and Risk Removal

What happens if, after all that, you find out your irresistible offer isn't so irresistible after all? To be clear, I'm talking Sage discernment (not Saboteur judgment) where you have spoken to your ideal customer prospects and you're seeing that they aren't as enticed by your offer as you were anticipating. Your offer is working, but you're finding it's not all that irresistible. It's at this point that some coaches prefer to add a money back guarantee.

Specifically, your money back guarantee ensures that your ideal customer prospect receives their outcome or you give them their money back. You've seen this everywhere from direct response television (i.e. "infomercials") to return policies on Amazon and other retailers.

There are certainly times when removing the risk of taking you up on your offer can push your offer from interesting to irresistible. There are other times when it can do the opposite. Let's explore both so that you have a good idea of when to use risk removal strategies and when not to use them.

Pros of Money Back Guarantees

At their most basic level, a money back guarantee removes the risk from your ideal customer prospect taking a chance on hiring you as their coach and puts that same risk squarely on you. I've used this approach effectively when launching my own coaching business and I can attest to how irresistible it can make your offer. When I first launched my course, *Millionaire Coaches Marketing Playbook*, my irresistible offer was:

Invest $5,000 in my 12-week course and double your money guaranteed.

Yep, that's what launched my business development course content that was eventually revised and updated to what you now have as part of Positive Intelligence's PQ Coach membership. It was as straight forward as you think. Participants invested $5,000 up front and then attended a weekly 90 minute live small-group conference (usually of about 15 people or less). Some quick math (15 x $5,000) shows you I received $75,000 for each 12-week course and sometimes I would do two of them in parallel for as much as $150,000 per three month term.

In addition to the group content, I would work one-on-one with each person to ensure they were making progress against their individual $10,000 revenue target. As contracts were signed, we'd celebrate each person's wins and work together to overcome fears, handle objections and ensure everyone finished successfully.

And yes, occasionally a coach would not hit their $10,000 revenue target and I would either give them their original $5,000 investment back or, in one case, a coach asked that I extend our individual coaching for another few months until she hit her target (which she did and then continued to hire me for individual coaching support).

If you're following along here, when you have 15 participants each investing $5,000 for a total of $75,000 per three-month term (and at least 13 of them hit their targets), you're looking at a total refund liability of $10,000 for a net positive of $65,000 in income. Would you be willing to risk $10,000 to generate $65,000? That's the bet I made on myself to launch my efforts. And yes, for someone who's never run a company before, that can be terrifying as your Hyper-Vigilant Saboteur keeps you up late at night stressing about your full liability.

Was it *possible* that I could have had 15 participants all miss their goals and 100% of that $75,000 must be returned? Yes, that's what a money back guarantee means. Worst case scenario, you're not only out the $75,000, but also the near 200 hours of time between your group and one-on-one coaching.

However, when you bring it back to a space of Sage discernment, is that likely to happen? No. Is it possible? Yes. That's the difference. If you're investing 15 hours or more per participant, you can bet you'll be clear on where each person is struggling and how you can help them overcome their biggest obstacles. And to ensure my own success, I launched my very first program as a *free* pilot. In other words, I assumed the risk of my very own worst-case scenario to prove to myself even the worst case scenario wasn't all that bad. In fact, I learned so much from my first program, I had every ounce of confidence I needed to go from free to $5,000 per person with that money back guarantee. I had worked out the bugs and knew precisely what was needed to ensure the outcomes of my participants. Game on!

So the bottom line for you is to really be clear on what it would take for you to take your own leap of faith. It doesn't have to be monetary like mine was. In the context of weight loss, it can be dropping a specific number of pounds or your money back. For new relationships, it can be overcoming your fear of dating and asking people out. Or it could be about eliminating your need for dating apps. For career focus, it could be getting the next promotion in six months or less. Every niche has a possible option to consider. The question is, where does making a money back guarantee actually *hurt* your irresistible offer? Let's see.

Cons of Money Back Guarantees

The most obvious con of having a money back guarantee is the risk it creates for you at the holder of that guarantee. More specifically, coaches will argue that there's no possible way that a coach could fulfill those guarantees while remaining an actual coach. After all, the coach is the "guide on the side" and therefore not responsible for doing the work necessary to reach the goal. So why would you ever do it?

What's missing in that premise is why the money back guarantee works in the first place. Yes, it's true that you, as the coach, are not the one doing the work that will ensure the outcome. You are, however, being a powerful stand for your client and in offering a guarantee you are building their own confidence in their own abilities to reach that outcome. Sometimes that's all that takes is for you, as their coach, to project confidence in their ability to reach their desired outcome when their own internal Saboteur self-critics are screaming that they can't. Breakthrough a limiting belief and you're already on the right trajectory to succeed.

The true con, however, is when a money back guarantee had the opposite effect. For CEOs and senior executives, for example, introducing a money back guarantee would backfire. They naturally assume that you're an expert in the coaching services that you are providing. When you offer a money back guarantee to C-Suite executives, rather than building confidence you are actually inadvertently injecting doubt where there previously was none. If you are so confident in your abilities, these C-Suite executives think, then why even open the door to a money back guarantee? The very act of doing so has them question if you can actually help them accomplish the outcome they desire. If you really could, they reason, why would you ever offer a money back guarantee?

Another big con to watch out for in money back guarantees is the precise language used to determine if giving money back is warranted. That is, imprecise language leads to grey areas and interpretation. Language such as "earn double your $5,000 investment or your money back" is easy to quantify and measure – the client either did or did not earn $10,000 in the term agreed to. That's easy to ascertain. Having a money back guarantee for overcoming imposter syndrome, for example is much more difficult to quantify. How would you know if your client did or did not without their own qualitative (and arguably biased assessment)?

What's important to note here is that while money back guarantees are a great strategy for mitigating risk for most niches, there are some niches where having one introduces doubt and this uncertainty makes your offer less irresistible instead of more. It's also critical that the outcome your guaranteeing is objectively quantifiable and that you and your client agree up front how accomplishing the desired outcome will be measured and verified. Otherwise, you open yourself up to an unmanageable level of financial risk that simply isn't worth doing.

Testing Your Irresistible Offer

Now that you have a solid draft of your irresistible offer, it's time to test out just how irresistible it actually is. Afterall, having the best, most carefully crafted language is of little value if your irresistible offer fails to convert your ideal customer prospects into paying clients. And while there's lots of ways to test out just how irresistible your irresistible offer actually is, nothing beats actual enrollment calls (which we'll cover in more detail in the upcoming chapter, *Converting Appointments: The Art of the Close*).

Beware of Feedback From Those Who Are NOT Your Niche

As we explore where to test out your irresistible offer, it's important to acknowledge that anyone who agrees to listen to your irresistible offer will have an opinion. The question is, if they're not your actual niche, how much should you act on this feedback? While you should most certainly pay attention to what feedback is offered, don't make any substantive changes until received confirmation on that feedback from individuals who are actually your niche.

For example, you may be using language that totally resonates with your niche, but if I'm not your ideal customer prospect (and I don't live in their world), I may be confused by the language you're using and urge you to change or eliminate something that would land powerfully for your actual ideal customers. While I urged you to avoid using "coach speak" in your irresistible offer, sometimes the most irresistible words in your offer are keywords from my industry that show to me you understand who I am and what I'm up to. Eliminating language that could support you because someone who is not your niche is confused by that language would be counterproductive.

Peer Coaches

Better than people outside your niche (but still not ideal) are your peer coaches – especially if they too are working on their own irresistible offer. By sharing your irresistible offer with them and providing your feedback on their irresistible offer, you are creating intentional learning opportunities for you and your peer coaches. As you lean into supporting one or more peer coaches with their irresistible offer, you begin to notice ways to refine your own. Said another way, "when you spot it, you got it." Helping others refine their irresistible offer is a surefire way to get better at yours.

Your peer coaches need not have the same niche, nor do they need to be PQ Coach members either (although that can be helpful). They just need to be a fellow coach who is working on building, growing and scaling their own coaching business. As long as they are clear on the power of an irresistible offer and why it's important to have one, their feedback can definitely support you in refining your irresistible offer.

People Who Know Your Ideal Customer Prospects

The closer we come to speaking directly with your actual ideal customer prospects, the more incredibly helpful the feedback on your irresistible offer will be. People who know your ideal customer prospects should light up when they hear your irresistible offer. Their reaction will something akin to, "This isn't for me, but I know someone who could use what you're offering. Can I make an introduction?"

Alternatively, if you know that they have access to your ideal customer prospects and are not interested in making introductions, that may be an early warning signal that your irresistible offer isn't all that irresistible. Just take note from a place of Sage discernment (not Saboteur judgment). If you talk to a number of people who know your ideal customer prospects, you should have a good sense how irresistible your offer truly is by the number of introductions or recommendations you receive.

Actual Ideal Customer Prospects

And finally, we're reach the actual gold standard. There is absolutely no better way to test just how irresistible your offer is than making it directly to your ideal customer prospect and tracking the number of nos and yeses. When we get into the chapter on *Converting Appointments: The Art of the Close* I'll go deeper there, but for now know that the average conversion rate is 1:10. That means for every ten prospects that you make your offer to, usually one of them will say yes. What you want to see is that number go up with a truly irresistible offer. Think about it, if you were able to close two clients (2:10) you're doing 50% better than the average and that means your offer is irresistible. The more irresistible your offer is, the more people will want to buy from you.

To get an average, however, you need to make your irresistible offer to at least 30 prospects. That's because you can get lucky and have the first two-three clients say yes and then have the next 27 say no. Remember that 1:10 is the average, which means that you could get 2:10 and then 1:10 and then 0:10 and still average down to 1:10.

As you ratchet up your conversion ratio, you will have the evidence you need to know that your offer is, indeed, irresistible (or not). Regardless of how irresistible your offer is, please don't think that this is a "one and done" exercise. Instead, see it as an iterative process of continued refinement and improvement. As you grow your coaching business, you're bound to learn more about the true needs of your ideal customers and, with this knowledge, will likely be in the position to make further refinements. Afterall, that's the value of testing out your irresistible offer: to learn, receive feedback and optimize as you grow and scale your coaching business.

Refining Your Irresistible Offer

As mentioned previously, your irresistible offer is not a "one and done" exercise. No matter how much you work on it, there are external factors and influences to consider. As you begin using your irresistible offer, you're going to continue to receive feedback both directly from your ideal customer prospects and indirectly by your tracking of your results (i.e. your conversion rate which we'll go into greater detail in the upcoming chapter, *Converting Appointments: The Art of the Close*).

Understanding that refining your irresistible offer is a continuous process helps you shift your perspective from a desire to have a perfectly crafted offer to understanding that it's more of a journey than a destination. In this journey, you have the opportunity to test out alternative approaches, new ideas and updated language. How you refine your irresistible offer is much less important than being mindful of your own continued journey towards Sage Mastery and the need to continuously improve. As you grow and expand, so, too, will your coaching business and it is important that this expansion includes regularly checking in on the effectiveness of your irresistible offer.

This is especially true if you adjust your niche, or deepen your learning of your ideal customer's biggest challenges and desired outcomes. As an entrepreneur, your business depends on your ability to remain curious and continuously listen for changes in the lives of those you serve. As the needs of your ideal customers change, so, too, must your irresistible offer follow suit.

When you notice that your irresistible offer is no longer delivering the impact and effectiveness it once was, it's time for refinements.

Designing Packages for Long-term Engagements

As you are playing with your irresistible offer, notice what you are optimizing for. When you're first starting out as a coach, "any client at any price for any length of time" tends to be the goal. Together, we've moved the "any client" part to becoming laser sharp focused by clearly defining your niche. What's next in the process is to be specific about the length of time you coach and shift to a long-term view of the work you do with your ideal customer prospects.

"Any client" and "any length of time" are typically driven by your Saboteurs and come from a place of scarcity. After building and growing businesses for nearly thirty years, I've come to realize that it takes just as much effort to enroll a client in a short-term engagement as it does to enroll them into a long-term one. Short engagements come from that place of scarcity where you, as a coach, are chiefly concerned about the revenue you're generating this month or the next three months. What that does is keep you on a proverbial hamster wheel where no matter how fast you move, you tend to remain stuck in the same space. To get off that hamster wheel, it's important to mentally shift from scarcity to abundance.

Abundant, Sage thinking, is not obsessed with the immediacy of your coaching business so much as thinking about the long-term growth and success you're truly after. Sure, you need some initial clients to build traction and you may optimize your strategy to just get out there and land your first client. That's fine. But once you begin building traction, remember you're also establishing your own parameters. If you're not careful, you will become comfortable with the short-term thinking and immediacy that got you started.

Living in abundance is different. Rather than your primary focus being on the short-term, you shift your focus to the long view and begin asking yourself questions such as:

- What is my ideal timeframe I'd like to have a client as part of my practice?
- What is the minimum timeframe I would need to make a massive impact on a client?
- When a new client seeks to speak with one of my current clients, how long do I want a current client to have worked with me when discussing our work together?

From my own work as a coach, I discovered that I was getting significant shifts and breakthroughs in as little as three months, but for some clients it could take five or even six months before they experienced a transformational shift. I discovered that it wasn't me that was the variable ... it was my client's readiness to take themselves on and truly desire a deep and lasting change in their life.

It is for that reason that I stopped taking on clients who wanted to "try me out" for a month or two and "see how it goes." After I shared, "I receive $1,000 a month for two 45-minute coaching sessions," I added, "and I coach my clients for a minimum of six months." That simple phrase, "and I coach my clients for a minimum of six months" made all the difference in my coaching practice.

"Why six months?" I would get asked. And I would speak my truth in response. "Because I find that it takes up to six months to truly see a transformational and lasting shift in our work together. While some clients have significant breakthroughs in as little as three months, I work with my clients for a minimum of six months to ensure the lasting change they hire me to create in their lives. After the first six months, most of my clients continue on and many have been with me for years."

What did you notice with what I just shared? While every word of that is true, what you may notice is the pre-frame I'm establishing with a potential client. Underneath my share, I'm planting a seed inside my prospect so that they can ask themselves questions such as:

- Is this me?
- Am I really ready to take myself on?
- Could I really have everything I ever wanted in as little as six months?
- Would it be worth a $6,000 investment to have what I desire most in my life?

I'm not asking these questions directly. They are subtly there in the background as I'm sharing my own direct experience with my current and past clients. If the person I'm talking with is not ready to commit to a six-month engagement, then I know I'm not the right coach for them. I say as much, thank them for the opportunity to connect and ask if they would like me to refer them to a coach who might be willing to engage for less than six months (perhaps even at a lower price point).

I know plenty of coaches – especially new ones just starting out in the industry – that would be thrilled to have a client seeking to pay less than $1,000 a month and for less than six months. By saying no to these opportunities, I'm saying YES to what I truly want: someone willing to make at least a six-month commitment at the investment level I seek. And my willingness to make an introduction often results in reciprocation from this person wanting to do the same – perhaps with a friend or college that they believe is more financially well off than they are and/or has a greater need then they are experiencing for themselves.

Regardless if they do or do not refer someone to me, I am leaving this person feeling held and cared for. Either they wish to have me make an introduction, or they don't. Either way I have offered to help them continue on my journey and I feel great about my part in their growth and success. Sometimes this one interaction can be the spark that ignites something deep inside of them. Their Sage is awakened to this powerful interaction and something inside of them knows that this is the work they need, even if I'm not the right coach for them in this moment in time.

Long-term engagements ensure your client's success. I urge you not to "sell out" on those you choose to serve. If your Sage knows that it takes a certain period of time (such as six-months) for your clients to truly experience a powerful shift and transformational breakthrough, then it's up to you to be a stand for their greatness. Holding them high ensures they sign-up for the work they are committed to doing and it gives you the space you need to perform your absolute best for them.

When you and your client agree on a long-term engagement, be it six months, a year or longer, there's a new level of commitment happening in your coaching business; one that will continue to pay massive dividends for you both.

Defining & Refining Price Points: When to Double Your Rates

Pricing is one of the more challenging aspects of building a coaching business. For many of the coaches I've worked with over the years, pricing and the broader concept of receiving money can be the most challenging aspect they face. Often, it required every bit of Sage discernment that they can muster. For many coaches, knowing what to charge is blocked by the resistance they feel to receiving in general. While coaches tend to give without expectations, they often struggle with receiving without resistance. If this is you, then defining and refining your price point could be your path to Sage Mastery. At the very least, you will stretch yourself as you grow into a new space of being open to receive without resistance.

In this section, I'll go over the core principles and in the next section we can take a good hard look at each of your Saboteurs and how they show up at precisely the wrong moments when money is involved.

Defining Your Price Point: Knowing What to Charge for Coaching

Your time is valuable. But how valuable is it? Many coaching schools do their "students" a disservice by introducing the concept of a "student rate" when you're first starting out. In my experience, nobody buys coaching. Period. Your ideal customer prospects are investing in the *outcomes* they want and believe they will achieve with you as their coach. Now there are many, many different approaches to establishing a price point. HubSpot published a great article[33] with several different strategies including:

- Competition-Based Pricing
- Cost-Plus Pricing

---

[33]   https://blog.hubspot.com/sales/pricing-strategy

- Dynamic ("Surge") Pricing
- Freemium Pricing
- High–Low Pricing
- Hourly Pricing
- Skimming Pricing
- Penetration Pricing
- Premium Pricing
- Project-Based Pricing
- Value-Based Pricing
- Bundle Pricing
- Psychological Pricing
- Geographic Pricing

And while all of these strategies are valid, well-researched and incredibly interesting to my Hyper-Rational Saboteur, they won't help most coaches establish their price point. If anything, seeing how many possibilities there are tends to active a coach's Avoider Saboteur.

Instead, I highly recommend the simplicity and elegance of Kendall Summerhawk's *Money, Marketing and Soul* program designed to help coaches establish their price point (among many other things). In this, she simply asks you to fill in the blanks:

1. Three years from today, my annual income will be $_____

2. Number of hours I want to work in a year is: _____

3. Amount your time is worth per hour = _____ [income / hours]

So let's say that as a brand new coach, I want to make $100,000 a year in coaching working a maximum of 1,000 billable hours. I divide $100,000 by 1,000 and come to a rate of $100/hour.

If you choose to work fewer billable hours, you'd need to charge more to still make an annual income of $100,000. If you're willing to work 1,000 hours a year, but want to make $200,000, then your hourly rate just doubled to $200/hr.

Now if that feels a bit arbitrary, I understand your concern. Your Saboteurs are likely screaming that there's no possible way you'll ever make that much per hour. As Henry Ford is famous for saying, "If you think you can, or you think you can't ... you're right."

Or, when Shirzad asks, "Which is true?" He then follows this question with, "Which ever you believe to be true becomes true." That's because whatever story we make up about how much we are able to charge clients is the story we live into. In the next section, we'll explore observing market dynamics and how to receive feedback in Sage, but for now please notice what you're telling yourself in this moment.

You are free to start out charging as little as you want as a coach. Some can't get past the notion of charging more than a government mandated minimum wage. For others, they pinpoint their price at the rate they were making at some other job before switching careers. What I'm asking you to consider is the under*lying* belief that's driving these assertions. Because this is elevating the "lie" or story that you've likely created for yourself which we'll explore in the sections that follow.

You need not believe me here. For many, you're "hearing" what I'm saying, but you don't believe it ... yet. Until you believe that it's possible, it's actually not as your Saboteurs will continue to mess with you whenever you attempt to share a price point that you, yourself, don't believe in. So for now, start with a number you *can* get behind.

Remember, this exercise said, *three years from today*, so you have some time to work up to the number you aspire to make. What I'm introducing at this stage is the notion that there's a lot more emotional energy behind what a coach charges than a "standard rate" that all must comply with. Especially in the United States where there is currently no regulation of the coaching industry, you are an entrepreneur and you get to set your price point. You can make that as low or as high as "the market" will bear. And that's what we'll examine next.

Refining Your Price Point: Observing Market Dynamics & Feedback in Sage

In the previous section, I urged you to begin with your own end in mind. Knowing how many hours you want to work and the annual salary you are looking to make each year are the foundations of establishing your hourly rate. It's that simple. And for some, it's that challenging as this simple formula has you take a good look at your own worthiness story. "Am I truly worth that much an hour?" is a question your Saboteurs may be challenging you to consider. Yes, you are. And sometimes you need to work toward building that confidence over time (rather than right out of the gate).

The next place to look (after exploring and reflecting *inside* yourself) is the market you choose to serve. Notice, I'm *not* talking about the *coaching* market. I'm talking about your niche. Different niches will have different market dynamics and it's important to pay attention to what's driving yours. For example, if you're working with established businesses at the C-Suite level, then premium pricing for coaching isn't just an option, it's expected. For senior leadership teams, pricing your coaching services too low will actually hurt your chances of picking up clients. If a company is used to investing $500 to $1,000 per hour for an executive coach, and you're asking for $100 per hour, that sends up a red flag that perhaps you're not a good fit.

That may sound strange, but observing market dynamics will help you have a better sense of what your niche is accustomed to paying so you can see if your rates are at least "in the ballpark." Even if they are higher than others in your niche, as long as you can share why you charge what you charge, you need not conform. It helps, however, to have a basis of understanding when possible.

Let's go the other extreme. Let's say your niche is underserved youth living in poverty. Before you give away your coaching services, explore who else is interested in serving this niche. What you will likely find is that there are several government grants available to support this same group of people; grants that you can apply for in order to be fairly compensated while also making a huge impact in the world. And if there are no established grants, you can seek out government agencies to request that a grant be established.

Not into grants? How about one or more non-profit organizations that serve this group? Non-profit does not mean "no money." In fact, the major donors of non-profits are actively seeking long-term sustainable solutions to the problem the non-profit was established to solve. When you can demonstrate that your coaching – especially your mental fitness coaching – provides these clients with a foundational operating system that helps them become self-sustaining, you have an incredible value proposition to offer.

From your own work in mental fitness, you know how powerful this operating system is. Imagine helping a non-profit by sharing this gift with the principles. Once they see that they themselves begin living in abundance and become proverbial self-cleaning ovens, how much more inclined are they to work with you to bring this work to their clients?

This is about tapping into your Sage Powers – especially Explore and Innovate. As you consider new possibilities, you no longer have to constrain yourself to a life of scarcity and minimum wage earnings. I'm confident that these approaches are barely scratching the surface. As soon as you align yourself to an established need in any community, you will see the magic of that community rise up to support you who is, in turn, supporting that community.

All of this information and these established norms are simply **feedback** for your coaching business. You are free to charge whatever you wish. At the time of this writing, you're operating in an unregulated industry (at least in the United States). That means you set your price point for your coaching services. When we switch over to the chapter on *Converting Appointments: The Art of the Close*, we'll go deeper into what this feedback means in real-time. That is, as you make your offer and quantify the number of times someone says, "Yes" or "No," we can determine if you're at, above or below the average conversion rates. Once you're clear on your targets, you can see how your overall performance is doing and make adjustments along the way.

And that is why, at least for now, you need not obsess over what you decide to charge for your coaching services. You need not publish your rates on your website or anywhere else for that matter. For now, you need only commit (for yourself) what you receive so that you can feel confident when delivering your irresistible offer.

When to Double Your Rates ... And Double Again

One of the scarier aspects of the growth in your coaching business is *after* you've generated some early success. As you're picking up momentum, you become comfortable with all that you've established for yourself. It's that comfort that tends to lock you into "fixed" thinking and can lead toward the opposite of what you want.

When you're first starting out, there is a deep desire to "coach anyone at any price." Let's use an extreme to illustrate a point, then we'll go the other direction. Since the 2020 ICF Global Coaching study has published data that the global average income for a coach is $47,100[34], we'll round up to $50,000 for easy math. Let's say you're working 1,000 (billable) hours a year to make $50,000 in coaching revenue. That means your hourly rate is $50.

What tends to happen is that as your coaching business is growing, you become more and more convinced that $50/hr is your rate, because it's working! Here's the thing, if most of the people you're talking to saying yes to you as a coach, that's a really great indication that you're not charging enough. At some point, you begin to paint yourself into the proverbial corner as your time is fixed. A law firm, for example, uses a 2,000 billable hours per year and most marketing agencies use 1,800 billable hours. What that means is that you're running out of "hours" you are able to offer up at any price.

Let's say that you're coaching your clients weekly for an hour a week at $50/hr. Assuming you take two weeks off a year for vacation, that means that each client you book is worth $2,500 annually ($50 x 50 weeks per year). If you secure 20 clients at $2,500/year you're at $50,000 coaching 1,000 hours.

Rather than allowing this scenario to organically play itself out, set a mental "alarm" when you achieve your eighth client. On an annualized basis, that means you've secured $20,000 in (projected) coaching revenue. This is the time to double your rates to $100/hr. It will take your Sage discernment in order to step into this next level, but trust me it's worth it.

Initially, you won't receive as many "yeses" as before and you'll wonder if you've made a huge mistake. You'll want to drop down to your previous rate. Instead, keep the faith. It will take longer and even slow your growth, but here's what happens next. Your ninth client says yes and suddenly, you have the *revenue equivalent* of landing not one, but two clients. You now secured your ninth AND tenth client at your old rate. See what's happening?

---

[34] https://coachingfederation.org/research/global-coaching-study

You're doing the exact same work, but receiving twice as much for it. Once you've secured yoru next seven clients at $100/hr., it's time to repeat the process. But before we double again, let's look at what this means to you economically speaking:

eight clients at $50/hr x 50 weeks a year   = $20,000
seven clients at $100/hr x 50 weeks a year = $35,000
Total   = **$55,000**

By doubling your rate at the eighth client secured, you're now working fewer hours for a higher rate of compensation. Rather than working 1,000 hours at $50/hr, you're now working a total of 750 hours at a *blended rate* of $73.33 ($55,000 / 750 hours). And because you've secured seven clients at $100/hr, you'll never go back to charging $50/hr ever again. In fact, as one of your first eight clients at $50/hr ends their coaching relationship with you (for whatever reason), then you'll replace them with another client at $100/hr.

If you *just* implemented this one strategy, didn't grow your business, but replaced each $50/hr client with a $100/hr client, then you will eventually have 15 clients at $100/hr or $75,000/year. With this approach, you'll already be making more than what the ICF is currently reporting most coaches make. And sure, you could add 5 more clients at $100/hr for your $100,000/year target of making six figures, but this would be a mistake.

The next 5 clients are your *premium* clients. You're in no rush to fill these seats. From this point on, you receive $200/hr which works out to $10,000 per year. Your coaching business now looks something like this:

eight clients at $50/hr x 50 weeks a year   = $20,000
seven clients at $100/hr x 50 weeks a year = $35,000
five clients at $200/hr x 50 weeks a year   = $50,000
Total: = **$105,000**

But it will never look this way (even if this is your target). Initially, it will look like this:

eight clients at $100/hr x 50 weeks a year = $40,000
seven clients at $100/hr x 50 weeks a year = $35,000
five clients at $200/hr x 50 weeks a year   = $50,000
Total: = **$125,000**

That's because as you begin building your five clients at $200/hr, your likely to have already replaced former $50/hr clients with $100/hr clients along the way. This strategy is called **stair-stepping** and it takes discipline. Your Saboteurs will scream at you to not mess with what's working. They will be incredibly vocal as you move from your eighth client at $50/hr to your ninth at $100. And if you thought that was loud, wait until you double again at your 15th client.

Remember, the way of the Sage is "ease and flow." This should feel like a natural evolution of your coaching business. If you're already feeling your Saboteurs going crazy just reviewing this strategy, help is coming. I'm going to share with you Sage Money Mastery before we end this chapter and help you see precisely which Saboteurs are messing with you and how to handle them so you can become a financially free coach.

Wait, Bill! What If I'm Already Charging $200 or More Per Hour?

Believe it or not, the same strategy applies and I speak from experience here. The very first year of my coaching, I charged $175 starting off with my first three clients just to test the waters. I wasn't sure if I could charge my former marketing billing rate of $250. But after my first few clients, I trusted myself enough to begin charging $250/hr. That wasn't quite a "double", but at that time I was just attempting to replace my marketing agency bill rate. I then followed the same process, but instead went from $250/hr to $500/hr to $1,000/hr.

I will fully admit that when I increased my rate from $500/hr to $1,000/hr I was hijacked by my own Saboteurs. "Who in their right mind would pay $1,000 an hour?" my Saboteurs chastised me. "It's just not possible," they said. "Nobody does that!" they argued. "You're destroying your coaching business!" they said. And if I listened to them, I still would have had a fine coaching practice with $500/hr clients.

But then something magical (a miracle?) happened. The very first person I shared my offer with replied with something so totally unexpected, it could only have been a love note sent by God, Source, the Universe, or whatever your spiritual belief system may be. It went down just as I'll share with you in the upcoming chapter, *Converting Appointments: The Art of the Close.* After the same pre-framing questions that I will share with you, I simply said:

> *"I receive $2,000 a month for two 45-minute coaching sessions, and I coach my clients for a minimum of six months."*

And yes, no number of PQ Reps would quiet my Saboteurs when I said this. I was anticipating being laughed at or receiving some sort of, "Are you out of your fucking mind?" response. I was totally hijacked by my Saboteurs, but I had committed to myself that it was time. And like I said, what I receive back was more of a spiritual wink and nod of a love note than a response.

"Sure, but can I ask you a question?" my ideal customer prospected asked. ***Why so little?***"

It took everything to hold my composure. It wasn't even a "Hell, yes!" My new client was genuinely confused why I wasn't charging *more*. That lead to a conversation about value and how important it is that my clients do their work between their coaching sessions. Blah, blah, blah. But inside I was like, "Holy shit! This was the kindest response I could have possibly received for taking such a big risk for myself. Thank you! Someone out there is definitely looking out for me and this was the most powerful lesson I could have received."

And it was. From that moment forth, I've never looked back. I don't apologize for my rate and I don't justify it. I know that it's not for everyone and that I've priced myself out of reach for many, many people who would love to hire me as their coach. I'm good with that. I've made peace with it. I've helped Shirzad build the coaching program of Positive Intelligence's PQ Coach Membership program so that thousands of coaches can have access to our work. And I'm sitting here writing this book in service to all coaches – not just the ones who are willing to invest in a one-on-one relationship with me.

And what's more, I know that if there ever comes a time when I am no longer part of Positive Intelligence, I will likely need to double my rates again. And I'm good with that too. After all, even at $2,000 per hour, or $48,000/year, if a coach I work with doubles, triples or quadruples their coaching business, then I'm confident that they will have received the value for their investment in our relationship. Remember, it's never about the coaching. It's about the desired outcomes a person is willing to invest in.

With this, I trust your Sage is listening closely here and seeing an entirely new possibility for yourself as you think about what you choose to charge your clients. Knowing that it's possible to receive $1,000 or more per hour for coaching, what do you choose to set as your rate today? And what will it be three years from today?

What If I Don't Want to Coach Weekly?

Perfect. For me, I find two times a month is optimal. Notice I didn't say "every two weeks." I tend to coach my clients on the *first and third* or *second and fourth* of each month. That works out to 24 sessions per year instead of 26.

Weekly works for many coaches and clients and I'm not discouraging this frequency. I've experimented with once a month and that didn't feel frequent enough to really make the impact we were going for, so I don't recommend that. But this is *your* coaching business. You get to decide how frequently you want to coach and what would work best for your clients.

At a C-Suite executive level, most business owners and senior managers deeply desire to accomplish more while doing less. Even at the same rate, they would much prefer a twice a month schedule vs. weekly *as long as* they are accomplishing their desired outcomes – personally and professionally.

Exploring Your Money Mindset

It only happened once, but a single event shaped my feelings about money for decades. After my parents separated and were in the process of getting divorced, my mom hadn't been to the grocery store and my brother and I realized we were really low on food in the house. We were down to the canned items that no one wanted and we were both hungry. Something deep inside of me turned on. I experienced a sudden and fierce survival instinct that I had never felt before. There was a part of me that was fighting to live and suddenly nothing else mattered – only finding food to eat in a perceived food scarcity moment.

Before that moment, I didn't have a care in the world. I was a kid and my biggest concern was how much time I had to play between homework, dinner and bed time. After that moment, I awakened a feeling of scarcity that there may not be enough to survive. No longer did I trust my parents to take care of me. I decided that I had to "be the man of the house" at the ripe old age of 12. I looked around for a role model as I had dismissed that either one of my parents were very good with money. So who was good with money?

I found my answer a few weeks later when at a family dinner at an upscale restaurant, my uncle Ron did something that created a lasting impression on me. As I was counting the number of family relatives around the largest restaurant table I had ever been part of, I began to wonder, who and how would someone pay for all of this? Just as I was pondering this question, I saw the waiter walk over with the bill. Without the slightest hesitation, my uncle Ron waived the waiter over and placed his credit card on top of the bill. He never even looked at the bill.

That was it. This simple gesture was enough to convince me that I needed to be a hell of a lot more like my uncle Ron. I knew he owned an electronics store in Los Angles, so I interpreted being an entrepreneur as the answer I was looking for.

Immediately, I looked for jobs and found that there were lots of options for an enterprising kid. I delivered newspapers, started door-to-door selling, and then started a lawn-care business with one friend. When another friend asked me to do the same with him, I kicked off a second lawn-care business on alternating weekends. Before I knew it, I was juggling five jobs all driven by this feeling of scarcity and my own survival.

None of this was real, of course. But my mind made it all feel real. I had established my own money mindset and allowed my Saboteurs in to drive me. Let's review.

Judge: Your parents are in capable of fulfilling your needs and will allow you to go hungry. You can't trust them to take care of you. If you want to survive your childhood, you will need to take matters into your own hands.

Controller: The only person I can truly rely on is myself. At 12 years old, my Controller convinced me that to take care of myself, I need to make enough money to support my mom my brother & myself.

Hyper-Achiever: The way to make money is to run my own businesses (paperboy, lawn care, door-to-door sales, and odd jobs). The harder I worked, the more money I would make — but only if I was constantly challenging myself and going "all out, all the time."

Bottom Line: I believed the lies of my Judge, Controller and Hyper-Achiever and operated a life of scarcity rather than abundance for the next 35 Years!

What's your money mindset?

As I shared my childhood story with you, can you recall an event that, at the time, had a profound impact on how you felt about money? Positive or negative, chances are something happened along the way that had you begin your story about money that in all likelihood remains with you to this day.

I believe everyone has a money mindset. In T. Harv Eker's *Secrets of the Millionaire Mind*, he goes deep into this work. Ultimately, what you believe to be true about money is how you will live into those beliefs.

If you believe that "money is the root of all evil," for example, is it any wonder that you will self-sabotage yourself when you begin to acquire wealth? If you have a deep-seeded belief that money is evil, then when you begin to acquire it, you will begin to find ways to get rid of money so that you can align with your belief system. As you don't see yourself as evil, you don't want any part of the root of all evil, money. Is it any wonder why it's so difficult to hold onto it?

Overcoming Your Saboteur Approach to Money

Each of your Saboteurs can have very different, but equally damaging beliefs about money. In this section, let's review some of the most commonly held Saboteur mindsets about money. This can support you in becoming aware of which Saboteurs are driving you and your approach to money. Once you are aware of which Saboteurs thoughts about money are driving you, we can then shift to the five Sage Powers in order to begin to shift these negative feelings and aversion to the very thing that will make you financially free.

How Your Judge Fuels Conflict With Money

- Your Judge generates a whole lot of negative feelings and assumptions about your financial future.
- These assumptions are often false and usually come from a mentality of scarcity.
- A powerful Judge also causes you to listen selectively, looking only for evidence to prove your own money blueprint (usually based in scarcity) right.
- Rather than experiencing life's true abundance, your Judge has you feeling scarcity, shame and guilt – especially when it comes to receiving money.
- **Big lie of your Judge:** There will never be enough money for you or anyone else … ever! It's a zero-sum game. If you have more money, then I will have less.

What Your Controller Says & Feels About Money

- The Controller wants money to go with their plan.
- Will pay bills when it suits your Controller in an effort to create power.
- Money is used to intimidate others; as a means to control.
- Money matters can make you appear confrontational and makes others uncomfortable
- Can also make you shut down others and cause them to feel that you are inflexible and only committed to your own way … even if that's not your true intention
- **Big lie of your Controller**: having more money solves problems by generating more control over your life.

What Your Stickler Says & Feels About Money

- The Stickler's certainty about the right way to handle money is often not shared by others.
- When your Stickler manages money, you might come across as self-righteous, rigid, or a perfectionist.
- Has trouble following through with "vague" financial plans, sticking with budgets, and moving money from savings to cover "frivolous spending."

- Anxious about things not getting done the right way.
- **Big lie of your Stickler:** There is a clear right and a clear wrong way to manage money. If you can't do it correctly, why even bother trying?

What Your Avoider Says & Feels About Money

- The Avoider has trouble making financial decisions as well as:
  o Sticking with Budgets.
  o Making regular / recurring payments.
  o Having crucial financial conversations.
  o Making important financial decisions.
- Large financial decisions generate fear / anxiety.
- Lacking a plan when money is owed; scared to discuss it.
- **Big lie of your Avoider:** Money matters usually work themselves out if you ignore them. My finances are never as bad as they may seem, so best to focus elsewhere.

What Your Hyper-Achiever Says & Feels About Money

- The Hyper-Achiever has multiple plans for multiple money streams and works hard to achieve them.
- Work becomes the number one priority justified by financial goals.
- Often paid top dollar and usually experiences burnout.
- Can make you too goal-focused, causing you to miss the more important relationship-building opportunities.
- The other person might feel you are treating them only as a means of getting to your financial goals.
- **Big lie of your Hyper-Achiever:** If I wish to meet my financial goals, I can never slow down or enjoy any of the wealth I've already created (or it will all evaporate).

What Your Pleaser Says & Feels About Money

- Your Pleaser will indirectly try to gain favor by paying for lunches, dinners, drinks and entertainment.
- Rather than asking for what you want, your Pleaser will discount your services and offer them for free.
- This leads to barely scraping by (i.e. "Breaking Even") let alone building financial freedom for yourself.
- Known to work for far less and only complain in secret.

- **Big lie of your Pleaser:** If I ask for what I'm worth, no one will hire me. Better to give it all away for free and trust that it will (eventually) come back to me over time.

What Your Victim Says & Feels About Money

- Your Victim will find fault with yourself and everyone else when it comes to money matters.
- Money is hard and everyone and everything has made it this way for me.
- Saving, planning, and paying my bills on time often leads to financial failure which is why I don't want to be in charge.
- Your Victim Saboteur wants someone else to handle the money matters (i.e. "Do it for me!") so that you can focus solely on spending the money.
- "Poor Me! I'll never by financially free. The system is rigged and out to get me."
- **Big lie of your Victim:** I am unfairly underprivileged when it comes to money. I will never be wealthy because I was set up to fail from the start. I am uniquely deprived and disadvantaged.

What Your Restless Says & Feels About Money

- Similar to the Avoider, the Restless causes you to avoid dealing with any pain or drama of money matters.
- You might choose to shift your focus to more exciting and pleasant things ...
- ...and be hard to pin down on issues of money
- The Restless has fantastic charisma, vision, and loves to talk about money and work.
- Doesn't like the details: budgeting, savings, and wants to create multiple plans with little support or structure to follow through.
- "I've got 10 money-making ideas & let's talk about it."
- **Big lie of your Restless:** There are so many ways to make money, whenever I find a short-cut or faster route, I should take it. Why settle for one path when there are so many options out there.

What Your Hyper-Vigilant Says & Feels About Money

- Hyper-Vigilant is about risk avoidance to the extreme.
- Constantly concerned about losing money, bad investments, and being taken advantage of in all things financial.
- Driven to have savings, compelled to have a job while owning a business, must have excellent credit, makes credit card charges extremely carefully.

- Seeks to have a good reputation but not a great reputation, never get too far ahead of themselves.
- Doesn't like to talk about money unless it's with a trained & trusted professional.
- "I work hard for my money, I won't spend it on much, and always look for 10 backup plans."
- **Big lie of your Hyper-Vigilant:** Never take any risk when it comes to financial matters. You can never be too careful when it comes to money. There's always someone out there looking to take advantage of me.

What Your Hyper-Rationale Says & Feels About Money

- The Hyper-Rational wishes everyone could see money the way they do.
- Financial matters are strictly numbers and common sense.
- Hyper-Rational Saboteur figures out the best ways to make money and shuns alternative approaches.
- They like to talk about money but only with their financial peers and those who have "made it."
- "I don't know what's wrong with them. My money works for me."
- **Big lie of your Hyper-Rationale:** Making money is predictable and completely logical. There's simply no place for feelings and emotions when it comes to money. Those who bring emotions into money matters are doomed to fail.

Did you discover which Saboteur lies align most to your own money blueprint? Remember that most of us have more than one, so if you discovered several Saboteurs driving how you feel about money, know that you're not alone. Is it any wonder why you have previously struggled to build financial freedom for yourself and those you love?

The objective here is to not allow your Judge to have you feel shame and guilt about how you've had it. That's double-dipping. Please don't allow your Judge to get away with that nonsense! Afterall, your Judge was primarily responsible for gathering your Saboteur committee to convince you of the may lies about money that have been likely plaguing you for years. Now is the time to let them go and cultivate your Sage Money Mindset.

Sage Money Mindset

Congratulations! In the previous section, you discovered many of the Saboteur lies that have driven a scarcity mindset and framed how you feel about money. Now is the time we get to let those lies go and begin our journey towards total abundance and financial freedom all while cultivating your Sage Money Mindset.

What Does a Sage Money Mindset Look like?

- Financially successful in ease and flow
- Discerning, calculating and committed to taking action.
- Goal-oriented, engaged in healthy competition, and is confident.
- Learns to detach from stress, anxiety and negative emotions about money.
- Fully present and conscious when making money decisions.
- Generous, optimistic, and open to a significant increase in cash flow.
- Offers little to no resistance when it comes to receiving financial abundance.
- Creates a financial and business vision, holds it, and maintains this vision by living into it every day.

And best of all, you're using the same Five Sage Powers to live into your Sage Money Mindset. All you're doing is applying what you already know to generate financial abundance in your life. Remember, money doesn't change you, it magnifies more of who you already are. As you become financially free, you will be empowered to do more, give more and live the life you choose for yourself and those you love.

How Empathy Fuels Your Sage Money Mindset

Empathy is the power that unlocks your other Sage powers. When it comes to cultivating a Sage Money Mindset, it's best to begin with empathy in all three areas: (1) Empathy for Yourself, (2) Empathy for Your Clients, and (3) Empathy for Your Situations.

Empathy for Yourself

Start with empathy for yourself. This focus shifts you from a scarcity to an abundance mentality. True empathy for yourself opens up the realization that your feelings and thoughts about money were imprinted on you. That scarcity feeling and negative emotions when it comes to all things financial were defense mechanisms that no longer serve you. Rather than allowing your Saboteurs to beat you up and tear you down, cultivate empathy for yourself. See the perfectly imperfect human being you are and connect with your Sage power.

It's true that you are powerful beyond measure. Abundance is all around you when you choose to see it. Have empathy for yourself that your previous Saboteur views of money blinded you to this abundance. Now that you have awareness of the nature of your abundance, you can begin to let go of scarcity and live into this new abundant way of being. Realize that your brain was operating with this scarcity mentality to keep you safe and out of harm's way. Knowing that you're safe and that you no longer need this protection, be grateful for the self-care cocoon you no longer need when it comes to your finances. Empathy for yourself will allow you to shift your focus and be open to receiving financial abundance as you support your niche and grow your coaching practice.

Empathy for Your Clients:

Having empathy for your clients and your ideal client prospects allows you to see them for the perfectly imperfect human beings that they are. Your clients are *not* their circumstances. When you choose to see past their current circumstances, you enter into the field of all possibilities. Regardless of whether your ideal client prospects choose to join you there, it's important for you to remain empathetic toward your potential clients and the struggles of life that they are doing their best to manage and overcome.

It is not your job to decide what your prospective clients can afford. Having empathy for your clients means trusting their Sage to discern if hiring you as their coach at the rate you receive is the right investment for them. It's not your job to convince them or pressure them in any way. You are here in service to them. When the time is right, they will enroll themselves. Having empathy for your clients is about realizing they are on their own journey too. If now is not the right time, trust that your discovery session with them has added value to their life and when the time comes, they will seek you out. You've planted a seed of possibility. Having empathy for your clients means being testifying to their greatness – even the times when they may not see it for themselves. This is just as true for active paying clients as it is prospective clients. Maintaining compassion and empathy for those you engage with will make you a powerful coach and one whom many will happily refer to their networks.

Empathy for Situations:

Much in the same way, you are not your circumstances. Your past does not have the power to define who you are ... unless you choose to allow it to. Empathy for situations is about a deep understanding that whatever struggle you are currently facing is temporary. The Sage Perspective, that everything can be turned into a gift and opportunity, will help you go even further. That is, to see the current struggle as a beautiful gift of knowledge, power or inspiration on your own path to self-actualization.

For example, what's the gift of having a pricing fear? Let's say you're considering asking for an amount that feels like a stretch for you. What's the gift of the fear that shows up in that moment? It could be the knowledge that you're stepping out of your comfort zone. Or it could be you are sharpening one of your Sage Powers such as empathy for yourself, your ability to serve clients powerfully and sustainably. Or perhaps it inspires you to be the best version of yourself and that fear is challenging you to step into an even more powerful way of being.

Remember, the fear is not there to stop you. It's to keep you alert to possibilities. When you feel that fear and do it anyway, you're strengthening your resolve and doubling down on you, your power, and your commitments. That fear of establishing or raising your pricing stops so many others in your industry. By having empathy for this one situation, you can use it as a powerful lesson and fuel your personal and professional growth.

Having empathy for situations allows you to see how overcoming temporary situations such as your pricing fears, uncertainties and doubts are all part of your Sage Mastery journey. We can be grateful for our situations as they challenge us to be the best version of our self. These situations invite our Sage to show up, speak up and keep up with the demands of life itself. As we cultivate our Sage Money Mindset, we stop seeing our circumstances as "bad" or "wrong" and instead begin to invite in more and more challenging circumstances as we see them as helping us to "level up" in our journey towards self-actualization.

How Explore Fuels Your Sage Money Mindset

Can you already see how each of these Sage powers plays a significant role in cultivating your Sage Money Mindset? Once you have established empathy for yourself, your clients and your situations, you have entered a neutral space and the field of all possibilities. Before jumping into innovation, it's really helpful to tap into Sage Power Explore as a means to see things as they are, rather than the previous filters of interpretations that plague us from facing reality.

Here's how Explore fuels your Sage Money Mindset:

- You become fascinated by your own earning and spending habits. Rather than judge these habits, you remain curious about why you behave the way you do.
- You begin to envision yourself as a seven-figure coach at an identity level. This leads to a deep probing question, "What would a seven-figure coach do?" The answer allows you to consider new ways of being and actions you can take toward that desired outcome.
- You remain fully present as you overcome your resistance to receiving increasing sums of money for your incredible coaching services. With each step, you see the progress and acknowledge it rather than question and judge your progress.

Your curiosity about the way you have money, how you behave with money, and feelings of tension and resistance around money-related conversations all strengthen your growth in your Sage Money Mindset. Staying in Explore leads to new breakthroughs. No longer are you living on proverbial autopilot in reaction to financial circumstances. With Explore, you stop, look and choose your actions rather than being in reaction to financial challenges and opportunities.

How Innovate Fuels Your Sage Money Mindset

By now, you probably already see it, don't you? Notice the speed at which your brain is firing as you go deeper in this work. Sage Innovate is about seeing new possibilities you hadn't considered before. When you ask a better question, you get a better answer. Leaning into your own innovation allows you to play around with any aspect of your coaching business and create new possibilities for future growth.

For example, you could:

- Play the "Yes, and …" game when it comes to doubling your rates. "What I like about that idea is …"
- Reframe your mindset. "As a seven-figure coach, I would …"
- Consider what you would charge for your coaching package three years from today.
- Play around with what would need to shift or change in order to double your rate. Then keeping going and innovate around how you would double them again.
- Ask yourself, "How would I incorporate mental fitness into a full year (or six month) program offering?"
- Continue this approach to overcome any resistance you have to receiving a premium price for your services.

As you tap into your Sage Innovate power, notice the excitement you feel in your body. Your Sage knows that you were born for this and these innovations charge you up energetically. The more you tap into your own creativity and innovation, the more possibilities emerge. This is the abundance of life that inspires us to play a much, much bigger game. As we elevate our thinking and trust our imagination, magic begins to happen.

Previous fears melt away. What remains are new possibilities previously unseen. What once felt impossible now feels down right probable … even inevitable. And for some, this process can even be a bit overwhelming. It's like you were living in a dark cave and just emerged to the blinding light of the mid-day sun. While your Saboteurs will encourage you to retreat to the comfort of the darkness, your Sage knows that remaining and basking in this light will quickly migrate from temporary blindness to long-term illumination to that which has always been there. You're smack dab in the field of all possibilities. Enjoy the realization of all the abundance around you. This illumination is showing you many paths to success. That's why Sage Power Navigate is so helpful.

How Navigate Fuels Your Sage Money Mindset

Having spent some time with your Sage Innovate, you're clear that there are many possible options you could choose. How do you know which is the best path for this moment? Some options are better suited in the months or years ahead, while others can support what you're up to right now. When it comes to your financial freedom, this is an important consideration. And this is where Sage Navigate can really support you and fuel your Sage Money Mindset. Here are some powerful questions to consider as you ponder your way forward.

- At the end of your life looking back, what kind of outsized impact could you make as a seven-figure coach? (Notice that this question helps reveal what's possible for you as you reach your own financial freedom.)
- Consider how becoming financially free aligns to your mission, purpose and values as a coach. This is another way to connect to what you're up to as a coach and how having financial freedom support your ability to accomplish all that you're up to.
- What would living in total financial abundance enable for your Sage?
  - Who would you choose to support financially?
  - What non-profit organizations would you start, join or participate in?
  - What do you now see as possible in your life?

Clarity emerges when you deeply embrace the understanding that money doesn't change you, it magnifies who you already are. Having a clear outcome illuminates the best way forward. And while many paths will lead you to your desired outcomes, some paths look easier than they actually are. Choosing the Sage path is about seeing which one has more light on it and moves you closer to your ultimate outcomes. As you align here with your Sage Navigate power, you reveal the day-to-day decisions that support you on your life's journey.

How Activate Fuels Your Sage Money Mindset

And finally, with the clarity of your mission, purpose and vision connected to a path forward that will get you there, it's time to take laser-focused action. It's no use to know what actions to take if you choose not to take them.

Stephen R. Covey was the one who said, "To know and not to do is not to know." In spending some quality time reflecting on this quote, I found this to be the essence of Sage Activate. How many times in my life did I "know" what to do and not do it? Besides, how I had it in my mind may not have been accurate. Only through the actions I take do I discover if I truly know.

Why this resonates with me so deeply is that I was taught a similar concept in my martial arts training. "Surprising things will happen when you meet your opponent."[35] As a fifth-degree black belt in Soo Bahk Do, Moo Duk Kwan, I've spent 30 years in martial arts training. There have been very few times in my life when I've needed to call upon this practice. No matter how much you practice in a dojang, meeting an opponent in real life is vastly different. The same is true in your coaching business. You can invest significant time learning, preparing and planning, but until you get out there and speak with real prospects who can hire you, it's mostly theoretical. It's the actions you take that produce the feedback you need to be successful.

This is equally true with your Sage Money Mindset. The more you weaken those Saboteur lies, reinforce your Sage discernment and strengthen your Sage powers, the easier it will become to generate financial abundance for yourself. The more actions you take toward your desired outcome, the easier it will become to achieve it and become it. Your Sage Money Mindset is as much being in Sage as it is acting in a Sage way when it comes to all financial matters. Each Sage action reinforces your Sage Money Mindset and sets you on the path to financial freedom.

You are always at choice – even when your Saboteurs do their best to convince you otherwise. Each choice you make brings you closer to your financial goals, or further away from them. When this clarity of action is top of mind, you will take consistent actions that produce the desired results. When they don't, you'll receive invaluable feedback that supports you in doubling down on your commitments to financial freedom.

- Action is where all these shifts in thinking change your financial future.
- Knowing all of this, what changes are you committed to making?
- By when will you make these changes?
- Declare your commitments to your accountability partner(s) to ensure you live into this Sage approach to financial freedom

---

[35] Kee, Hwang, *Moo Do Chul Hahk: A New Translation by Hyun Chul Hwang.* ©2009. Self-Published. p178.

Frequently Asked Questions About Your Irresistible Offer:

As I've continued to work with thousands of coaches in developing their irresistible offer, I've short listed the most common questions I receive in our live Q&A sessions. This can help you continue to refine and adjust your irresistible offer for maximum effectiveness.

1. **How important is it to offer a money back guarantee?** This depends on who your niche is, what stage of business you're in and how irresistible your offer can be on its own without a money back guarantee. As we mentioned in this chapter, for some niches, having a money back guarantee can actually backfire so it's not for everyone. If you find you can create an irresistible offer without a money back guarantee, then go for it. If you're a coach just starting out, you can likely afford to take more risk early on as you look to build and scale your coaching practice. After you've established yourself with passionate testimonials and a core of at least five clients, you may not want or need to include a money back guarantee in any case. So while a money back guarantee can help make your offer irresistible, it's by no means required. Use your best judgment here and give yourself permission to experiment.

2. **Is it okay to have different irresistible offers depending on who I'm talking to?** Yes, as long as you're not juggling so many irresistible offers that you can't keep them straight. For large enterprise clients, for example, it's a best practice to have two irresistible offers: one for the client you want to work with and one for the sponsor who pays for the work. In a business-to-business context, it's rare for your client to also be the sponsor (i.e. the person who pays for your coaching), so it's extremely helpful to have two separate irresistible offers. It's also important to have different irresistible offers depending on what stage you are in the process. You will need one irresistible offer that gets prospects onto your calendar and one that converts them from being a prospect to being a paying client. You might also consider any adjustments you might make to your irresistible offer when it's shared on your website, social media, email and from the stage. It's okay to make adjustments, as long as the essence of your irresistible offer is something you can easily remember and use whenever you need it.

3. **What do I do if I'm not clear on the desired outcomes of my niche?** For the first iteration of your irresistible offer, make your best guess to start. While you may not know precisely what your niche wants as their most important desired outcome, you likely have a good feel for what the possibilities are. You're Stickler Saboteur would have you wait and take no action until your

irresistible offer is perfect including properly researched, vetted by your peers as well as your ideal customer prospects and proven. Whereas your Sage will have you begin the ongoing process of learning by testing out your best assumptions and continually refining your irresistible offer until you believe you have crafted one that is effective for the current needs of your coaching business.

4. **What if I have multiple niches?** If you really can't land on a single niche (which is recommended for maximum scale), then you owe it to yourself to at least prioritize which is your top, number one niche, which one is secondary and which is tertiary. And if you have more than three, you don't have a niche and I recommend that you go back and repeat the niche exercises in the previous chapter. While you are free to work with anyone, when it comes to building and scaling your coaching business, less is more. Having a single niche is optimal as it simplifies your marketing and sales efforts. In some cases, it's wise to have two as both niches complement each other. As long as you're not coming from a Saboteur scarcity mentality, and instead have a strong business case for why you have more than one niche, then prioritize them. And stay in the question if having more than one niche is Sage discernment or being driven by one of your Saboteurs (especially Hyper-Achiever, Controller, Pleaser and Hyper-Vigilant).

5. **What do I do if I have multiple offers I want to promote?** Choose your primary offer that you want to use to build and scale your coaching business. Are you currently focusing on building your one-on-one coaching, group coaching, masterminds or mental fitness practice? While you're free to have all of these and more, it's important to recognize that having too many choices will inhibit your growth. Simplicity is your friend. The best practice here is to focus on one offer and have the others as a back-up when you learn in a one-on-one discovery call that the needs of your ideal customer prospect are different than what's included in your primary offering. Forcing your ideal customer prospects to choose between multiple offers tends to have the unintended negative impact of making them choose not to work with you at all. And making choice between two options is certainly better than having them make a choice between three or more options. The best option, however, is that you're clear on your best and primary offering and the real choice for your ideal customer prospect is whether to hire you or not.

6. **How is your irresistible offer statement different than your niche statement?** When crafting a niche statement, it can sometimes feel like it's naturally evolving into your irresistible offer statement. While there can definitely

be some similarities, the core difference is that your niche is a description of *who* you help and *what* problem(s) you solve, and your irresistible offer statement is an actual *offer* that includes the ability to accept or reject. So while your irresistible offer could include elements of what you worked on in your niche statement, it should be able to be made in the context of your ideal customer prospect considering whether to hire you or not. Upon hearing your irresistible offer, your prospect should be able to decide for themselves if they want to engage you and say "Hell Yes!" or "No Thank You." We'll get into more detail on this in the upcoming chapter, *Converting Appointments: The Art of the Close*).

7. **What if I'm not confident in my pricing? How do I know what to charge?**
Determining what to charge is an important part of building your coaching business and tends to be more of a reflection of your own mindset than a specific pricing strategy. From a Saboteur scarcity space, you'll hear all the arguments in your own mind about how little you can charge or what your ideal customers are willing to pay. From a Sage abundance space, you will find that the pricing need only be less than the monetary value of the problem your ideal customers are committed to solving. The higher value the problem is that they wish to solve, the more you can receive for your coaching and mental fitness programs. So while there's no "correct" answer to what to charge, it's more important to look inside yourself than it is to pay close attention to what others are charging. We'll revisit the overall concept of Sage Money Mindset in the upcoming chapter, *Converting Appointments: The Art of the Close*.

8. **I think my irresistible offer statement is too wordy. How do I shorten it?**
Wherever you can shorten your irresistible offer statement, you are likely to increase effectiveness. Remember the concept of a prime number equivalent? To the extent that you can remove parts of your irresistible offer and still have it land powerfully, then go for it. The biggest mistake that most coaches make is explaining *how* they do what they are offering. Please don't fall into that trap. The more you focus on how you help your niche overcome their problem and reach their desired outcome, you less your ideal customer prospect can retain and respond with a "Hell Yes!" While all the details you are sharing may be important, these details are not important at the very moment of decision making. Less is more when it comes to your irresistible offer. Wherever you can simply your irresistible offer, do it. If there's a one-word option that would replace three or more words, then make that substitution. You want to get your irresistible offer down to one or two short sentences. If you need

to read or memorize your irresistible offer, then chances are it's too long and needs further refinement. That's part of the process and remember that all of this effort now will shorten the timeline to building and growing the coaching business of your dreams (so it's well worth the upfront effort).

9. **Every time I go to say my irresistible offer, my mind goes blank. What's going on?** Hello Saboteurs, what took you so long? Remember that the domain of building and growing any business will activate your Saboteurs and challenge you to grow your Sage powers. Having your mind go blank in precisely the worst moment possible, is your Saboteurs way of "protecting" you. Let me explain. Your Saboteurs were designed to alert you as a means of keeping you safe. Think "hand on the hot stove". That's helpful for a few seconds as an alert signal that you can immediately switch to Sage to determine what action to take. When your mind goes blank, it's your amygdala surfacing your freeze response (as in "fight, flight or freeze"). When you focus on the freeze itself, you perpetuate that blank space rather than move past it. So if you're finding this is happening to you, then do your PQ Reps in anticipation of delivering your irresistible offer and during the process of delivery. Stay with the blank mind and trust that your Sage will move you past it. Having a blank mind is just another form of a Saboteur hijack. It's no different than your Judge screaming at you as a means to stop you from making your irresistible offer. Why? Because not offering your services is what your Saboteurs consider "safe." It's not, but they don't know any better. So instead of getting upset and extending the Saboteur hijack, lean into it when it happens, and do your PQ Reps even as you hold the space with your prospect. If it helps, speak into what you're experiencing as a means to let it go. While you don't want to get into a practice of doing this, it's perfectly fine to share what's happening as a means to model the process of just as quickly getting out of it. Now that you know what's going on, you can take steps to reduce or eliminate this from happening in the future.

10. **How do I know if my irresistible offer is specific enough?** If you were an independent auditor, how would you know if your prospect's desired outcome was achieved? This is especially important if you choose to offer a money back guarantee. Would an independent third party (think mediator or analyst) be able to look at what was promised and confirm completion in the time specified? If you are using vague words like, "happiness," "better," "more," "less," "reduce," and similar notions that are difficult to measure, then they lack specificity and should be refined to something concrete. To become better at something is not to master or accomplish it. Having more

of something is anchoring the result to something vague. How much more? By whose standards is this more? You want to be as specific as you can be and ideally be in a position to independently verify the outcome. If you sense your irresistible offer isn't specific enough, then chances are you're right and your irresistible offer could use some additional refinements.

And you may have a different question than these. Or answering one question may lead to another question. That's why it's so important to work with your pod. Having accountability partners in your journey towards building and scaling your coaching business is critical. In the last section of this book, we'll go into these best practices so that you have the systems of support that will ensure you continue your journey both in Sage Mastery and building and scaling your coaching business.

Irresistible Offer For Getting Appointments On Your Calendar

At the beginning of this chapter, I shared that there are actually two irresistible offers we need to focus on: (1) The irresistible offer to convert prospects into clients and (2) Your initial irresistible offer to get prospects on your calendar. It's important to have both in your coaching business in order to scale efficiently and effectively. While most of this chapter was about crafting an irresistible offer that has your ideal customer prospects wanting to buy from you, it's time to turn our attention to the irresistible offer that will generate more appointments on your calendar.

Win, Free & New

When I was studying marketing way back when, I learned that the three most powerful words you can use in a direct response campaign to generate response are: (1) Win, (2) Free, and (3) New. While we won't spend much time on *winning* (as that comes with its own set of promotions and gambling laws), we can do a lot with the other two words, *free* and *new*.

Think about the last time you received something for free. It might have been anything from free samples at the grocery store to a free eBook or worksheets. In a world driven all too often by Saboteur scarcity, Sage abundance thinking pays off handsomely. You just have to ensure that whatever free thing you're giving out has value to the recipient.

That's why a *Free Discovery Call* is a gold standard offer in the coaching industry – especially after a podcast, keynote, article or a myriad of other possibilities we'll cover in the next chapter on *Generating Appointments*. That's because when your ideal customer prospects get to know you, they have a desire to get to know you directly in a one-on-one.

What's important, however, is not to name this a Free "Discovery Call", but rather something that directly aligns to the needs of your niche. A prospect looking for a health coach doesn't want a free discovery call from a (generalist) life coach. You'd much rather receive a free health assessment or a free lifestyle optimization call. By taking some time to rename your discovery calls to a specific deliverable, the more attractive your offer will become.

Using some of our prior examples, a C-Suite executive might be interested in a Legacy Blueprint Session or a Retire Right Strategy appointment. Someone struggling to generate wealth in their life would very much be attracted to a Financial Freedom Plan. A newly divorced mother might be interested in a Free Divorced & Effective Dating Strategy. You get the point. While you can still run all of these as typical Discovery Sessions, coming up with a name that aligns to the needs of your ideal customer prospects will generate more appointments on your calendar.

The word *new* is just as powerful in attracting your ideal customer prospects, but it may be best to use the word *new* to describe one or more of your alternatives to discovery calls which we'll address below. If you wanted to include new to describe your discovery call, it might be something like "Build Your New Legacy" or "Build A New Dating Plan" or "New Money Plan for Free." Play around with what your niche is most interested in and see how you can weave the words *free* and/or *new* into the mix. Sometimes the changes are that simple to make a standard discovery call appear irresistible and drive your ideal customer prospects to jump at the chance to get onto your calendar.

Not Everyone Wants A Discovery Call

It's equally important to recognize that not everyone wants to spend an hour or so on a discovery call with you – despite how much value they will get out of the exchange. Busy C-Suite executives, for example, would love to receive value long before the two of you speak. If you can come up with alternatives to discovery calls that your ideal customer prospects are excited to receive, then they will be more likely to give you time on a discovery call. It's possible your ideal customer prospects have their own Saboteurs urging them to use caution and be careful by looking for "the catch." Before you jump on a discovery call, consider what alternatives you could gift your ideal customer prospects to support them in the journey they are most interested in pursuing ... possibly with you as their coach.

A mistake coaches make is assuming the "one size fits all" approach. Discovery calls are great for some and not so irresistible for others. To make your irresistible offer of getting on your calendar, well, "irresistible," then you need to revisit your niche worksheets and determine what information products you could create and turn into lead magnets. It's easier than it sounds and incredibly effective. Let's explore this concept of lead magnets further together.

Lead Magnets

A lead magnet is what attracts your prospective clients to connect with you. Think of it this way, before I want to invest time and money with you, I first need to explore whether you know what my problems are and are likely to be able to help me overcome these problems. If I've heard you speak at a conference or liked what you shared via a podcast, I have a nagging suspicion that you could help me overcome a pain point that's been bothering me. But before I decide to get on your calendar, I'm more inclined to download something from your website or receive something from you via email.

Lead magnets are important because:

- 96% of your website visitors aren't ready to buy yet
- 63% of consumers need to hear your claims three to five times before they believe them[36]

At its most basic level, a lead magnet is a "value for value" exchange. You know that having my contact information and the ability to follow up with me is valuable to you. I believe that whatever you have created and talked about could very well be valuable to me. Therefore, I agree to give you my contact information in exchange for the valuable thing you're giving me.

Digital information products, for example, are relatively inexpensive to create and can be delivered just as soon as they are requested. A digital information product is just a fancy way of saying you've accumulated a bunch of insights and packaged them up. What you name your digital information product is just as important as what's inside. Similar to a really great article, it's the headline that grabs someone's attention, so it is important to come up with a name that you know will be interesting to your ideal customer prospects.

Joanna Lott, an early pioneer of our PQ Coach membership who joined as part of Cohort Two, shared a number of example titles for lead magnets she used to generate clients. Take a look at these titles and be thinking about what your ideal customer prospects would need from you:

- Six Steps to Finding a Job You Love... Get Unstuck in Less Than 10 minutes.
- How to Build Confidence to Land Your Dream Date: Three Things You Can Do Immediately.
- Free Resume Cover Letter Template (That Will Land You in the *Yes* Pile).
- DON'T DO THIS: Five Mistakes Women in Their 40s Make That Ruin Their Diet.
- Five Ways To Find Happiness: Powerful Ways You Can Transform Your Life.

---

[36] https://autogrow.co/sales-funnel-follow-up-statistics/

Each of these lead magnets allow your prospects to go deeper with you vicariously by better understanding how to tackle the problem with which they are currently struggling. These lead magnets also give you a powerful referral source because even if they don't take the action to get on your calendar, they are likely to share what they've learned with others who are struggling with a similar problem.

These lead magnets are usually in post document format (or PDFs), so they also reduce the need for shipping and fulfillment. This is why digital assets are a popular lead magnets. You spend some quality time up front thinking about the short version of how to help your prospects solve a particular problem, then you can utilize what you've created to attract your prospects to reach out to you and connect.

Successful lead magnets will quickly solve a pain point of your ideal customer prospects. They also build goodwill, credibility and begin building a relationship with someone you have not yet met. Think of them as the first step toward enrolling your clients into your coaching program(s). You're not likely to get an immediate sale with a lead magnet, but you are certainly increasing your odds to getting prospects onto your calendar.

Include Your Single Call to Action In Your Lead Magnets

Lastly, it may seem obvious, but you don't want the relationship to end with the lead magnet itself. Afterall, the point wasn't to solve the problem with an information product. The endgame is to enroll clients into your coaching practice. To that end, it's important to be direct about the next step after completing the consumption of the information product. This is your call to action embedded in your lead magnets and it might look something like this:

Want to personalize all of this information? I recognize that your needs are unique and that we have the opportunity to go deeper. If you'd like that, then reach out via [your email address] or grab some time on my calendar using this link: [insert your calendar link here].

I trust that this information has been valuable to you. Now that you have a better sense of what I'm all about, I invite you to go deeper here with my [insert new name of your discovery call]. You can sign up for that via [insert your website or calendar link here].

Now that you've learned about [insert your lead magnet title here], I invite you to grab time on my calendar so that we can go deeper: [insert your calendar link here].

What's important in this step is to ensure that you're only focusing on *one* call to action. Giving more than one next step will likely result in your prospect not taking any next step at all. That's why you want to think about what's most important to you in order to enroll this client. Perhaps you want them to attend an upcoming webinar or invite them to hear what other clients have said about you (via testimonials). For most coaches, however, the call to action will be to get on your calendar to go deeper with the issue you've identified and branded with the lead magnet you just gave them.

How Your Irresistible Offer Leads You To Generate Appointments

With your niche well defined and your irresistible offers mapped out, it's time to begin generating appointments on your calendar. That's what we're going to cover in the next chapter. For now, I'd like you to see how all of these four foundations of any coaching business are fitting together. Your niche helped you identify your ideal customer prospect and the biggest pain points they have. Then, in this chapter, we worked on how to create an irresistible offer to both have them get on your calendar and then sign up for your coaching program.

In the next chapter, we'll continue to build from here. Using your irresistible offer, we're going to lean into the best ways for you to generate appointments. The best part is that your path will be unique to what you already love doing. No need to follow the path of other coaches when you have a number of unique skills that will help you build and scale your coaching practice. This is going to be about doing what you already love doing and doing it with the intention of generating appointments.

Once you have an appointment on your calendar, you can assess if this prospect is, in fact, part of your niche. If so, you're prepared to deliver your irresistible offer and enroll them into your coaching practice. All the while, you're remaining in Sage and not allow your Saboteurs to stop you from successful alignment with your deep sense of mission and purpose. As you do all of this in ease and flow, you Sage will ensure that you achieve your desired outcomes. That's what Sage Business Development is all about.

CHAPTER SEVEN

Generating Appointments

Now that you have a clear picture of your niche, ideal customer and your irresistible offer, it's time to shake the proverbial trees and begin generating appointments for your coaching business. The following chapter will dive into how best to convert those appointments once they are on your calendar. So, for now, let's focus on your unique way of generating appointments.

Beware the "Done For You" Trap

Before I launch into your unique way of generating appointments, I want to serve up a word of caution. Part of you would just rather coach and have someone else deal with the sales stuff. I mean, wouldn't it be wonderful if all you ever had to do was coach?

Be leery of anyone who approaches you with this compelling offer. There are a ton of "done for you" services ranging from joining a network of coaches to marketing experts who swear they can help you generate more leads than you can handle. The problem with these services is that you are skipping over the part where you learn how to grow and scale your own coaching business to any size you choose. Shortcuts look great until you realize the price you pay either in upfront dollars and/or in long term opportunity costs.

Let me break this down just a bit further so you are forewarned if you find yourself tempted to go down this path.

Let's say you meet up with someone who is a lead generation expert. Wonderful! They know how to make Google, Facebook, LinkedIn and several other platforms work for you. They've worked for many small businesses like yours and they are confident that they can help you scale. This is good news, so what's the catch? In order to deploy these proven lead generation strategies, they need to know your target audience (i.e. your "ideal customer") – so far so good. They also need to know your call to action (i.e. your "irresistible offer"), we're still on solid ground. And then they want to know your lead magnet and any content you have to attract your ideal customers. What's that, you say? You haven't developed your lead magnet and content strategy yet? No problem, we'll use something off the shelf. No big deal, right?

It's actually a very big deal. What your lead generation expert is asking you for you haven't created yet: the thing that's uniquely you. It turns out that until you have paved a track record for yourself where you know what content your ideal customers respond to, in what medium and at what frequency, you're going to burn a lot of advertising dollars while you attempt to figure out what your lead generation expert wants. It's not that you can't hire a lead generation expert – you're just too early in the process when you haven't already created a foundational proven track record that they can leverage to help you grow and scale your business.

Okay, but what about a network of coaches. If my niche is more or less the same as theirs, what's the harm in teaming up with a company who bands together a ton of coaches and sells your services (along with many others)? Usually, it comes down to price. When you sign-up, everything sounds great. They will do the stuff you don't want to do including the branding, marketing, lead generation, lead qualification, and even setting the appointment. All you have to do is show up and coach. Dream come true, right?

Well, if you're a brand-new coach, this isn't a terrible way to get started, but the hourly rate they offer you is a small fraction of what you can get on your own. What's more, because of the low rate they pay you, it's a high profit margin for the company who represents you. Their goal is to fill your calendar. That's great news at first, but then you being to realize that when you amortize out what they are paying you, you're right in the ballpark of the ICF coaching salary survey we discussed at the beginning of the book. You end up getting by, but by no means are you creating the financial freedom you desire in your coaching practice. So what should you do instead? Simply put, do what you love.

Do What You Love

As mentioned earlier, one of my favorite quotes from Shirzad Chamine is that "The way of the Sage is ease and flow." Notice that he did *not* add, "...except when it comes to business development." To build the kinds of coaching practice you desire, generating appointments needs to be an extension of what you already love to do. Otherwise, if you experience difficulty here, your Saboteurs will show up and block you from the growth you know you're capable of.

Your Judge will convince you that you're not cut out to handle how hard business development is supposed to be and then judge you for not already having a financially lucrative coaching business. Your Avoider will find all the reasons not to spend time generating appointments. Your Restless will suddenly find all these other interesting things that seem to need your attention. And we could keep going down the list.

So before we set out to generate appointments, it's important that we spend some quality time with your five Sage powers to ensure what you set out to do will actually lead you to the outcome you desire. Here we want to use Sage Power Explore to observe that which you already love to do … naturally and with relatively little effort.

For example, if you had one hour to invest in building your coaching business today, which would you naturally gravitate to? Please notice which options jump off the page and immediately resonate with you (and which immediately activate your Saboteurs):

- Give a keynote speech in front of 200 or more of your ideal customers
- Be interviewed on a podcast that your ideal customers listen to regularly
- Write a guest column for a publication frequently read by your niche
- Record a video that captures the essence of the kind of coaching you offer
- Network at a local event and introduce yourself to at least five to 20 prospects
- Look up your ideal customer on their social media platform and direct message them
- Comment on a post that your ideal customer recently shared
- Craft a compelling email and send it out to a list of prospective clients
- Build a landing page for interested prospects wanting to learn about your offer
- Take pictures that capture the essence of the problems your ideal customers face
- Offer a free workshop on a topic you know your ideal customers would love
- Send a handwritten card to someone you know could benefit from your coaching
- Other: _____

And we're just scratching the surface here. And yet, that's enough variety to allow you to think about which of those options excite you and which ones you'd put off in order to finish your taxes or watch paint dry.

I'm asking this upfront because your path is unique to you. As long as your ideal customers can benefit from any of the options mentioned, you already have a head start in thinking about the best ways to connect with you niche.

Generating Leads In Ease & Flow

Perhaps you're already seeing your Sage path to generating leads in ease and flow. What we absolutely do not want is to take on activities that our Saboteurs tell us we *should* be doing when we know with certainty that we don't enjoy doing them. That's the sure-fire way to start and stop. If you've ever been on a roundtrip and so engrossed in a conversation or an audiobook that you ran out of gas, you know what I'm talking about. Before your car comes to a complete stop there is a rather aggressive lunge followed by what feels like a braking of the car while your foot is still on the accelerator.

That's the best visualization I can come up with when you choose to generate appointments the way others are doing it when your Sage knows your heart isn't into that particular activity. Just because one of your colleagues is having great success with public speaking doesn't mean you should try it if you don't enjoy speaking to audiences. Nor should you jump on the latest social media craze because others are successful doing it. These are all Saboteur fears of missing out and they aren't helpful in your *Sage Business Development* journey.

So what actions might you choose as alternatives to what everyone else seems to be doing?

Rather than looking "out there," trust your Sage wisdom and look "in here." Whenever you have an important strategic decision to make, the best practice is to do a long PQ Gym session (20-30 minutes or more) and ask your Sage the important questions you're contemplating.

Your Sage Power Explore will guide you here. Deep down, you already know what you love to do. Rather than allowing your Saboteurs to convince you that what you do naturally and effortlessly is "not enough," see the beauty of who you already are and the gifts you naturally have (and, for that matter, have *always* had). If you see yourself as an extrovert and love to talk, then double down and use your voice. If you prefer to sit down and write, then make time for yourself to allow your Sage to share your wisdom through the written word. If you know you're truly a social creature who loves meeting new people, then arrange your schedule so that you are getting out there regularly.

The historic saying that "all roads lead to Rome," applies here in your appointment generation. Simply put, there's no "wrong" way to generate appointments. The point is to develop a habit of regularly generating appointments. Inaction is the only thing that will prevent you from building and scaling your coaching business. Doing *nothing* produces the zero-result guarantee. That is, you're guaranteed to produce exactly zero appointments when you choose not to take action on any appointment generation strategy.

In the pages that follow, we're going to focus on a number of ways to generate appointments and they are categorized by the big arcs of what's possible (and by no means comprehensive). If you don't see what your Sage is naturally gravitating you towards in the pages below, I urge you to following your own path here. Just be sure to track your progress along the way. In the last part of this chapter, we dive into just how important tracking and measuring is to ensure you are making the progress you want to see in order to have the coaching business you desire. If you've decided to take a different path, be sure to design your own tracking and measurements so that you can ensure your unique path is delivering results.

Use Your Voice to Generate Appointments

When I think about using my voice to generate appointments, I imagine singing a siren song from the ancient Greek myth of sea nymphs – seductive and alluring without being deceptive or dangerous. That's because when you are crystal clear on the needs of your ideal customers, what you have to share is powerful to the point of being intoxicating. Seriously. When you let go of any and all fears about looking good, saying things the right way, and whatever other nonsense and lies your Saboteurs are spinning, what's left is your Sage brilliance. Nothing is more illuminating than the truth that you are unafraid to share with the world.

And yes, there are many critics out there who will feel the urge to challenge you, trip you up and make you feel small. When you can see that these are just another person's Saboteur fears manifesting as a result of your Sage brilliance, you won't even react to them. In Brené Brown's Netflix special, she made a point to share that just because someone tosses something your way, you are in no way required to catch it. In fact, her point was that people sitting comfortably in the stands are not showing up vulnerably in the arena. Therefore, we shouldn't care about their feedback. Have the courage to be in the same arena in which I'm in and *then* we can talk.

That's why that siren song, for me, is such a powerful metaphor. I know when I use my voice, I'm not attempting to reach everyone – just the people I'm committed to supporting in the world (i.e. you, my niche). I know that when I light your fire, you are empowered to let go of your fears, uncertainties and doubts and create something magical that makes the world so much better than when your Saboteurs convinced you to play small. As you light up, so will those around you. They will feel your fire and be attracted to your light. That's what using your voice is about. And it's ridiculously enticing. Your ideal customers are drawn to your words and see a different future for themselves. In seeing a new possibility, they can't wait to get on your calendar and spend some quality 1:1 time with you. That's what generating appointments in ease and flow is all about.

Even as I write these words, I am keenly aware that while they may be coming through me, they are not the egoic version of "me." I'm tapping into my Sage wisdom which has a deep connection to the interconnected web of life. All I've done is set aside the time to allow my words to flow through me. That's the beauty of using your voice to generate appointments. You are, in essence, declaring to the world your intention to be a positive influence with the niche you have decided to support. What happens next is an alignment that is so much bigger than you and your egoic self. Often when I look back and read the words I wrote, I wonder where they came from.

I have the experience of knowing my fingers were moving on the keyboard, and yet I know there's a deeper Sage wisdom that flows through me. All I'm actually doing is providing the space and time to allow this flow to continue.

My brother, Brian Carmody, a professional Jazz drummer, once told me, "When I'm really present and connected to my fellow musicians, my drums play me." As I write these words, I know precisely what he's referring to. That's my inner Sage coming out to play with me. It's such an incredibly powerful experience and one that I know is serving the greater good. So let's channel your brilliance in a way that generates appointments in total ease and flow for you.

Develop Your Key Message Architecture

As my grandfather, Reginald McLean used to tell me when we were building some wooden project, "Measure twice and cut once." Developing your key message architecture is about precisely that. While you may have some incredible stories to tell, it's important to take the time to outline what it is you want to share. Time spent outlining is the equivalent of measuring twice before sharing your words (i.e. cutting once).

To do this effectively, imagine that you were writing an article for a national publication. What headline would you use to capture the essence of your key message? Then what are the three salient points you want to make sure your audience hears clearly and concisely from you? For example, if you were highlighting mental fitness with your audience, it might look something like this:

Key Message: Mental fitness is your capacity to respond to life's challenges with a positive, rather than a negative mindset.

Mental fitness impacts your:

1. Peak performance
2. Peace of Mind / Wellness
3. Healthy Relationships

Now, from this key message architecture, I can build a one-hour keynote presentation, a 15-minute TED talk, a 30-minute podcast, or join an AMA ("Ask Me Anything") Clubhouse event. While I can adjust and tailor the specific language I use to maximize the impact on any given audience, I'm constantly considering the needs of my ideal customers and designing my irresistible offer as part of this effort. No good giving a talk if I haven't made a specific call to action that results in that audience eager to reach out to me in some capacity to follow-up.

By developing your key message architecture in advance, you give yourself the freedom to make modifications and changes to fit the needs of any medium while still holding to the integrity of what it is you choose to share. Let's see how you can take your key message architecture into different mediums that help amplify your voice in ways that will generate appointments on your calendar in ease and flow.

Audience-Centered Storytelling

Before joining Positive Intelligence as its Chief Coaching Officer, I spent several years perfecting a training called *Masterful Storytelling & Persuasive Presentations*. I helped several media and marketing agencies train their account teams so that they could become more effective in their sales presentations by becoming audience-centered storytellers.

What I discovered from my own research and training[37] in this field is that there are only five story archetypes. I know, that felt mind-blowing to me when I first heard it, but it's true. Every book you've ever read, every movie you've ever watched and every story you've ever heard can be categorized into one (or more) of the following five archetypes:

1. Love
2. Revenge
3. Stranger In A Strange Land
4. Rags to Riches
5. Holy Grail

To deliver truly audience-centered storytelling, you must first understand the needs of your audience. To do that, ask yourself, "What is it that my audience need to hear?" If you were speaking at a start-up business event, then the audience is pre-disposed to listening for the *Rags to Riches* archetype. Whereas a technology innovation event is more in tune with the *Stranger In A Strange Land* archetype. Or, if you're going into a company that just had their intellectual property appropriated by a competitor, they will gravitate to the *Revenge* archetype. And so on.

For more on this topic, please check out on my TEDx talk, *The Power of Audience-Centered Storytelling*.[38] This is a really fascinating topic and a wonderful way for you to wrap your key message and story into an archetype that is sure to land with your audience, provided that you've done your homework and understand their needs.

---

[37] For more on this topic, see http://micdropcourse.com/ and Morgan, Nick. *Working the Room: How to Move People to Action through Audience-Centered Speaking*. HBS Publishing. ©2003.
[38] https://www.ted.com/talks/bill_carmody_the_power_of_audience_centered_storytelling

Public Speaking

There is nothing quite like standing in front of a crowd of people and sharing the very thing that moves them. When you choose to stand and deliver, you are given an opportunity to make a deep and lasting impact in the lives of your audience members. I believe that the only reason to give a speech is to change the world. When given the chance to do so, I encourage you to really tap into your Sage so that you present the best version of yourself. When you show up fully in Sage, you encourage your audience to step into their Sage. What happens is a powerful Sage contagion effect where your words touch the hearts of your audience and they, in turn, call upon their inner Sage wisdom to decide how best to shift their lives into the direction they believe is best for themselves.

With this intention, you can see how the right public speech can be a powerful platform for generating leads for your coaching business. It's not a place to show up as a Saboteur-driven, hard-closing sales person. If you've ever been to a presentation that is all about the hard sales tactics, you know it's such a turn off. You're looking for how quickly you can exit without having to directly confront the speaker or the ushers. It's a far better way to generate massive value for your audience by remaining in Sage throughout.

At the heart of it, your speech is about addressing a known problem or issue that the majority of your audience is experiencing. As such, what you want to do is address that problem head on, show your audience the what, how and why of that problem and, where possible, offer a potential solution that would support them. You realize, of course, that whatever brilliant insights you share won't actually solve their problem. At best, it helps them see what's in their blind spot and gives them an opportunity to realize something that they hadn't previously considered. That's why offering to go to the next logical step is so powerful.

Once your audience realizes you have what they have been looking for, they will be motivated to take a small action (as long as it is, in fact, small). In order to effectively generate leads, you don't want to display your entire offer, but rather create an invitation to continue together. That could materialize in several ways such as:

- Display the link to your calendar platform[39] in order for them to grab time with you
- Create a QR code that they can scan with their phone to book time with you
- Offer a lead magnet that captures the best practices and have them text your mobile number with their name and email address to receive it directly from you

---

[39] This can be Calendly, Schedule Once, Acuity, or several other calendar software programs. Most have a free version to get you started.

- Create a supplemental workbook or eBook to go along with your talk and offer this as a means to continue their learning journey (using any of the techniques above)
- Give them the first two chapters of your book, or, if you've self-published, the entire PDF of your book so that they can reinforce what they have learned today
- Have them sign-up for your newsletter to go deeper with this topic

And again, these are just to get your creative juices flowing. What you want to do is offer something of value in exchange for their permission to connect with you. Doing this will maximize the outreach from participants who enjoyed your speech. Then you can track and measure what percentage of the audience took advantage of your offer from the stage. Generally, somewhere between 10–25% will take you up on your offer depending on how compelling it is and how related it is to the content of your speech.

Lastly, don't forget about the conference organizer. The person (or team) who put this event together is interested in adding more value for their attendees. As they have the email address of every registered attendee, see if what you have created would be of value to share with everyone as a follow-up. This makes your conference organizer look good and allows a second chance for audience members to reach out to you and continue to engage with you.

TED Talks

If you have the opportunity to give a TED talk, it's very much worth your time. The format of your TED talk will require that you deliver incredible value in about 15 to 18 minutes. Think of a TED talk as the cream of your keynote or executive summary version. There are some really great books on how to give a great TED talk including *TED Talks* by Chris Anderson (one of the pioneers of TED Talks) and *Talk Like TED*. In both books, the authors unpack the power of the TED format and why it's so appealing to audiences.

While you can't use them to offer a lead magnet from stage, the sheer fact that you've been elevated to deliver a TED talk means you can leverage this in every other part of your marketing efforts. For example, I have this included on my LinkedIn profile. At the time of the writing of this book, my LinkedIn profile reads, "TEDx Speaker | Bestselling Author | Chief Coaching Officer for Positive Intelligence." I believe that having this designation elevates you as an expert and will support how your ideal customer prospects see you. While it's by no means required to build and scale your coaching business, it becomes an industry nod indicating a special achievement. That, in turn, helps people who don't know you increase their ability to trust you.

From there, you can include the link to your TED talk in your email signature line, your speaker's bio and any other profiles you use to promote yourself. What happens then is that your ideal customer prospects will often click over to hear your 15-to-18-minute TED talk and see if they can imagine hiring you as their coach. In this way your reputation very much proceeds you.

Be sure that your TED talk is relevant to your ideal customer prospects as well as addressing a problem that they have. I selected the topic of "The Power of Audience-Centered Storytelling" because, at the time, my goal was to teach storytelling to large enterprise companies. It sure did help whenever I was soliciting companies to train their teams. When the Chief People Officer, Head of HR or Director of Talent would watch my talk, they could see instantly how I could support their teams to become better public speakers and presenters. This also led to some multi-client coaching contracts that filled my calendar with precisely my ideal customers at the time – C-Suite executives of large enterprise companies.

The key to having all of this work in your favor is to design, practice and deliver one of the best speeches you've ever given. I hired a coach to work with me, wrote out my speech, obsessed over the pacing and delivery of every word, and practiced my speech over 100 times out loud and to real people. It's that level of practice that allows you to be great. And it pays off. If a TED talk is in your future, begin preparing now. Take the time to craft your speech and really get it down to a point where you've nailed it before walking on stage. As my jazz brother Brian used to tell me, "Don't practice until you get it right. Practice until you can't get it wrong."

Podcasts As A Guest

Whether or not physical stages are your thing, another fabulous way to use your voice is to become a guest on podcasts that are relevant to your niche. As of 2022, there are over two million podcasts worldwide.[40] You don't need to be on the most popular ones. In fact, the more specific the podcast is to your niche, the better. When I first started out in my coaching business, I was happy to join a podcast that measured their audience in the low hundreds because I knew that they were targeting the very people I wanted to reach with my message. What's more, I had refined my own content strategy so I had a few interviews "at the ready" for when I reached out to a particular host of a podcast I wanted to be on.

And while you are certainly free to reach out directly, there are a number of established and emerging platforms that exist for matching podcast hosts with

---

[40] https://earthweb.com/podcast-statistics/#:~:text=least%20one%20podcast.-,There%20are%20over%202%20million%20podcasts%20worldwide.,home%20to%20over%20700%2C000%20podcasts.

potential guests. Head on over to Google and search, "How to get on podcasts as a guest" for all sorts of articles and platforms to help you do just that.

For the more established, mature and sophisticated podcasts, they will send you to their vetting form which asks you for the standard information a host needs to decide if you're a good fit for their audience. When you anticipate these needs, it will make it so much easier for you to be booked on multiple podcasts. They are going to want things such as:

- Your bio (including your background, accomplishments and why you'd be a great guest)
- Your headshot (so that they can drop you into their marketing and promo materials)
- What you want to talk about (think headline and brief description of your topic)
- Your social media handles (this is so they can see if you can help the host promote their podcast via your platforms)
- Any previous podcast recording links (so the host can see you in action, but don't worry if you're new to this and don't have any)

And of course, each host will have slight variations of what they need to ensure you're a solid fit for their podcast. It helps if you take the time to listen to one or more episodes so you have a feel for the kinds of guests this podcast host is looking for.

Keep in mind that active podcasters are looking to book out as far in advance as they can to keep their show active and interesting. They want great guests with topics that they know will be interesting to their audience. All you need to do is anticipate these needs (hello, Sage Power Explore & Innovate) and do some of your own brainstorming on topics of interest. The more you anticipate the needs of your podcast hosts, the easier it will be to get booked on their shows and the more frequently you'll be asked back (and referred) as a top guest.

Similar to the previous sections, if this is your desired medium to generate appointments, then in addition to all of what your host will want from you, you'll want to take some time to consider what additional value you can deliver in the podcast to anyone listening. I've been successful offering the most basic- such as a free one hour discovery call to the most robust where I've written a well-researched eBook I know my audience would enjoy. Whatever it is you choose to offer, make sure it's relevant and valuable to the audience listening to you via this podcast interview.

And the great news is that you're planting seeds that will continue to pay off in the future. That is, while you may receive some initial individuals who take you up on your offer, podcast interviews are "long tail" strategies. That is, because they are recorded and generally kept alive in perpetuity, don't be surprised if six months *after* your podcast aired, you're still generating appointments on your calendar.

As you can see, there's no need to launch your own podcast unless you do your research and find out that of the more than two million podcasts that exist, your audience really doesn't have a solid podcast that fits their unique needs and situation. If, after doing your research, you determine that this really is the case, then perhaps you consider making the investment in launching your own.

Podcasts As A Host

In my experience, you don't need to host your own podcast to leverage this powerful medium, but if you have done your homework and discovered a truly unmet need by your ideal customer prospects, then go for it. With more than two million podcasts in existence as of 2022, there are many tools and resources available to you to make it easy to launch your own podcast. To look like a pro, there are a few things you'll want to invest in:

1. Name of Your Podcast. This helps your audience discover you when the name helps them have a good sense of what your podcast is all about.
2. Cover Art. Check out Fiverr.com and do a search for "Podcast Art" to see a plethora of artists that are here to support the launch of your podcast.
3. Intro & Outro. While it helps to have custom music, the most important part are the bookends that anchor your audience on your show and then help wrap up each show.
4. Hosting Platform. Where will your podcast episodes reside? Which service(s) will you use to host the audio (and/or video) content so your listeners can enjoy your show?
5. Show Notes Templates. As you get rocking and rolling, you're going to want to have a simple format to provide show notes to your audience. This includes what the topic was about, the guest details, how to contact the guest, and any relevant materials referenced in the episode.
6. Promotion. How will your audience find out about your podcast? Before you launch, it's best to think through how you'll promote your podcast so your audience can find you.
7. Editing Support. When you're first starting you, you might be tempted to do all the post-production yourself. You'll find that having a good podcast producer will help you focus on working with guests and growing your audience rather than post-production editing.

This is by no means a comprehensive list. It's intended to illustrate some of the foundations needed in order to launch a professional podcast. Because of the millions of podcasts that already exist, there are many suppliers who are happy to work with you to take on as much of this part as you're willing to invest in. The purpose of having this list to so that you can enter into the launch of your podcast with your eyes wide open and know what you're signing up for.

Don't get me wrong. Having a podcast can be a blast. It's a great way to help authors promote their books, for example, that are relevant to your audience. Once you establish your podcast, you can use it to get access to guests you might not otherwise have access to. And, the more work you do on the back-end to promote each of your episodes, the more likely a popular guest will be willing to return for a second (or third) interview.

It's equally important to free yourself of the *need* to have guests at all. There are many successful podcasts that, instead, focus on the core content needs of their audience and commit to a regular publishing schedule to attract and retain their niche. Every podcast is different and while there may be some established norms, your Sage discernment will ensure that you focus on the needs of your niche rather than conform to what's been done already.

And the best part about launching your own podcast is that you are your first sponsor. That is, you are allowed to "interrupt" your own podcast with your very own call to action such as urging your audience to get on your calendar for a free discovery call or to download the latest content you've pulled together. It's also perfectly appropriate for you to establish a newsletter that your audience can sign-up for to be reminded of your latest episodes and get supplementary content (including show notes) on your latest episodes. All of these efforts will support you in generating appointments on your calendar.

Clubhouse & Audio Social Networks

Lately, another channel has been opening up and I'm curious as to its longevity. When Clubhouse first launched, I was bombarded by my well-intentioned friends sharing their limited invitations with me. Kudos to Clubhouse for their launch strategy because it was really effective. So many people who knew me and my public speaking background urged me to dive head first into Clubhouse. Despite my initial resistance, enough people shared their invitations with me that I decided to check it out.

What I love about Clubhouse and the emerging audio social network industry is that they've resurfaced a successful audio-only strategy by enhancing the good old-fashioned party lines (for those of us who are old enough to know what that means). Back when there existed a concept of "Long Distance" (whereby you paid per minute based on the value of how far someone was from you), to reduce the cost the telephone industry created "party lines" where multiple callers could join in to the (relatively) expensive conversation. What it did is allow multiple people to enjoy a single conversation and reduce the friction associated with talking on the phone Long Distance.

What Clubhouse realized is that even when the cost was all but eliminated, there was still a need to have real conversation with real people – especially with the rise of artificial intelligence and other technologies rising inside of social media. Rather than obsessing about the perfect Instagram post or Tic Tock video, Clubhouse allowed you to connect with likeminded individuals and have a real conversation. Or, as an audience member, to listen to interesting people talk to each other in real time.

As a featured speaker on Clubhouse, you can usually make your offer from the virtual stage. As a guest, it's important to be clear on your host's boundaries around making offers as part of the discussion. If they have a strict "no selling" policy, you're still free to establish your offer as part of your profile. Clubhouse allows you to have a single link as part of your profile and that can take prospects to your Calendar link or a specific landing page where they can learn more about how to connect and engage with you.

If this is your platform to generate appointments, then get familiar with the best practices of Clubhouse regarding generating appointments before you dive head first into all the conversations that you can have on this platform. In general, you can provide your offer in your profile and generally share the details of your offer as part of your engagement with the host, but as this platform continues to evolve, so too will the means of generating appointments.

Video Content Both Live & Recorded

Later in this chapter, we'll dive into organic and paid search methodologies for generating appointments. In this section, what's important to remember is that YouTube (which is also owned by Google) is the second largest search engine. That matters because when you choose to generate video content and publish it on YouTube, you're also increasing your visibility to the most powerful search engines in the world. It's called Universal Search and it's Google's way of acknowledging that, given the choice, many people would rather watch a short video than read an article about a particular answer to their search question.

The videos need not be particularly long in order to be effective. I worked with a production company to create a series of "Marketing in a Minute" videos on YouTube. The goal was to address some of the more common marketing questions in about a minute. While this effort supported my efforts to increase my search rankings, they also attracted the attention of licensing company. As an unexpected, but happy benefit of my marketing efforts, I received a licensing deal for my short videos for more than ten thousand dollars. I was just as surprised as you are. Afterall, these were essentially free videos published on YouTube and yet there were outside interests who wished to represent them for licensing deals. Who knew?

Similarly, Facebook, LinkedIn and other social networks began adjusting their algorithms to promote live video. So if you are planning on hosting video podcasts, you're in luck. By tapping into Facebook Live, LinkedIn Live and similar platforms, not only will you be producing video content, but by also doing so live you get the added benefit of having your preferred social platform supporting your efforts. Specifically, these platforms will alert your network whenever you choose to go live. This can help you build and grow your audience which leads to your ability to generate more appointments via the offer you include in your videos.

Where Else Can You Stand & Deliver?

As stated previously, this is by no means an exhaustive list. Please do not allow your Stickler Saboteur to convince you otherwise. From a space of Sage discernment, what other insights and ideas does this spark for you? As the ancient proverb goes, "Do not seek to follow in the footsteps of the masters, seek what they sought."

Perhaps you are recognizing an opportunity to join an association that is attended by your niche and find opportunities to present there. Or perhaps you know of opportunities to meet with the senior executives of an organization that would love to have you speak at their next event. If it supports you to tap into your Sage Power Innovate and play the "Yes, and ..." game as demonstrated in an earlier chapter, take the time to lean in here and identify all the different places where you have an opportunity to use your voice.

If your passion is public speaking, then begin to see that there are opportunities all around you to stand and deliver. As the comedian Jerry Seinfeld would say, "According to most studies, people's number one fear is public speaking. Number two is death. Death is number two. Does that sound right? This means to the average person, if you go to a funeral, you're better off in the casket than doing the eulogy."[41] Said another way, most people's Saboteurs stop them from public speaking. When you allow your Sage to overcome the fear that most people experience when speaking in public, your words become a sounding beacon for your niche to connect with. This is a great platform to generate appointments. But if this is not your Sage "ease and flow," then there are several other paths to choose from. Let's explore them together.

---

[41] https://www.goodreads.com/quotes/162599-according-to-most-studies-people-s-number-one-fear-is-public

Use Your Written Words to Generate Appointments

Using your voice is not limited to public speaking. There are many authors out there in the world who prefer the written word to delivering keynote speeches. If your ease and flow occurs in front of a computer when you're writing, there are plenty of opportunities to generate appointments from your written words. This is especially true when you are clear on how your ideal customer prospects consume their media. Ask yourself where your ideal customers would most likely discover your writing.

If there is a particular platform where they like to read content, that will help you focus your written efforts to appear where they are already spending their time reading. With that in mind, we'll explore some areas where you can generate appointments in ease and flow with your written words. But first, it's important to develop your content strategy so you're clear on your key messages regardless of where they end up being published.

Develop Your Content Strategy

No matter where you end up writing, it will really help you if you take the time to develop your own content strategy. A content strategy is simply a map to the most important topics that your ideal customers care about. Think of a content strategy as your architectural blueprint you'd design before building a house. Before picking up a hammer or pouring concrete, you'd want to have a clear vision of the structure you're looking to build. The same is true when it comes to your writing.

Back when I was writing for Inc.com, the entrepreneur audience was always on my mind. On my phone in my pocket was a running notebook page of possible article ideas I was playing with and planned to write. What I discovered was that there was an infinite number of topics I could write about that would benefit entrepreneurs who were building their businesses. I could explore the latest trends in technology to make their lives easier or I could interview a subject matter expert when it came to hiring the best employees. Once I was clear on the audience I served, everywhere I looked I saw possible articles I could write that would support them. This is why I was able to write hundreds of articles. There was no end to the number of topics that would interest my audience.

The same is true for you. Developing a content strategy is about considering all the possible topics that your ideal customer cares about. By starting with Sage Power Empathy for your audience and their situation, you can begin to envision all the challenges that they face and the questions they most likely have. That naturally leads you into Sage Power Explore as you become fascinated by all the challenges they are seeking to overcome. Start here. As you put yourself in their shoes, capture the essence of what they would like most to know and better understand. Notice how one simple idea can generate a dozen possible article ideas.

For example, when I thought about how I could support coaches to build a six-figure coaching business while remaining in Sage, this entire book was born. But imagine for a moment that rather than this being a book, it was a series of articles. They might look something like this:

First article idea: *"Only Four Things Matter When Building Your Coaching Business."* This is a provocative declaration that helps to simplify what appears to be a massively complex challenge for coaches looking to build their business. Underneath that first idea are several others including each of the four foundations of the coaching business, the idea that none of this works when driven by your Saboteurs and how important it is to remain in Sage while taking any action. That would lead to the following articles:

- Define Your Niche. The Paradox of Casting a Wide Net and Struggling to Grow.
- Create Your Irresistible Offer to Grow Your Coaching Business.
- How to Generate Appointments in Ease & Flow
- How Your Saboteurs Stop You Despite Your Knowing Precisely What To Do
- Building Your Coaching Business in Ease & Flow
- Applying Sage Business Development for Sustainable, Predictable Growth
- The Art of the Close: How Best to Enroll Clients in Ease & Flow

And you can see that each of these articles can be broken down even further. That's the exciting part about building your content strategy. When each article idea can only be between 500 and 1,000 words, it allows you to take a big idea and break it up into smaller, *snackable* parts. That is, if your book idea is the full meal, each of these article ideas would be more like a snack with no more than a page or two from your book.

Depending on the altitude you can see developing both big picture articles and highly granular ones. Some articles will fly at that ten-thousand-foot altitude so that your audience can see the big picture. Others will drop down and get extremely tactical showing them precisely how do accomplish a single task.

This becomes your go-to architecture whenever you sit down to write. The architecture itself is important because it helps you maintain a vision for what you're writing at any given time. Rather than getting lost and wondering where to go next, your content strategy highlights where you are and what topics you've already covered. In this way, you're strategically sharing the value you wish to deliver to your niche by mapping it out ahead of time. Going back to the home building example, you're free to build extensions onto the home at any time. You just want to make sure the basics are covered so that you have enough bedrooms, bathrooms, a kitchen, living room, dining room and garage. Your early work in building your content strategy will help you remain focused and know what to write next.

Blog Posts

With your content strategy mapped out, you can easily see the path towards regularly publishing blog posts on any platform. That is, if you choose to publish this content on your own website as part of a regular blog, you'll rise quickly as a powerful resource for your niche. If you prefer to publish on a third-party blog site such as LinkedIn, Medium, Tumblr, Blogger or any of dozens of others[42] you will use most important ingredient: your content roadmap.

What's great about having a blog is that you can create a custom signature at the bottom of each article you publish to support building your personal brand and exposing more of the efforts you've already made in the world. That might look something like this:

> *Bill Carmody is the bestselling author of the* **Three Rules of Marriage***, and is the Chief Coaching Officer of* **Positive Intelligence***. Watch more of his interviews on his* ***YouTube*** *Channel or follow him on* ***LinkedIn****.*

Or, if you prefer to be more direct in generating appointments directly from a single article, it might look something more like this:

> *Bill Carmody is an executive leadership coach who works with world-changing visionaries to create a better future. If you're ready to leave a legacy your grandchildren will be proud of, you are invited to* ***start here*** *with an hour on Bill's calendar.*

Notice the difference the signature line makes. The first one is about building awareness (i.e. "Who is the person that wrote this article?") while the second one is a true call to action; an invitation to begin a conversation with your ideal customer prospect. This is that first irresistible offer needed to get your ideal customer prospects to grab time on your calendar. And it can just as easily be about having them share their contact details in exchange for a lead magnet such as a relevant eBook, whitepaper, or custom designed workbook that will support them in going deeper on the subject you were just blogging about.

The more time you take up front to plan the path you envision your niche taking when interacting with you and your content, the easier it will be for you to generate

---

[42] https://www.wpbeginner.com/beginners-guide/how-to-choose-the-best-blogging-platform/

appointments on your calendar – either immediately via your calendar link or through a softer ask such as signing up for your newsletter. If this part is unclear, keep going. We'll cover eBooks, whitepapers, lead magnets, newsletters and email marketing in the pages that follow. Blogging is just one avenue available to you and your written words. Remember, the way of the Sage is ease and flow, so if this part isn't feeling particularly easy, rather than allowing your Saboteurs have you do nothing and opt-out, your Sage will encourage you to remain open to new possibilities (even if this one isn't appealing to you).

Think of these diverse options like a buffet. Feel free to take the ones that appeal to you and leave the rest for someone else. Knowing all the choice you have available to you will support you in deciding which areas to focus on and which to leave for someone else to do. There are plenty of mediums to choose from. Your written words have the power to enroll your niche into learning more about you as well as becoming attracted to what you stand for in such a way that they choose to reach out to you and hire you as their coach. That's why we're taking all this time to look at each option individually. You don't need to do all of them, just the one that really appeals to you. And sometimes, it doesn't even need to be you who's doing the work.

Guest Posts

No matter how prolific a writer you are, there will be times when you want to take a break for a number of reasons. Perhaps you want to take a month off or perhaps you are gearing up for an intensive workshop program. Whatever the reason, if you've established a regular publishing schedule (i.e. weekly), you have the option to provide your audience with other points of view in the form of guest posts.

Guest posts are just like they sound. There are many other people in the world who are catering to the content needs of your same niche. Once you have established your own publishing schedule on your blog, you will attract others who like your work and want to contribute to your efforts. Why would they want to do that? By being featured in a guest post, you are lending your brand and credibility to someone else who is equally passionate about your niche. The important step for you is to ensure they do, in fact, represent the same Sage qualities you have established for yourself. In other words, it's incumbent on you to do some due diligence on the backgrounds of any potential guest contributors. Make sure you've reviewed their work and identify what you're looking for before allowing them to contribute.

Assuming the person you've identified has a relevant background and appears to be genuinely interested in the same niche that you are focused on, then having one or more guest posts can help build a diversity of insight for your audience. And this works both ways. In the same way you are willing to allow others to contribute content to you, there are many highly regarded content producers out there who would love a guest post from you! When you're just starting out, this can be a fabulous way to get noticed by your niche. When publishing on someone else's established platform, you yourself are being held up as an expert vetted by them. When you're willing to do the work of writing the content and sharing it with someone else who caters to your niche, you're adding value to both them and the same ideal customer prospects you're looking to attract into your coaching business.

When you're first establishing your own brand as a coach, guest posts for others can be a great way of establishing your voice and your reputation. Just be sure you've taken the time to research the blogs or other publishing platforms you intend to contribute to in order to ensure they are legitimate. The digital content industry has exploded over the last decade and shows no signs of slowing down. The important part for you is to see where you'd like to be featured and work towards becoming a guest there.

To that end, you may want to go old school and begin with the most established names in the industry. These are usually traditional magazines and news organizations which have catered to your niche for a long time and have taken their work online. As they continue to grow and expand, so do their needs for having great writers who can help contribute to their growth.

Articles (Interviewed & Written By You)

Where does your niche go to get their news? When you have answered that question for yourself, consider how you can contribute article content to those very news organizations. If you have chosen a niche that mirrors your own previous experience, this can be a powerful way to publish your content in the form of articles in their news channels.

After I had been featured on the *Inc 5,000* list two years in a row, I was approached by *Inc.com* to start writing for them. They had asked me to support my fellow entrepreneurs with regular articles that would demystify what it means to be a successful CEO of a fast-growing company. At first, this was a daunting task as Inc had asked me to commit to a minimum of 6 articles a month and that was during the time I was still running a multi-million dollar marketing agency.

Rather than allowing my Saboteurs to have me, I tapped my wiser, elder self to see what writing for *Inc* could mean for me and the growth of my business. I started small by writing about the biggest problems and challenges I had overcome. Simple insights like, "How saying no can help you grow." But soon I began to think bigger. I realized I had access to some incredible human beings that I was sure had all kinds of wisdom to share. When I asked them if they would like to be interviewed by me for *Inc.com*, they were equally excited to share.

This snowballed into more than 350 articles between *Inc*, *Forbes* and *Entrepreneur*. I was put on the short list of several book publishers who were happy to send me pre-release copies of both their established and up and coming authors. I loved to read, so this became a partnership whereby I would read some really great books and share what I loved about them with my growing audience of entrepreneurs. That lead to conference organizers inviting me to attend their conferences as their guest and interview their keynote speakers. At first, these were relatively unknown conferences, but as I continued to publish more and more articles I received invites from top industry conferences and some incredible keynote speakers including Malcolm Gladwell and Sir Richard Branson.

My point here is that you never know how far a channel like this will take you. The more I leaned into writing, the more opportunities opened up for me. I would say the pinnacle of this effort was sitting in Tony Robbins' hotel room along with Joe Berlinger, doing a video interview for their Netflix special, *Tony Robbins: I'm Not Your Guru.* That was a surreal experience and would never have been possible without all the foundational work that I had invested in these publications for over two years prior to that event.

This all falls under the law of reciprocity. No matter how much you attempt to selflessly give to someone else, the universe will not allow the unbalance to remain unbalanced. You will end up receiving so much more than you give no matter how much you choose to give of yourself. The more you lean into your giving, the more abundance you will receive in return – especially when it's your intention is to give without expectation. This was the magic I found from my experience writing for other publications.

And yes, you can imagine the coaching appointments it generated as a result. At the time I was writing, I wasn't even a coach. When I decided to become a coach, I had built up a powerful head of steam that I was able to redirect to my coaching business with incredible ease and flow. The abundance didn't stop with generating appointments, either. I found many an entrepreneur who was looking for an executive coach they could work with to help them take their business to the next level. I found my sweet spot and I'm confident you can create your own success path to accomplish a similar or even better outcome. And this path need not focus on writing articles, either. There are many other proven success paths with the written word, so let's keep exploring together.

Books

While I'll do my best here, if you believe there's a book in your future, I urge you to check out two books about writing books from author Adam Witty. The first is *21 Ways to Build Your Business with a Book* and the second he co-authored with Dan Kennedy, *Book the Business: How to Make Money With Your Book Without Even Selling A Single Copy.* The content contained within each of these books justifies the powerful titles.

Let me dispel a common myth. The vast majority of authors won't make money writing their books. This will be my third published book and I expect to make nothing financially from it. At least, not directly from the book itself. My first book, *Online Promotions: Winning Strategies & Tactics* was written out of frustration. During the late 90's, I either had people who understood promotional marketing, but very little about digital marketing and those who knew lots about digital marketing, but very little about promotional marketing. This book was a crossing of the chasm in order to help each learn about the other.

Wiley Publishing ordered a book proposal and then advanced me $10,000 to write the book. I was ecstatic, mostly because I wanted to write it anyway and having an advance of $10,000 was just icing on the cake. In fact, I decided I'd spend most of that money to help promote the book. And that's when things went sideways. You see, I had been a guest writer for the industry's largest trade magazine, Promo Magazine, and when I told the editor I was writing the book, he offered to do a six-page spread in an upcoming issue to help promote the book. I thought I had won the lottery. Just about every person I wanted to read my book also subscribed to that magazine, so I was thrilled to share this big win with the marketing team at Wiley.

Instead of popping the champagne and celebrating with me, they killed the deal. They told me that Promo Magazine would have to pay royalties for the insertion of my excerpt into their magazine. WTF? I was mortified and so frustrated. Rather than accepting this loss, I asked them instead how they planned to market the book. Their answer was to have me make a list of 100 of my top influencers and they would send out a free copy of the book to them. That's it. I later learned that this is common with publishers and first-time authors. Publisher prefer to make their big strategic bets on the sure things. If you're J.K. Rowling or Stephen King, then they will make sizeable investments in your work because you have a built-in audience and proven track record. If you're just starting out, you're on your own and limited in what you can do on your own even if you want to.

So rather than having an excerpt available to my ideal customer prospects, I had to follow my contract and allow them to do the limited "marketing" of sending out free books to a short list of influencers. Predictably, the book didn't do well and I later bought the rights back to the book and published a second edition with a self-publishing company whereby I had control over how and where I marketed my book. The second edition did much better, but it wasn't the book sales that mattered to me. The book became a sort of long-form informercial for both of my marketing agencies. Rather than opting for a $25 dollar book sale, I gave it away for free to help me land multi-million-dollar promotions and digital marketing projects. The book was a fabulous way to open doors, secure meetings and even provide a valuable leave-behind to the influencers who swayed the opinions of the key decision makers.

And that's what you can do with your own book – especially if you self-publish or work with a hybrid publisher. While there are many out there, take the time to find a publisher who cares about helping you get your message out to your niche. There are *so many* ways to leverage your book to generate appointments and scale your coaching business. In Adam Witty's *21 Ways to Build Your Business with a Book*, he shows you how having a book will:

- Increase visibility, credibility and clout
- Increase the quantity and quality of referrals
- Create passive income streams
- Become a darling of the media
- Attract new customers and increase revenue
- Reach more prospects
- Build your list and acquire leads
- Become a highly paid speaker
- Generate multiple revenue streams

And while going into the details of each of these approaches is beyond the scope of this book, it's important to understand the underlying philosophy. When you publish your book, you are an author and that milestone generates credibility. You can then leverage this credibility to gain access to conferences as a keynote speaker (if you so desire), get attention of your ideal customer prospects (by sending an autographed copy to them for free), and use your book as an incredible lead magnet (which we'll talk about in the pages that follow).

The bottom line is that when you put all your best thinking into a book, you're sharing what you know with the audience you truly care about. As you read these words, ask yourself, if you knew you could grab an hour on my calendar would you do it? Just reverse that question for you and your ideal customer prospects. When you take the time to write your book, your niche will appreciate all your efforts and see that you're whom they would like to spend more time with. That's the credential that opens doors and helps you generate more appointments on your calendar. And there are more ways to leverage this approach then the traditional printed hardcopy books.

eBooks

An eBook is just another format of the hardcopy book. However, because it's electronic, it makes for a powerful digital asset or lead magnet (which we'll go into detail next). That means, that unlike having to pay for shipping, you can instantly give someone a copy of your eBook when they take an action such as: (1) Grab time on your calendar, (2) Sign up for your newsletter, (3) Complete a lead generation form, or (4) Share their thoughts with you about something you'd like to learn about them.

Because your book is digital, you can grant instant access. Use your Sage Power Explore and Innovate to discover all the ways you can share your brilliance packaged in an eBook with your niche. The key is to ensure a value-for-value exchange. By giving someone a copy of your eBook, you're receiving their time, contact information, insights or permission to share with them in the future.

One brilliant strategy I love is combining eBooks with podcasts. As a guest on a podcast, you're usually allowed to give listeners something of value. What most authors do is give away their first two free chapters. For an example of this visit my previous bestselling book's website: https://www.threerulesofmarriage.com/two-free-chapters and you can see how this is done. But that's not the brilliant part. What's truly brilliant is taking the extra step of adding in the option to receive the FULL eBook. Why? Because when your niche takes the time to read your full book, they have a much higher propensity to want to grab time on your calendar.

While the first two chapters is great for your ideal customer prospects to get a good feel for your writing and what the book is about, giving the full eBook away feels so much more valuable and leads your niche to want to learn more about you and what you offer. By giving the full eBook away, you're activating the law of reciprocity. Your ideal customer prospects are going to want to thank you for the valuable information you've provided and that will lead them to want to get on your calendar and book a discovery call with you.

If you've *also* self-published a hardcopy version of the book, then you can offer to send an autographed copy of your book for free or for the cost of shipping. Why? Because in order to do so, they need to provide you with their physical address and that helps you fill out your database of your ideal customer prospects. The more you know about your niche, the more you can market to them now and in the future. Knowing their birthday (and having their physical address), for example, means you can now send them a birthday card and remain top of mind – even if they choose not to hire you as their coach. Remember, they weren't a "no forever," just a "no for now." If you like where this is headed, let's dive deeper into this world of possibilities using lead magnets.

Lead Magnets

Did you know that as much as 96% of your website visitors aren't ready to buy yet?[43] The vast majority of the people you meet and connect with just aren't ready to jump

---

[43]   https://www.autogrow.co/sales-funnel-follow-up-statistics/

on your calendar and be enrolled into your coaching offerings. That's where lead magnets come in.

Simply put, a lead magnet is any digital asset that your niche wants. The magnetic part is the attraction your digital asset creates for your niche to entice them to connect with you in some way. That's the lead part. This can be an eBook like we were just discussing in the previous section, or it can be any packaged content that is interesting to your ideal customer prospects.

I was working with coach Joanna Lott on a webinar for our PQ Coach members, and she shared how book titles and magazine headlines can be great inspiration for developing your lead magnet. Check out these titles as examples:

- Six Steps to Finding A Job You Love... Get Unstuck In Less Than 10 Minutes.
- How to Build Confidence to Land Your Dream Date: Three Things You Can Do Immediately.
- Free Resume Cover Letter Template (That Will Land You in the Yes Pile)
- DON'T DO THIS: Five Mistakes Women in Their 40s Make That Ruin Their Diet.
- Five Ways To Find Happiness: Powerful Ways You Can Transform Your Life.

While each lead magnet is unique to the audience it serves, you can see how each one would get the attention of its desired target. For "Six Steps to Finding a Job You Love... Get Unstuck In Less Than 10 Minutes," you could see how someone who's feeling stuck in a dead-end job would perk up seeing that title – especially if they had some other connection or introduction to you.

The idea of the lead magnet is that your ideal customer prospect is just getting to know you. Perhaps they saw you give a presentation, met you at a networking event, or read one of your blog posts. However they discovered you, they are now checking out your background and capabilities. They see something that catches their eye and they decide to give you their contact details in exchange for this lead magnet. What you're doing is thinking about one problem you believe your niche has and you're taking the time to share your insights in the form of a lead magnet.

For Positive Intelligence, this is our Saboteur Assessment (see https://positiveintelligence.com/assessment). Here, you take about five minutes to answer questions about yourself and receive real-time feedback about your top Accomplice Saboteurs. In order to receive the completed assessment, you provide your name and email address so that we can send the results to you along with some context of what you can do to reduce your biggest Accomplice Saboteurs.

At the time of the writing of this book, we are receiving tens of thousands of leads every month. We then encourage these individuals to seek out the review of their results with one of our Certified PQ Coach members (see https://www.positiveintelligence.com/find-a-coach/). This is how we channel these leads to our

PQ Coach community. The Certified PQ Coaches, in turn, review the results with these individuals through one hour discovery calls and determine if any of them would be a good fit for their service offerings.

In the next chapter, *Converting Appointments: The Art of the Close*, I'll go into more detail as to how to masterfully convert this lead into an enrolled client. For now, the focus is how to use lead magnets to get more appointments on your calendar or at the very least make an initial connection with a potential prospect for your coaching business.

The deal is, your niche wants what you have to offer and you're willing to give it away at no cost – as long as they agree to give you their contact details for a future interaction. One of the best ways to go from an initial exchange of information to an opportunity to enroll a prospective client is through newsletters and email marketing which is what we'll dig into next.

Newsletters & Email Marketing

While social media tends to get much of the attention these days, according to Constant Contact, email's return on investment (ROI) is 3,600% vs 26% for social media.[44] The same report shows that 60% of consumers say they've made a purchase as the result of email they received vs. 12.5% for social media.

And while it used to quite a lot of work to set up an email nurturing campaign, today's platforms make it really simple to both establish and automate these efforts. By automation, I mean once you take the time to script out a series of emails (which we'll walk you through in this section), you can use a platform such as Constant Contact, MailChimp, or dozens of other platforms to automatically send out a series of emails to nurture your lead and entice them to get on your calendar where you can enroll them.

In the same webinar I worked on with coach Joanna Lott, she recommended the following email nurture sequence:

- Email one: Initial welcome and deliver your lead magnet.
- Email two: Get to know you email where you let your prospects know the real you.
- Email three: Answer a burning question or a common mistake (and address a belief).
- Email four: Reason most people fail (or go deeper on a topic/worry/belief).
- Email five: Why they are stuck - answer a common objection (that may prevent them from taking action on your offer). Introduce your offer.

---

[44] https://www.Constantcontact.com/blog/email-marketing-statistics

- Email six: Talk about your intro session and why they need it. Get concrete. Share a case study/testimonial.
- Email seven: Remind them to take action on your offer, stressing why it will help them. Remind them of what you've shared, why you're passionate, a testimonial. Do you still need my help?

While there's no *perfect* email nurture sequence, you can see how the receipt of the lead magnet can grow your audience's understanding of who you are and how you can help them with what they are struggling with. The emails are sent out over about a two week period (one every other day). Coach Joanna Lott shared an example that follows her own sequence approach for prospects looking to find a new job:

- Email one: "Here's the six steps to find work you love!" (Welcome and deliver your lead magnet).
- Email two: "Welcome to the club".
- Email three: "The number one mistake about finding work you love". (Answer a burning question or big mistake that will start to address a belief.)
- Email four: "The difference between passion and a hobby". (Reason most people fail.)
- Email five: "Are you stuck because you need an income? There is a solution – here's why…" (Answer a common objection/belief + intro your offer).
- Email six: "Want to know how to go from overworked to purposeful work? (Dedicated email about your intro package and why they need it. Share a testimonial if possible.)
- Email seven: "Did you see this help on work you love? Time sensitive!" (Remind them to take action!)

One technique that I like is that in the seventh email, telling your prospects that if they're not interested in what you're sharing, no problem, as this will be the last email they receive from you. That way, you can clean up your list and only focus on those who are interested in hearing from you. Alternatively, you can offer to share your monthly newsletter if you want to give more time to build out the opportunity to convert this lead into a paying client.

If we go back to the beginning with our content strategy, you can plan out a series of monthly topics so that you can establish a regular publishing schedule. This will allow you to plan ahead and tease out the topic of what's planned for the next month's newsletter. Taking a page out of traditional magazine's publishing calendar, the more predictable you can make your newsletter, the easier it will be for you to continue the journey of having your prospects get to know you while they are learning about how best to overcome the challenges identified. As they better understand how you can support them, the more interested they become in hiring you as their coach (which is why your content strategy is important to map out).

As with each of these topics, the point is to have you consider the ones that feel that you could complete with ease and flow. If this is calling to your Sage, then know that there are so many more insights and best practices waiting for you to discover. Any email marketing platform you choose to focus on will help you get started and point you to a wealth of great resources you can use to strengthen your own email marketing skills.

Whitepapers

Similar to an eBook, a whitepaper is a kind of lead magnet that is used to package up your wisdom on a particular topic and typically includes either primary or secondary research. The term "whitepaper" came from the US government where the color was used to indicate the distribution and white meant it was available for the public.[45] The business industry followed suit and individuals became accustomed to whitepapers being made available for providing insights and solutions to particular problems.

When I first began building websites in the early 1990s, we soon realized that it wasn't enough just to *build* a website. In order to connect with our desired audience, we needed to find ways to *promote* the website. For business audiences, nothing worked better than whitepapers. While the government distribution of whitepapers was before my time, it became evident that most leaders inside of companies were using the internet to search for whitepapers. When we began building and providing what people wanted, we discovered we could drive tremendous traffic to our websites and begin creating a direct relationship with those visitors.

Seth Godin's bestselling book, *Permission Marketing* changed the industry as he correctly pointed out that just because someone gave you their contact information didn't mean they wanted to be added to every marketing effort and distribution list you were building. The concept of permission marketing was about ensuring you received explicit permission for future marketing efforts. This simple concept lead to government regulation including the CAN-SPAM Act of 2003.

"Among other things, the CAN-SPAM Act of 2003 prohibits the inclusion of deceptive or misleading information and subject headings, requires identifying information such as a return address in email messages, and prohibits sending emails to a recipient after an explicit response that the recipient does not want to continue receiving messages (i.e. an "opt-out")."[46]

---

[45] https://www-cdn.law.stanford.edu/wp-content/uploads/2015/04/Definitions-of-White-Papers-Briefing-Books-Memos-2.pdf
[46] https://www.law.cornell.edu/wex/inbox/what_is_can-spam#:~:text=Among%20other%20things%2C%20the%20CAN,recipient%20does%20not%20want%20to

Whitepapers became a bridge between what both parties wanted. In exchange for your permission to share relevant content with you (permission, you can revoke at any time), you can receive this whitepaper that addresses a problem you're looking to solve.

To this day, there are many problems that your ideal customer prospects are interested in solving. If you've taken the time to research the problem and feel you've come up with a solid solution that will support your niche, then offering a whitepaper can be a powerful way to generate leads for your coaching business.

In addition to the traditional methodology of seeking permission (i.e. opt-in), you can offer to have your ideal customer prospect grab time on your calendar (once they've reviewed your whitepaper) for additional support via a discovery call. This is your opportunity to think through the journey your audience will go through once they have discovered you, your whitepaper and your service offerings. While your whitepaper with your packaged insights is very informative, many would love to speak with you directly to apply those insights to their particular current challenge. While a one-on-one session simply isn't practical for most large enterprise companies, you have this distinct advantage and can offer it up to generate appointments for your coaching business.

Website

When building your website, it's really important to focus on your niche and not yourself. One of the many Saboteur traps of building your website is the natural gravitation toward wanting to create a monument to yourself. Your egoic self wants to share all about your accomplishments and your life story. While there are opportunities to weave that into your website, your Sage discernment on the purpose of the website will help you here.

Your primary objective of having a website should be to generate leads for your coaching business. There are quite a number of ways to make that happen, so rather than diving into the how, let's begin with the why of your website. Why have a website at all? In truth, you don't need one. There are plenty of other ways to generate appointments as outlined in this chapter. So if you're not experiencing joy and excitement to build your website, then don't. You can accomplish everything you need with a digital calendar link (such as Calendly, Accuity, Schedule Once and many others) and an "About Me" page such as your LinkedIn profile. That's really the minimum information needed to launch our coaching business. So why have a website at all?

If you choose to build a website (from a place of Sage discernment), then think of your website as a digital playground for your niche. How would they want to interact with you in real life? What insights, for example, would you want to share with them?

Your website can be a powerful resource for your niche when you take the time to walk in their shoes. That's why we spent so much time working on your niche up front. Having gone through the exercise of discovering your niche, you already have a sense of what is important to them, what they struggle with and what problems they are looking to solve.

Rather than build a website as a monument to yourself, consider building a digital monument to your niche and all the complex needs they have in their journey towards self-actualization. The more you shift the focus and make it about them, the more interested they will be to learn about you. Sure, you can have an "About Me" page and share your background. But even then, make sure you're filtering what you're sharing to ensure it's relevant to your niche. You and your family may be proud of all your diverse accomplishments, but unless you can share how this is relevant to your niche, less is more. So share what is relevant to your niche. Your certifications, educational background, work experience and accomplishments all work to establish your credibility and why you're the right coach to support your ideal customer prospect on their journey.

The main part of your website should be a clear and well thought out call to action. This could be to book available time on your calendar to have a free discovery call with you, or it could be to provide their contact details in exchange for your lead magnet as we've discussed earlier in this chapter. Or perhaps, you're looking for them to join your newsletter for regular content updates and ongoing support.

Start with the primary action you want your website visitors to take and then build out from there. This is where you can launch your blog and provide regular content updates, just as long as each of these blog posts reinforces the primary action you want them to take.

When you consider carefully the actions you want your niche to take on your website, you can work backwards from that strategy to identify what core elements you need. This gets back to the 80/20 rule previously discussed. Remember that 20% of your efforts will produce 80% of the results. Your Saboteurs will have you obsess over the 80% effort that only produces 20% of the results, while your Sage will focus on the opposite. A launched website is infinitely more valuable than one that remains hidden in a staging area as you work on it. Do your best to map out the minimum viable website you need to launch. A few well thought out pages that generate leads for your coaching business are far superior to a complex multi-page behemoth that ultimately produces very few appointments.

At the end of this chapter, we'll review the importance of tracking and reporting so that you can continue to grow and optimize your efforts. For now, begin with the end in mind. Your website is here to generate appointments for your coaching business. Anything that doesn't directly connect with that mission should be eliminated or pushed out to a later date. Once you launch and begin promoting your website, you should see the desired results. If not, keep streamlining your website until you generate the appointments you seek.

Use Networking to Generate Appointments

Do you fancy yourself a "people person?" In other words, do you love meeting new people? Networking, at its most basic level, is about meeting new people and creating authentic connections with them. One of my closest friends, Jen Nash, wrote a great book on this subject called, *The Big Power of Tiny Connections*. In it, she describes that everyone you need to succeed in life is all around you (and often in unexpected places). She shares a story of how a seemingly random interaction with a coffee barista can lead to fabulous opportunities.

In this section, we're going to explore a number of ways to strengthen your networking muscles. The important point to understand before we do that, however, is that networking is not "event" based, it's something you can do everywhere you choose to take action.

This is one of the most fabulous things about successful entrepreneurs: they can't shut up about what they're building. When entrepreneurs launch their businesses, they see the businesses as extensions of themselves. As such, they want to share their creation with the world. This is your opportunity too. With a well-defined niche, you know precisely who you are looking to serve. Now it's about striking up conversations with everyone around you to seek out your ideal customer prospects. Along the way, you're going to find people who are *not* your niche equally interested in what you have to offer. That's great. Just because you've crafted a well-defined niche doesn't mean you can't coach people outside of your niche. It just means your clear on the bullseye of your coaching business. That level of clarity will lead to some fabulous introductions and business growth from unexpected places.

Think about it. At your barber or salon, you have a choice. You can talk about the weather and local sports teams, or you can be intentional and talk about your coaching business. You never know the network of the person you're speaking to. They might have a brother, cousin or friend who is precisely your niche. That's the power of networking. It's not just the people you know, it's the second and third ring out that has such incredible value to you. Your network has an even larger network of people you've never met and could very well be your ideal customer prospects. Spending time deepening the relationships you already have can lead to some fabulous new introductions and opportunities.

At its core, I see networking as the ultimate expression of Sage Power Explore. Assuming you're in Sage and already have empathy for yourself and the person your speaking with, there's a great opportunity to explore the people in the life of the person you're speaking with to see if you might be a great resource for them.

Assuming yes, the person you're speaking to has a high probability of making an introduction as they, too, are looking to add value to the people in their network (otherwise known as their sphere of influence). This is a natural Sage response when striking up a conversation with someone. When you have available resources that can support the people in their lives, they naturally want to share, make introductions and strengthen the bonds with their colleagues, friends and family members.

Simply put, we're here on this earth to help each other. When it's clear you're in Sage and genuinely desire to help someone else, that authenticity is extremely appealing and leads to fabulous introductions. The more networking you do, the better you become at it and the more natural it feels. And there are designated places to really work out your networking muscles. That's what we'll cover in this section.

Develop A Business Card & Mobile Strategy

One of the most important actions you can take is to craft a well thought out business card. As the old saying goes, "Luck is when opportunity meets preparedness." In order to generate your own luck, be prepared. Your business card is so much more than your contact details. Most coaches "phone it in" when it comes to their business cards. I say your business card is one of the most valuable pieces of collateral you'll ever create. It's small, fits in a wallet or purse and done correctly can feel like a mini gift card coming from you. Let me explain.

When I launched my *Millionaire Coaches Marketing Playbook* training program, I realized that I had created something really valuable for the coaching industry. The trouble was, most of my network were C-Suite executives. I was going to need to enroll coaches and, at the time, I didn't know very many personally. I started with the networks I had access to that did have coaches. And rather than giving out my corporate business card, I designed a brand new one that looked like a mini magazine advertisement on the front and contained an invitation for my (free) live workshop event on the back.

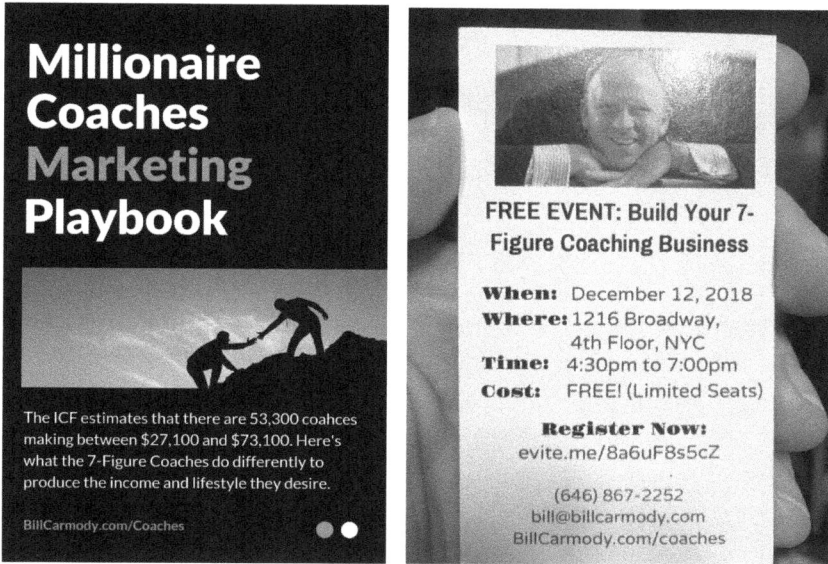

On the front of the card, I went right for the central pain point that I knew most coaches were struggling with. "The ICF estimates that there are 53,500 coaches making between $27,100 and $73,100. Here's what the Seven-Figure Coaches do differently to produce the income and lifestyle they desire." Immediately underneath that, I included a "deep" link to my website (BillCarmody.com/Coaches) which took them directly to my video overview of the event and why they should attend.

On the back of the card, I had my picture (something I picked up from the Real-Estate industry) along with a bold title that read, "FREE Event: Build Your Seven-Figure Coaching Business"

> **When**: December 12, 2018
> **Where**: 1216 Broadway, 4th Floor, NYC
> **Time:** 4:30pm to 7:00pm
> **Cost**: Free! (Limited Seats)
>
> **Register Now:** evite.me/8a6uF8s5cZ
>
> (646) 867-2252
> bill@billcarmody.com
> BillCarmody.com/coaches

Notice that I didn't include any of the "traditional" business card elements of my title, my company, my logo or even my own physical address. None of that is important to the person I'm handing off my card to. And because my website is my name, I didn't even include my name in my contact details. I truly went for minimum viable.

And all of this cost me around $25 including shipping from Vista Print. It took me about an hour to set up everything including the free evite invitation link and then lay it out on Vista Print's digital layout editor. Even if it cost me $50 to $100, it would have been a very small price to pay in order to enroll my ideal customer prospects into my live event.

I gave myself three months from the time the cards were in hand to going to regular networking events where I knew coaches would be. I'd strike up a conversation, confirm they were a coach struggling to make the kind of money they wanted to make, then tell them about my event and give them this customized card.

Even those who couldn't make it asked for time on my calendar to talk more about my program to see if it was a good fit for them. With this effort, I kicked off my first round of paid participants and enrolled each of them into my 12-week course charging $5,000 each. While your program may be vastly different than mine, creating a custom business card is a relatively inexpensive way to generate leads for your event(s) and get your ideal customer prospects to get on your calendar to spend time with you.

Why settle for a boring business card, when you can use a customized one to move your business forward? Before taking this action, at both my former agencies I had crazy fun cards. At Seismicom, our business cards were circular and slightly smaller than a drink coaster. In fact, they were so often referred to as "coasters" that we went ahead and designed custom actual coasters we gave away as a premium. This was so effective that at my next agency, I made triangle business cards. The point was that neither of these cards "fit" in the stack of networking cards you ended up with at the end of the night. Even if you had to fold my card, you were physically interacting with it and that by itself made it stand out and be more memorable. I never apologized for having a physical business card that stood out. It got me noticed and generated millions of dollars of business for both of my agencies.

When you're willing to stand out, you get noticed. When you're willing to go above and beyond what anyone could reasonably expect from you, you're going to build, grow and scale your coaching business quickly. Allow your inner Sage to "play" here and be as creative as possible. Don't settle for a "normal" business card. Be willing to stand out and be noticed. After all, that's one of the cornerstones of all marketing efforts: to generate awareness.

Networking at Conferences & Events

Now that you've taken the time to create a stand-out business card, you're ready to give it out to as many of your ideal customer prospects as you can. The only "rule" of networking is to ensure that your niche is present, or, at the very least, the people who know and can refer you to your niche are present.

When I was first starting out in business, I discovered the "Association of Associations" yellow book which was essentially an old-fashioned directory of all the associations registered in the US. Pre-Google, this book served as a way of discovering all of the thousands upon thousands of associations that exist in the US alone.

An article from back in 2017 estimated that there are over 1.8 million meetings and events held every year in the US alone.[47] Despite the impact of the 2020 global pandemic, there are still millions of physical meetings and events held every year. Remind your Hyper-Achiever Saboteur that you don't need to attend very many to build a fabulous network of contacts from your niche. In fact, over-networking produces far inferior results as you tend not to follow-up effectively, which leads to wasted effort.

Your niche likely has somewhere between one to six conferences and events that they attend. This could be informal "Meet-Ups" (see meetup.com) or events listed on LinkedIn, Facebook and Eventbrite. Many are free and some require an investment to attend. While you might be compelled to become an official sponsor of an event, it's best to first go to an event as an attendee so that when you do invest money you'll know the likely impact of your investment. Conference organizers would love to have you believe that your sponsorship dollar is well spent at their event and in some cases they are right. But before investing, you're better off attending and seeing how many actual appointments you generate.

There's so much you can do organically before turning to paid services. It's not that you shouldn't invest in your coaching business, it's that you need to deliver your own initial success that you can then amplify with financial investments. Otherwise, you'll end up spending money to learn what works and what doesn't. And those can be both expensive and painful lessons. Much better to build a track record of success that you can then share with others who are asking you to make financial investments with them.

Join Relevant Industry Associations

Membership fees tend to be relatively nominal when compared to the access you get to your niche. The main considerations before joining are: (1) Can you confirm that your niche is active with this association? And (2) Are you committed to making the time to show up to their regular events yourself? If the answer to both of these

---

[47] https://askwonder.com/research/events-planned-united-states-vendors-average-per-event-zujıxzyyq

questions is "yes" and "yes," then joining relevant industry associations can be a great way to generate leads for your coaching business.

Often, when about to join, the person in charge of membership acquisition can give you a crash course in the best events to attend and how to become a contributing member of the association. Share your super powers with the person in charge of membership. Typically, in addition to enrolling members, they also have a number of volunteer slots they need to fill each year. If you're sure your niche is present, it can really help propel your coaching business to volunteer for a leadership position. This elevates you among the group participants and can lead to more of your ideal customer prospects approaching you to discover who you are, what you do and how you might be able to help them. It's a great way of generating more appointments on your calendar.

Meet-Ups & Speed Dating

There are many great platforms that have developed for people who want to meet others who share similar interests. Meetup, for example, launched over two decades ago with the primary objective of helping people meet each other in real life. Today, there are thousands of events[48] happening every day, according to their website. The goal is to help you meet people, develop friendships, grow your business and discover people who can support you. As a coach, you are one of those people offering support to those who need it most – your niche.

What I have particularly enjoyed about the Meetups I've attended is meeting the leadership and regular participants who enjoy attending and opportunities for making introductions, deepening connections and traditional networking.

Before you attend, practice your "elevator pitch." This is idea that if you were on the ground floor riding up an elevator, you'd have about a minute to share who you are, what you do, the people you serve and how you help them. At Meetups and similar venues, you're going to have a short amount of time to make yourself known to the person in front of you. The time you practice in private will support you when it's time to share in public. What you'd want to do is have a brief way of introducing yourself that's clear and powerful.

When we were going over your niche statement, recall that we started this process with: "I help [people] go from [problem] to [promise] by [process]." This is a good place to start. Then you can embellish and evolve this statement based on the group of people you're expecting to connect with. The less you include, the more powerful your statement, and the higher the probability that someone will remember who you are and what you do.

---

[48]   https://www.meetup.com/ as of June 2022

It's also perfectly acceptable to ask for help. "Do you know anyone who ..." and then describe your ideal customer prospect, and their biggest problem. That way, you're planting a seed with those who are not part of your niche, but perhaps know someone they can introduce you to. If it turns out you *are* talking to your niche, then they will likely respond something to the effect of, "That's me! You're describing me and the problem that's been haunting me for the last several weeks/months/years."

Some events have a "speed dating" aspect to them. I love these structured meeting opportunities. This is when the event organizers want you to meet with 15 to 20 people in 30 to 40 minutes. You essentially have about two–three minutes with different people and you both need to share who you are, what you do, what you're looking for and how the other person can help you. It's fast and exhilarating. It really helps you streamline your elevator pitch and the facial feedback from the person in front of you instantly gives you feedback as to what's landing, what's confusing and how well you're doing.

If you have an opportunity to use the "speed dating" methodology in your networking, I highly recommend it. You'll never have such powerful feedback in such a short amount of time without going through an experience like this. If you're struggling to find something like this for your niche, talk to the event organizer and offer to help set it up at a future event. You can get all the details of how to host a speed dating session online. And, if you happen to be single looking for a new relationship, this is an excellent way to meet a ton of prospects in a single evening. Business or pleasure, speed dating is a great way to generate a ton of appointments on your calendar when you're looking to grow.

Host Your Own In-Person Gatherings

Let's say that you do your homework and discover that there really isn't a good fit for the kinds of networking you'd like to do. Your Sage might whisper to you that that's a beautiful gift. Why? Because it turns out that you're the one you've been waiting for. Your niche may very much be in need with what you have to offer, but they've never found an event quite like the one you know you're capable of creating. Go for it!

This is especially true if hosting events is one of your superpowers. Perhaps you're the friend that everyone turns to when they want to throw a really great party, barbeque or even help with wedding plans. If you enjoy creating all the elements for people to have a great time, then perhaps this is your opportunity to apply these skills to generate more appointments on your calendar. With the rise of WeWork and similar coworking spaces, you can get a relatively inexpensive great meeting space for a single event like never before.

Or perhaps you know someone who works in a fabulous space. Consider asking for after-hours access. When I was working in New York City, I was surprised to find just how empty all these incredible office buildings were after six or seven pm at night. By asking the right people for permission, I could usually get access to an incredible conference room for the price of inclusion. If I'm throwing a really great event that my "conference room sponsor" would love to attend, then all I need to do is share my vision of what I'm planning.

While security hurdles have certainly increased over the years, that all can usually be overcome with some extra time and planning reserved for jumping over said hurdles. Guests are usually required to bring their identification and may be required to sign wavers ahead of time depending on the security of the building itself and that of your sponsor's company. Regardless, if you give yourself enough time to plan, you can have all the elements: great space, food, beverages and an incredible experience that you've planned out.

This can be a fabulous way to build your own personal brand among your niche. All the while, your event can help you generate all sorts of new opportunities for relatively low financial investment. When you are managing the space, you have the power to generate the kind of experience you desire for your niche to have. Your preparation and planning can deliver an incredible experience that motivates your ideal customer prospects to want to spend even more time with you in the form a one-on-one discovery coaching session.

Virtual Networking

Perhaps the greatest gift of the global pandemic was the rise of Zoom and other virtual platforms. Technology has always been available for us to connect globally. Post-pandemic, however, virtual meetings and networking has become normalized and common. Just like hosting your own physical event, there's no reason you can't come up with a powerful virtual experience that you can provide to your ideal customer prospects.

This can be as simple as preparing a short presentation with a longer discussion, or designing one or more break-out sessions where your niche members have a chance to meet with others who are going through the same or similar experiences. If you are the host, you have a really great opportunity to design a virtual meeting that has your niche receive a ton of value from you as they deepen their own understanding of the challenges they face.

If you are attending a virtual networking session, I encourage you to treat it as if you were there in person … physically. That means being prepared with your elevator pitch that you've already practiced and are ready to share. That also means finding a quiet space where you are not likely to be interrupted so that you can focus on the event. Please do not allow your Restless, Hyper-Achiever or other Saboteurs to convince you to multi-task. If you're driving in a car, checking email, or doing the dishes, you're not present and it shows. Virtual networking is about giving your undivided attention to those who are there and have chosen to show up. Be respectful of their time by managing yours.

In addition, there are several add-on opportunities you can play with in a virtual setting. Since you can't give out a physical card, you can prepare to connect on LinkedIn, for example, by having your link to your profile at the ready. When appropriate, you can drop your LinkedIn link in the chat (i.e. https://www.linkedin.com/in/billcarmody/), along with your other relevant contact details such as your calendar link for booking time with you, your email and phone number. You could even share your bio or one-page offer if you have these available.

In other words, at a traditional networking event, you're limited to what you can share physically. No matter how proud you are of your book, for example, you can only physically carry so many copies to give away. Your eBook (or other lead magnets), for example, can be shared with a link. Keep this in mind as you're thinking about the virtual networking you're considering. The more you prepare for these networking events, the more likely they will generate the appointments you're looking to get on your calendar.

Weaving In Casual Parties & Gatherings

One thing I learned as an entrepreneur is that you're never really "off." I'm sharing that as you're going to end up at a neighbor's barbeque, a family friend's birthday party or perhaps a sports or religious gathering, and as part of this casual party or gathering, you will invariably be asked, "So what do you do?"

Your Saboteurs will (loudly) urge you to minimize this question, change the subject and otherwise play small. Afterall, you're a guest, not the guest of honor, right? Don't make a big deal out of this or you might not be invited back. Whatever your Saboteurs are telling you, they are doing their best to have you turn off who you are, what you do, and sharing your purpose.

Instead, listen to your Sage. The person in front of you could hold the keys to opening up your coaching business even if they are not your ideal customer prospect (and you know because you've been authentically listening to them for some time). Rather than deciding for them, answer their question authentically. You are a [state your niche] coach and you [solve this particular problem this niche has]. You want to have created a compelling niche statement that has even people outside your niche intrigued and wanting to learn more.

To the extent that you can further personalize and make your niche statement relative to the person you're speaking to, go for it. This is an incredible opportunity to practice – especially since you have low expectations that the conversation will lead to generating an appointment on your calendar. So why do it? Every time you speak your niche out loud to another human being, you reinforce for yourself (and the universe) what you're up to. You don't know where your next client will come from, so begin to see every opportunity in front of you as a means to practice and improve.

The only thing you do NOT want to do is create an impromptu coaching session. Seriously, don't do it. Not ever. You wouldn't go to a party in order to get a diagnosis from a doctor, would you? If you met a top orthopedic surgeon, you'd be free to ask her all about her career and what it's like. The minute you asked her for a diagnosis, she'd invite you to make an appointment for a follow-up visit. That's what you want to be doing too. Treat your coaching business *like an actual business.* That means you can share who you are, what you do, how you do it and any aspects of your business you choose. But if the person you're talking with is a prospect or knows someone who is, move the next step to generating an appointment on your calendar. The more professional you act, the higher the probability that there will, in fact, be a next conversation that can lead to an enrollment.

Appointment Setters & Done For You Services

I'm not opposed to using the services of others – especially those who are in alignment with your desired growth. When it comes to hiring someone to get appointments on your calendar, that can seem like such a "no brainer" solution to scaling your coaching business – and it can be … at the right stage of your growth. When you're first starting out, it's so tempting to take short cuts. Facebook, Instagram, Google and LinkedIn ads have a great track record. There are many "done for you" services available. But before you press the "easy" button, make sure you already have a track record of success that others can help you grow and scale.

When you dive into third party services too soon, you've missed all the learning opportunities that come with boot strapping your own business. They will argue that this is the point. "Why go through all the pain and struggle when you can have it all done for you?" Sounds like a great argument until you realize that it's never about the technology or even the human resources. The ability to launch, grow and scale your coaching business is about working on each of the four foundations: Niche, Irresistible Offer, Generating Appointments and Converting Appointments. You want to know that you've nailed all four of these foundations by actually producing clients that invest in your coaching business.

Then, and only then, should you consider using "done for you" services to elevate and extrapolate on the success you've already achieved. Otherwise, you risk throwing a lot of money at a problem you yourself haven't clearly solved. How can someone who isn't you answer the questions you yourself are struggling with? Who better than you knows the audience you choose to serve? Who else knows the problems your niche is grappling with? Or how to engage them via any of the approaches outlined in this chapter?

Please don't allow Saboteur fear and judgment to stop you from experimenting. Because that's what this is all about. You are a perfectly imperfect human being. The very fear your Saboteurs have of making mistakes and "failing" is the very thing preventing you from learning, growing and scaling. Instead of fearing failure, your Sage is inviting you to embrace it ... seek it out, even. It's not about the number of times you stumble and fall. It's about the number of times you get back up and dust yourself off. That's what every seasoned entrepreneur knows. To play it safe is to not try at all. Only when we're willing to risk failure, do we truly discover our unique gifts, talents and resilience.

When you're ready to hire appointment setters and "done for you" service, be prepared to share what you already know that is working, as well as what you've tried that didn't work. Without that, you're entering a taxicab and turning on the meter without really have a precise destination. It can be an expensive ride. You feel like you're making progress (because the taxicab is moving), but you can wonder up and down several streets until you finally find the one that produces results for your business. That's why I urge you to go first and know where you're headed. There really are no shortcuts here, as much as you'd like there to be.

Use Traditional Marketing to Generate Appointments

Once you have established a few success paths for your coaching business, then you are ready to tap into traditional marketing efforts in order to scale up your coaching business. That is, only after you've successfully generated appointments and are confident that you're reaching and attracting your niche, can you turn to more traditional marketing methodologies. Remember, I built and successfully exited two multi-million dollar marketing agencies so I'm a huge fan of marketing ... as long as you have the foundation of a business that's ready to scale. I've seen way too many start-up businesses fail because they assumed they knew their niche and had an irresistible offer that ended up being a very expensive "test."

If you haven't market-tested your niche with actual outreach efforts and enrollment attempts, then you are guessing about who your ideal customer prospect is and their biggest needs. Adding more expense to a business without revenue is not a wise move. Your Sage would encourage you to have Empathy for yourself and Explore some alternatives to spending a lot of marketing dollars on a product that has yet to launch with a "proof of concept."

A proof of concept is a way to validate your assumptions. By actually speaking with members of your niche and delivering your irresistible offer, you can test your assumptions. If your offer lands and they are willing to book time on your calendar (or better yet, hire you as their coach), then you have validated your assumptions. Nothing paves a success track like actual sales. Short of converting appointments (which we'll talk about in the next chapter), generating appointments on your calendar is the next best thing. It means your niche is interested in giving you a hour of their time to engage with you. That's a great first step. Now let's go deeper.

Develop Your Go-To-Market Strategy

Before you dive into more traditional marketing methodologies, it's really helpful to have a go-to-market strategy. As my grandfather used to say, "Measure twice and cut once." In the same vein, having a go-to-market strategy allows you to think through what will be most effective to reach your niche and accomplish your objectives before investing (wasting?) money trying to figure that out on the fly.

At its most basic level, a go-to-market strategy contains a clearly defined marketing objective such as, "To generate 50 new appointments on my calendar from my niche, defined as [describe your ideal customer prospects], by [date]." Notice you have identified the who (your niche), the what (appointments on your calendar) and the by when (the date).

When working with other marketers, it helps to share with them your irresistible offer and any lead magnets you've developed and would like to use as part of this effort. The more you can share of whom you're looking to reach with what offer and by when, the easier the job will be for someone who can support you in reaching this goal.

Sage Power Navigate will also support you here. Your high purpose can help guide the strategy. Knowing *why* you desire to help this niche can influence *how* you tell your story and in *what* medium you choose to tell it. As we explore different tactics, you can see how different mediums offer different advantages to generating awareness and making your offer in unique and creative ways. By spending time thinking through these possible options, you're helping to craft the outline of your go-to-market strategy which will, in turn, help you narrow your focus and increase the results of your efforts.

Direct Response & Dimensional Mail

To this day, my favorite book on direct response is Lester Wunderman's *Being Direct*. Not only is he considered one of the pioneers of direct marketing, he shares his approach to "making advertising pay." In other words, the direct response industry pioneered the concepts of expecting a return on investment (ROI). For every dollar you spend, if you get more than a dollar back, you have a positive ROI. If you get back less than the dollar you spent, you have a negative ROI. This can help you decide if your efforts are working and therefore should continue or are not working and therefore should be closely examined before adjusting one or more elements associated with the effort.

Most people know direct response from the "junk mail" you receive in your physical mail box. You know, the ones addressed to "Resident" or "Current Homeowner." Even the more sophisticated mail with your name on it often feels impersonal and clearly a broadcast approach of "spray and pray."

That's not what you're up to. You've done your homework. You know your niche and the biggest problems they struggle with. What's more, you've spent time thinking about how you can support them with your irresistible offer. Rather than broadcasting and casting a wide net to grab anyone, you've fine-tuned your strategy and know who you're targeting. Now it's time to get their attention. And there are so many ways to do this!

When looking to reach C-Suite executives, I thought I was clever by FedExing a signed copy of my book. It was expensive, but it got the response I was looking for. But there's always someone who goes the extra mile and it shows. In Jeffrey Gitomer's *Little Red Book of Selling*, he shared a story of needing to get the attention of a single CEO that he was told was "nearly impossible" to reach. Challenge accepted. What Gitomer did was called up FedEx and asked what the largest box they would deliver. They responded a refrigerator sized box. Perfect. He strung a piece of string from both sides of the giant box and hung his business card with a simple, "Call me" note. It totally worked. The CEO picked up the phone and called Gitomer, opening the call with, "You have my attention."

"But Bill, that would be so expensive!" I hear you, but it's a very small price to pay to speak to a prospect that could land you a multi-million-dollar contract. And that's the point. What are you willing to invest to land your next coaching client? When I first started out, I received $350 a month for coaching. Then I quickly raised my prices to $500, $1,000 and $2,000. What I was willing to invest to land a $350/mo client was very different than one for $2,000/mo.

That's the calculation you'll need to do. Think of it this way. If you land a client, how long are they likely to engage with you? Three months? Six months? A year? Multiple years? That will give you the projected "lifetime value" of a client. Using my $350/mo example, if I know that my minimum contracted amount is six months, or $2,100, then what am I willing to spend on a single client? That begins to open up some possibilities for you. Rather than trying to hit a large number of unqualified prospects at $5, you might invest $50, $100 or more on highly qualified prospects – the ones you *know* are your ideal customers.

Regardless of what budget you decide on, consider the dimensionality of what you're sending physically. A box is like receiving a random present. By nature, you're curious what someone you don't know has sent you. You are actually curious and excited to open it. A letter has much less of that same appeal. So consider investing in dimensional objects that help tell your story and get you noticed. Even a really well-designed coffee mug or T-Shirt can grab the attention of your audience and have them curious to speak with you.

That said, don't expect a "one and done" approach. The research keeps changing, but most marketers will tell you that you need to make up to nine "impressions" before someone will take the time to reach out and connect with you. That can be a combination of email, social media messages, phone, text, and direct mail. While some of your niche are already seeking out a solution to the problem you've well defined, many are vaguely aware that they have it and are not yet "buy ready." That's part of your marketing plans. You want to anticipate multiple out-reaches and not get discouraged if your niche isn't ready to enroll when you're attempting to enroll them. We'll dive deeper into that in the next chapter.

Search Engine Marketing (SEM) & Local Paid Search

Google and other search engines have made it incredibly easy to purchase ads on their platforms. What many people don't realize is that the second largest search engine after Google is YouTube (which is also owned by Google). What this means is that you can be very selective about where you place your advertising messages in order to generate appointments. What is also important to understand is the level of sophistication that has grown in the search engine marketing (SEM) space.

Today, you can get extremely granular which means the more you know about your niche, the more effective your media investments will be in reaching them. This goes all the way down to their local geography. One of the most popular searches that has shaped the industry is adding "near me" to the search. If you're in new town and need a haircut, you might look up "Barbershops near me." Or perhaps you're in the mood for Ethiopian food. Searching "Ethiopian restaurants near me" will produce a list of the closest Ethiopian restaurants along with their menus and point-to-point directions by any mode of transportation you choose.

Knowledge is no different. If you are wondering about something, chances are someone has the answer and likely created a YouTube video on the subject. Want to know how to change your own oil? Don't search for an oil change. Instead include the year, make and model of your vehicle and find a qualified mechanic showing you step-by-step how do change the oil and replace the filter on your exact car. Want to learn how to play the guitar? Sure, you could hire a guitar teacher to give you lessons. And, there is an abundance of free videos showing you how to play any song you'd like to learn on the guitar. "Do it yourself" and "how to" videos are some of the most popular ones available to you.

In the context of generating appointments on your calendar for your coaching business, it's helpful to remember just how convenient it is to search for anything you desire so that you can align your business with what's already the normalized behavior of your niche. What's unique about SEM and local paid search is that you don't even have to be the content generator to benefit from all of this incredible content that exists out there. You can become a paid sponsor of the content that your niche is interested in watching, reading or otherwise interacting with.

For example, let's say that your niche is a mid-level manager looking to get promoted, but they really struggle with imposter syndrome. A quick search produces over 575,000 videos on the subject. If you were so inclined, you could place an ad for overcoming imposter syndrome with a free one hour discovery call with you. What you'd want to do then is to see how many appointments your ad produces on your calendar as well as the quality of the person who accepts your offer. That is, are they your niche? If not, what's missing that would help you further refine your offer to target your ideal customer prospect? As you refine your campaign, you will generate more appointments with the precise ideal customer prospects you seek.

At the same time, the main Google search for "imposter syndrome" produces nearly 25 million search results. At the time I'm writing this book, there were also zero paid search ads. Now that can be for a myriad of reasons, but if your ideal customer prospect is struggling with imposter syndrome, there is currently (at the time of this writing) no competition to place a paid search ad to capture leads on this highly relevant topic for a niche that focuses on this issue. And that's the point. You don't need *all* the people searching on this subject, you just need to generate qualified appointments on your calendar. You might even want to go local and start with people searching in a specific geography (rather than all people globally searching on this subject).

When you're ready to ease into the world of paid search, Google (and many others) are happy to guide you to invest wisely. That might sound counter-intuitive. Your Judge might ask why you would ever trust the platform taking your money? Your Sage would answer that it's in their best interest to have you be successful generating appointments with your niche so that you'll continue to invest (rather than experiencing a "failure" and ceasing your investment).

Organic Search Engine Optimization (SEO)

While paid search can help you test the waters on what are the best search terms (i.e. "keywords"), once you have designed a proven track record, you may want to ease off the amount of money you're investing in paid search. In order to reduce or eliminate your paid search advertising investment, you'll need to leverage the power of organic search engine optimization (SEO). What that means is that rather than effectively sponsoring someone else's content, you begin building your own content.

Remember all those "how to" videos on YouTube we covered in the last section on SEM? How do you feel about creating some of your own? Or perhaps video isn't your thing and you'd much rather write articles on blog sites. That too can help you generate leads on your calendar. The trick for effective SEO is to work with an expert who can help you map out your content plans including the best keywords and meta data to use. Meta data is how search engines identify the essence of your content. You're essentially declaring what your content is and then what Google or other search engines do is verify your claims and see who else is referencing / linking to your content. The more people who think your content is relevant to the subject you're focusing on, the higher your content will rank in the search results.

Yes, I'm totally oversimplifying SEO and there are entire books, courses and service providers dedicated to this subject if you're interested. What matters here is highlighting that there is a non-paid advertising method to generate appointments on your calendar. You're trading off your time for your dollars. Rather than spending money to generate appointments using search, you're investing your time (and patience) to grow organically. To that end, a well-thought-out SEO strategy can take six months or more to be effective. That's why most SEO efforts happen in parallel to some other marketing tactic. Long-term, however, SEO can be a very effective and inexpensive way to generate leads on your calendar.

Paid Social Media Advertising

Social media sites like Facebook and LinkedIn are free to their users because they receive the bulk of their revenue from advertising dollars. What makes social media platforms so compelling to advertisers is the rich amount of consumer-generated data to make advertising campaigns relevant. Said another way, social media sites are not "free", as anyone who uses them is funding their participation with their data -- personally identifiable data as well as their unique preferences.

The line between creepy and cool is a fine one. Most people would be shocked if they knew just how much of their information was available to advertisers. That's why the government has gotten involved with privacy protection and companies are beginning to do a better job protecting their consumer's privacy ... or at least wish to be perceived as making an effort to do so.

If you choose to jump in here and participate in paid social media advertising, you'll quickly discover that all the work you did previously in crafting your niche and getting clear on your ideal customer prospects will serve you well. It's easy to get lost with all the available options you have at your disposal when creating a paid social media advertising campaign.

You can define a specific targeted audience based on all the insights you have on your niche including their age, industry, marital status, career, interests, geography and several other factors. You can create custom audiences based on past client profiles or even people who have previously visited your website. And once you have confirmed the most important criteria for generating appointments, you can develop lookalike audiences. A lookalike audience tells a social media advertising platform precisely who your ideal customers are by sharing what you know about real people. An algorithm is then used to look for others who match similar demographic and psychographic profile characteristics (and help you more efficiently target).

Simply put, the media industry has become data-driven and the more you know about your ideal customer prospects, the easier it will be to reach them efficiently with your advertising investment. When you add in your irresistible offer, you'll be in a great position to launch highly efficient campaigns that will generate leads at a predictable cost per lead. That is, you'll know how much you need to spend (in dollars) to generate a lead on your calendar. That will help you define your estimated return on investment (which we'll spend more time on making it clear in the next chapter).

Despite how wonderful all the advances may be for helping you reach your niche, don't get so wrapped up in the technology that you lose focus on what you're trying to accomplish. You're only spending money on social media advertising to generate appointments. While you may feel compelled to use these platforms to increase your friends, followers and boost your content, keep checking these impulses against your Sage Power Navigate. Remember your purpose and why you are doing any of this. If your investments are not directly generating leads for you, you may be inadvertently sabotaging your effectiveness. Sage Power Activate is about fierce, laser-focused action. In the world of social media advertising there are may compelling rabbit holes. Be forewarned here and do your best to remain focused and diligent. If your investment isn't producing the desired results, don't be afraid to end the campaign and try something else.

Organic Social Media

Similar to SEO, there are organic approaches to using social media that don't require paying for advertising. Back in the heyday of early social media, these strategies were similar to SEO for websites. The concept that "content is king" reigned supreme. The more money you invested in generating compelling content, the more you were rewarded in terms of sales opportunities without investing advertising dollars.

Social media platforms put an end to much of that when they introduced the concept of "boosting." That meant sub-optimal content could receive a burst of awareness through advertising support. Slowly, organic content was diminished in the algorithms and replaced by advertising supported posts and shares. But that doesn't mean organic social media efforts are a waste of time.

On the flip side, social media platforms elevated the concept of "live." When you choose to broadcast on Facebook Live or LinkedIn Live, you will get support from these platforms – especially to your established network of connections. So now, having great content on your social media feeds creates a foundation so that when someone comes to visit you, your presence feels fresh and relevant, inviting new ideal customer prospects to review what you've been up to. Going live helps get you noticed and your content shared organically. And it doesn't end there.

After a few years writing for Inc and Forbes, I turned my attention to LinkedIn's publishing platform. I realized that most of the people I wanted to attract were either coaches or business people and their platform of choice was LinkedIn. By publishing an article, my efforts were rewarded by being exposed to my connections and followers. But that's not how I generated appointments. Instead, I grabbed the direct link of the article and reached out to select individuals I knew would find it interesting. I would direct message them and ask them if they would be open to commenting on my article. Or, if I didn't know them particularly well, I'd ask if they would be willing to like my article.

Why? Because likes, comments and shares are the feedback loop that let's LinkedIn know that a relevant article is getting traction. The more comments and likes I received, the higher the article would show up as relevant to more of my audience's content streams.

At the bottom of the article, I would invite people to book time on my calendar to speak with me directly and go deeper. I also experimented with lead magnets such as whitepapers, eBooks and other relevant content in exchange for a connection. I could then measure the effectiveness of my article (and outreach efforts) by the number of appointments I generated on my calendar.

What's great is that once you move onto your next article, the previous one is still generating appointments. As new people comment, like and share, the article continues to remain relevant. This allows you to update the article pointing to the next one you just published so that you continue to gain traction. So while you may be responsible for keeping your own articles relevant, you can still generate appointments through organic social media efforts.

Outdoor

As you grow and expand your coaching business, you may want to experiment with non-traditional methods of getting the attention of your niche. This is especially true as you deepen your own knowledge and understanding of your niche. Let's say that you choose to work with medical professionals and there's a bus stop right in front of the hospital or administration office where your ideal customers reside. If you were given free space on the side of that bus shelter, what would you want to tell them?

Perhaps you'd share your empathy for them and their situation. Or perhaps you'd like to invite them to an upcoming event or webinar. The more specific a call to action you can give them, the more likely they will respond if you offer is irresistible, timely and relevant. What would you want to give your niche if you were standing there in person?

What outdoor does is create a geographically relevant delivery of your key message and offer. As you grow and expand your practice, perhaps you've launched regular group coaching and are looking to fill spots. Or perhaps you want to create a regular cadence of new prospects that are interested in joining you for in-person events, retreats or your membership program.

What outdoor does is help generate awareness and can be a great vehicle when combined with other methods of reaching your niche. Just be sure you've started small with other methods outlined in this chapter. The wrong message in the wrong geography can be an expensive lesson. Typically, outdoor is reserved for scaling your coaching practice after you've nailed your foundations. It's not advisable for coaches who are just getting started. But if you have traction and are looking to scale, select locations for outdoor advertising can be a great way to remain top of mind as you're growing the number of leads you'd like to generate consistently.

Sponsorships

With all the same caveats as shared in the previous section on outdoor advertising, sponsorships are best as a scale effort. I associate sponsorships with goodwill. When my son was young and playing T-Ball, the local restaurant that sponsored his team made me want to reciprocate and eat at his restaurant more frequently.

When I go to a tradeshow, I like to browse the sponsors who have worked hard to put compelling offers together knowing that you're not there for them as much as the content at the event. Still, they made an investment to be there and I do what I can to support them since they helped make the event happen. That's why I associate it with goodwill as the primary benefit. It can also generate leads when you create a powerful sponsorship activation approach and strategy.

Sponsorship activation is what flips an awareness and goodwill effort into a viable lead generation platform. In general, you're going to want to invest two or three dollars for every dollar you allocated to the sponsorship fee itself. So if you spent $1,000 to be the sponsor, make sure you have another $2,000 to $3,000 on top of that to invest in activating that sponsorship.

Using my kid's T-Ball example, an activation of that sponsorship might be hosting a party for all the parents and families at the sponsor's restaurant so that everyone can taste the food, drive to the specific restaurant location and have the full meal experience. This is what leads to repeat business and future event parties being booked.

At one of the tradeshows I decided to sponsor, I staffed my booth with my strategy and creative teams and offered on-the-spot free breakthrough campaign strategies.

This was a highly engaging brainstorming session where the prospects brought in their most challenging problem, we asked a bunch of questions, brainstormed solutions and sketched out an initial marketing campaign that would solve the problem.

At scale, we helped one of our GPS clients become known at the Consumer Electronics Show (CES) by bucking the trend of even buying booth space, but instead offered free wrapped London Cab services all week because we knew how hard it was to hail a cab (or even catch an Uber) during the peak CES start and end times.

Sponsorship activation allows you to go way beyond what the conference organizer had envisioned. It allows you to show up powerfully and add massive value to the event or organization you choose to sponsor. Think of the sponsorship fee as the "opening bid" for what you really want to do and then double or triple the sponsorship fee to create a memorable experience that will lead to appointments on your calendar. As you consider the needs of your niche, tap your Sage Innovate power to "Yes, and ..." your way to a really fun and creative solution that will help you generate the leads you're looking to gather.

Radio & Internet Radio

Radio has gone though some significant changes over the last few decades. What hasn't changed is its attractiveness when it comes to delivering key messages to your target audience. When you're clear on which channels your niche tunes in and listens to, you have a platform for delivering your key messages and encouraging them to connect and engage with you. This could be another way to promote your newly designed lead magnet, an upcoming event or webinar, or as a means to directly generate appointments on your calendar.

As radio is a broadcast medium, the downside is that in addition to your ideal customer prospects, there a many people who are not your niche who may also choose to participate. That's why broadcast media such as radio can be powerful awareness generators as a means to provide air coverage while other more targeted direct response approaches are used to narrow the focus and optimize the success.

For example, Google and the Radio Advertising Bureau completed some research on the positive impact that terrestrial (traditional) radio advertising has on SEM (search engine marketing) campaigns. Among other findings, this study reported that "Radio generated an average of 29% lift in Google search activity."[49] And it makes logical sense. When you're listening to the radio and hear something compelling, your natural inclination is to look it up on Google to explore the new information or insights you have just heard.

---

[49] http://www.rab.com/secure/radiodrivessearch/rdsexecsummary.pdf

A combination of radio and SEM also allows you to track and measure the direct impact of your radio efforts – something that was previously difficult to do prior to the rise of the internet.

Internet radio stations go one step further with this trend as they can embed links directly from their ads to online campaigns. Many internet radio stations are driven by mobile apps which means they can track your engagement and responses to various offers thereby tailoring advertising to each individual listener. What this means to you is that you can reduce some of the wasted advertising dollars you experience in a more traditional broadcast campaign. By narrowing your target with internet radio campaigns, you can begin to apply your learning from other digital marketing efforts (such as your social media advertising efforts) to leverage what was once relegated to awareness generation campaigns only.

As stated previously, radio (and to a lesser extent internet radio) is a broadcast medium which works for scaling your coaching business as you look to generate even more appointments. Before venturing into radio, be sure you're clear on how best to attract your ideal customer prospects including a proven irresistible offer that you're confident will generate appointments because you've tested out the offer elsewhere and have achieved the desired results. Think of radio as a way to add fuel to your already successful campaigns rather than the place to begin testing and learning what works and what doesn't generate appointments.

Alexa, Siri & Voice Advertising

When Amazon launched Alexa, there were mix reviews ranging from, "this changes everything" to "I wouldn't be caught dead allowing an 'always on' spy device in my home." Similar to every other advancement in technology, there are those who resist the advancements (and erosion of privacy) and those who embrace the advantages (despite the erosion of privacy). Regardless of how you personally feel about an always on listening device in your home, Alexa has proven itself to be part of the next generation of shopping, listening and search.

What this means for your coaching business is that you can apply what you're learning to new and emerging mediums such as voice advertising. This is especially true when you begin to look for geographically local opportunities. By some estimates, more than half of US consumers have used voice search to find local businesses.[50] And this is likely to continue to rise as people ask Siri, Alexa and "Okay, Google" to help them find what they are looking for. As the coaching industry grows and expands, so too will the ways in which your niche seeks to find you.

---

[50] https://www.dbswebsite.com/services/voice-search/

If you're already investing in SEM and SEO, this is a natural extension of your efforts. You're simply optimizing for voice commands so that you can be found on smart devices – phones as well as voice activated devices such as those powered by Alexa and Google at home.

Direct Response Television (DRTV)

What, you say? Television? Your Saboteurs are likely messing with you as you read this section. Most coaches see the cost of television prohibitive and rarely give it a second thought. And yet, the right media strategy coupled with an established proven track record from other approaches outlined in this chapter could propel your coaching business to new heights.

This is precisely how Tony Robbins became a household name. Sure, he was doing well before diving into direct response television (DRTV), but most of his events were driven by word of mouth and limited advertising support. When Tony Robbins decided to use DRTV, he had developed his line of information products. He chose to work with outside investors who saw his potential and wanted to partner with him. The rest, as they say, is history. His audio programs took off and so did his event business with each one feeding the other. The more successful his information products became, the higher attendance his events had which, in turn, ended up with more of his information product selling on-site at the events. At his *Unleash the Power Within (UPW)* events, Tony Robbins shares that, collectively, his businesses are worth in excess of $5 billion dollars. Not bad for a coach whose business partner is reported to have stolen everything from him, forcing Tony Robbins to start over from scratch.

Stepping out of the coaching industry for a moment, perhaps you've heard of Proactiv. "Proactiv," also known as Proactiv Solution, is an American brand of skin-care products developed by two American dermatologists, Katie Rodan and Kathy A. Fields, and launched in 1995 by Guthy-Renker, a California-based direct marketing company, that features endorsement by famous celebrities ... As a result of its celebrity endorsements and infomercials, Proactiv is one of the most popular skincare brands of all time, according to the Journal of Clinical and Aesthetic Dermatology. Sales amounted to $800 million a year as of 2010, with a media budget of nearly $200 million and $12–15 million for celebrity fees."[51]

In talking with experts from the DRTV industry, I learned that Proactiv started with a $50,000 media budget. Now that may sound like a lot to you if you're just launching your coaching business or your business only produced $50,000 to $75,000 in revenue last year. But if I told you that a $50,000 investment would lead to more than $800 million a year in revenue, would I have your attention?

---

[51]   https://en.wikipedia.org/wiki/Proactiv

Just like the other traditional media vehicles, DRTV isn't for everyone. But unlike traditional brand advertising, DRTV focuses on a highly targeted niche and often a local geographical one. By focusing your television dollars and continuously testing along the way, you can determine just how effective your media investment dollars are against generating sales. True, DRTV is likely overkill for generating appointments on your calendar, but it could be quite an effective tool for launching your membership program, filling a local event, selling an information product, and building a core foundation into a much larger business venture. As you begin to scale your coaching business, you're going to see new opportunities to grow beyond individual one-to-one coaching, group coaching and masterminds. As you look to scale your business, you may need to make more strategic investments to ensure your long-term success.

DRTV can be a power tool as you look to scale. When working with experts in this field, you can build a customized go-to-market program that builds upon itself. In other words, the campaign becomes "self-funding." The more successful your program is, the more media dollars become available to reinvest. This is how a company like Proactiv can start with a $50,000 budget and ratchet it up to an $800 million-dollar annual revenue company.

Working with a Media Partner

In all of these avenues, when you begin to feel the need to invest thousands to tens of thousands of media dollars, it's best to look for a strategic media partner to work with. Back in its heyday, you would need hundreds of thousands to millions of dollars in media to attract a decent media partner. Today, there are so many solopreneurs out there that it doesn't take more than a few thousand dollars to attract the attention of a small media shop looking to bring on new clients.

Take your time here. Meet with a few and ask how their fee structures work. Some take a percentage of your media spend. Others work on a flat fee or monthly retainer. Nearly all media partners are now transparent with their fee structures, but before you engage them, be sure to have that part in writing. You don't want to find out that the dollars you thought were being invested in media were actually eroded by hidden fees.

A great media partner can save you all sorts of time navigating the everchanging landscape that is today's media. Despite how "simple" you believe your campaign is, a great media partner can help you invest wisely and minimize waste. They earn their spot on your team by advising you on the best avenues to accomplish your sales and marketing objectives.

Avoiding Overwhelm When Generating Appointments

If all of this feels like a lot, please engage self-empathy here. The point of this chapter is to show you just how abundant your choices are when it comes to generating leads. From a Sage discernment space, there is no need to take any action that doesn't excite you. If you feel like a kid in the candy store and want to dive into all of this, then wonderful. If you are feeling a bit intimidated by all the options, then please do your PQ Reps and tap into Sage Power Explore. You don't need to do more than one single path here.

Rather than experience overwhelm, consider that your ability to generate appointments is as abundant as the ocean. Remember, as Shirzad has shared with us, "You can't control the wind or the waves, but you can learn to surf." That's what this chapter is all about. Choosing the path that feels right for you to begin generating appointments for your coaching business. You need only select one path to start and start small. Like a child learning to ride her bike, be okay with falling down a number of times before you nail it. Rather than getting upset or feeling defeated, look to the gift of each challenge you uncover.

Perhaps you are driven by the gift of knowledge as you discover precisely what is needed to effectively generate appointments in your coaching business. Or perhaps you see each challenge as a gift of power as you strengthen your own Sage Powers through Empathy, Explore, Innovate, Navigate and Activate. Or perhaps you see the gift of inspiration so that each challenge you face inspires you to go bigger and connect with your own vision, mission and purpose in an even deeper way.

Whatever it is for you, remember that this is a *journey*, not a destination. Business development is here to help you develop your Sage Mastery and to self-actualize. All of your top Saboteurs will show up as you look to generate appointments on your calendar. Isn't that amazing? What better arena to develop and strengthen your PQ Muscles than in business development? Remember that as you grow your coaching business, you are also becoming a master in mental fitness. They feed off each other. Your Sage Mastery will bolster your coaching business, and growing your coaching business will strengthen your mental fitness mastery.

Tracking & Measurement: Trust and Verify

Peter Drucker is known for saying, "What gets measured, gets managed." What I love about that simple philosophy is that it underlines the idea that what you focus on tends to improve. If you were looking to drop 10 pounds of weight, stepping on the scale every morning would continue to give you feedback on how you're doing. It would also give you time to reflect each day on what's working, what's not working and what you might want to change in order to reach your desired outcome.

In the context of generating appointments, you want the same thing. While it doesn't matter which path you choose in order to generate appointments, you do want to track and measure the effectiveness of your actions. To keep this simple, you're looking to uncover how many actions you would need to take in order to generate a single appointment on your calendar. Each of the different options we've reviewed in this chapter may have very different outcomes based on what actions your taking and how much (or little) these actions resonate with your niche.

For example, let's say you believe that posting on LinkedIn will attract your niche to get an appointment on your calendar. You commit to posting every day for 30 days, and then see how many appointments that generates on your calendar. Your theory is that by the end of the month, you will have generated 10 appointments on your calendar. Assuming that you post only once a day, you are hypothesizing that Every three posts should generate one appointment on your calendar.

So you begin tracking the number of posts on LinkedIn. After the first three posts, you still don't have a single appointment on your calendar. Rather than give up, you continue through the first full week. At the end of the week, you celebrate that you've posted seven times as you promised to yourself, but haven't yet generated a single appointment. At this rate, you see that something needs to shift if you want to generate 10 appointments by the end of the month. You consider your options. Perhaps posting generally isn't as effective as reaching out individually. You do some research on using LinkedIn's search options effectively and begin to narrow your focus on your ideal customer prospects.

For the next seven days you continue posting generally, but now you've doubled your efforts by also posting individually to known ideal customer prospects. And it works! By the end of week two, you've posted 14 times on LinkedIn and another seven times individually directly to your ideal customer prospects. So, for week three, instead of posting general, you focus on 100% individual outreach efforts to see if that continues the momentum. And instead of two people a day, you decide to reach out to three people each day for a full seven days. YES! You just generated two more appointments this week. Let's see what that looks like in a very simple table. Here's what you have generated thus far:

	Posts on LinkedIn	Number of Appts	Notes / Feedback
Week One	7	0	General posts do not appear to be generating results. Will add individual outreaches.
Week Two	14	1	Individual outreaches more effective than general posts.
Week Three	21	2	Appears 10 individual outreaches produce one appointment on my calendar

Notice that there's no "perfect" way to track and measure your progress. You might notice your Judge, Stickler or other Saboteurs looking to chime in here with some negative commentary. Instead, invite your Sage to the conversation. What do you notice from this simple example? How might you use your Sage Explore and Innovate powers to generate other ways to track and measure your individual efforts?

Your Saboteurs will have a field day pointing out all the reasons why this isn't important, doesn't work, or how much more information you need to get started. That's how our Saboteurs hold us small and feeling stuck. Instead, I invite you to see the underlying value of tracking and measuring your activities while remaining curious. Invite your childhood self to be curious and fascinated by your efforts rather than your Judge to use this information to make you feel bad, wrong and generally like you're failing. You're not. And that's the lie of your Saboteurs. Tracking and measuring is about learning. Reframe the "failures" into experiments where you are seeking to learn. Therefore, the more "failures" the better. That means you're learning and growing rather than remaining stuck and frustrated.

What I trust your Sage can see here is that there's no "right" way to track and measure your progress. You need only set a target and track your daily progress against that target. If I can lean on the brilliance of BJ Fogg's book *Tiny Habits*, then I'll even urge you to begin with something far easier and simpler than you think is necessary to build and grow your coaching business. In his book, Fogg makes the point that we tend to over-index on motivation which comes and goes. To make a habit stick, we need to start tiny. I love his example of doing two push-ups every day or flossing a single tooth. It may sound silly, but something so ridiculously easy means there's no excuse not to do it every day.

When you're starting out, consider tracking the smallest action you can take that still moving your coaching business forward. Once you've seen you're able to stick to a daily habit, then you can begin to grow your habit from tiny to transformative.

Staying with the LinkedIn example, perhaps you don't know what to say exactly. Instead of doing nothing, perhaps you reach out to one of your ideal customer prospects and share vulnerably what you're up to. The gift of not having a well-crafted "pitch" is that you don't sound like you're using marketing automation and data tools to cast a wide net, instead, someone receives a heart-felt personal exchange that's hard to ignore.

You did your one outreach for the day. Now, CELEBRATE! If you just did that every day, by the end of the year, you'd have 365 outreaches. Assuming that it takes about 10 outreaches to generate one appointment, that's 37 appointments on your calendar and in the next chapter we'll share how to convert those appointments. On average, those 37 appointments will generate between three-four net new clients. And, in truth, that success will have you increasing your tiny habit well before the end of the year, so your probability of having more like 10 new clients is very high.

While you want to trust that you're doing the right efforts here to generate appointments, your ability to track and measure your efforts allows you to verify your progress. We tend to over-estimate what we can accomplish in a month and vastly under-estimate what we can accomplish in a year. When you track and measure your activities, you can see how each of your efforts leads to a sustainable long-term result in your coaching business.

Can't wait a year to generate those 10 clients? You don't have to. If you're a full-time coach and looking to scale your coaching practice, you're going to want to reach out to as many as 50 prospects *per day* so that you can generate as many as 10 discovery calls *per week* which will result in one client per week. We'll go over this in detail in the next chapter, but some coaches are looking for targets to hit. If that's you, then now you have it. By working backwards from securing a single coaching client, you can see how your efforts in reaching out to people will ultimately result in appointments generated on your calendar and new client wins.

More is not necessarily "better," but it does show you the lengths that some coaches are willing to go to in order to generate the clients they desire. Just be sure that's not an invitation to your Hyper-Achiever Saboteur. We know where that leads: negative emotions and burnout. Instead, start small and build your success as you go.

Establishing daily habits that you can commit to for the long-term is much more important than "overnight success." Sage discernment knows that sustainable efforts trump short-term bursts of activity. Think marathon runner, not sprinter. Sprinters require longer recovery times but as a marathon runner, you continue to build your momentum over time. Your coaching business is a marathon, not a sprint.

Now that you have ample ways to generate appointments on your calendar, let's go over how best to convert those appointments to clients in your coaching business. Afterall, as David Ogilvy of premier advertising agency, Ogilvy & Mather was famous for saying, "Nothing happens until the sale is made." For our purposes, we're enrolling, not selling, but the underlying principle holds true. To build and scale your coaching practice, you need paying clients. Let's figure that part out together.

CHAPTER EIGHT

Converting Appointments: The Art of the Close

ere it is. This is *the* moment. You did all that work of clearly defining your niche. You've gone deeper in identifying your ideal customer. You crafted your irresistible offer. And you discovered how to generate appointments with ease and flow. You've done all the heavy lifting to get to this moment and what happens? Yep, you guessed it. For most coaches, this is where they fall short and allow their Saboteurs to stop them from growing and scaling their coaching business. Logically, this should be the easy part. You demonstrate how awesome a coach you are and you give your prospective client an opportunity to hire you. That's Sage Business Development. But that's not how it usually goes down, is it?

In this chapter, we'll review the ten Saboteur hijacks and see if you can spot which ones you're most familiar with. Perhaps you'll find that there is a combination of Saboteurs who gang up on you to ensure you don't complete the final step in the business development process. Then we'll review each of the Sage powers you can use to ensure you enroll clients in ease and flow.

But before we get into all that, most coaches find it extremely helpful to have a plan when it comes to converting appointments. This isn't "science" in the sense that you have a precise formula that works every time. It's much more art in that you have some core principles that maximize your highest probability of success, and then you call upon your Sage to be fully present to whatever shows up after that. When you are truly in Sage, you will trust whatever shows up is exactly what is supposed to happen.

Remember, you can't control the winds or the waves of the ocean, but you can learn to surf. Each and every time you enroll a client, you get better. Not incrementally better, but exponentially better. That's because you continue to learn from each experience. Think of this chapter as a guide on "how to ride a bike." No matter how much I share with you, it's not the same as getting on the bike and wobbling and even falling down. The first few times you're going to fall – guaranteed. But then after a few falls you get the hang of it. Eventually, you find your balance and you learn from experience.

Then, even if you haven't been on a bike in more than a decade, if you suddenly needed to ride one, you know you have the skills to push off, pedal and glide with ease and flow. That is what you're working towards. If you give up after a few falls, you'll never want to get back on that bike. All you'll associated with it is pain and disappointment. But once you've found your balance and discover you're good at it, you'll want to ride more and more often; perhaps even enter a bike race or a triathlon.

It's the same with enrollment. Once you've enrolled about five or so clients, you'll realize you're actually pretty good at this enrollment stuff. Moreover, as your bank account begins to grow and your cash flow increases, you'll want to do more of it. In fact, when you have confidence that for every eight or nine "no's" you will receive one "yes," your attitude will change. You'll begin to *celebrate* each no you receive. First, because you are confident you still added massive value to this person's life. Second, you have most certainly learned something from the experience. And third because you know that each no is getting you one step closer to a yes. The more you practice your art, the more masterful you become.

You may already be well on your way to becoming a masterful coach. Now it's time to become a masterful enroller. As David Ogilvy liked to say, "Nothing happens until the sale is made." In other words, it doesn't matter how awesome a coach you are if you don't have clients. The world needs you to become a masterful enroller. In doing this, you can continue to practice and hone your coaching skills and deliver the incredible value your Sage knows you're capable of. So let's get to it, shall we?

Art of the Close

You are a *professional* coach. When it comes to enrollment, your Saboteurs are going to want to challenge you here and make you doubt yourself. We'll explore how each individual Saboteur gangs up on you to prevent you from successfully enrolling a client later in this chapter. For now, assume you've handled all of that. You are in total Sage mode.

As a professional coach, when it's time to talk about the business side of your coaching business, there are some important aspects to keep in mind. Specifically, the business side of your coaching business must be / feel:

- **Natural**: You're a professional and this is what you do. The conversation of engagement will either be brought up by you or the client. Otherwise, it's just talk.
- **Professional**: You are clear on what you receive (i.e. "how much") for the value you deliver (i.e. "for what") and over a specific length of time (i.e. "how long?")

- **Confident**: Because you've rehearsed this part several times, there's no hesitation, stumbling or wavering on your part. You're strong in your resolve.
- **Thoughtful**: You've already considered whether you think the person you're speaking to would benefit from your work and would be a good fit.
- **Direct**: There's no sense of "talking around" the subject of your offer. You choose to bring it up at the appropriate time, or you are ready to get into it when they want to talk about hiring you.

Notice that these are all Sage qualities. When you are in Sage, you are natural, professional, confident, thoughtful, direct and a whole lot of other positive qualities. It's your Saboteurs that stop you from being, well ... you! The best version of yourself isn't nervous because there's nothing to be nervous about. When you live in abundance, all you're doing is making your offer to a person who you've already identified as being in need of your services. What is there to fear? Any fear you experience here is generated from your Saboteurs and we'll take a look at each of them individually.

For now, I want you to continue to lean in and trust that you'll be your Sage self here. When you're nothing but Sage, you show up powerfully and your ideal customer prospects are naturally drawn to you – your Sage self – and want to engage you as their coach.

The ultimate expression of the Art of the Close, therefore, is your being in Sage as you transition from a powerful coaching session into a discussion about hiring you as their coach – all in ease and flow. While that may sound too good to be true, I'm going to show you how to do just that.

And, just like riding a bike, the first few times you do it will look *nothing* like what I describe. Why? Because you're most likely going to stumble and fall the first few times. So what? If you allow your Saboteurs to win here, you're doomed. All I ask is that you get back up, dust yourself off and try again. Even if you do this part ineloquently ten times, you're going to be ten times better than the first time you did it and chances are you'll enroll one client anyway.

The best part about this is that every enrollment call you have *after* your first dozen or so will be far superior to your first ones. So much so, that you'll likely have a good belly laugh at those first ineloquent attempts and rest assured that you've learned so much you'll never have to do *that* again. Whatever the mistakes, just keep going. You're learning so much more than you even realize. As long as you keep going, you will master the art of the close and it will support you for the rest of your life.

So here's what you'll want to do:

1. Bring the coaching session to a close.
2. Ask pre-frame questions to shift the focus.
3. Make your offer.

4. Remain "cathedral" silent.
5. Stick the landing.

We'll go over each of these in detail so you know precisely what should happen at the end of a discovery call so that you can enroll a client into your coaching practice. Then we'll see how your Saboteurs attempt to sabotage you in precisely the worst possible moments. And then we'll call upon each of your Sage powers to ensure that your Saboteurs are handled well in advance of your enrollment conversation.

One- Bring the Coaching Session to a Close

Before you begin an enrollment conversation, it's vital that you first bring your coaching session to a close. Whenever I start a discovery call, I share how we'll use the time allotted. I'm clear that I will leave about 15 minutes at the end of our session to get some feedback on the coaching session itself and then ask, "Does that sound okay with you?" I do that to get any objections out on the table before we even begin. I have yet to have a prospective client object to leaving time at the end of our session to discuss their experience and give me feedback.

When you take a few minutes at the start to share your intentions, there's no surprise when you bring the coaching session to a close in order to leave time to get feedback. For me that sounds something like any of the following:

- *With your permission, I'd like to close the coaching portion of our session in order to ask you a few questions about your experience.*
- *In the 15 minutes we have remaining, I'd like to close the coaching portion of our session in order to hear from you about your experience.*
- *Is this a good place to end the coaching portion of our session today? I'd like to leave some time to get your feedback.*

The words themselves are much less important than the intention you bring. You're a professional and this is how a discovery call goes. For most people, they've never had a discovery call before so you're modeling what it's like. In nearly every case, the person you're speaking with is already in deep gratitude for the support they received from you. While you could certainly spend another fifteen minutes or even an hour and fifteen minutes going deeper, that isn't what your prospective client truly needs. You want to give them an opportunity to process their experience and decide for themselves if they want to continue with you as their coach.

Once you have received permission from your prospective client to close the coaching session, you can proceed to the next step. Just be sure you receive a verbal "yes" or other verbal confirmation that you have permission to close the session and proceed to the next step. Without this part of the process, you don't have permission to proceed and the rest of this work will feel Saboteur driven instead of coming from your highest Sage self.

Two- Ask Pre-Frame Questions to Shift the Focus

Having just finished an incredible coaching session, you're now asking your prospective client to reflect on their experience. This gives them a chance to process what they just experienced before having them decide if they want more of it ... or not.

When it comes to the pre-frame questions, what you're looking to better understand is, money aside, would this potential client truly benefit from a relationship with you and your service? Is what you're offering likely to be worth the investment they would need to make in order to get it? The more context that connects directly to result they are looking to achieve, the more interested they become in the possibility of hiring you as their coach.

Ultimately, what you charge is of little importance if they are not already convinced that you are what they need in order to achieve what they want to accomplish / solve / grow into. This is why having a powerful coaching conversation is so vital to your success. When they have that "aha" moment, that clarity will help them experience the true value of coaching.

While you can certainly come up with your own pre-frame questions, I've found the following pre-frame questions to allow a prospective client enough time to consider what just happened, understand where they are in their journey and to think about whether they might want to hear more about hiring you.

- *What value did you get from today's coaching session?*
  - Alternatively: What did you like most about today's coaching session?
  - The key here is that you want your prospective client to tell *you* what value you they received. If they are struggling to come up with something, then chances are they don't feel they had a powerful coaching session and this in itself is valuable feedback. It means you have the opportunity to sharpen and refine your coaching skills so that the next time you coach someone, the answer to this question comes pouring out of them.

- *What clarity or awareness do you now have?*
  - The key to this question is that they are now seeing their problem and possible solution(s) in an entirely new light. (Hello, Explore power!) With deeper clarity and awareness, they now see what was previously in their blind spot. When they recognize that clarity and new awareness has been generated in your work together, they can begin to see what's been

missing previously. Remember, nothing is "wrong" with your prospective client. They just were blinded to something that they now see clearly. Only with new awareness can new actions be taken to solve the problem they were working on.

- *How will you move forward after our session today?*
  - o The key to this question is to help them recognize that a "one and done" won't be sufficient. It's not enough to "see" what was in their blind spot. Action is needed in order to make change happen. What actions are they truly committed to taking? Even if you already covered this in the coaching portion, it's best to see the building blocks from value to awareness / clarity to action. You're guiding your prospective client here to see they've previously been missing in life.

- *What accountability support do you have in place to ensure your continued forward momentum?*
  - o This question gets at the heart of commitment. Even if they previously declared an action they will take, without accountability they are most likely to return to their previous routines. Change is hard. Without having someone to support you and champion you towards that which you say you want in life, we all tend to return to our comfort zone – that space where our Saboteurs are most comfortable having us live out our life. There's no growth in it. Sage accountability (which we'll talk about in more detail later) is about holding your clients high and capable of having what they declare they want. Without accountability, it's not likely to happen.

- *Is coaching a form of support that would serve you?*
  - o And now we're getting to the heart of it. Regardless of what they answered in the previous question, you want them considering a coaching relationship – ANY coaching relationship. If they answer is, "no," then you're done. Thank them for their time, wish them luck and end the call. Seriously. Your job is *not* to convince them. If coaching is *not* a form of support that they see would serve them, then move on. Even if you work your magic and convince them otherwise, at best you'll have a flaky client who constantly reschedules, pays late (if at all) and isn't willing to do the work required between coaching sessions. However, if they answer in the affirmative (i.e. "yes") or even maybe (i.e. "perhaps" or "I think so"), then go to the next question.

- Would you like to hear about working with me?
  - Again, if the answer is no, you're done here for the same reasons as stated above. Thank them and end the session. Most people, however, are curious enough that they want to hear your offer. Only once you get a yes to this question should you proceed. When your prospective client answers in the affirmative to this question you are granted permission to make your offer.

Three- Make Your Offer

Having just received a "yes" to the question, "Would you like to hear about working with me?" It's time to shine, baby. What comes out of your mouth next needs to be clear. simple and to the point. Under no circumstances should you discuss the *how* of the coaching relationship. That is, if you ramble on with all the details of what you do, how you do it, the benefits, etc. then you've lost your prospective client. Less is more here. In as few as words as possible, make your offer.

Said another way, the way you land a conversation solidifies its value. If you're clearly nervous, rambling and unclear in your offer, you're sending an non-verbal message that you're not the right coach for your prospective client. That's why this is the *precise* moment when your Saboteurs will have a field day with you. If you haven't practiced in front of a mirror – out loud and at least 100 times – then chances are your Saboteurs will hijack you here.

Instead, we want to be 100% Sage (or as close to 100%) as we can be in this moment. I find that while I'm asking the pre-frame questions, I'm also doing my own PQ Reps. Yes, I'm listening to my prospective client *and* I'm activating my Sage. I know what's coming and rather than interpreting those sensations as "fear" I choose to experience them as "excitement" for the offer I'm about to make to this incredible human being.

I'm assuming that you're doing your part to be in Sage here and handle your Saboteurs as best you can. And remember, this is you riding your proverbial bike. No amount of preparation will replace actually delivering your offer out loud to a real prospective client who can hire you. Accept that your first dozen attempts will likely suck. Do them anyway. Each time you make your offer, you'll strengthen your resolve to keep going. You'll weaken the grip of whatever Saboteur has a hold on you and strengthen your Sage muscles. By the twelfth time you've done this (assuming it's within 30 to 60 days of the previous attempts) you'll be in great shape barely noticing your Saboteur interruptions. Instead, you'll be deep in your Sage brain and fully present to what your prospective client is experiencing in this moment. You'll know you're there when your focus is no longer on you and how ineloquent your offer sounds, but instead are focused on your prospective client and how they are receiving your offer.

Here's what you want to say in this moment:

"I receive [money] per month for [quantity] [# of minute] coaching sessions and I coach my clients for a minimum of [number] months."

"I receive $2,000 per month for two 45-minute coaching sessions and I coach my clients for a minimum of six months."

Then move to step four.

Before we do that, a couple of things point out. Notice I'm using 21 words. I'd love this to be less, but feel that this is the minimum I need to use in order to get my offer across. I have experimented with sharing a "$12,000 for a six month coaching engagement," but I have found that establishing a monthly payment process is optimal for getting a much longer than six month engagement.

Why six months? Because even if my client receives significant breakthroughs in the first two to three months, some clients need more time to truly experience the value of a coach. No matter what, I want my clients committed and I've found less than six months to be challenging to have my clients achieve the outcomes they are committed to having in their life.

Monthly payments also have the added benefit of not "ending" the coaching relationship prematurely. Take a page from all the "subscription" services you currently have: mobile phone, internet access, streaming services, car payments, house payments, etc. Once your client has adjusted to this monthly payment routine, continuing your work is much, much easier than having to renegotiate and re-enroll in six months' time. Instead, you give them the option to opt-out any time after the six months and most don't.

Are there other ways to make your offer? Sure thing, but for most coaches, simple is best. Deliver your minimum viable offer and then allow your prospective clients to decide what's best for them in this moment. The more you add to your offer, only complicates the message and ensure confusion rather than having them make their own buying decision.

Four- Remain "Cathedral" Silent

If you've travelled through Europe, chances are you've explored ancient cathedrals with all the grandeur and reverence available. When you walk inside, you might notice the stained glass, the high ceilings or any of the incredible feats of architecture in the building itself. In addition to all this beauty and extravagance, you probably also noticed the silence that surrounds the entire environment.

When you deliver your offer to a prospect, this is the experience you want to create immediately following your offer. I call this "cathedral" silence.

Your Saboteurs will want to add all the "how" and justify the investment that you just articulated. Don't allow your Saboteurs to ruin this sacred moment. Talking past the offer you just made would be the equivalent of playing bag pipes in the cathedral. Each sentence you utter after making your offer is just a distraction and stops your prospect from being able to think for themselves if they want to hire you or what they want to ask about next.

Please do yourself a favor and SHUT UP!

When I do my live workshops on the *Art of the Close* I demonstrate this technique over and over again. It doesn't matter how much I emphasize the point of remaining silent after making your offer- the majority of the demo participants fall into the trap of talking right past their offer. It's human nature to want to justify and explain away your offer. It's also ineffective.

Your Sage knows that once you make a clear and concise offer, the best thing you can do is remain cathedral silent until your prospect responds. This will feel like an eternity, but usually lasts only a minute or two. As your discomfort builds, know that your discomfort is the price you pay to give your prospect space to make the best decision for them.

After that long period of silence, your prospect will either be a "yes", "no" or more often a "maybe with questions." This is how you finish strong and stick the landing. Regardless of the final outcome, you are a professional coach in Sage ease and flow. When you detach from the decision of your prospect, you remain in service to ensure they get what they truly need – even if that's not what you may want for yourself and your coaching business.

Five- Stick the Landing

No matter if you're just starting out as a coach or you've been coaching for more years than you care to admit, when you're having an enrollment call, you want to stick the landing. What that means is that no matter what the outcome, your prospect feels great about how the call ended and was glad they choose to spend time with you. Since there are three ways this call can go, we'll explore all three of them and ensure you're prepared to stick the landing of your enrollment call regardless of which way it goes.

If they say, "Yes," "Let's Go For it," or any variation that is clearly a positive affirmation and commitment, be sure to make it about them (not you). Celebrate their decision to take themselves on, but under no circumstances do you share your experience of what just happened from your perspective. There will be time to share that with your own coach and accountability buddies later. For now, you're celebrating their decision by congratulating them and acknowledging their decision. From there, you will share the next steps such as:

- Setting up the regular coaching schedule
- Sending out a recurring calendar invitation
- Confirming method of payment and frequency (i.e. automatic credit card processing)
- Sharing by when you'll send them the coaching agreement
- Any pre-work you'd like them to complete before your next coaching session

You're a professional coach, so you're prepared to share the coaching agreement and related engagement materials necessary in order to solidify the verbal "yes." Statistically, you can expect to receive a yes approximately one out of ten enrollment calls. This is an average, so you may get your first yes the third enrollment session you have or the fifteenth. On average, if you do ten enrollment calls, one will say yes. That means the other nine or "no" or "maybe."

When you receive your "no," remember they are not rejecting *you* (despite what your Saboteurs would have you believe). Rather than becoming defensive, be grateful, compassionate and curious. Specifically:

- Thank them for having such clarity in their decision making
- Acknowledge them for the work they did in today's discovery call
- Assuming you're in Sage, inquire if there's anyone who they know would benefit from a session you just had together (i.e. ask for a referral)
- Let them know that if they ever change their mind and would like to engage you as their coach, you'd love the opportunity to coach them

This is perhaps the most difficult part of any enrollment call as you will receive so many more "nos" than "yeses." If you allow your Saboteurs to take each "no" personally, you'll quit coaching or limp along for years rather than building a thriving coaching practice that creates financial freedom for you and your family. When you allow your Sage to see clearly that this is not a personal rejection, but rather a snapshot in time, you will reframe a "no" to a "no for now" and trust that you've planted a seed that will eventually bear fruit down the road.

Each "no" gets you one enrollment call closer to a "yes." Ideally, your Sage would have you remain in child-like wonder and excited for each "no." Seriously. When you can playfully connect with each "no" as a step *forward* to your financial freedom, you'l actively seek out these "nos" rather than feeling rejected by them. That's the critical difference between coaches in Sage who thrive and coaches driven by their Saboteurs who struggle.

Often, you won't get a clear "yes" or "no," but rather a "maybe" equivalent that might sound like any of the following:

- I don't know.
- Let me think about it and get back to you.
- I need to ask my spouse.
- I never make any decisions on the fly, I'll need to process further.
- I could see how that might help me down the road.

What you absolutely do NOT want to do is spend your time chasing maybes. A "maybe" is so much worse than a "no." The best way to handle a maybe is to simply turn it into a no right there on the spot. In *The Prosperous Coach*, Rich Litvin said it best when he shared his response to maybes:

> *"Basically, unless this is an absolute yes for you, let's leave today being totally clear that it's a no. That way if the desire begins to build in you to be coached you can come back to me. But only when you are ready."*[52]

Brilliant! With a statement like this, you're leaving the possibility open for a future engagement and letting go of any follow-up. Notice what Saboteurs show up with this approach. Remember, your Saboteurs live in scarcity and your Sage lives in abundance. Or, as Confucius said, "The man who chases two rabbits catches none."[53] If your prospect isn't ready to say "yes" to hiring you as their coach, then the best thing you can do for *both* of you is to thank them for their time and move on.

Turning a "maybe" into a "no" does two things for your prospect. First, it lets them off the hook. If they are feeling any guilt or shame about not hiring you, you just gave them a perfect opportunity to release any of that Saboteur negativity. Second, if they really do want to hire you as a coach, removing this option will have them fight for it. In other words, rather than you wasting your time chasing a "maybe," upon losing the option to hire you their Sage speaks up and asks for what they truly want – support from you as their coach.

---

[52] Chandler, Steve and Litvin, Rich. *The Prosperous Coach: Increase income and impact for you and your clients*. Maurice Bassett. ©2013, page 85.

[53] https://www.goodreads.com/quotes/8688305-the-man-who-chases-two-rabbits-catches-neither

Either way, you both win. Your prospect has one less thing to think about and you don't have to chase someone who isn't ready to hire you as their coach. Now, before we exist this space, it's really important to get ahead of your Saboteurs as they will most certainly be hyper-active during your enrollment efforts. In the next section, we'll break down what each Saboteur will do in order to trip you up and attempt to prevent you from growing your coaching business. Then, we'll look at how each Sage Power will ensure your ability to overcome these Saboteurs and ensure you remain in Sage throughout the enrollment process.

Judge Alternative Path: Judgment of Self, Your Prospect and/or Their Circumstances

As we know, your Judge is the master Saboteur; the one who invites all the accomplice Saboteurs to the party. There are three flavors of how your Judge stops you from Sage Business Development in precisely the wrong moment. By unpacking each of them, we can weaken the power of your Judge and anticipate the very patterns that prevent you from enrolling clients into your coaching practice.

Judgment of Self

Imagine this. You've just spent a good 30 to 45 minutes having a powerful coaching session with a prospective client. Your discovery call couldn't have gone better. This prospect is on fire having all kinds of insights and breakthroughs. You can feel the door open to a future relationship with this prospect. They are, after all, your ideal customer and you've served them powerfully. Just as you begin to start down the path of enrollment, your Judge begins loudly taking over your thoughts. It sounds something like this:

- *Who do you think you are?*
- *You are only a few months out of being certified! You're not ready!*
- *Do you really think you're ready to be this person's coach? And have them pay you?*
- *You're going to charge HOW MUCH??? [Hysterical Laughter] What makes you think you have the right to charge that much money? Be prepared to be laughed at.*
- *If you think just because you had a good session this person is going to shell out that much money to hire you as their coach, you're an idiot.*

And of course, your Judge may use more expletives, be louder or softer in your head. While everyone's Judge sounds different and unique to them, you get the essence of the communication. You're not _____ enough. Your Judge fills in that blank with your deepest fear. You're not good enough. You're not experienced enough.

You're not worth that much. You're not ready for this. And that list only scratches the surface. Let's face it, your Judge is ruthless. Ironically, your Judge was created to "keep you safe" and yet you know you're capable of so much more than your current circumstances. But it doesn't stop there does it? This would be bad enough on its own, but oh no, your Judge is prepared to absolutely convince you that what you're about to do is a terrible idea and comes with insurmountable risk.

Judgment of Your Prospect

Even if you're able to overcome all the seeds of doubt your Judge has planted on you, the next tactic is to attack your prospect directly. Your Judge has a laundry list of all the reasons your prospect is not, in fact, your ideal customer. Remember that the power of your Judge is their ability to find a kernel of truth and then build their lies on that kernel. If you could clearly see their lies, you'd never believe them. But see if can spot how your Judge judges your prospect as a means to discourage your enrollment into your coaching practice.

- *This prospect can't afford you. There's no scenario in which (s)he agrees to hire you.*
- *Even if this prospect says yes, you know that's the last thing you'll ever hear from them.*
- *You've been ghosted before. Is this what you want?*
- *You had such a great session with them, don't ruin it by asking them to hire you.*
- *When will you ever learn? Everyone will take a free hour or two of your time, but no one will invest in your coaching beyond your free session. Take the win and let it go!*

There your Judge goes putting its hand in your prospect's pocket. Your Judge does it's best to convince you that they are the wrong prospect. Or that this prospect can't afford you. Or that even if the prospect says yes, they will change their mind and you'll never hear from them again. Why are these arguments so convincing? Because chances are you've had one or all of them happen to you before. Yes, it's true that *some* prospects fit this description. But by pre-judging every prospect, you're significantly decreasing your effectiveness at enrollment. And yet, it doesn't stop there, does it? Indeed, your Judge has even more in store for you.

Judgment of Circumstances

Here's where your Judge really has a field day. Even if you are able to get past their Judgment of you and your prospect, the Judge is ready with their alternative: an infinite number of circumstances that would prevent this particular prospect on this particular day from hiring you. It might look something like this.

- *Weren't you listening? You were JUST told this person lost their job. They have no income. How can they afford to hire you as their coach? It's not going to happen!*
- *What kind of monster are you? She just told you she's about to get divorced and her deepest fear is running out of money. Why would you ask her to pay you anything?*
- *Are you crazy? There's no way someone who has just had their business partner run off with all their profits is looking to invest in you or anyone else. Don't go there!*
- *Haven't you been paying attention to the news? We're in a bear market. That means the economy is currently down! No one invests in coaching in a down market.*
- *The housing market is tanking … again! No one in their right mind would invest in coaching when the real-estate market is going belly up. Try again in six months.*
- *In case you haven't noticed, it's an election year. There is great uncertainty right now and the political climate is more extreme than it has ever been. How can someone invest in coaching without knowing who will be elected?*

And, of course, we're only scratching the surface here. Any circumstance can be used by your Judge to create an argument for not enrolling clients … ever. That's the game of your Judge. Your limbic system was established to keep you safe. You're safe now, so whatever you were previously doing must be working. Your brain, therefore, doesn't want you to change. Not now. Not ever. Any possible circumstance that could stop you from your current survival trajectory is getting in the way and must be stopped (according to your over-protective Judge).

And this is only your Judge! Now pile on what each accomplice saboteur has to share and is it any wonder why most coaches fall apart at precisely the wrong moment in their efforts to enroll clients into their coaching practice?

What Your Accomplice Saboteurs Have to Say About Enrolling Clients

Take a moment to see which voices you hear clearly when enrolling clients. Despite having completed the Saboteur Assessment (PositiveIntelligence.com/assessment), don't be surprised if an accomplice saboteur that's relatively "low" on your list shows up with gusto when attempting to enroll a client. It's the relatively dormant ones that often show up and blindside you in precisely the worst possible moments.

Avoider

Your Avoider looks to focus on the positive and pleasant in an extreme way. This means avoiding difficult and unpleasant tasks and conflicts. For someone who doesn't regularly enroll clients into their coaching practice, the Art of the Close is considered difficult and unpleasant. How that shows up is right at the moment when you're planning on talking about your coaching practice and deliver your offer, your Avoider kicks in as an effort to shut you down before you generate potential conflict. It might look like any of the following:

- *Silence.* Your mind goes completely blank. It's as if your brain was suddenly unplugged and you are left with nothing. Each second the passes, you feel more and more embarrassed and that only deepens your feeling of being lost and without words.
- *Fear.* Suddenly a wave of fear rises up inside of you. While you can't put your finger on it, you sense extreme danger proceeding as planned.
- *Anxiety.* You become aware of how anxious you're feeling. This subject of enrollment has you fidgeting and feeling off-balance.
- *Nervous.* Having just had a powerful discovery call, you notice how nervous you are feeling about an enrollment discussion.

All of these uncomfortable feelings are your Avoider quietly, but persistently convincing you to stop and not proceed as planned. Unlike your Judge and other Accomplice Saboteurs, your Avoider often remains hidden in the shadows. Rather than being overt about telling you what not to do, negative feelings like fear, anxiety and nervousness land like a tidal wave crashing over you. When you go blank, it's often in reaction to the feeling of being short circuited by your own brain. This is the "freeze" experience in the "Fight, Flight, or Freeze" response.

You can experience this much like a deer in the headlights. Intellectually, you know what you're supposed to do next, but you experience a paralysis that has you feel stuck in an extreme way. The more you desire to "get over it," the stronger the feeling remains. In other words, fighting the feeling generally doesn't work. Instead, fighting the feeling gives it more power and has you feeling even more powerless. Only through deep breathing, PQ Reps, and any of the methodologies to drop back into your body can you let go of these feelings and recover. We'll dive into this as we explore the Sage Alternative in the next section.

Controller

When your Controller experiences anxiety, this triggers the need to take charge and control the situation, including other people's actions. Your Controller is actually quite good at bending people to your will. This may even lead to a temporary agreement for your ideal customer prospect to hire you as their coach. But then you never hear from them again. Your prospect essentially ghosts you.

If you are experiencing receiving a yes, only to find out the person who said yes no longer wants to take the next action, chances are your Controller is sabotaging your enrollments. At the point of offering your coaching services, you might hear things inside your mind like:

- *If I don't force this person to make a decision, we'll never make the sale.*
- *Here we go again! I've just delivered a powerful coaching session and (s)he's waffling. Why can't anyone just make up their minds?*
- *I better not leave too much time to think of excuses and reasons not to hire me. I should just go for it and convert this prospect into a client.*
- *Time to make it happen. My family is depending on me to get this client. Here goes!*
- *I am the master of my domain. Time to make it rain.*
- *I can see (s)he just needs a push to hire me. Otherwise, we're just talking. Let's do this!*

The result is predictable. The pressure of your Controller is not welcomed. Your prospects shame and guilt for taking up your time kicks in and they end up verbally agreeing to keep going. As soon as they are out of the meeting with you, they regret saying yes. Rather than facing their own fears and telling you bluntly, they'd rather not put themselves in the position of being manipulated again, so they disengage. You're left wondering why so many of your prospects are flaky and unreliable.

Rather than looking inward to your own Sage discernment, the tendency is to allow your Controller to have the last word. "See, they weren't ready. I dodged a bullet there. If they don't have the common decency to say no to my face, who needs them?" This is your Controller's knee jerk response in an effort to maintain control of the situation … even when it's clear that your ideal client isn't interested in hiring you. Your Controller blinds you to the truth of the self-inflected sabotage that's at the root of the problem of your enrollment. Only through Sage discernment will you be able to see what's really going on.

Hyper-Achiever

Your Hyper-Achiever is dependent on constant performance and achievement for self-respect and self-validation. The near obsession with external success leads to unsustainable workaholic tendencies and loss of touch with deeper emotional and relationship needs. This shows up in a few different flavors when it comes to enrollment. First, your Hyper-Achiever will exert unsustainable pressure on you to perform. If you're not generating the number of clients that you'd like, the only answer your Hyper-Achiever can accept is that you're not working hard enough. So "do more" becomes the constant mantra and that leads to burnout.

On individual enrollment calls, your ideal customer prospects begin to feel like objects rather than human beings. No one wants to feel like a stepping stone in someone else's journey. And yet, that's exactly how your Hyper-Achiever makes them feel. By obsessing over the performance of successful enrollment, you miss out on authentically connecting with the very person you are committed to supporting as their coach. At the point of offering your coaching services, you might hear things inside your mind like:

- *Don't screw this up!*
- *What's the best way to win in this sales game?*
- *Now is my time to convince them to hire me. Better turn it up so that I can convert this prospect into a client.*
- *This is a no brainer decision. After what we just discussed, (s)he would be an idiot not to hire me.*
- *If it's to be, it's up to me.*
- *I've suffered enough losses already, I'm overdue for a sale. This one is MINE!*

All the time that your Hyper-Achiever is focused on "the win," you are no longer being present to the actual needs of your ideal customer prospect. In essence, the coach has left the building and what's left is your Hyper-Achiever doing everything in its power to close the sale. This could lead to high-pressure sales tactics, pressure to make a decision, or simply ignoring the needs of the person you're engaging with in order to convert the sale. By having your Hyper-Achiever focus on the performance aspects, you are, in essence, performing, not coaching.

Your Sage self is pushed deep down inside of you as your Hyper-Achiever does everything in its power to achieve, win and be the best. The person you are speaking with no longer feels valued or appreciated and whatever trust was built during the coaching session is replaced with feelings of judgment and concern about the shift that just occurred. Even if the prospect agrees to hire you, there is an intrinsic feeling that something is "off." This leads to a shaky foundation as you kick-off your work together and can even lead to your clients having buyer's remorse from saying yes to you in the first place.

Hyper-Rationale

Your Hyper-Rationale can have you be perceived as cold, distant and intellectually arrogant. None of these traits will support your enrollment conversations. Your

Hyper-Rationale's intense and exclusive focus on the rational processing of everything will also have you miss the emotional cues that are important in successful enrollment into your coaching business.

When your Hyper-Rationale is at the forefront, the feelings of your ideal customer prospect are disregarded and seen as irrelevant. It will have you over-calibrate on knowledge, data and insights. This leads to surfacing other aspects of the coaching call as "evidence" that your ideal customer prospect "needs" to hire you as their coach. Rather than being keenly interested in how they are feeling, your Hyper-Rationale is only considering the rationale behind being hired or not being hired. At the point of offering your coaching services, you might hear things inside your mind like:

- *Obviously, (s)he needs to hire me as their coach. I just need to help them see that fact.*
- *Can't (s)he see it? Without coaching, they are doomed to repeat the same endless cycle of mistakes and regrets.*
- *Logically speaking, this is the only choice. I've made it clear the value I create.*
- *If this person says no, it's their loss. Clearly, they need me and I've demonstrated how I can help them. If they don't say yes, it just further proves my point.*
- *What's there to think about? It's so aggravating when someone asks for time to consider my offer. How do they not just know?*

The result of your Hyper-Rationale driving your enrollment conversations is that you miss out on all the emotions that come with any buying decision. Human beings buy on emotion and backfill with logic. By not understanding just how emotional a buying decision is, your Hyper-Rationale is blind to the most important cues associated with making such an important decision – the emotional ones. Logic comes *after* the decision to buy has been made, not before. Not understanding or skipping this part of the enrollment leads to predictable difficulty in meeting your ideal customer prospects in their authentic experience; one that's raw and real.

Hyper-Vigilant

Your Hyper-Vigilant can never rest. You'll notice intense anxiety about all the "dangers" of enrolling clients into your coaching business. Your Hyper-Vigilant is adamant that so much could go wrong in an enrollment call, why even bother? At the point of offering your coaching services, you might hear things inside your mind like:

- *You're not ready! Even if they say "Yes" it will be a disaster. Best not to proceed.*
- *What if (s)he laughs at you when you share what you receive? That would be devastating. It's not worth the risk!*

- *Were you listening at all to that coaching session? (S)he is traumatized. You're not a trauma expert. Don't even think of offering your coaching services. You'll get sued.*
- *Liability alert! Having this client is nothing but a liability. No matter how hard you work, they will ultimately be upset, unsatisfied and bad mouth you.*
- *Think of your reputation. What if things go off the rails and they disparage you? Your reputation is so much more important than adding another client to your roster.*
- *There is so much that could go wrong. You need a lot more practice, guidance, mentorship and support before you should even consider bringing a client on.*

Do you hear the red thread through all of this noise? While there are tiny kernels of possible outcomes, they are not probable. It's the same thing as winning the lottery. Is it possible? Yes. Is it *probable*? No. Fear lives in the shadows. When you shine a bright light on any individual fear, it dissipates. Any individual fear can't stand up and survive a good hard look at what's probable. Is there risk? Always. But can you mitigate the risk? Of course.

In the United States, anyone can sue anyone for any reason. It's absurd. Often these frivolous law suits are tossed out in the very early stages. In most cases the threat of a lawsuit is enough to get someone who's "out of bounds" to correct course. But unless you are egregiously and maliciously mistreating your clients, the probability of you ever getting into a lawsuit is extremely low. And, as a coach, you can mitigate this extremely low probability by carrying business insurance.[54]

There are inherent risks in life. Vigilance is good. Your Hyper-Vigilant Saboteur will stop you from taking any risk at all. You'll end up "freezing" at precisely the wrong moment. Or you'll decide taking on clients is not worth the risks, so you won't. If you feel your Hyper-Vigilant showing up in your enrollment conversations, then do your PQ Reps as you close out your discovery call and begin the process of enrollment.

Pleaser

Your Pleaser is an interesting one. During an enrollment call, your Pleaser indirectly tries to gain acceptance and affection by helping, pleasing rescuing or flattering. This blinds you to your own needs and leads to resentment as a result.

During your coaching session, your Pleaser will have you elevate the needs of your ideal customer prospect over your own. This may have you not offer your coaching services at all. Or, it might have you offer them in such a way as to not be understood that an offer is being made. According to your Pleaser, expressing your own needs

---

[54] ICF members qualify for coaching insurance. See https://coachingfederation.org/partners

directly feels selfish, so you end up obscuring your offer in such a way that it can't be understood by your ideal customer prospect. At the point of offering your coaching services, you might hear things inside your mind like:

- *Look at the incredible trust we've created on our call today. It would be rude/ wrong/tactless to enroll this person now. I can't do this to them.*
- *Rather than offer up my coaching services, perhaps the best thing to do is schedule another call. That way we can go even deeper and they are sure to hire me.*
- *This person really needs me, but probably can't afford me. I'll offer up my services for free. It's the right thing to do in this situation.*
- *It would be so selfish for me to ask for money at this stage. I'm not a selfish person.*
- *If I don't take care of this person, who will? Of course they can't afford me. I shouldn't even create an awkward request. That would be rude and put them on the spot.*
- *Why don't they just hire me? Clearly, they had a great session with me. Can't they see the value I bring? Why do I have to be the one to make an offer?*

Notice how putting your prospects needs above your own actually does the opposite. That is, by intending to serve your ideal customer prospect at the highest level, you end up doing them a disservice by not making it clear how to hire you and for how much. By obscuring, minimizing or neglecting to even present your offering, they won't be empowered to make the best decision for themselves and likely won't hire you. In an effort to please them, your Pleaser inadvertently denies them the opportunity to hire you. That leads to your ideal customer prospect not benefiting from your gift and adding a much more difficult time for you to grow and expand your coaching business.

Restless

One of the biggest risks of your Restless Saboteur showing up its impatience with what is happening in the moment. Your Restless will have you begin thinking about "what's next" even before the deal is done. That's extremely dangerous because you're no longer present to what's happening in real time with your ideal client prospect. By thinking about how much time you need to send the contract, what form of payment they might choose, or a myriad of other possible "next steps," you miss out on the subtle cues given as to where your prospect is in their buyer's journey.

Your Restless will have you constantly in search of greater excitement in the net activity or constant business. By not being at peace with the enrollment process you'll most certainly miss important information along the way thereby reducing your chance of enrolling a client. At the point of offering your coaching services, you might hear things inside your mind like:

- *What's next on my calendar?*
- *After this enrollment call, I wonder if I should …*
- *I think I just heard my phone alert me to a new message, I wonder who's messaging me?*
- *What a beautiful day outside today. I wonder if I should get some exercise afterwards?*
- *I wonder what I'll have for dinner tonight? I'm craving sushi, but haven't had tacos in a while.*
- *I think this person has a dog. I keep hearing a dog barking in the background.*

And, of course, there are so many flavors of questions, comments and distractions surfaced by your Restless. Why? Because having an enrollment conversation can be uncomfortable. Rather than staying with the discomfort, the Restless looks for "pleasant" distractions to take your mind off what's happening and instead think about something more pleasurable. It could be something happening in the future, or something else that's going on in the background that your Restless decides to pull forward.

None of this helps you remain present to what's happening in your enrollment conversation. This, in turn, makes it so much harder to listen deeply, be present and have the best possible success. If you notice your mind wandering, the best thing you can do is refocus your attention to the present moment. This can be any form of PQ Reps of your choosing – visual, audible, kinesthetic, breath, or whatever drops you right back into the present moment. If you know this is a pattern (based on previous efforts), begin doing those PQ reps early and often so that you remain in Sage.

Stickler

One of the unique characteristics of your Stickler Saboteur is that it can be activated at the very beginning of the discovery session. If, for example, your ideal customer prospect is even one or two minutes late, your Stickler is already acting up. Because your Stickler is highly critical of yourself and others, you may notice a game of mental ping pong going on between self-criticism and criticism of your prospect. Throughout your discovery session, you might hear things inside your mind like:

- *Did I just say that? What an idiot! I'm so stupid!*
- *What is this half-ass amateur hour?*
- *Who does (s)he think (s)he is, anyway?*

- *No wonder (s)he has all these problems. A five-year old could see what the problems are.*
- *Damn it! I didn't hear what was just said. How can I be an awesome coach if I still keep missing important details? I'll never get this right.*
- *Ahhhh! I'm so FRUSTRATED right now I could scream!*

If your Stickler is particularly judgmental of your prospect, they will feel like a failure not living up to an impossible standard and won't want to spend any more time than they have to with you. Despite how great a coach you may be, your prospect won't be able to get past the ridiculous standard your Stickler holds for them (and for you), which leads to the reason most prospects choose not to hire you when you're in Stickler mode. It's simply uncomfortable and exhausting to try and remain at a perfectionist standard. Most people won't want to continue in this kind of pressure-cooker environment. They will do whatever they must to gracefully get out of the session and avoid you like the plague. No one wants to feel that way.

Victim

When your Victim shows up in a discovery session, you will notice your Victim attempts to turn the conversation to make it about you. Your own emotions and temperament will show up as a means to gain attention and pity. You might even find yourself in dramatic flares or breaking down on your discovery call as your Victim's repressed rage is triggered. Your Victim gets attention by having emotional problems or being temperamental and sullen.

While there should be not space for any of this in a discovery session, your Victim doesn't care when and where to have emotional outbursts. In fact, the more "inappropriate" the better as a means to gain attention and pity. As unhealthy as this attention is, your Victim lies to you in order to convince you that any attention is good. At the point of offering your coaching services, you might hear things inside your mind like:

- *Here we go again! I'm going to make my offer and get rejected ... again!*
- *I must be Sisyphus destined to roll my boulder up this hill of rejection.*
- *If (s)he rejects me after the coaching session we just had, I'm going to LOSE IT!*
- *Keep it together, you can do this. Afterall, it's your lot in life to get rejected. You should be used it by now.*
- *I can't get a break! No matter what I do, how hard I try, I just can't win. WTF?*
- *How is it I'm the only coach who can't get clients? It's so not fair! I'm jinxed*

All the time your Victim is having a pity party in your head, you're missing the opportunity to focus on your ideal customer prospect. Once again, your Victim has made the enrollment process about you rather than about the person it should be about ... your prospect. This perspective of "I'll never be successful" becomes a self-fulfilling prophecy. The more you focus on how unsuccessful you are, the more you ensure your losing streak will continue. Or, as Henry Ford used to say, "If you think you can, or you think you can't, you're right."

Only once you shift your Victim's "poor me" perspective can you truly hear what's going on for your prospect and how you may support them in their journey. The moment you stop focusing on your own needs is the moment you become fully present with the opportunity in front of you. This is the work of your Sage as you shift from your Victim Saboteur.

The Sage Alternative to Enrolling Clients

Your best shot at enrolling a client is when you remain in Sage no matter what. It's helpful to think in terms of Improv here. By accepting whatever premise your client shares with you, you are able to remain fully present to what is offered and "dance in the moment" with your prospect. That is, rather than experience the need to justify yourself, your coaching offering, or anything else, just be fully present with your prospective client.

How? Through PQ Reps, of course. Right before you begin the enrollment process, make sure you, yourself, are in Sage. Better yet, no matter how Sage you believe you are, begin doing PQ Reps as you bring the coaching portion of the call to a close and begin the enrollment portion.

Saboteur Intercept

The most important thing you can do to increase your odds of enrolling a client is to be in Sage. That's it. No amount of process, research or even practice can take the place of being fully present in your Sage. Intercepting your own Saboteurs will allow you to be fully present with your prospective client and notice more than their words. In Sage, you'll hear the nuance in their tone of voice, inflections and body language. Instead of making up stories of what's going on with your prospect, you'll be actively present and listening for what is needed in the moment.

Remember the Sage contagion effect? Being in Sage will also have the positive impact of enrolling your prospect into their Sage. Even when your prospect's Saboteurs emerge, your ability to intercept your own Saboteurs will ensure the two of you don't engage in a Saboteur dance. For example, when you give your offer, the knee jerk response from your prospect might feel like a judgment. If you were to take that personally, you'd miss the opportunity to be curious with empathy and explore what's really going on for your prospect. Alternatively, by remaining in Sage, you'd side-step the Saboteur trap and instead uncover deeper insights from your prospect – ones that would either help you turn a "no" into a "yes" or lead to more powerful enrollment calls in the future.

Saboteur Intercept ensures that your prospect has a powerful coaching session with you even during the enrollment portion of your time together. By not allowing yourself to become hijacked, you increase your odds of having a future opportunity with this prospect and possibly a receive a referral. Afterall, by not exerting pressure to buy from you, your prospect will feel free to share their experience with others in their network and these referrals have a much greater chance of turning into clients.

There are many reasons you'll want to intercept your Saboteurs in these discovery calls, but perhaps the most important one is to deepen your own Sage Mastery and continue your path towards self-actualization. With every interception, you weaken your Saboteurs and strengthen your Sage powers. As you regularly take this action, you are increasing and strengthening your neuro-pathways. In other words, the most challenging aspects of enrolling clients isn't just helping you become financially free, it's also helping you to become the best version of yourself. How cool is that?

How Empathy Helps You Enroll Clients

In addition to doing your PQ Reps, another way to remain in Sage is to increase your compassion for your prospect. When you can see your prospects as the five-year-old version of themselves, you can't help but love them holistically. Your empathy grows as you see the perfectly imperfect human being in front of you. You realize that everyone of us is doing our best. We are all seeking growth and desire fulfillment. Having true empathy for the struggle that your ideal customer prospect is experiencing will help you authentically connect with their Sage. You can't fake this part and your prospect knows it. That's why when they experience you in your Sage with genuine empathy towards them, they tend to drop their façade and get real with you. Remaining in empathy will illuminate the best path forward.

Having empathy for yourself will allow you to see the incredible value you are delivering to the person in front of you (instead of beating yourself up for not being perfect). As you grow your self-empathy, you will tune out the negative self-talk of your Saboteurs and see how you are living your mission and purpose as you support those who need you most. And this truth will help you experience empathy for the enrollment itself.

Empathy for situations like your enrollment call allows you to see just how necessary they are. Nobody wants to be "sold", but individuals like to buy. Enrollment is about allowing your ideal customer prospects to opt-in to your services. You're not forcing anyone to buy something they don't need. Rather, you're offering up your services to support your niche in their self-development. As you connect to this purpose, it's easy to have empathy for the enrollment process itself and the value that it brings not only to you but also your prospect.

See how all of this helps you maximize your odds of successfully enrolling a client? Empathy can be a powerful ally in your efforts to enroll clients. It keeps you authentic and vulnerable. You are now open to receive the opportunities your prospective clients would like to give you.

Using Explore Power to Enroll Clients

From a place of empathy, you remain in your Sage and it's much harder for your Saboteurs to hijack you. This is important when you choose to invoke your Explore power during your enrollment call. Rather than taking personally the decision not to hire you as their coach, your Explore power allows you to remain curious and open to a possibility you might otherwise have missed. Rather than feeling judged or experience being rejected, your Explore power allows you to remain curious as to what's driving the decision. When you detach from your own desired outcome to be hired, you create the space to truly explore what's driving your prospect's decision not to proceed.

Embodying a fascinated anthropologist who simply wants to understand – not to change or influence the outcome – your Sage begins to see new possibilities. Perhaps the timing is not right and with deep empathy and compassion you see this truth. Or perhaps a deep feeling of scarcity is keeping your prospect blind to their own financial abundance. Whatever is driving the decision becomes an opportunity for you to see things as they are – not as you wish them to be.

Being clear on the situation that your prospect finds himself in gives you tremendous power to do several things including:

- Anticipate similar rejections in future enrollment conversations.
- Explore root causes for the objections that are surfaced in the conversation.
- Continue the powerful coaching session you're having by asking powerful questions associated with what's coming up as part of the rejection.
- Consider possible solutions in partnership with your prospective client.
- Identify a condition or future-state whereby a desire to engage in coaching would occur.
- Uncover a different opportunity altogether – perhaps one that isn't coaching, but taps into other skills you've developed and can offer up.

The possibilities are as infinite as the unique human being you are speaking with. The moment your Saboteur voices convince you that you know why your prospect has rejected your coaching offering, you close off possibilities and remain "stuck" in a decision. No growth can occur in the space of, "I know." Your Sage Explore power has you remain curious and seeking new insights rather than closing off alternatives and new possibilities.

Having just had a powerful coaching session with you, your prospect will likely be open to sharing what's driving their decision not to proceed. When they are clear you're not here to make them wrong or to convince them of why they "need" coaching, what remains are new paths forward that neither one of you may have considered.

All too often we get stuck in our thinking ruts. We think we know why things are as they are. In reality, we know far less than we think we do. When you tap your Sage Explore power, you are acknowledging that there's far more you likely don't know that, even if it doesn't change today's enrollment outcome, having that knowledge will most definitely support you in your journey to build and grow your coaching business. The gift of knowledge here will pay significant dividends for years to come, so stay curious and open to possibilities.

Innovate New Possibilities & Paths Forward

With the knowledge you've gained from your Sage Explore power, you are free to Innovate and come up with entirely new possibilities. Perhaps you learn something that has you consider a different coaching service or frequency of coaching than you were previously offering your prospects. When I first heard Kendall Summerhawk speak into her VIP Days, it totally changed my concept of what individual coaching could be. I had a fixed mindset that you could only coach for 30 to 60 minutes. After hearing her talk about what she would do with her clients, I began to see an entirely different approach that would powerfully serve my clients.

My work with Shirzad in developing the business development training track came as a direct result of seeing how powerful a combination of his PQ Operating System was in combination with my business development experience. Even this book came from a Sage space of Innovate. The moment I let go of thinking I knew what would serve my clients best, I engaged my Innovate Power to consider vastly different approaches to helping coaches achieve financial freedom through their coaching businesses.

Where have you uncovered a "fixed" mindset? Perhaps one driven by your Saboteurs convincing you that you "know" what your prospects need and why they choose (not) to hire you as their coach? Sage Power Innovate would have you play the "Yes, and ..." game to see entirely new possibilities driven by your Sage Explore power. The more you're willing to explore possible alternatives, the faster new paths forward will emerge.

This doesn't mean you want to activate your Restless Saboteur and bounce from idea to idea. What's important is to tap your Sage Innovate power to consider several new approaches you *could* take before activating your Sage discernment on which of these approaches is the best to *actually* take. How do you know which new path forward to take in enrolling clients into your coaching business? That's where your Sage Power Navigate comes in to light the way forward.

Use Navigate Power to Connect With Your High Purpose

Your Saboteurs live in scarcity and your Sage lives in abundance. Part of the challenge of living in abundance is the realization that there are, in fact, many diverse and distinct paths you could take to be successful. So which path do you choose?

Your Sage Power Navigate connects you with your high purpose as a means to illuminate the best path forward for you right now in this moment. While so many paths are available to you, the one that stands out is the one that connects you with your purpose.

When I struggle to decide which path I choose to take, I ask myself which path will empower me to help more coaches become financially free through their coaching business? As that's my north star, it helps guide me on my way. Those actions that take me closer to this outcome connect me with Sage Power Navigate. Those that don't, while certainly viable alternatives, become more of a distraction or detour to my best way forward.

If you're not clear on your high purpose, there are several approaches you can take, including:

- Consulting your Wiser, Older Self (i.e. your Future Self) for Sage wisdom.
- Begin with the ultimate "end" in mind and write out your eulogy for your funeral.
- Write out what you wish to be remembered for when you're gone.
- Ask yourself what's most important to you in life, then ask "Why is that important?" five times to reveal what's driving you.
- Do a long PQ Gym session to shift to Sage and ask yourself which path to choose.
- Consider what your niche would have you do if they could direct your actions.
- Simply choose the path of love, not fear.

When you are clear on your high purpose, you'll know which path to follow. What's even more important to understand is that just because you choose one path doesn't mean you have to remain on it forever. If it turns out you choose the wrong path, you can always pivot. Your Navigate power will guide you on your way. As new insights and information become available, trust that your Sage will know what actions to take. After all, knowing the path is not the same as committing to and living that path. That's the next step in this process.

Activate: Take Bold Action & Ask for What You Want

Do you see how all of your other Sage Powers lead you to this single moment? No matter how much you may lean into thinking about enrolling clients, only the act of enrollment will produce your desired outcome. Having handled your Saboteurs (or at least quieted them down significantly), doing your own PQ Reps in order to engage your Sage self, it's time to act. Even if you are still experiencing body sensations that you interpret as nervousness or fear, feel those sensations and take action any way.

Being brave does not mean you are void of the feelings of nervousness or fear. Being brave means you acknowledge those sensations in your body, quiet the negative self-talk from your Saboteurs and take bold action anyway. Remember, our brains were not designed to keep us happy and positive. Our brains were designed to keep us safe. By default when your amygdala acts up, your body enters that fight, flight or freeze mode. This isn't helpful right at the moment of enrollment. Rather than allowing our brains to stop us, this is the precise moment when we must activate our Sage brain and take action.

For me, I began to reimagine what those sensations in my body actually mean. Rather than interpreting my heart racing and that butterflies in my stomach feeling to mean fear, I choose to connect those sensations to excitement and anticipation. I realized that those same exact sensations happened when I was on a rollercoaster, rock climbing, in a karate sparing tournament, whitewater rafting, skydiving and so many other pleasurable moments in my life. In those moments, I didn't experience those bodily sensations as fear, but rather excitement and pleasurable anticipation of what was about to happen.

As soon as I reframed the same "fear" sensations to "excitement" they no longer stopped me. Sure, for a nanosecond, my heightened awareness had me "check for danger", but just as soon as that happened, I smiled and instantly reassured my body that I was perfectly safe and doing something that I loved.

Imagine being forever free of the fear and nervousness associated with enrollment. How would your life change when you experienced peace and calm as you offer your coaching services to a prospective client? That's what will happen after about a dozen offers where you reframe your sensations of fear and nervousness as excitement and passion.

When that happens, you'll boldly ask for what you want. You will stop seeing enrollment as an awkward and uncomfortable process to be avoided at all costs. Instead, you'll see that it fuels your ability to live into your mission in life. Your ability to give is only inhibited by your inability to receive. As you open up to receive, you will massively expand your ability to give. Think of it this way, you're playing full out right now, right? Well chances are you have turned on your garden hose full blast, but you're restricted by the circumference of your garden hose itself. When you open up to receive, you expand that circumference to a fire hose and can give even more.

This is what you have chosen to do in this life. This is you living your highest and best self. Just as soon as you conquer this (previously unhelpful) rush of energy and direct it towards what you're really up to, you will be *on fire!* Or for me it's "UnstoppaBILL."

Yep, I actually named it for myself. When I choose to step into my highest and best self, I'm *UnstoppaBill*. That's my Sage name. When I'm truly living in Sage, I am, in fact, unstoppable. That's because I never allow any circumstance to stop me from my mission, purpose and vision. Everything is a gift, which is what we'll focus on next.

Sage Perspective: Even a No Is A Gift

Remember what Shirzad has taught us? The Sage perspective is that *everything* can be turned into a gift and opportunity. Lean into that. What's the gift of a no? What's the gift of receiving a rejection when you make your offer to have a prospect hire you as their coach? Let's explore a few possibilities to get your creative juices flowing because those gifts are ridiculously abundant – but only when you choose to see them. For most people, these gifts are summarily ignored because way too much focus goes to the Saboteurs in these moments. But not you. Your Sage is calling out to you. Let's listen to your Sage's call.

The Gift of Knowledge

When a prospect rejects you, the opportunity exists to actively seek out the gift of knowledge. When you stop making it about you, you create the space to explore what really happened. Were they your ideal customer prospect? If not, how did they end up on your calendar? If so, did they share with you a deep issue or problem for them, or were they holding back? Did you deliver an epic coaching session for them, or were you playing it safe? Get deeply curious about what transpired. The gift of knowledge you can get is infinitely more valuable than the sum total of the financial value this client would ever deliver to you – but only if you actively seek it out.

And don't expect your prospect to be the one to tell you. Sure, you can ask some questions and probe alongside them, but the real work happens in the ten or 15 minutes *after* the call has ended. What is *your* lesson? What will you commit to doing differently next time? What incredible insight does your Sage have for you when you stop judging yourself and listen to what your Sage has to share? Reflect on the session you just had. Who cares if it didn't go your way? You're living in abundance. There will be as many more of these enrollment calls as you choose to have in your lifetime. Refocus your efforts to ensure you know why they said no and what you'll do differently to get a yes on the next enrollment call.

The Gift of Power

Which of your Sage powers either grew or would need to grow for the next enrollment call? Did you expand your Empathy for yourself? Your prospect? Your enrollment session itself? Are you practicing Explore and being a fascinated anthropologist looking at what worked, what didn't work and what could be changed for next time? Have you decided to Innovate in some way so that the next enrollment call will be even better than this one? Are you taking bold action and lining up your next enrollment calls?

So many ways to increase your Sage Powers here. Every single time you participate in an enrollment call, you are confronting your Saboteurs, growing your Self-Command muscles and strengthening your Sage Powers. Ironically, receiving a yes is not nearly as powerful as receiving a no. Yes is what you want so nothing really changes. When you receive a no, you are challenged to strengthen your Sage Mastery, so get excited for your nos. They truly are here to shape and serve you at the highest level. By actively seeking out your nos, you lose your fear of them and instead begin to see them as your Sage Mastery black belt trainers.

The Gift of Inspiration

What would need to happen in your coaching business (or in your life) in order to make each no meaningful? What inspired action can you take? When answering these questions, I connect with my own Sage Power Navigate. I connect with my high purpose as a coach and it inspires me to do even more.

When it comes to receiving a no, you have a very simple choice: Better or Bitter. When your Sage allows the message of "no" to represent feedback, it naturally makes you better and generates inspired action. That's a true gift. When your Saboteurs allow the message of "no" to represent feelings of negativity, it makes you bitter. That has you ignore any possible gifts associated with the no. You are always at choice as to how you receive a no and you'll immediately connect with your Saboteurs or Sage based on how you're feeling.

From a Sage Discernment perspective, all feedback is neutral. It's information that can be used or ignored. When you receive the gift of the "no" as nothing more than feedback, you are empowered to generate inspired action; to turn neutral feedback into positive, inspired action. This can be as simple as getting excited about the next enrollment opportunity where you continue your learning journey. Or it could be as awesome as having you want to invest more energy in your marketing as you double down on the core needs of your niche.

The actual inspired action isn't nearly as important as the inspiration to take action. When you associate the inspired action with the no generated, you're continuing your journey and building momentum. The opposite is allowing the no to feel like a set-back and hindering your momentum. Both are always available to you, so why would you impede yourself when you are being called to your own greatness? Even when you're not feeling all that inspired, remember what Winston Churchill said, "When you're going through hell, keep going." Your Saboteurs would have you stop and feel sorry for yourself. Your Sage would see it for what it truly is: an invitation and opportunity to take even more action and increase your momentum. So keep going!

Regular Tracking & Reporting: How Measuring Helps You Improve

As we wrap up this chapter, there's one more thing that will support you living in Sage as you look to convert appointments: regular tracking and reporting of your efforts. As Peter Drucker said, "What gets measured, gets improved." Said another way, what gets measured gets managed. Regular measurement of your efforts will allow you to see what's working, what's not working and what you want to change.

So what might you want to track when it comes to converting appointments?

I find it best when you work backwards from your desired result. Let's say you want to build a six-figure coaching business. While there's many ways to get there (and you are free to adjust any numbers you wish), let's take ten clients at $1,000 per month each. That would get you to $120,000 per year (ten clients x $1,000/mo x 12 months). On average, it will take you about ten discovery calls in order to enroll one client. What you'd want to track is how many outreach efforts does it take to get a single ideal customer prospect onto your calendar. An outreach can be a one-on-one direct approach (such as a call, text, email, social media direct message, etc.) or a one-to-many indirect approach (such as a podcast, speaking engagement, newsletter, social media post, advertising, etc.).

Your tracking might look something like this:

	Outreach	Calendar	Enrollment	Conversions
Day One	30 via LinkedIn	1	0	0
Day Two	25 via Email	1	0	0
Day Three	1,500 Podcast	0	0	0
Day Four	20 via Text	2	0	0
Day Five	10 via Phone	0	0	0
Day Six	10 via Letter	0	0	0
Day Seven	22 via LinkedIn	1	0	0

And when you look at this first week's efforts, it's easy to allow your Saboteurs to have you feel discouraged. "It's not working! Look how much effort I put in this week and I only got five people on my calendar. I'm terrible at this!" When, in reality, you're just getting started. Your first efforts will often feel futile as there isn't a direct correlation between the efforts you make in outreach with the number of people who agree to a discovery call and get on your calendar. Instead of thinking of instant gratification, consider each of these outreach efforts as seeds you've planted that will bear fruit in the future – some sooner than others.

The purpose of tracking your efforts is not to give your Saboteurs data to beat you up with, but rather to have a sense of what's working and what's not working *over time*. That means, the early tracking efforts are not likely to be all that helpful (which is why most people don't stick with it). Where these efforts become hugely insightful is when you keep with them three, six and twelve months out. When you play the long-game, you begin to see patterns.

For example, you might notice that when you are interviewed for podcasts, it takes more than three months for someone to book an appointment with you. Why is that? It could be that the podcast is growing its audience and it takes a while for your episode to be consumed. Or it could be that your episode finally got indexed on Google Search and now pops up whenever someone is looking to solve the problem that you were being interviewed about. Whatever the answer, you are starting to see an influx in podcast appointments despite doing fewer of them.

Or perhaps you notice that your speaking engagements tend to lead to more speaking engagements, but not many appointments. This leads you to change up your offer from the stage and spend some quality time creating a powerful lead magnet. The next time you present, BANG! You suddenly see a dramatic improvement in booked appointments.

While you may think you "know" some of this intuitively, without tracking and measuring consistently, you are going to miss out on patterns emerging. Besides the patterns themselves, you'll also tend to drift in and out of generating appointments. Without tracking your efforts, you'll be left to your feelings. That is, when you *feel* like generating appointments, you'll do it, but often you won't. This leads to inconsistency and all sorts of fits and starts. Only consistent action leads to significant improvements. Consistent action comes from making a plan and then tracking your projected actions versus your actual actions.

When you can see in black and white that you're not spending the quality time needed to build and scale your coaching business, your Sage will discern that new efforts are needed. Sure, your Saboteurs may have a few choice words as well, but we're not listening to them – at least not for more than a second.

The flip side of this is also true. You can't manage what you don't pay attention to. If you're ignoring your efforts by not tracking and measuring them, then how do you optimize for what's working? How do you know if your time spent on LinkedIn is more effective than your time on stage or in a podcast, for example? Intuition only gets you so far. By tracking your efforts, you can begin to see those patterns that will support you in optimizing what's working and adjusting that which isn't in order to deliver the results you expect. Which leads us to understanding the ROI of your efforts.

The Return on Investment (ROI) of Your Efforts

Do you know what your time is *actually* worth? Most coaches over-index on the billable hours and tend to lose track of the hours spent building their coaching business. For example, let's say that you currently make as little as $25/hr for your coaching sessions. That means, to make $50,000 a year you'd have to coach 2,000 billable hours. But that's nearly impossible. First of all, that would mean you'd need to coach clients 40 hours a week for 50 weeks a year. Even incredibly successful law firms that bill their clients $500 to $1,000 per hour tend to struggle to fully utilize 2,000 billable hours – and they have all sorts of paid staff who are there to help them.

Conversely, most coaches are solopreneurs. That means you're the only one working in your coaching practice. So you're responsible for *delivering* your coaching service as well as:

- Acquiring New Clients
- Invoicing Clients
- Collecting Payments from Clients
- Reporting Your Earning to the Tax Authorities
- Responding to Inquiries about Your Coaching
- Building and Maintaining Your Website, Social Media Presence, etc.

You get it. You're the one juggling all these balls. So when you look at how much time do you *actually* have to coach, it's not 40 hours a week – at least not when you're just starting out. It might be closer to 10 to 20 hours a week. And that's assuming you're a full-time coach. If this is your side-hustle then this is just one of the ways you make money.

That's why it's so important to understand how much time you're investing in all of the non-coaching activities. Every hour you spend not coaching is an opportunity cost to your coaching business. In other words, you're investing in generating more clients so that you can spend more time *delivering* coaching sessions.

But don't get discouraged here. This is all part of the process. The return on your efforts can actually be quite great. It just takes knowing the value of your next coaching client and how many hours you're investing to land them. At $25/hr, for a full year of coaching the value is about $1250 per year ($25/hr x one hour a week x 50 weeks). At $100/hr, your next client is worth $5,000/yr. At $150/hr it's $7,500/yr and so on.

Once you begin tracking and measuring how many hours it takes you to land your next client, you can measure the ROI of your efforts. You'll see how long it takes you to secure a single client and the value of that client based on what you currently receive for your coaching. At $200/hr your next coaching client is worth $10,000 per year. If it takes you 20 hours to land that client, your actual hourly is $142.85 (not $200). Or, said another way, it cost you $4,000 (20 hours x $200/hr) in opportunity cost to land your $10,000 client.

The ROI of your efforts will begin to move you towards the places you are most efficient. If that first client took 20 hours, but the next took only 10 hours, you've cut your opportunity cost in half. Instead of $4,000 of invested time, it only took you $2,000 and you're making great progress towards maximizing your growth and efficiency as a coach.

Look, you don't need to calculate all of this out. I'm illustrating this point to you because your time is valuable and most coaches don't stop to consider how much time they are investing in order to build their coaching business. When you quantify and measure the value of the time you're investing to land a client, it helps you really focus your efforts on the appointment generating efforts with the highest return. Once you master the art of the close, you're going to want to pay closer attention to how much time it takes you to get your ideal customer prospects on your calendar so that you can quantify your efforts. Just because you didn't pay out of your pocket doesn't mean there was "no cost." Organic (non-paid) marketing efforts still take time and when you quantify the value of that time it helps you see the big picture so that you know where to better focus your efforts.

Life Is An Enrollment Game

The final point I'd like to make here is that your entire life is an enrollment game. Think about that for a moment. Every moment of every day you are either being enrolled or you are enrolling someone else. What do you want to have for dinner tonight? What movie would you like to watch? Where would you like to go on vacation? Where do you want to live?

Your life is a perfect reflection of the choices you make. So many of us have been on autopilot for so long we barely recognize all the choices we make every moment of every day. To that extent, we can become unconscious to these choices and fall into a pattern and routine. If you want a different life, you need only make different choices. It's just as easy or difficult as that. Our Saboteurs want us to make one set of choices and our Sage would like us to make different choices. Who do we choose to listen to?

It's no different for anyone you connect with. When you are in a discovery call, you are listening deeply and being fully present to the needs of the person you are coaching. When it comes to enrolling them into your offering, you are either enrolling them into your coaching services or being enrolled by them and their circumstances. The outcome is often based on who is the more compelling enroller.

For example, if your prospect has a high Victim Saboteur showing up in the conversation, you may be enrolled by their terrible story of tragedy. That would have you believe that their current (or past) circumstances rule. In effect, you are enrolled in the story they are telling you as to why they could never afford you as their coach or why this timing can't work. Alternatively, your Sage has the power to be fully present to all that is shared and through deep empathy and curiosity, present a viable alternative as their coach. Both are possible.

It would be both an oversimplification and incorrect to believe that this is a win / lose paradigm. Enrollment is quantum in that you are entering a field of all possibilities. Even when a person's circumstances are presented as fixed and impossible, know that this is not true. When you remain in Sage and invite the other person into their Sage, new possibilities present themselves; ones that neither of you may have imagined possible previously.

Life is an enrollment game. Every moment of every day you are either being enrolled or are enrolling. Your Saboteurs wish to enroll you to play it safe, comfortable, and status quo. Your Sage wishes to enroll you into being the absolute best version of yourself by doing what's right despite your own fears, insecurities and other Saboteur negative emotions. This holds true for yourself as much as it does for anyone you are interacting with.

There's something profound here when you come to realize just how much power you wield in every moment of every day. When you choose to use this power for the benefit of others, you Sage calls upon the Sage in others and you generate a Sage contagion effect. As you go deeper into your Sage, so too does the person you're interacting with. The result is that you both are in a field of all possibilities as you genuinely seek the best path forward. This is the path of the Sage. The one with more light in it. The one with more love in it.

When this is your deepest desire, you transcend "selling your coaching services" and emerge as a powerful ally in service of others. When someone recognizes that you care more about them than you do about your own needs, the pretense of "being sold" evaporates. What's left is a genuine conversation of possibilities examined in Sage. This is the essence of enrollment.

You are not here to sell anything to anyone ever. No one likes to be sold. But most people like to buy. When people buy, they tend to buy on emotion and backfill with logic. This is why your being in Sage is so enrolling. There is a plethora of positive emotions being shared that gravitationally pull someone else into their Sage so that you both can choose a path that serves humanity best. I know that may seem far-fetched to your Saboteurs, but that's the real game we're playing here.

You have the power to make the world better and so does your ideal customer prospect. Together you support each other to live your best lives; ones filled with service to the world. Think about that for a moment. What if every person lived in Sage for the majority of their life. Think about the global impact that would have – from parenting to schools to careers to legacies. This is how I see the high purpose of coaching. This is our high calling. To live our best life in service of others. To live an epic life as an example and permission for others to do the same. Nothing enrolls clients like your Sage living your best life.

That's why your own mental fitness practice is vital to your success. As you grow towards self-actualization, you inspire others to do the same. This isn't about "following in your footsteps" as much as seeing what's possible. Or, as Matsuo Bashō put it, "Don't seek to follow in the footsteps of the wise. Seek what they sought."[55]

Mastery of your own Sage is appealing to potential clients. You are living your best life. In doing so, you shine a bright light on what is possible for anyone. While we are imperfect human beings, we have this incredible power to grow and evolve. Being a coach is about being the guide on the side. You enroll others to be their guide when you yourself live this work. As you grow your Sage, so too will you strengthen your ability to enroll others and grow your coaching practice.

---

[55] https://www.brainyquote.com/quotes/matsuo_basho_107176

CHAPTER NINE

Creating Daily Habits & Applying What You Know

Having made it this far, I am clear that you're committed to your coaching business. According to Tony Robbins in his book *Money: Master the Game*, "...statistics show that fewer than 10% of people who buy a [nonfiction] book ever read past the first chapter."[56]

Change can be difficult, but it doesn't have to be. Sometimes when my wife asks me what I'm reading, after she hears me describe the contents of the book she replies, "Sounds like you're eating your mental broccoli." And she's right. While I love fiction books too, I've made it a habit to continually read books from the people I admire most. While these books may not be a "fun" read, I continually walk away with an expanded wealth of knowledge as well as a short list of actions to take. And that's what this chapter is about – defining the actions you choose to take in order to apply what you're learning (as well as what you already knew coming into this book). In other words, putting Sage Power Activate to work.

Red / Green Filter

Up until this point in the book, you may have been reading with what I call a red / green filter. Red represents the parts of the book that you disagree with and green represents the parts of the book you either agree with or are open to seeing if they work. For any red parts in the book, the chances of you trying them out are slim to none. The green parts, however, are inviting you to see if this may be the thing that's been holding your coaching business back and you're open to trying them.

---

[56] Robbins, Tony. *Money Master the Game: 7 Simple Steps to Financial Freedom*. Simon & Schuster. ©2014, page 28.

Are you aware of the thought distortions we all have when reading something? Those are your internal filters that either agree or disagree with what you're reading. Even right now as you read the last line, there was something inside of you that either said, "Yep, I know exactly what he means," or, conversely, "No, I don't have that going on in my head."

That's actually what I'm talking about right there. We can't help ourselves. Rather than remaining open to what information is being presented, our brains are designed to interpret what we read and choose to absorb the information or summarily reject it based on our own filters. Our filters are created by our own life experiences and we can't help but apply our own life experience to any new information that is being presented to us.

Regardless of what you believe based on your own personal experience, the time has come to put what's been presented here to the test. As a reminder, the purpose of this book is NOT merely to intellectually challenge or stimulate you. The worst thing you can do would be to put this book down, change nothing and continue to either struggle with your coaching business or have a coaching business that is a fraction of the success you know you're truly capable of achieving.

Ready to Start Your Quest?

In Joseph Campbell's Hero's Journey[57], this is your *Call to Adventure*. It's time to say goodbye to your *Ordinary World* where your coaching business has not accomplished the desired impact you originally envisioned. Sure, you could stay in this same space longer doing the same things you've been doing and getting the same or similar results. But there's something inside of you the yearns for something more. That's your Sage whispering to you that you were meant for something greater and it's time to step up to begin your quest.

This quest will combine elements of your physicality as you take consistent actions every day until you have the kind of coaching business you desire. It will also challenge you to stretch your emotions. Beyond the actions you'll be taking, you'll also notice how you feel about these actions. Our emotions will either support our desired outcomes or will get in the way of what we say we want. That depends entirely on which voice we are tuning into: our Sage or our Saboteurs.

Ultimately, this is a spiritual quest. The Latin root word for spiritual is *spiritus*, which means "the breath of life"[58] It's your choice if this has a religious context for you ... or not. Either way, you are deliberately breathing life into your quest to build

---

57   https://www.movieoutline.com/articles/the-hero-journey-mythic-structure-of-joseph-campbell-monomyth.html

58   https://www.omicsonline.org/open-access/constructing-and-deconstructing-the-terminology-of-spirituality-a-journeyback-to-the-greek-roots.php?aid=94448

and scale your coaching practice. Even if you believe this is divine, it is you who puts the breath into the life you choose. This is your opportunity to align your abilities with your mission, purpose and vision so that you have the coaching practice you want and the world needs right now. This starts with a declaration and a commitment to this desired outcome.

Make Your Declaration

The time has come to make a declaration -- even when you're not precisely sure *how* you'll do it. Establishing your *what* and *why* are more important than *how*. It's so easy to get lost in the details which is the reason *how* deters most people from getting started. Besides, when you're committed to something, you'll find a way because you won't allow anything to stop you. As stated earlier, when you're committed, you find a way. When you're not committed you find an excuse. Your *how* will continue to shift, evolve and grow as you strengthen your Sage powers.

A declaration means to declare without evidence. Anyone paying attention can observe and make a prediction based on patterns. A declaration is different. To declare without evidence is to give birth to a new possibility; one that previously didn't exist until you willed it into existence. That's what you're invited to do right now. What is it that you wish to declare? If you already know, write it down:

_____

_____

_____

_____

_____

And if you're not sure or need some support, start here:

Big Picture (Begin With The End In Mind):

1. What **size** (in dollars) of coaching business are you committed to creating?
2. How many **clients** will you have in the next three years?
3. How **much** (in dollars) will each client invest with you as their coach in three years?
4. What are the **number of hours** you'll coach each week in three years?
5. Why is all of this **important** for you to accomplish? (In other words, is this a *should* or a *must happen* for you? Why?)

Your Declaration Might Look Something Like This:

*In three years' time, I will earn **$180,000 dollars** per year as a coach working with 15 **clients** each investing **$1,000 per month** for two 45-minute coaching sessions. I'm committed to accomplishing this outcome in order to more than triple the median coaching salary globally.*

Now, $180,000 may seem too low for you, so feel free to double that:

*In three years' time, I will earn **$360,000 dollars** per year as a coach working with 15 **clients** each investing **$2,000 per month** for two 45-minute coaching sessions. I'm committed to accomplishing this outcome in order to more than triple the median coaching salary globally.*

Remember, we're not allowing *how* to stand in the way of your declaration. In this step, we're only focusing on the *what* and the *why*. To test that you've done this part correctly, check in with yourself. Are your Saboteurs have a bit of a field day with you? If so, **good!** It wouldn't be much of a declaration if it didn't feel uncomfortable. You know what to do: PQ Reps so that you drop back into your body for what's next. Allow your Saboteurs to have their say, then smile (or laugh) and keep going. You've got this!

Double Down On Your Commitment

A declaration is only a dream if you are not committed. In order to move an idea or dream to a declaration, you must be committed. "This is going to happen no matter what!" Here's the thing. Motivation comes and motivation goes. In the moments you are motivated, you can feel fully committed. However, commitment isn't about *those* moments, are they? In fact, it's really hard to stay committed to anything that's uncomfortable or feels difficult.

Take it from BJ Fogg, author of *Tiny Habits.* He points out that entire industries are created around this false premise of motivation. I know that if I eat right and exercise I'll lose weight, so why don't I do it? We think it's a matter of motivation, but it's not that simple. The Fogg Behavior model states that a, "behavior happens when motivation, ability and prompt converge at the same moment."[59]

So doubling down on your commitment may not look the way you imagined. When I began writing this book, I was 100% committed to writing it. My motivation was high because I knew how many coaches this book would support. What was missing was my prompt and a tiny habit that would ensure this book would go from idea to reality.

---

[59] https://behaviormodel.org/

For me, this meant building accountability and systems of support that would ensure my declaration to write this book and my commitment would not wane when other priorities were vying for my attention.

Sometimes doubling down on your commitment is about recognizing that your current motivation will inevitably weaken long before you achieve the results you're going after. That's what the rest of this chapter is about to ensure you achieve your desired outcome. When you are fully committed you find a way. When you are not fully committed you find an excuse. While your motivation is high, let's ensure you have your clear path forward to ensure your successful outcome.

Building Accountability & Systems of Support

When I sat down to write this book, I was incredibly excited to share all that I have learned with as many coaches as I could inspire. I also knew that the only way this book would be written is if I created a daily habit of writing about 1,000 words a day. Even before I stared, I knew there would be days that I wrote more and days that I wrote less. That's fine. What I didn't want was to go several days or weeks without writing anything.

I also knew that doing this on my own would allow my Saboteurs to convince me there were more pressing matters that needed my attention and that while this project was important, it wasn't particularly urgent. That would be a problem for me. So, I made a commitment to myself to track every word I wrote and then share my word count with my accountability partners.

What's more, it was an incredibly easy ask of my accountability partners. So as not to burden them with my own fluctuating motivation, my request was simple. I told each of my accountability partners that every day I will text you a word count. Even though my target is 1,000 words or more per day, the number of words is not important. What is important is that I text you every day. If I miss one day, that's fine. But if I miss two or more days, that's when I ask you to check in with me because something is wrong.

Notice, the request was simple. They agreed to receive a daily text from me with my word count. Only when a second day passed without receiving a text would they be prompted to reach out and check in with me. Now, I can count on one hand the number of times I missed a second day of writing. That's because I knew when this happened I would be asked to share what was going on. Not wanting to have to explain my circumstances motivated me to sit down and write for about an hour every single day.

Another system of support was my Google Calendar. I set a recurring meeting invite every day at seven am to remind me to write my 1,000 words. That showed up on my phone, computer and even when I asked Alexa about my schedule for the day. With all my devices proactively reminding me and my accountability partners expecting a word count from me, I had what I needed to stay focused, disciplined and committed to my outcome.

Your accountability or system of support may look different from this. That's totally fine. The goal is to *establish* accountability and systems of support. What you choose to have need only work for you. But design some check-ins for yourself to evaluate if what you set up is, in fact working. If you're not progressing, it may be time to change up your systems of support.

Importance of Establishing & Maintaining Daily Habits

My daily habit for writing this book was sitting down for about one hour every morning and writing 1,000 words. Let's switch back to the daily habit you need in order to build and scale your coaching business. After you've established your niche and developed your irresistible offer, the most valuable daily habit that you can create is generating appointments. How you generate appointments is far less important than the daily habit of doing so.

Let's say for purpose of illustration that you think articles on LinkedIn is your best bet. Make a commitment to write every day. Most articles are between 300 to 1,000 words, so if you are so inclined, you can write a single article daily and within three months you'll have about 90 articles. Talk about becoming a content generating machine!

Or perhaps you want to become known to your ideal customers via podcasts. With so many podcasts out there, chances are your prospects are listening to many different ones. Reach out to podcasts hosts every day. You can use a platform to become a guest or go direct. The method is less important than the daily habit itself.

If BJ Fogg was here, he'd recommend that you go *tiny* in order to create sustainability. Ask yourself what's the very least you can do every day. In his book he talks about the value of doing just two push-ups or flossing a single tooth. That may seem crazy, but it works like a charm. Perhaps your daily habit is as simple as going through LinkedIn and reviewing which of your current first-degree connections *are* your niche. Or, if that's not enough people, then check out second and third-degree connections. Or perhaps you keep a five-year journal, writing only three or four sentences each day.

Only once you *establish* a daily habit can you improve upon it. By heeding BJ Fogg's advice, starting tiny allows for sustainability. Consider what you truly want in terms of your path to generating appointments and start tiny. Consistent daily action will trump infrequent and sporadic highly motivated actions. If you want to run a marathon, you need to get out there and run just about every day. If you want to build your financial freedom and a significant coaching business, establish your daily habits.

And, of course, I'd be remiss if I didn't point out your number one most important daily habit: long 12-to-20-minute PQ Gym sessions. None of these other daily habits matter when done in Saboteur. Only Sage habits will produce the results you seek, so make your first daily habit doing PQ Reps of your choosing. That single habit taken out over the next six months will transform your life. I know it did mine.

Celebrate!!!

When was the last time you celebrated? I mean *really* celebrated. Jumping up and down, pumping our fists and yelling like a crazy person? Well if you're committed to building and scaling your coaching practice, it's time to reintroduce this step back into your life. That's because when you celebrate, you release dopamine and continue to reinforce the behaviors you want to see in your life. The more you celebrate, the faster your neuropathways grow and the more frequently you'll take continued right actions toward your desired outcome.

Can you build a successful coaching business without celebrating? Of course you can – it will just take longer and require more PQ Reps. But if you want to strap a booster rocket on your business growth, then tap into your childhood self and celebrate like it's your fifth birthday party and you're about to eat CAKE!

And that's not the occasional celebration. I'm talking about each and every time you finish your daily habit. When I finish writing this section, you can bet I'm going to fist bump high in the air and say "YES!" out loud. Why? Because it means I finished my 1,000 words and I'm proud of myself. This simple action reinforces my Sage connection to my writing and has me wanting to do even more. I actually have to stop myself now or I will end up spending the rest of my day writing instead of all the other items on my calendar.

Can you imagine what that will be like for you in the context of generating more appointments and scaling your coaching business. That's the power of celebration. If you want more on the neuroscience of celebrating, I highly recommend you read BJ Fogg's *Tiny Habits*. There's more insights and data on the power of celebrating than anywhere else I know.

Applying What You Know

Stephen Covey has often said, "To know and not to do is not to know." There is profound wisdom in this short phrase. I take it to mean that your daily actions are so much more important than your intellectual understanding and this goes for every domain in your life. In the context of health, how many of us struggle to lose ten pounds? We are generally clear what foods make us gain weight and which make us lose weight. So what's the issue?

Simply put, by not taking consistent action, we lack the discipline to achieve the outcome we say we're committed to. Only through consistent action do we truly apply what we know and achieve the outcome we desire.

Mental fitness is another great example. You can achieve the 20% insight needed on the topic of mental fitness in a single half-day workshop (or about three hours of time). That's the acquisition of the "knowing" through the insights needed. But to truly know mental fitness is to act in Sage by quieting our Saboteurs and developing our self-command muscle. That 80% muscle building requires no more insights. Instead, it requires a regular daily practice every morning for at least 20 minutes as well as brief interruptions throughout your day to continue your practice.

And when it comes to building and growing your coaching business, the requirements are the same. You now know how important it is to clearly define your niche, have an irresistible offer, regularly practice generating appointments and regularly practice converting those appointments. No mystery here. You know what to do. Now it comes down to doing it regularly and with a frequency of committed action that ensures your success.

Chet Holmes, author of *The Ultimate Sales Machine* referred to this as "stubborn pigheadedness." When crafting a sales team, he believed the number one predictor of success is an individual's level of stubborn pigheadedness. Those who are willing to repeat the tried and true formulas over and over and over again will enjoy the fruits of their labors. Results are predictable when the right actions are repeated on a daily basis.

It's time to stop intellectualizing this work and put it into your daily practice so that you can enjoy all the benefits of a thriving coaching business.

One Day or Day One – You Decide

What will it be, then? Is having a thriving coaching practice a far-off dream, or are you committed to taking the steps necessary to have it happen. That's the difference between "one day" and "day one." A perspective of "one day" means it's somewhere "out there" waiting to be discovered. While a perspective of "day one" means starting NOW.

Today really can be the first day of the rest of your life. Every person you admire had to take the same journey you're stepping into right here and now. No one magically steps into greatness. Greatness happens when you decide to remain in Sage (no matter what) as you begin your journey. What makes anyone great is the resilience they develop from overcoming any and all obstacles in their way.

That's why we should be extremely grateful for our challenges and setbacks. Every challenge tests your resolve. Will you rise to the challenge or walk away? If today truly is day one for you, then you have begun your path towards mastery and nothing can stop you. If it's "one day" then it's little more than a pipe dream. The minute challenges show up, the dreamer is on to the next thing.

Day one is about starting your journey even if you're not completely clear about the path before you. Allow Sage Power Navigate to guide you along your way even when you're not completely clear on every little detail. I trust you're committed to this work and see the value of getting started. Allow this to be your "Day One" and celebrate your commitment to being the best coach you can be regardless of what obstacles you will encounter along your journey.

S.M.A.R.T Goals & Metrics of Success

How will you know you're making progress in your journey? It helps to define clearly what success for you is so that when you've achieved it, you'll know. That's where S.M.A.R.T. goals come into play. S.M.A.R.T. stands for:

- Specific
- Measurable
- Achievable
- Realistic
- Time-Bound

Specific

"I want to have more money" is not specific. "I will have $100,000 in revenue from my coaching business in the next 12 months" is so much more specific. When setting a S.M.A.R.T. goal for yourself, begin by being as specific as you possibly can be. The more specificity you can include, the easier it will be to know when you've achieved your goal.

Measurable

How will you measure the success of your goal? Notice in the previous example, "more money" is not measurable. For example, I find $1 on the ground on the way to my car then technically, I have more money. How will I measure $100,000 in revenue from my coaching business? I can see each and every month how I'm tracking in my financial software such as Quickbooks and even in my bank account.

If I'm measuring how many clients I've achieved, it would also be helpful to know which methods generated those clients. That's why I like to measure the number of appointments on my calendar after each podcast, speech, webinar, LinkedIn outreach, etc. Once you begin measuring, you begin revealing powerful insights about what's working and not working in your coaching business.

Achievable

Make sure your goal is achievable so that you're setting yourself up to succeed. That's because success begets more success. You may have a goal of acquiring ten or even 20 clients, and that's perfectly fine. Make your first goal significantly more achievable by focusing all your efforts on the first client. Or, if you have clients, focus on the next client you wish to bring on. By focusing one client at a time, you make the task easily achievable. And, if success eludes you, instead of allowing your Saboteurs to have you be hard on yourself, you're able to bring in your Sage Perspective and get curious about what you may not be clearly understanding.

Smaller, more achievable goals will activate your continued success. Once you bring one client on, you'll be motivated to turn your attention to the next client and so on. So make your goals easy to win. Remember that the way of the Sage is ease and flow. Making sure your goals are achievable from the start ensures the ease and flow you want in your efforts. If at any point your goal feels insurmountable and unachievable, then ask yourself what would need to shift or change to ensure your success. Making it easy to win is half the battle. The more achievable your goals are, the more likely you will stick with them through completion.

Realistic

Even when a goal is achievable, is it realistic for you right now in this present moment? For internal coaches (i.e. those working for a non-coaching company as an in-house coach) and coaches who are coaching as their side-hustle, this is a really important question to consider. What happens when I'm successful? Is it realistic to think I can keep my day job and also grow my coaching practice? What happens when both my day job and my coaching business are demanding my attention?

If you know you're intention is to ultimately transition from your current day job to become a full-time coach, then are you ready to make that transition now? If not, what would need to shift or change so you could make this transition. As the saying goes, "failing to plan is planning to fail." Being realistic is about anticipating what's ahead and being ready to make the changes necessary to ensure your success. Said another way, success is when opportunity meets preparedness. You are preparing your coaching practice to grow and scale. Make sure it's realistic for you to remove any obstacles that might prevent this outcome from happening.

Time-Bound

Lastly, by when will you achieve this goal? "Someday" is not a S.M.A.R.T. goal. Giving yourself a hard deadline allows you to work backwards from that date to ensure it's the R in S.M.A.R.T. (realistic). Having your goal be time-bound also allows you to share your goal with your accountability partners. "By [date], I will ..." allows someone else to check in with you to see if that goal has been achieved. If it has, then they can celebrate with you. If it has not, there's a wonderful opportunity to explore the gift in not achieving the goal you set out to achieve.

Deadlines are also a powerful motivator. Having too much time to accomplish something can make it hard to ever accomplish it. That's why "someday" is a dream, not a goal. When you add a timeframe to your goals, you're making a commitment to yourself to have it happen. Otherwise, it's just another "should." (And as Tony Robbins likes to tease, "Don't Should All Over Yourself!")

The Ultimate Sage Growth Experience

Once again, I want to acknowledge you for the work you're doing here. Building and growing your coaching practice is the ultimate expression of your Sage showing up in the world. Who you become in the process of building and growing your coaching practice is the ultimate expression of your Sage. You're about to grow your Sage in ways unimaginable before you began this journey.

Shirzad has said on more than one occasion that, "Business development is your Sage black-belt teacher." Meaning, the challenges you'll face in growing your business will strengthen your Sage and help you become the best version of yourself. Along your path, you will encounter each of your Saboteurs and usually at the most inopportune times. As you let go of how you believe it should look and begin to see things as they are, you can begin to shift your perspective and truly see all of the challenges you face as gifts along the way. Each challenge, each set-back, and each encounter with your Saboteurs empowers you to strengthen your Sage Powers and Self-Command.

That's why business development is the ultimate Sage growth experience! You can't help but grow your Sage as you take on the building and scaling of your coaching business. While your Saboteurs would have you believe that you're not ready or don't have strength necessary for this journey, you already know that's a lie. Everything you need is already inside of you just waiting to come forth (and play).

I urge you to remain in Sage ease and flow throughout this journey. If something feels difficult, rather than trying to "push through it," pause and reflect on what's making it difficult. Ask yourself how it could be easier. How would your Sage approach this particular challenge? When you maintain that level of curiosity, you can see past the business development game itself. After all, while it may not seem like a "game" because you have so much riding on your success, it's that very pressure to succeed that activates your Saboteurs.

The moment you let go and accept the journey you are on is the moment you invite your Sage forward to have fun and enjoy the ride. Imagine your five year old self doing all of this. Would (s)he be all stressed out and frustrated? Or would that child inside have a grin from ear to ear seeing how incredible it is to have the opportunity to serve? At a heart level, there's no greater calling than supporting your clients to be the best version of themselves. When you take the time to remember why you're doing all of this, you can see that all the effort pales in comparison to the seismic impact you're making in the world.

In the next chapter we'll focus on how to ensure that nothing gets in your way as you choose to level up your coaching business and your life.

CHAPTER TEN

The Importance of Building Community & Accountability

One of the more challenging aspects of building your coaching business is how alone you can feel. This is especially true if you left a corporate job or switched your career after having been part of a team. If this is the first business you've ever created from the ground up, it's important to ensure you've built sufficient community along your journey. Despite how it may feel from time to time, you need not be alone.

Similarly, when you are working for yourself, you may be experiencing challenges with accountability. It's different when you work for someone else. When someone hires you to work for them, there's usually a job description and some form of key performance indicators that track your job performance. Before you ask for a raise or negotiate your next promotion, it's important that you're clear on your own job performance and know what your new job requirements would be should you be promoted and advance your career.

As a solopreneur, it's different, isn't it? In the back of your mind, you have a sense that you can improve in some areas, but the person you're accountable is to you. In this chapter, we're going to explore the importance of being part of a community of coaches who are committed to the same or similar outcomes as yours. We'll see how having built in accountability can help keep you on track and focused on your continued growth.

Simply put, the only person you can't coach is yourself. If you knew what was in your blind spot, you'd deal with it. Yet despite how powerful a coach you are, it's incredibly challenging to coach yourself; especially when you experience yourself in a plateau with little to no growth. Having outside perspective supports your ability to grow and expand. As the African proverb goes:

"If you want to go fast, go alone. If you want to go far, go together."

You've done the heavy lifting on designing your niche, so you know who it is you're looking to attract into your coaching business. While you don't necessarily need other coaches who are focused on the same ideal customer, it certainly can help to have like-minded coaches supporting you in your journey.

Building Your Community of Likeminded Coaches

Our Saboteurs perpetuate a scarcity mindset: if you win, I lose. But our Sage lives in abundance: advocating for your wins supports my winning. This is important to remember when building your community of like-minded coaches. Check in with yourself around any resistance to sharing your best practices, what's working and opportunities to collaborate. If your Saboteurs have convinced you to live in scarcity, you'll be reluctant to share what's working. Conversely, when your Sage supports you in trusting others who are with you along the way, your abundant mindset opens up all sorts of possibilities.

Building your community of like-minded coaches begins with your Sage abundant mindset. At the heart of it, you know deep down that there is plenty of business to go around. There's no reason to be Hyper-Vigilant and overconcerned about another coach benefiting from what's working in your coaching business. If anything, having another coach model what's working in your coaching business can either help validate the path you're on, or identify potential pitfalls before either of you get knocked off course.

It is with this foundational principle that we can be free to share our learning with others with whom we choose to be in community. This mindset ensures that you and the other coaches you choose to be in community with are able to share freely with one another and be vulnerable in asking for support when things aren't going according to plan.

Enter Communities of Practice

In 1995, I was part of an incredible community called the World Wide Web Artists Consortium (WWWAC) founded by some of the earliest pioneers of the Internet in New York City. Our group was lovingly referred to as Silicon Alley playing off the incredible growth of Silicon Valley some 3,000 miles away just south of San Francisco, California.

While we each had our own companies and diverse interests in how we could apply what we were learning about the Internet in a vast number of ways, we realized that without standards and foundational principles, this "Wild West" mentality wouldn't scale. There was also concerns about the biggest of the big players calling the shots and stifling innovation. Together, we could tap into our collective wisdom and apply what we knew.

Soon, however, we realized that we needed a way to organize the many diverse needs of the group. Someone offered up a solution with what they called, "Special Interest Groups" or SIGs. That way, we could narrow the focus outside of the main WWWAC meeting and have sub-groups that tackled the big issues impacting all of us. In very little time, we were able to address the diverse individual needs by coming together in different combinations of diverse team members. It worked really, really well.

So when I saw something similar happening at Positive Intelligence, I suggested we try something similar for our coaching efforts. In one of the very first meetings we held, Jim Millner, who was already leading a Diversity, Equity, Inclusion and Belonging group suggested that we not call this effort SIGs, but rather Communities of Practice. The name of what we called our effort was important, he argued, and SIGs has too much association with government and politics. So we agreed to create Communities of Practice instead.

What Are Communities of Practice?

Communities of Practice are groups of people informally bound together by shared expertise and a passion for something they do. As they work together and interact regularly, they grow their expertise and improve their skillsets. The word "practice" is key. To have an interest in something tends to lead toward intellectual curiosity. To be a member of a community of practice means that you are a practitioner, regularly working on your craft so that it will continuously improve.

Many Communities of Practice develop shared resources from tools like case studies, stories, experiences, and strategies to tackle problems – especially recurring ones. By working together, each practitioner gains from the experience of the others in the community. Over time and sustained interaction, the value of the community grows as each member contributes for the benefit of all.

Doesn't that sound like something that would support you in your journey? For me it was foundational to my exponential growth, albeit in a different industry. Anytime you have an opportunity to practice with others who share a passion for what you do in the world, I urge you to take advantage of it. Your combined experiences will minimize the setbacks that inevitably occur when honing your craft.

Applying Mental Fitness To Your Niche

At Positive Intelligence, we initially launched our Communities of Practice as a means to empower our PQ Coach members to gather their wisdom together and apply mental fitness to their niche. The concept was that while the foundations of mental fitness are universally applicable, there are important nuances when applying the principles of mental fitness to specific niches. For example, how you would introduce mental fitness to lawyers would be very different from working with young adults or C-Suite executives.

After a full year of a beta test, we realized that there were universal applications and categories that would serve the greatest good. Version 2.0 of Communities of Practice began to look very different. The core principles of applying mental fitness began to emerge into broader categories such as relationships, performance, belonging, spirituality, and profession.

Once we were able to see the larger container that would support tens of thousands of coaches, it became clear how to scale our Communities of Practice while ensuring that individual coaches received the interaction and support they craved while working together toward a common desired outcome.

After all, every one of us is committed to changing lives. *How* we change the lives of others depends on where each of us is in our learning journey and the experience and support we need along the way. What exists today is the outcome of so many incredible pioneers who were willing to "play" with the community of practice model and figure out what served the greater good. I am forever in the debt of these leaders that I continue to learn from to this day.

The Power of Sage Accountability Partners

Being in a community of practice by itself may not be enough to help keep you on track. I can't underscore enough how powerful it is to have an accountability partner (or multiple partners). Deciding you want to take an action is great. Telling someone else what you've decided to take action on helps reinforce your commitment to yourself. Having someone else check in with you at regular intervals to support your progress is priceless.

This is especially true for coaches. Think about it. You joined this industry for a noble cause. You decided your profession was all about being a servant leader. As such, you are committed to being in the service of others. The risk, however, is that you end up doing more for others than you do for yourself. Recall that your journey in coaching is about opening up to receive. You're already an incredible giver (otherwise you wouldn't be drawn to this profession).

The power of having an accountability partner, is that you are allowing someone else to support you along your journey. The reason most people shy away from accountability is that their experience has been around Saboteur-led accountability, not Sage accountability.

Saboteur-led accountability comes from another person's Judge, Controller, Stickler, Hyper-Achiever, or other Saboteur. You experience being judged, feeling controlled, never being enough, never achieving enough and all the other negative feelings associated with *their* Saboteur's view of what you're doing bad, wrong or not enough. Underneath all of this is a sense of fear, scarcity and negativity. Who would ever want that?

Contrast that with Sage-led accountability based in love. Love can be fierce. Love can challenge you to be your best. But at all times, you are experiencing Sage discernment, not Saboteur judgment. If you're a parent, you can totally relate to the difference. When your toddler begins walking toward a busy street, your Sage Activate takes over. You are swift and you bring your toddler back to safety. They may not like it, but there was never any intent other than to keep your child safe. It's done in love even if the action is swift.

That's what we want here. Sage-led accountability is about having someone else hold you high. To align with the brilliance of your own Sage, challenge you in love, and all the while hold empathy and compassion for all that you're up to. If you've never experienced Sage-led accountability, it's no wonder you have an aversion to being held accountable. Now is your opportunity to anticipate what might throw you off your course, identify your support needs and design your own Sage accountability.

Identify & Design Your Own Sage Accountability

How would you like to be held in Sage accountability? What would that even look like? Put aside any negative Saboteur accountability from the past. This is different by design. Let me give you an example to get you started and we'll go from there.

In order to write this book, I knew I would need to write about 1,000 words every day for approximately 100 days. Some days would be more than 1,000. Some days would be less than 1,000 or none at all. What I didn't want was to go more than two days with zero words written. If that happened, then I was in trouble and likely needed support. I also didn't need to add another "to do" to my list requiring a long check-in with my accountability partners. That would likely lead me to Saboteur accountability as I would feel negatively about the meeting, judge myself for my lack of progress, feel judged by my accountability partners, etc. I knew that wasn't going to work for me. So what would?

I told my accountability partners what Sage accountability looked like so that they could support me in a very Sage way. Every day I would sit down and write for about an hour. My target would be 1,000 words. When I was done writing, I would text them both what my word count was. I made it clear that I wasn't fishing for any comments such as "Nice work!" "Good Job!" or emojis of positive reinforcement. Instead, if they noticed that two days had gone by without a word count from me, then something was off. Then, and only then, would I really appreciate support such as a check-in, question, or offer to talk about what's happening.

Notice, I put the majority of the accountability on me. In only asked for the support I actually needed (and in Sage). I would do the heavy lifting and they would receive daily evidence of my progress. Only when there was no evidence would it help me if they inquired. That was precisely what I needed to keep going in my journey. Writing a book is often about keeping momentum. Some parts are easier than others, but when there's no momentum, it's easy to focus elsewhere and have the project go completely off the rails.

Now it's your turn. Where do you need accountability support from others? Depending on where you are in this moment, that might look like carving out time to practice and refine your Niche statement. Or perhaps you'd like to ensure you're offer is irresistible. Or maybe you'd love to practice converting appointments. Or if you have all of that, then it's about exploring the best ways for you to generate appointments consistently by doing what you love. Even if you're nodding your head and saying, "Yes to all, please!!" you want to start somewhere. When you chase all four rabbits you catch none, so start with one and grow from there.

Designing your own accountability means knowing what you specifically need to be successful. If you know the number one challenge you're up against is generating appointments, then you could make a target list of the number of appointments you need to generate and begin sharing your daily progress toward that end. Early on it won't be as simple as "take action, get result." So design pre-appointment setting accountability such as number of outreach efforts (text, email, phone calls, LinkedIn messages, etc.) or podcast interviews booked or keynote presentations you have firmed up. It can be a word count (like I described when writing articles) you'll post to attract your niche or anything else that would support your forward movement.

Just ... keep ... going.

This is about aligning your Sage Power Activate with your accountability partner(s). Sage accountability is designing the flow you choose to be in and ensuring you're staying there. When you inevitably get knocked off your game, it really helps to have Sage accountability partners there to support your getting back onto your path– the path of the Sage. Remember that the path of the Sage is ease and flow, so if you'd over-engineered your (Saboteur?) accountability, take a good hard look at it and make it easier to win. When done correctly, Sage accountability feels like a warm blanket of love and support on a cold winter's night. You will want to have it as it keeps you connected to your mission, vision and purpose. Without Sage accountability, you are likely to wander off your own Sage path and end up in activities that simply don't lead to what you're committed to having in your life.

Identify your Key Performance Indicators (KPIs) of Coaching

But Bill, all who wonder are not lost, right?

Sure. And there are many, many paths that will lead to your success. You live in a time of unfathomable abundance. So where do you place your focus? How do you know if what you're working on is optimal? This is where having key performance indicators (KPIs) are so helpful. Any KPI tells you that you're either on-track or off-track. When you're on-track you keep going in that direction with the confidence that what you're doing will eventually lead to the outcome you desire. When you're off-track, you see it and adjust accordingly.

KPIs are metrics. When done correctly, you should be able to share with anyone and they can objectively see that you're taking the right actions in accordance with your desired outcomes. For example, one very important KPI of coaching is number of discovery calls. Knowing that the average coach needs 10 discovery calls to generate one client, then the more discovery calls (with your niche) will lead to having the number of paying clients you seek.

Most Common KPIs of Coaching

While you can adjust any of these to suit your needs, I'll share with you the most common KPIs of any coaching business. By tracking and paying attention to these numbers, you can quickly determine the success of your efforts.

- Number of active, paying clients
- Conversion rate on your discovery calls
  - Total number of clients divided by total number of discovery calls
  - Average is 10% (i.e. one client for every 10 discovery calls)
- Number of discovery (enrollment) calls per week
  - Knowing it takes an average of 10 discovery calls to get one client, this will help you project when you will have the number of clients you seek
  - Want more clients? Generate more discovery calls
- Number of outreach efforts to generate one discovery call
  - Varies by effort, but this also tells you how irresistible your offer is
- Conversion rate on your outreach efforts
  - Allows you to compare time spent direct messaging in LinkedIn vs. a speaking engagement (Divide appointments generated by total audience in attendance or outreaches made directly)

While these are the most common when it comes to growing your coaching business, you could also measure scaling KPIs such as:

- Average lifetime value of a client
- Average length of a client engagement
  - Total number of months actively coaching with you
  - If you require a minimum of six months, what's the longevity post-six months?
- Amount of support time between coaching sessions
  - Capture total time invested in each client beyond individual coaching sessions
- Percentage of late-paying clients

As you begin to provide clarity for yourself around the core KPIs of your coaching business, you can spot trends and understand your biggest areas needing improvement. Do your clients stay with you for years or drop out after a few months? This will tell you if you have a churn or retention challenge that needs attention. How much effort are you spending getting a single client? That will tell you the true value of a client engagement once you factor in the value of the time it took to land this client in the first place.

The more you capture the easier it will be to ask and answer questions about the growth of your coaching business (or what's hindering that growth). KPIs allow you to focus on what truly matters at each stage of your development. Early on, it's about generating clients. Then it becomes more of a focus on retention, then about optimizing the rate and value delivered. Knowing which KPIs to focus on ensures you're not distracted by the entirety of your business, but rather focusing on the areas you most want to improve.

Learning from *Traction* by Gino Wickman

There are so many incredible resources out there. Sometimes, it's hard to know what to pay attention to. This is especially true when you realize that our brains were designed to seek out the "never ending" 20% insight rather than the 80% muscle building that we need to be successful. If we're not careful, we can spend all our time and attention listening to the experts and precious little time embodying and acting on our own Sage wisdom.

That said, when you are looking to build and scale your coaching business, there are core principles that every business owner (that's you) needs to know. For example, Gino Wickman point out that, "Your processes are your *Way* of doing business … Most entrepreneurs don't understand how powerful process can be, but when you apply it correctly, it works like magic, resulting in simplicity, scalability, efficiency and profitability."[60]

You have a way of doing business. The question is, is your way of doing business driven by your Sage or your Saboteurs? When I first began, my Controller was in the driver's seat. God help you if you attempted to stand between me and my desired outcome. I was known for railroading anyone that got in my way. My process was simple and yet highly inefficient. Whatever I decided was important got done – usually by me and usually at the cost of other equally (or even more important) aspects of the business.

It was a hard lesson to overcome. I damaged many relationships in my overwhelming desire to build and grow my business. And I was confused because my Saboteurs had convinced me that "the ends justify the means." Who cares whose feelings get hurt as long as we reach the most important outcomes. Soon, I became the bottleneck of my own business because even if I asked someone else to do something, I'd ultimately decide it wasn't good enough, and I'd end up doing it myself. This proved very inefficient and frustrating to me and my employees.

What's your process? Have you ever taken the time to map out each step? For example, how does your niche find out about you? What action do they take to connect with you? How do they get on your calendar? What notifications / confirmations do they receive? What reminders are sent out if any? And so on.

As you map out your existing process, you can begin to see gaps or opportunities for improvement. You're not looking for "the perfect" process, but rather a mapped-out process that anyone could follow. Even if it's just you as a solopreneur, when you map out your process you get it out of your head and on paper where you can evaluate it and improve upon it.

What Gino Wickman has developed is the *Entrepreneurial Operating System (EOS)*. It's an elegant and simplified way to look at the foundations of your business and continuously improve upon each of them. What's more, if your niche includes small and medium sized businesses, chances are they are actively using the EOS framework or something very similar to it. By mapping out your own process, you are empowered to improve on your business model and bring in support for the areas where you could use some extra help.

Applying Objectives & Key Results (OKRs) to your Coaching Business

I've brought up Gino Wickman's *Traction* book to help elevate the importance of understanding your own business process. In the context of building community

---

[60] Wickman, Gino. *Traction: Get a Grip on Your Business*. BenBell Books. ©2011, page 7.

and accountability, understanding your own process will empower you to receive accountability support in any aspect of your coaching business you desire.

This leads you to the understanding that your time is your most precious resource and so in Sage ease and flow, you're going to want to spend the bulk of your time focused on the 20% that drives the 80%. That is, the 20% of the tasks and actions that deliver 80% of the outcomes you're looking to create. That's the Sage approach to building your coaching business in ease and flow. The Saboteur alternative is to obsess over the 80% effort that delivers only 20% of the outcomes you desire.

To avoid time wasters in your coaching business, it's important to get clear about the outcomes that matter most to you right now in this moment. Businesses tend to break down the year into quarters. January to March would be Q1, April to June, Q2, and so on. We tend to over-estimate what we can accomplish in one month and underestimate what we can accomplish in a year. So quarterly planning tends to be just right. Begin to break up your year by quarters and then determine the most important objectives that will lead to the outcomes you seek. Successful outcomes are determined by your "key result." It's what you want to have happen by knowing the results you'll need to have as evidence that your outcome was achieved. Your objective is what actions you must take in order to achieve the key results.

Examples of Objectives & Key Results (OKRs)

You'll want to customize the objectives and key result that are right for your stage of growth. While you may desire to have $1MM in revenue from your coaching business, you would want to map out the steps to get there. So when you're first starting out, your ORKs might look like this:

1. Determine My Niche for My Coaching Business
   a. Schedule a two-hour time block to complete the niche worksheet
   b. Meet with my pod to share what I've come up with
   c. Receive feedback from my pod and refine my niche further
   d. Practice saying my niche out loud in the mirror 100 times or more
   e. Attend a networking event to practice sharing my niche with referral sources
   f. Further refine my niche having practiced sharing it with prospects
   g. Update my LinkedIn profile and website with my niche profile

2. Develop My Irresistible Offer
   a. Research the biggest pain points that my niche has
   b. Select one pain point that I can focus on in my coaching work
   c. Complete the irresistible offer worksheet

    d.   Meet with my pod to share what I've come up with

    e.   Receive feedback from my pod and refine my irresistible offer further

    f.   Practice saying my irresistible offer out loud in the mirror 100 times or more

    g.   Attend a networking event to practice sharing my offer with referral sources

    h.   Further refine my irresistible offer having practiced sharing it with prospects

    i.   Update my LinkedIn profile and website with my irresistible offer and include my calendar link

3. Generate Ten Calendar Appointments

    a.   Determine method I'll use to generate appointments on my calendar

    b.   Update this OKR with the appointment generating actions to take

    c.   Having determined my method will be direct outreach to start, schedule two hours per day to conduct direct outreach efforts

    d.   Determine number of outreach efforts needed in order to generate one scheduled calendar appointment

    e.   Repeat sufficient outreach efforts to generate 10 calendar appointments

4. Generate Three Clients

    a.   Determine if method chosen to generate appointments on my calendar is effective or should be changed to something else that I already love doing

    b.   Having generated ten calendar appointments, practice mock conversion (*Art of the Close*) with my pod

    c.   Receive feedback from my pod and refine my *Art of the Close* conversion further

    d.   Track success rate of all ten discovery call appointments on my calendar

    e.   If other than one YES for every nine Nos, adjust number of calendar appointments necessary to generate a single client.

    f.   Repeat the steps above in order to generate two more clients

Setting up your OKRs at the beginning of each quarter allows you to regularly check in with yourself and your pod on how much progress you're making (and where you could use some support). Or, as Benjamin Franklin said, "If you fail to plan, you are planning to fail."[61] This is where many coaches struggle and get stuck. By neglecting to plan out the way that they will spend their time, they end up dealing with whatever circumstances are in front of them.

---

[61] https://www.goodreads.com/quotes/460142-if-you-fail-to-plan-you-are-planning-to-fail

Conversely, when you choose to develop then execute on your plans, you are designing your life instead of managing your circumstances. These plans will also illuminate where you are stuck so that you can ask for support. All too often, all you know is that you don't have the result you want. Building OKRs will help you map out precisely the steps you believe are necessary in order to succeed. Then, when you see what doesn't get done or you are unable to accomplish the next task, you can get curious and deploy your own Sage Powers of Explore and Innovate (after having deep empathy for yourself and your situation) so that you can learn from whatever challenge shows up on your path to mastery.

Your Saboteurs would like to point out that you're not an expert in any of this, and then ask "so why bother?", while your Sage understands that this is the learning journey towards your own self-actualization and Sage mastery. The journey itself is the path to mastery.

Take Time to Review Your Progress

The importance of building community and accountability is so that you continue your journey towards self-actualization and Sage mastery. How we view this journey is determined by who (inside us) is looking. While our Saboteurs are quick to point out all the challenges and struggles that are to come ahead of us, your Sage enjoys turning around from time to time to see all the incredible progress you've already made.

I highly recommend scheduling out regular celebration points. This can be as frequently as daily or weekly, or as infrequent as monthly or quarterly. The more you condition yourself to celebrate your progress, the more progress you will make. It may sound strange to celebrate receiving six "Nos" this week; that is, until you consider you're more than half way to securing a client (as it typically takes nine "Nos" for every one "Yes!").

Each time you review your progress, ensure that your focus is on the positive and celebratory aspects. What progress can you celebrate? What breakthroughs were had today? What lessons have you learned? How will you apply these lessons to help shape and expand your coaching business in meaningful ways?

Reviewing your progress is an opportunity for you to stop and smell the proverbial roses along your journey. Laser focus on the outcome can blind you to all your progress, invite your Saboteurs in and lead to burnout. By building breaks in along the way to acknowledge and celebrate your progress, you have a much higher likelihood of continuing your journey – even when you experience challenges and headwinds.

I come from a family of musicians. My father and brother are both Ph.D.'s in music (theory and performing arts respectively). My mom was an elementary school music teacher. While I've learned everything I know about music from my family, I'm choosing to bring it up here because of a simple family of symbols you will find on every sheet of music: the rest symbols.

Whole Note ○	4 Counts
Half Note ♩	2 Counts
Quarter Note ♩	1 Count
Eighth Note ♪	½ Count
1/16th Note ♬	¼ Count

While music can be soft and gentle or loud and fierce, no matter what is being played, without rest the music wouldn't work. The balance is between playing and not playing. Making beautiful sounds and then stopping to allow those last few notes to "hang" out there and dissipate. It's what makes music so magical.

And rests are built in by the composer. When a composer designs his music, he is purposefully designing in rests. Rests build anticipation as well as allow you to savor what has just been played. So too will you want to design in these breaks that allow you to savor your coaching progression. It can be a short 15-minute acknowledgement each day (I like to do mine in the mornings before breakfast), or a longer pause at the conclusion of a week.

Decide up front where you choose to place your rests in your day, week, month and quarter. The more you choose to celebrate your progress, the faster you'll experience growth. Each celebration releases a bit of dopamine in your brain and encourages more of the same. Taking time to pause and reflect will give you the space to acknowledge the progress you're making so that you can progress even further in your journey.

Ideally, you can bring this into your support and accountability pod and make this a regular practice that you all do together. At first, this may feel like bragging and be uncomfortable. Notice the Saboteurs that do their best to shut you down. But soon, you'll actually crave this part of your work together as you truly and authentically celebrate yourself and your buddies.

This practice will support you through the hard times and ensure you keep going even when you experience a feeling of being lost, unsure or confusion. This is a natural part of growth. Remember, no one grows safely *inside* your comfort zone. It's the act of leaving your comfort zone that allows growth to occur. This is why building community and accountability are important to your success. This is you going the distance and ensuring your success.

CHAPTER ELEVEN

Continuing Your Journey of Sage Mastery

When I received my black belt in Soo Bahk Do, Moo Duk Kwon, my instructor said to me, "Congratulations! Now you can *begin* your training." That was quite a paradigm shift. For most people, achieving the level of black belt in a martial art is the desired outcome. A true martial artist, however, sees this accomplishment as the beginning of a lifelong quest. It was also pointed out to me that my black belt was actually midnight blue. Why? Because perfection is an illusion and can never be reached despite all of our best efforts.

Your journey of Sage Mastery is a similar quest in that mental fitness is a life long journey. Every effort that you put into your own mental fitness will yield an improvement. The goal is your own peak performance, happiness, healthy relationships and well-being. The journey continues as you go deep inside yourself and let go of your Saboteur fear and negative self-talk.

Will you ever be rid of your Saboteurs? Unfortunately, no. But what was once an automatic response to outside stimulus will become a whisper in the background of your day-to-day life. As your Sage becomes your dominant way of being, the power of your Saboteurs will continue to weaken. While they will remain present, they begin to be nothing more than an early warning signal that can be helpful to keep you alert.

Sage Mastery embodies the five Sage Powers of Empathy, Explore, Innovate, Navigate and Activate as each power is ever present and immediately accessible in everything you do. This is what's next as you continue to build and grow the business end of your coaching business. Let's explore what's next for you as you lean into this way of being.

Sage Power Empathy Applied to Your Coaching Business

Your Sage Power Empathy is how you remain open to whatever shows up in your coaching business. To have empathy for yourself is to understand that you are a perfectly imperfect human on your journey towards self-actualization. As you progress in your coaching business, you will continue to be tested, reminding you of where you are on your journey and what's to come.

When Your Business Hits a Plateau, Remain Curious

Inevitably, your business will rise, fall and plateau. The early rise invites a near state of euphoria as you put all of the four pillars of business development into practice. Having done the work to really figure out your niche and ideal customer, you're regularly talking to those whom you choose to serve at the highest level. And yet, at some point you notice that what was working initially appears to have hit an invisible glass ceiling. No matter what you do, you appear to have reached a threshold in your business where you desire more, but the efforts you're making are no longer producing the results you had previously achieved.

This is when your Saboteurs jump in. Your Judge uses this temporary set-back to beat you up mentally. "See, I knew you couldn't succeed! You're doing everything you were taught and still you're not getting results. This will never work. Why even bother? You're just setting yourself up for pain, frustration and disappointment. Better quit now while you're ahead!" And that nasty Judge enrolls your top accomplice Saboteurs to convince you that continuing down this path is a futile effort and you should stop.

For many, this is the end of the road. These limiting beliefs become a self-fulfilling prophecy. The risk is that we trap ourselves by looking for evidence that we don't have what it takes. "Sure, these other coaches were successful, but that's just not me!" When you truly believe something, you look for (and usually find) the evidence that proves you right. This is the trap that so many of us fall into.

The antidote is Sage Power Empathy. Rather than allowing your Saboteurs to beat you up, you begin to focus on empathy for yourself. "Yes, I'm having some resistance to my efforts. How can I shift my focus from all the self-limiting beliefs to remaining curious around what's actually going on?" Empathy for yourself begins with seeing all the efforts you have invested in your coaching business and trusting that this plateau will reveal something insightful. Perhaps there is a powerful gift here if we remain curious and see what's really going on.

In addition to empathy for yourself, keep going back to the needs of your ideal customer. After all, when you can have empathy for them and what they are going through, you can quickly shift your focus from all the reasons your efforts do not appear to be successful and instead reconnect with just how much your ideal customers need you. Your focus on their needs will help you realign to why you choose to be a coach in the first place.

And to go even deeper, imagine having empathy for the situation you find yourself in. Recognize that every coach goes through plateaus in their business and experiences temporary setbacks. Having empathy for the situation you find yourself in allows you to remain curious and see what you might otherwise have missed.

And so I ask you, how committed are you to your own Sage Mastery? Building a six or seven figure coaching business will reveal every Saboteur you have and challenge you to leverage all of your Sage Powers – starting with Empathy for yourself, your ideal clients and the diverse situations you find yourself in.

Having Empathy When Your Business Declines

Another set-back occurs anytime your business is in decline. Despite your best efforts, you're going to lose clients – not just one, but multiple clients. In fact, the more successful you are, the higher the expectations your ideal customers will have when they engage you as their coach. Rather than acknowledging the perfectly imperfect human being that you are, your clients may choose to hold you to a fairly unreasonable bar with high expectations. The worst of these expectations is that *you* will end up doing the work *for* your clients. While you're clear that your clients must be the ones to do the work, that doesn't stop the Saboteurs of your clients from judging your ability as a coach to help them succeed.

Here again, Sage Power Empathy will reconnect you with the truth and remove much of the perceived power your Saboteurs believe they have to control you. When you authentically connect to empathy for yourself, you will accept who you are and what you can (and cannot) do as a coach. When a client inevitably decides it's time to move on, deep empathy for yourself will ensure you see this choice for what it is – your client's choice for what's best for them – rather than the Saboteur lies they would have you believe. Lies to the effect that you're a terrible coach, no one should hire you, blah, blah, blah.

Having empathy for your (former) client will have you see that they are making the best decision for themselves in this moment. In fact, they may not even be "good bye" as much as "good bye for now." Some clients do recognize their own Saboteurs and with the benefit of time change their mind. If you take the position that life is happening *for* you rather than *to* you, you'll trust that this decision is best for you both. And, if it's not the best decision, that one or both of your Sage selves will learn a powerful lesson that will support future growth.

This is how having empathy for the situation of losing a client can be so powerful. Our Saboteurs would have us ignore any possible gifts in losing a client and simply dwell on why it's such a terribly bad thing to happen. With reduced income there are some very real consequences that must be addressed. However, dwelling on all the negative repercussions will blind you to any positive aspects of no longer having this particular client. For example, losing this client could free you up to bring on a new client at a higher bill rate. Rather than replacing this lost client with a new client at the same rate, why not take this opportunity to see about raising your fee? Your Saboteurs will hold you in scarcity mode and deny this possibility, but your Sage knows better. Why not continue your appointment generation and try out closing with a higher rate?

Having empathy will ensure that you see what's right there in front of you rather than making up stories about what's actually happening. This is the important distinction between "fact" and "interpretation." The fact is, you lost a client. The Saboteur interpretation is that losing this client is *bad* and the loss of income is *devastating* and ultimately this is a reflection of just how *terrible* a coach you are. These are all Saboteur lies, but when you're feeling down, these lies can sound very convincing. Empathy shines a bright light on these lies and allows you to see the truth.

Yes, you lost a client. Who knows if that loss is *bad* or *good*? Five years from now, what action(s) will you be most proud of in having lost a client? How will wallowing in your own suffering help you in any meaningful way? When you realize that suffering is, in fact, a choice, you'll choose differently. Yes, pain is inevitable, but suffering is a choice we make when we choose to dwell on something we don't like. Our suffering is our interpretation of what actually happened (i.e. "the facts"). Sage discernment is about acknowledging and dealing with the facts, while our Saboteurs prefer interpretations used to manipulate us into playing it safe and avoiding any potential growth – especially when it comes to growth that requires taking risks.

Choose Sage Power Empathy. And continue your journey of Sage Mastery. Empathy isn't where the journey ends, but it's a great place to begin – especially when you experience yourself as feeling "low" or in Saboteur mode.

Sage Power Explore Applied to Your Coaching Business

Be curious. Be fascinated. And when it comes to your Sage Mastery in your coaching business, just be. Think of your coaching business as your ultimate playground. Think back to when you were a kid at recess. The playground was where it was at. Swings. Slide. Climb. Run. So much to explore, play and have fun. So much fun, that when the bell rang and it was time to go back inside, there was a feeling of loss and missing out.

Imagine if that's how you felt every day in building your coaching business? Instead of a bell to go outside, you have your morning alarm clock. All day you get to play and be fascinated by who else is on the playground with you. When you were a kid, did you worry about how to play with other kids? Maybe when you were older, but when you were first in school, chances are that playing was fun with anyone. New kid? Old friend? New game? Didn't matter. Recess was fun and you were here to play and maximize your time having fun.

If you can embody that perspective in your coaching business, you'll crush it. Being curious and fascinated means you see yourself on that proverbial playground having fun playing the ultimate game called Sage Mastery. In this game, you're a coach and there are hundreds (if not thousands) of your ideal customer prospects out there. They need you, but they only discover that they need you by hearing you share how you help them reach their greatest desired outcome. You choose what, when and how often you want to share. But the more you share, the more prospects you attract into your coaching business.

This whole book has been about sharing with you the "rules" of the game. To build a thriving coaching practice, you'll need your niche, irresistible offer, and methods of generating and converting appointments. But the game isn't building your coaching business, is it? The real game is Sage Mastery. That's when you choose to self-actualize through the art of building your coaching business.

Explore Your Performance

From a place of fascination and curiosity (not judgment), how's your performance as a coach? When you can explore without judgment, you are open to where you are in your journey as a coach and how you can continue to increase your performance. This could mean signing up for more training in a particular aspect of your coaching, hiring a mentor, or simply working regularly with fellow coaches looking to improve their skills.

Your number of hours spent as a coach help you keep track of the amount of time you're investing in your coaching practice. That's why the International Coaching Federation has you keep a log of all your compensated and uncompensated coaching hours. When you remain fascinated by your own performance as a coach, you'll look for ways you can continue to improve. Just because you were accredited doesn't mean you're "done" improving your performance. Regular practice will ensure that you continue your learning journey and apply your ever-improving performance to the benefit of your clients. This, in turn, ensures that the value of your coaching continues to grow and that you will continue to be in demand.

As you explore your own performance as a coach, understand that it's not about being critical of yourself. Rather, this is an opportunity to reflect on what's working so that you can do more of that and what can be improved so that you can be an even better coach. This is a super power you have in your life. The more you use your coaching skills, the stronger they become. The more you work to improve your skills as a coach, the easier and more fun your coaching will be as you continue to grow your own performance.

Explore Your Relationships

When is the last time you got curious about all the relationships you have in your life? Who have you attracted into your life? Who have you chosen to remove? What relationships could use some love and attention? Coaching is very much a relationship business. Even if you self-identify as an introvert, your relationships matter a great deal.

As you explore your relationships, allow your curiosity to drive you here. Why is this person in my life? What am I learning? How am I growing from this relationship? How will I apply what I'm learning to growing and expanding my coaching business? Exploring your relationships with your clients, for example, will illuminate important aspects of how you choose to model your coaching practice. When it comes to clients, what actions do you choose to take between your designated coaching session? How do your clients know that you are committed to their success? While you're not required to take any actions, when you begin to explore your relationships, patterns begin to emerge.

One client of mine made birthdays his thing. He systematically collected every birthday of everyone who was important to him in his life. He then wrote out a birthday card for every person he wanted to build a relationship with. He would send out hundreds of hand-written birthday cards each year. That doesn't mean you should do any of this. It's just an example of when someone explores their relationships, they can see opportunities (like celebrating a person's birthday) to deepen important relationships.

As you explore your relationships, what can you discover that will help you grow and expand your coaching business? Your Sage can and will illuminate all sorts of possibilities. Before taking any actions, just capture them as options to consider. Generating awareness is a wonderful first step in seeing new possibilities that will help you grow. Taking the time to explore is a powerful step towards building and scaling the coaching practice you desire.

Explore Your Health & Well-Being

How's your health? I know the first two businesses I ever built took a heavy toll on my health. Granted, I was being driven by my Controller and Hyper-Achiever. I truly believed that being a "workaholic" was a badge of honor and not taking breaks was a sign of strength. How misguided I was. I now know those were the lies of my Saboteurs; lies that I bought into fully and lived at the expense of my own health and well-being.

The paradox I discovered was that when I slowed down, I sped up. When I took on martial arts, figure drawing, reading books, and spending quality time with the people closest to me, my business didn't decline, it flourished. I was so charged up when I started my work day that I was incredibly irresistible to prospective clients. My powers grew as I ensured my own health and well-being took priority. While I was still disciplined and put in the hours my business needed to grow and expand, I became very choosy as to what I spent my time on.

By prioritizing my own health and well-being, I left myself sufficient time to focus on the 20% of tasks that delivered 80% of the value. What I was forced to let go of was the 80% of the tasks that only delivered 20% of the value. In essence, by focusing on my health and well-being, I built a sustainable business model that grew and grew. As I charged myself up, so too did I charge up my team, my clients and anyone I chose to work with. My health and well-being encouraged others to take care of themselves. In other words, taking time to explore my health didn't just increase my own health and well-being, it positively impacted the health and well-being of everyone around me. Talk about Sage contagion!

Explore Your Coaching Business

From the space of fascinated anthropologist, what can you objectively learn about the way you run your coaching business? When you seek to truly and authentically understand what's driving (and what's inhibiting) your coaching business, let go of any judgments. Instead, get curious about what you're naturally compelled to do and what you appear to resist.

For example, if you see yourself as an extrovert, chances are the more time you spend with other people, the more energized you feel. That positive reinforcement will have you seek out more and more opportunities to get in front of people in various different ways. However, when it comes to contracts, billing, schedules and administrative tasks, you may find yourself avoiding these seemingly unpleasant aspects of your business.

What can you discover about yourself through the lens of your coaching business?

How you do one thing can show you how you do most things. What can you learn about yourself as you explore the different aspects of your coaching business? How are you when it comes to charging for your coaching services? What happens when a client wants to "pause" or wind down their work with you? What actions do you take (or choose not to take) when your business isn't performing in the ways you want it to?

Your coaching business is an extension of you and therefore will reflect both your strengths and your opportunities to grow, expand and improve. While your Saboteurs would love to point out all your faults and make you feel bad about them, your Sage has an uncanny ability to see your business with clear eyes and laser focus. When you give yourself time to pause and reflect, you will begin to explore the parts of your business that require more of your attention – or support from someone other than you.

You need not be the expert in all aspects of your coaching business. As you grow and expand, you may choose to hire individuals to take over the aspects of your business that you neither enjoy nor want to improve on your own. Saboteur scarcity will prevent you from taking these actions, but Sage abundance will support you in clearly seeing the value of having a team – once you can reasonably afford one.

Part of exploring your coaching business is better understanding the road ahead. In five, ten or more years out in the future, what will your business need? How will you maximize your financial freedom? What tax planning would support your future growth and eventual retirement? When should you hire a fiduciary (a financial advisor legally required to put your needs over their own) to support your investment strategy?

Each stage of business growth leads to more opportunities as well as new challenges that ensure your own continued growth towards self-actualization. Scheduling down time to review where you are in your coaching business, where you desire to be, and what's needed to get there ensures your continued growth as well as strengthening your Explore power.

This is the beauty of your coaching business journey. Each time you "level up" you are invited to new and different opportunities that will allow you to tap into your Sage in deeper and deeper ways. As you grow your coaching business, so, too, do you grow personally and professionally.

Explore Your World

Lastly, when considering how you apply your Sage Power Explore to your coaching business, continue to explore your world. What kind of impact are you having? Is this what you set out to do? Early on in your coaching business, you may find that Saboteur scarcity has you make decisions that align toward your basic survival needs. Specifically, making enough income to support the financial needs of yourself and your immediate family.

Once your core needs are met, it's easy to keep going in the same direction without considering viable alternatives. This is the "auto-pilot" that we can easily find ourselves falling into. When our Saboteur brains are no longer bothering us with any survival-related urgency, we tend to get comfortable and continue the path we began.

Taking time to explore your world will give you the time and space to see what impact you're currently having and the trajectory you're currently on. This is important to do periodically as you may find a need to change paths to ensure alignment towards your ultimate desired outcome.

For example, I never intended to join Shirzad at Positive Intelligence. As you read at the beginning of this book, I had successfully created the kind of coaching business

I had always dreamed of having. I was well on my way to having a seven-figure coaching practice while taking a minimum of one month off a year and travelling the world. I "made it" as far as I was concerned. I had studied the most successful coaches I could find, combined my insights and expertise with theirs and my trajectory appeared to be set for the foreseeable future.

When Shirzad became interested in having me join him, he didn't challenge any of that. He saw that I was happy doing my thing. To his credit, he asked an even more powerful question about impact. When he had me see that despite my financial success, I would have a "limited" impact on a few hundred clients in my lifetime, he had me dream bigger. Once I could see that I had an opportunity to impact millions of lives before I die, I couldn't "unsee" that vision.

By exploring my world, I could see a different path towards creating a seismic shift in my lifetime. By supporting 100,000 coaches (or more) impacting their own hundreds (or more) of clients through a mental fitness platform, the aggregate impact would easily reach into the millions (or more).

When thinking about Malcom Gladwell's book, *The Tipping Point*, I began to envision what a global impact mental fitness could have on all of us- from parents to school children, government agencies to large private companies, and so many non-profits, causes and neighborhoods. It was just too incredible not to "go for it."

Exploring my world led me to dreaming bigger about my contributions to the world. I invite you to do the same. What's your ultimate outcome? What kind of impact are you committed to making in the world? What vision is so big that it almost scares you at the possibility of happening? When you realize just how powerful your Sage actually is, even the sky doesn't feel like a limit – just another plane of existence. We were born into this world to do incredible things with the limited time we have here. This is our opportunity to step into what's possible and explore the incredible depths of our individual and collective capabilities.

Sage Power Innovate Applied to Your Coaching Business

Inspired? I hope so. You were meant to do amazing things in your lifetime. Sage Power Innovate supports you in expanding and widening your vision. When we first begin the process of building a coaching business, it's easy to get "tunnel vision." You see a specific outcome and you go after it. You see the next hurdle and you figure out how to go over, under or through it. Each step in your coaching business brings you to the next logical step. But left unexplored, this leads toward incremental growth and misses out on any exponential opportunities.

Incremental growth is about doing five-10% better. Exponential growth is about doing 25 to 100%+ better. Exponential growth doesn't happen with focusing on the thing right in front of you. Exponential growth happens with Sage Power Innovate as you begin to see what's been in your blind spot. Or, as Peter Theil likes to ask, "What's something you see that others don't?" That's where the exponential growth happens.

For me, Sage Power Innovate began when I was appalled at just how little money the average coach made according to the ICF. Relative to other industries, this just didn't seem fair. How could such a noble profession generate such little income? I saw a future where coaches make as much or more than the highest paid professions out there. And why not? Why not generate financial abundance while doing something you absolutely love?

To accomplish this, however, would require new and innovative thinking. This wasn't about doing incrementally more. This was about reimagining what success as a coach looked like. This was about playing the "Yes, and ..." game as we innovate into entirely new ways of working in this industry. Sage Power Innovate would ensure new thinking, new innovation, and new possibilities that would forever change the coaching industry. Woo Hoo!

What's the Biggest Challenge You Face in Your Coaching Business?

Whatever you see as the biggest challenge in your coaching business is a wonderful place to start with your Sage Power Innovate. Rather than being flummoxed by this challenge, you have the opportunity for a powerful breakthrough. Challenges are not here to stop us. Think of each challenge you come across as a heavy weight in your mental fitness gym. As you strengthen your own mental fitness around a particular problem, you grow yourself so that you can not only handle this particular problem, but others like it that you will inevitably face sometime in the future.

When you choose to reframe "challenges" into "opportunities" you can shift your entire perspective about what a challenge means for you. Rather than imagining a particular challenge as an obstacle to overcome, you can choose to see it as an opportunity to grow your Sage mastery and take one step closer to self-actualization. With each new challenge, viewed through the lens of an opportunity, you continue to grow and strengthen your own mastery. Your ability to handle any challenge that shows up in your coaching business is a sign of just how incredible your inner strength has become.

For many coaches, their biggest challenge tends to be "getting clients." Let's use this example to illustrate how your Sage Power Innovate grows your coaching business. Begin with the problem statement as a powerful open-ended question that is as clear as you can make it. For purposes of this illustration, we'll use, "How can I attract my ideal customers into my coaching practice?" And then let's start with the *worst* possible answer we can think of and build from there using the "Yes, and ..." technique.

- Set-up a child's lemonade stand in front of my house and give away FREE Donuts.

Now, using the "Yes, and ..." technique, we respond (to ourselves, in this case), "What I like about that idea is ..." and build from there. Witness the magic that can happen from the *worst* idea I could come up with. And remember that I'm doing this solo. Imagine how much more value you could generate by doing this work with your peer coach(es).

- What I like about that idea is giving something away for free. Instead of donuts, I can create a lead magnet such as "How to increase sales without spending a dime on advertising."
- What I like about having a lead magnet is that I could offer it on my website in exchange for a prospective ideal customer giving me their email address and permission to send them similar content in the future.
- What I like about generating a database of prospects is that I can then invite them to a free webinar where I address their biggest challenges and offer to have them book a discovery call with me.
- What I like about hosting a webinar where I address the customers' biggest problems is that I can use the feedback from that session to generate even more powerful lead magnets through actively listening to the biggest challenges my prospects face.
- What I like about having more lead magnets is that I can create a library of content that I can use to generate even more prospects, webinars and ultimately calendar appointments.
- What I like about booking more calendar appointments is that all I need is 10 appointments from my ideal customer prospects to generate a single client.
- What I like about generating a single client is that I can likely ask for a referral and that single client can easily become two, three or more clients in just a few months' time.

Wow. That took me precisely five minutes. Imagine if I dedicated 20-30 minutes and had the benefit of other peer coaches to play this game with me (and for the benefit of all involved)? That's the power of Innovate. As we build from the worst idea we can think of, we can slowly move toward the outcome we seek and capture all sorts of possibilities along the way. With this exercise, I'm energized to dive in and experiment with several of these ideas. Even if these are not right for you, try this process yourself and see what you can generate ... on your own or with a group committed to the same outcome you seek.

Using Sage Power Innovate to Exponentially Grow Your Coaching Business

Imagine if the challenge you choose to Innovate around was the entirety of your coaching business? The question might be, "How do I double my current coaching business?" Or "How do I 10x my coaching business?" The same rules apply as we just demonstrated in the previous section. While our Saboteurs might chime in here and say something like, "That would never work because …" our Sage discernment will counter that, "We'll never know until we try." Shall we give it a go?

Let's see what we can come up with together. Remember, just because I'm sharing the exercise doesn't mean I'm "right." This is simply illustrating what's possible when you choose to play the "Yes, and …" game on the opportunities that are most important to you.

- *Worst Idea:* To double my current coaching business, I could rob a bank.
- What I like about that idea is generating more cash flow in the business. And that idea inspires me to get clear on precisely how much money I would need to charge to precisely how many additional clients to double my coaching business.
- What I like about knowing precisely how many clients I need and at what rate in order to double my coaching business is that it feels manageable and achievable. And that idea inspires me to get clear on who within my niche could afford my coaching at this higher billing rate.
- What I like about narrowing my focus to clients who can afford a higher rate is that I can be really specific when doing my outreach efforts to these individuals. And this idea inspires me to host a dinner party exclusively to these individuals.
- What I like about hosting a dinner party is that it's an in-person event where each person gets to meet and connect with others who have similar backgrounds and likely struggling with the same issues.
- What I like about connecting these people together is that they will soon discover that they all share the same challenges and that will likely inspire them to be open and vulnerable about what they are struggling with.
- What I like about clients sharing what they are struggling with is that it allows for deeper and more honest conversation and that includes the value of solving the problem in very real terms.

What I like about quantifying the value of a problem is that my billing rate pales in comparison to the problem my client's face. Once that is fully understood, enrollment into my coaching program will feel like a no-brainer.

And so on. What's so fun about this exercise is that you have *no idea* what wisdom your Sage has just waiting to be unveiled. Our subconscious minds are incredibly powerful. The moment we commit to our own creativity and ingenuity, ideas begin to flow freely. And sure, you may not *love* all of the ideas that emerge, but many of them have real potential.

Hosting a dinner party was an idea my subconscious had stored from many decades ago when American Express Financial Advisors bought me a steak dinner and gave me some powerful insights about investing – both what it could and could NOT do for me. While I learned a lot that night, I remember thinking, "I need this person on my team!" My subconscious mind tucked that away until I did this exercise and suddenly it emerged to remind me of when I was the ideal customer prospect and was buying financial advisory services.

Today, it may serve just as well to set up a virtual meeting and send a care package with everything your prospect needs to enjoy the virtual session. That can be as creative as I choose and be a three-dimensional packaged reminder of both the challenge they face and why joining the virtual meeting would be so beneficial, fun and supportive.

Suddenly, growing my coaching business exponentially doesn't feel so "out there." Instead, I'm seeing multiple paths to make that possibility become a forgone conclusion and very probable reality. All it took was a commitment to Sage Power Innovate with a problem I very much would like to solve for myself. What resulted was not only ideation, but inspiration to go out and do something fun, entertaining and effective. I already know it works because I've been on the other side as a buyer. Now it's my turn to be the host. Game on!

Continued Innovation Year After Year

Momentum is your friend. If you want continued growth and scale, keep reimagining the next phase of growth in your coaching business. Sage Power Innovate will help you expand your view to see the big picture. Our brains tend to "spotlight" our focus so that we only see what's precisely in front of us. That's why our Saboteurs urge us "play it safe" and remain in our comfort zone. Unfortunately, there's little to no growth inside our comfort zone.

Continued innovation year after year is about getting outside of our comfort zone. We do this by identifying the next big challenge and then inviting our Sage self to innovate new and different approaches to grow ourselves and expand our practice. Will each new innovation work? Of course not. But the act of expansion is about stretching ourselves – especially through challenging and difficult times.

During the Covid-19 epidemic, there were lawn signs in my neighborhood that read. "We grow through what we go through." So true. Our most challenging and difficult times strengthen us as individuals and specifically grow our Sage powers – as long as we remain in Sage. When it comes to growth, Sage Power Innovate helps us break out of our comfort zone and come up with creative solutions that not only grow our coaching practice, but also grow our Sage. Self-actualization comes from that continued growth mindset from Sage. As we innovate, we challenge ourselves to be our best and that keeps us open to new and different possibilities.

Even when one of our ideas flops in a fantastic manor, we can still find the gifts of knowledge, power and inspiration. Our Sage doesn't see it as failure, but rather a learning opportunity and deeper growth. Continued innovation year after year is about constantly learning. And we learn so much more from our "failures" than we do from our successes. The gifts emerge from some of our most difficult times and shape us in ways we don't always understand or appreciate at the time that growth is happening.

Sage Power Navigate Applied to Your Coaching Business

"The best way to find yourself is to lose yourself in the service of others," said Mahatma Gandhi.[62] For me, that's one part of what we do as coaches. The other was summed up by Muhammad Ali when he said, "Service to others is the rent you pay for your room here on earth."[63] The power of connecting to your purpose supersedes all others when you meet your biggest obstacles along your path of Sage mastery and self-actualization.

No amount of money, power or status will motivate you as much as the impact of knowing how much you've changed the lives of the people you truly and deeply care about. When you're having a "bad day" (yes, Shirzad, I hear you when you say, "Who knows, what is good and what is bad?") we can forget why we do what we do as coaches. When a client chooses to end a coaching relationship, not pay a bill, or simply doesn't show up for a coaching session, our Saboteurs enjoy getting really vocal making up all sorts of lies about us, our ineffectiveness as a coach and our coaching business. It can get really dark really quickly, if we're not mindful.

That's why it's critical to connect with your preverbal "North Star" to remind you of why you do what you do when things don't go your way. When I think about the thousands of coaches who's lives I've already touched as part of my work, I'm inspired to take more action and not allow any set-back stand in my way. When I imagine each of those coaches helping dozens, hundreds or thousands of clients over their lifetime, it's easy to imagine the millions of lives I will indirectly impact in my lifetime.

Then I think about all the people who have supported me in my journey. I still marvel at the thought that I have the honor and privilege to work with Shirzad Chamine himself. I remember the half day I spent in a hotel room with none other than Tony Robbins. Or the time I was flown to Brazil to deliver a keynote presentation

---

[62] https://www.brainyquote.com/topics/service-quotes
[63] Ibid.

after Sir Richard Branson (and then enjoy a Scotch with him). When I think of any of these moments, I can't help but be eternally grateful for the epic life I have already enjoyed and the insane amount of fun that still awaits me.

At the time of the writing of this book, I'm also preparing to interview Cynthia Covey Haller, who is about to launch her co-authored book with her late father, Stephen R. Covey called *Live Life in Crescendo: Your Most Important Work is Always Ahead of You*. Isn't that just perfect? When I stop to think about just how many incredible experiences are ahead of me, I get lost in the wonder of this life and how damn lucky I am to be alive ... today ... in this moment in history. I share these as examples of what's possible when you live your legendary life. The world needs you to play full out and shine your Sage light as bright as you possibly can.

So I ask you, what's your North Star? What do you see as your purpose for being a coach? Yes, we touched on this earlier in the book, but how present is the answer for you? Can you immediately connect with it upon request? If not, perhaps it's time to write it down so that you have it handy and can reference it anytime you choose.

Getting Crystal Clear on Your Mission, Vision & Purpose

Simon Sinek asks us to *Start With Why*. Our vision for why we do what we do influences and drives every action we take. Our purpose for being begins with a vision that has us see the ultimate outcomes of our efforts. When you look past any immediate challenge or problem, what do you see? When you take your coaching business out five, 10, or 20 years or more into the future, what impact have you made in the world?

Remember when I shared the exercise from Stephen R. Covey about scripting out your funeral – your ultimate end? Who shows up? What do they say? This is all to help you see just how much you matter in the world and what impact you can have when you set your sights on making a difference. And you don't have to "change the world" in order to make a seismic shift in someone's life. You can help a single client be the best version of themselves and witness the ripple effect of that person on all the lives of their family, friends and community.

To get clear on your vision, you need only see possibility. Tony Robbins asks us not to allow the "tyranny of how" stop you from creating a powerful vision for your life. He's so right about that. When you obsess about *how* you do something, you can fall into the trap of never even starting. So, instead, use your creativity to imagine *what* is possible and *why* having that outcome would be so important to you and those you choose to serve.

Connecting with the big reason you're dedicating so much of your life to this thing called coaching will have you see the big picture. Your Sage already knows how precious your life is and why you matter, and sometimes your Saboteurs blind you to seeing the truth of just how powerful and important you are in the world. When you can see that the only person who can stop you is ... you guessed it ... **YOU**, then you won't allow anything to stand in your way – not even your self-sabotage.

Your mission is simple. To live your purpose and manifest your vision for your life. If you're not clear on your vision, then it's not possible to live your purpose. Conversely, when you *are* clear on your vision, the individual set-backs are trivial. In fact, they force you to slow down, learn valuable lessons and double your efforts and commitment to realizing your vision.

This is how you apply Sage Power Navigate to your coaching business. By taking the time to reflect on why your work in coaching truly matters today and decades into the future, you're paving your path forward toward the future you are committed to building for yourself and your niche.

What If I'm Lost?

When you experience darkness and are unable to navigate toward a clear path forward, then do the next best thing: take one step closer to the light. As dark as you may experience the world around you, the moment you realize it's your own Saboteurs that are blinding you, the veil over your eyes begins to fall away. As the light seeps through, the picture may not be clear, but you can see any that choice before you takes you closer to (or father from) the light.

Even if you're not clear on your path, you take one step closer to the light and immediately discover the next step is even easier to distinguish. That is, with each step closer to the light, your path becomes illuminated with more light. What keeps us in darkness is fear and the subsequent lack of any movement in any direction. Even if you take a step deeper into the darkness by mistake, you'll see that the (often very low-level) light has gone even more dim and you can reverse your course of action back towards the light.

Sometimes taking a step requires faith and intuition. You won't always "know" what's best. But as you begin to take steps, you receive feedback and that builds your momentum. Action leads to feedback which helps you further refine your next action.

At the End of Your Life Looking Back ...

When in doubt, it's helpful to tap into your future self. After doing a long PQ Gym session, connect with your wiser, older self with healthy mind and body. What have you accomplished in your coaching business? How many lives have you positively impacted through your work as a coach? See the indirect ripple effect not just for your clients, but their families, friends, and community members. See what happens in the world when more and more of the people you serve show up mentally fit and focused in their Sage selves.

Listen for the sounds of success. What do you hear? How does that sound support you in your coaching journey? Is there a smell that fires up your olfactory senses and anchors you in the powerful work you do in the world? Really allow all of your senses to connect to your wiser, older self and fully immerse yourself there. When you experience the incredible innate power of your Sage inside you, notice your deep desire to unleash that power into the world and the incredibly positive impact that can have.

At the end of your life looking back, you are as wise and powerful as any being on this earth. You live in abundance and have access to everything you need. In fact, everything you need is already within you. All that is needed is to realize this truth and allow your resourcefulness to well up inside you and guide you to where you need to go. As you trust your Sage, all fear evaporates. What's left is your interconnectedness with all beings and the incredible power that is generated from those connections as you do the work you were put on this earth to accomplish. That's the power of your Sage and knowing your purpose.

At the end of your life looking back, you'll have no regrets because you allow fear to neither stop or hinder you. You took your shot and did everything in your power to make the seismic impact you know you're capable of making in the world. Do that and you are unstoppable. Know you are meant for great things and don't allow your Saboteurs to keep you from the greatness already inside you. You already have all that you need. The path before you is inviting you to be your best self and live your best life. Answer the call of your Sage. Allow yourself to embrace all the gifts you've been given and maximize your contribution while you still have time to do so. This is your path. This is where the light shines brightest beckoning you to live a life of purposeful contribution.

Sage Power Activate Applied to Your Coaching Business

As Nike's advertising campaign so eloquently states, "Just Do It."

Sage Power Activate beckons you to act. It's not enough to simply "know" the path. It's the daily walking of the path that builds Sage mastery and leads to self-actualization. Remember as Stephen R. Covey has shared, "To know and not to do is not to know." I know that eating healthy food will ensure that I have the healthy and fit body I desire. To know that and not to actually eat healthy food is not to know it. My depth of knowing is limited because I've not taken committed action and utilized the depth of knowledge waiting for me.

The same is true in your coaching business. As we near the end of this book, you unquestionably "know" all of the knowledge that has been shared and can go back and re-read the most salient parts. But not taking action means you won't truly know any of this. Sure, you'll know it at an intellectual level, but until you take action, that's where it will stay – an idea or concept waiting to be acted upon.

I love it when at a Tony Robbins event, he says, "Don't judge me by the way my lips move, judge me by the way my feet move." Same concept. None of what I've shared would matter in the slightest if I hadn't already gone out and done the work myself. In today's self-publishing world, anyone can write a book and many do. You know who to listen to based on the results they have already achieved for themselves and their commitment to the world.

I have zero doubt about Stephen R. Covey's commitment to the world. He studied the habits of the most successful people he admired and discovered his *Seven Habits of Highly Effective People.* He then spent the rest of his life living these principles which lead to *The 8th Habit* where he highlighted the importance of everyone finding their own voice and encouraging others to do the same. Stopping at the voice-level, however, he knew would not be enough. Action was necessary for anyone's vision to become a reality.

The time has come to take action on your coaching business. To ensure the time you've spent with this book isn't wasted, it's time to apply what you believe you've learned. I say "believe" deliberately. Whatever you *think* you know is untested until you take action. That's when you discover what you *actually* know as your ideas are proven or disproven in a myriad of contexts.

Your coaching business is your blackbelt level dojo for Sage mastery. It's time to get out there on the mats and try out all the techniques you've learned. Soon you'll discover that you're thrown to the mats despite your best efforts. Getting back up, dusting yourself off and going again is how you develop mastery.

Same with riding a bike. You could read every manual on "how to ride a bike" and intellectually understand every aspect of the gears turning, wheels rotating and tires giving you traction. Until you wobble on that bike and fall over a few times, you don't really know how to ride a bike. For some coaches, that first fall is so "bad" that they refuse to try again. For others, just knowing it's possible (and even probable) that they will fall stops them from ever trying.

Not you. You're clear that these are all Saboteur-based fears and lies. Tapping into your Sage has you see clearly that setbacks are a natural part of the learning journey as you build, grow and scale your coaching business. Your journey has already begun. The opportunity to take action is all around you. Wherever in your coaching business you choose to focus your energy, that part will experience growth (as will your Sage).

Where Do I Focus My Energy?

Your Sage already intuitively knows this answer. The best place to focus your energy is listening to the Sage wisdom and insights already inside of you. You already know what needs attention in your coaching business. Sure, there may be some Saboteur fears around taking bold action in these areas, but the outcomes you seek require that you take some risks. When you allow fear to prevent you from taking action, you've allowed your Saboteurs to get in your way. Instead, do as many PQ Reps as you need to connect deeply with your Sage and simply listen to your innate wisdom. Then, as Nike urges us, "Just Do It!"

Where your focus goes, your energy can't help but flow. When you focus on fear, uncertainty and doubts, no action will be taken. Instead, when you focus on just how incredibly abundant your life is and the needs of your ideal customers, you'll take all the committed actions you need to be successful. Anytime you catch yourself feeling sorry for yourself or beating yourself up for making an inevitable mistake, redirect that focus to being of service to your niche. When you focus on the needs of your niche, you'll immediately see how you can add value and connect with their deepest needs. That's where to focus your energy for continued growth and unstoppable momentum.

What Do I Do When I Inevitably "Fall"?

Smile. Then acknowledge yourself for having the courage to try. Quiet your Saboteurs who are verbally beating you up and diminishing your efforts. Listen to your softer Sage voice offering insights and wisdom that will help you grow personally and professionally. Whatever mistake you made can be corrected. Start by acknowledging what went wrong – just the facts, not the Saboteur interpretations which often get piled on. What can you learn from this mistake? How can you apply this learning to be even more effective in the future? What Sage strength can you work on here? Might you need more empathy for yourself? Your niche? Or empathy for the situation you find yourself in? How would exploring this mistake deeper uncover even more lessons you can apply in the future? What are you inspired to do now that you have learned this valuable lesson?

You see, it's your "failures" (or, as I prefer to call them, your "lessons") that make you stronger and more resilient. We learn next to nothing from our successes, it's those really difficult situations that call forth our Sage to work through them. And work through them you will. Keep seeking the lessons and you'll find them everywhere. That's why I loved that phrase that "We grow through what we go through." There's tremendous growth in our set-backs. We need only open ourselves to what lessons are in front of us. They make us stronger, more resilient and ensure that we continue on our path towards self-actualization and Sage mastery.

How Do I Keep Going?

In order to keep going – even in the darkest times – keep connected to your Sage Navigate power. It's your vision, mission and purpose that will have you continue to take committed action despite any circumstance you find yourself in. When you connect to the truth that you are not your circumstances and that you are powerful beyond measure, you will see that any setback is simply there to test your resolve. How committed are you to reaching your desired outcome? Are you living your mission, vision and purpose?

It's easy to *say* what your committed to. Our true commitment is tested when the circumstances around us grow increasingly challenging. What are you willing to sacrifice in order to have the life you most deeply desire? What more are you willing to take action on to ensure that your vision is realized? To live your mission and align to your purpose in life is among the greatest gifts you will ever experience. This is your birthright, but you are not "entitled" to this life. You receive it by your committed actions that are in alignment with your purpose.

As you make the seemingly difficult choices, you eradicate the illusion that life needs to be hard. Sure, it can be, but when we take a good look at what makes anything hard, we can determine a simpler path of ease and flow. As we remove the barriers that stand in our way, we are clearing our path towards our own success.

Many years ago, I wrote on my whiteboard, "I live my Legendary Life as an example and permission for others to do the same." I put it there to remind me to live legendary. And that my living legendary shows all those who choose to pay attention that if I can do it, so can you. I wasn't born with wealth, power or influence. I experienced my own false sense of scarcity at a very early age and allowed my Saboteurs to drive me. When I saw the alternative path of the Sage, I pivoted to a life of ease and flow.

Live Your Legendary Life

That is my request of you. All you need is within you now. Your Sage knows this. Taking action on this deep-seated belief will ensure you live your legendary life. Living legendary means being in total alignment with your Sage and being committed to your own greatness. You were not born in this day and time to play small. You were given an extraordinary gift of life that has unlocked and will continue to unlock an unlimited number of gifts until the day you die.

In the next chapter we'll explore how you continue to find the gifts of your epic life everywhere you look and especially inside your coaching business. You have the power to change the lives of more people than you can even imagine. Your impact will ripple through the lives of your clients and positively impact their families, friends and community. Your Sage *contagion* is one of positive committed action that inspires those around you to live their best lives. And as Henry Ford said, "If you think you can, or you think you can't ... you're right!"

CHAPTER TWELVE

Sage Perspective: Finding the Gift

The Sage Perspective is that everything can be turned into a gift or opportunity. This is easy to remember when coaching others and easy to forget when working on the business end of your coaching business. What is the gift of your prospective ideal client saying no? What is the gift of your seemingly inability to generate new appointments on your calendar? What is the gift of a client dropping out and/or choosing to end their coaching engagement with you?

In this chapter, we're going to dig into these and other hard questions where the answers may not be immediately obvious when they are happening. Rather than waiting until the time that they do happen (as they inevitably will), this is your opportunity to anticipate the biggest challenges in growing and scaling your coaching business so that you can get out in front of them. By anticipating where you see your biggest struggles are likely to be, you can develop a plan for how you'll overcome them and actually be better because of them.

By going through these thought exercises now, you can pre-frame your Sage Power Activate. In this way, you are less likely to allow your Saboteurs to mess with you when these very normal and predictable events happen. Your plan of action designed now (ahead of these events) will prepare you for your adventure ahead. By seeing the biggest problems as nothing more than obstacles to overcome, you can remove all (or at least much) of the emotional attachment to them. What remains is a clear strategy to overcoming any obstacle that shows up on your way to designing your coaching business.

Jim Rohn, an early mentor of Tony Robbins, said it this way, "If you really want to do something you'll find a way. If you don't, you'll find an excuse." For me, the doingness comes after the beingness, so I'll say it slightly differently with the same underlying principle:

When you're committed, you find a way. When you're not committed, you find an excuse.

Sage Power Activate happens when you're fully committed to something ... no matter what. All of your Saboteur voices are the ones which quickly present all the alternative excuses you need to justify not taking action.

Some powerful questions and insights I've used when going deeper in this work have come from my early coaching mentors:

- "Are you designing your life or managing your circumstances?" asked Chad Cooper
- "Every time you open your mouth, you reveal your whole life," says Bettie Spruill
- "If your life were a movie, are you the main actor or are you playing the part of an extra?" asked Chad Cooper
- "Bold action beats great ideas seven days a week!" proclaims Tony Robbins

When in doubt, tap into the Sage Perspective; it will guide you along your journey so that you know what next action to take. And since there are three possible gifts to help you in your journey, let's apply each of them to the most common challenges you'll experience along your coaching journey.

Gift of Knowledge

Whenever you're feeling stuck, the gift of knowledge is a wonderful place to start. Ask yourself, "What am I learning from this experience?" Be mindful of the Saboteur knee jerk responses such as "Nothing!" "That I suck at this," and similar lies that reinforce the problem rather than illuminating possible solutions and ways forward.

It's helpful to align with the philosophy that there's no such thing as "failure" – you're either succeeding or learning. Either outcome leads to a growth mindset. Even as you succeed, it really helps to stay curious. "What's working right now? How might I replicate this success? What am I noticing about the actions I'm taking?"

Similarly, when your business isn't expanding in the ways you imagined, curiosity is still your greatest ally in revealing the lessons you have not yet learned or applied. The gift of knowledge is revealed when you are able to lean into the concept that "I am NOT my results. And results don't lie." I suspect it's beneficial to expand on that dialectic.

To say, "I am NOT my results," you are connecting to the truth that your efforts are just that – efforts, not the entirety of your being. You are not the sum total of the results you achieve, despite your Hyper-Achiever doing its best to convince you otherwise. When you see clearly that you are not your results, you can detach from the desire to have what you want in your coaching business for long enough to see clearly what's going on. That's the second part, "And results don't lie." What are my results telling me? What deeper knowledge can I tap into because of these results?

Let's use an example for illustration. In the context of the gift of knowledge, **what can we learn from your prospect saying no?** Here are several places to look:

- Is this prospect actually my ideal client or not?
- Is my irresistible offer actually irresistible enough?
- Did I ask open-ended pre-frame questions leading up to making my offer?
- Was my offer clear, concise and easy to understand?
- Did I use silence for impact and stop talking after I made my offer?
- Knowing that I likely need nine "Nos" in order to get one "Yes", can I accept this as one of my nine "Nos" that this is just part of the process and keep going?
- What, if anything, would I do differently the next time I have a discovery session?
- How can I apply what I'm learning to the next discovery session I have?
- Why is it important for me to learn from this experience and apply what I have learned?

Even as you read these questions, what other questions are formulating in your mind? See what happens naturally when you stay curious? As you get curious about what's really happening, you activate Sage Discernment rather than judgment from your Saboteurs. This is an important distinction and foundational to your learning journey. I'm sure you can come up with a whole list of questions that are NOT helpful and driven by your Saboteurs. Just for fun, imagine if you asked these questions instead:

- Why am I not successful?
- What is it that stops me from succeeding?
- How is it that success continues to elude me?

Notice that these questions assume you're not successful and when you look for evidence as to why, your brain will also fill in the answer – usually with lies, half-truths and limiting beliefs. Knowing that what you focus on, expands, this is a dangerous Saboteur-led question, so if you hear yourself say something like this, then STOP. Do PQ Reps and ask a better question.

The quality of your questions matters and is the key to unlocking your Sage Perspective; especially the Gift of Knowledge. When you choose to receive the gift of knowledge, it's important to go beyond basic understanding and challenge yourself to look deeper to see what you might not otherwise know.

The Three Circles of Knowledge

Imagine you have a dart board in front of you. The bullseye is that smallest circle right in the middle of the dart board. This first circle of knowledge is all that you know. These are the things you know that you know. For example, my name is Bill and I know that I know my name. Then, the next ring out is all the things I know that I don't know. I know that there is a whole language of Chinese that exists in the world and I know that I don't know how to speak Chinese. But what's so powerful is the next ring out. The third circle of knowledge is everything else. It's all the things I don't even know that I don't know. What's an example? Yes, that's a trick question.

But to illustrate the point, we can go back in history. There was a time when mobile phones didn't exist. Prior to their availability, someone was working feverishly in a lab somewhere trying to invent them. During that time, I didn't even know that I didn't know what a mobile phone was. Only after it was invented, could I become aware that I didn't know what a mobile phone was. Then, eventually, I learned what a mobile phone was and how useful it could be and it went from something I didn't even know I didn't know, to something I knew I didn't know, to something I know I know about and use every day of my life.

When we talk about the Gift of Knowledge, see if you can reach for that third circle. What's something you didn't even know you didn't know prior to having this happen to you? What can be revealed as part of remaining curious? If you are only coming up with the first circle of knowledge (i.e. the things I know I know), don't settle for a weak answer. Asking better questions will help you break through the first circle of knowledge and begin to identify the things you know you don't know and could surprise you with the third circle of knowledge. That's where the real breakthroughs happen. When you begin to discover the things you didn't even know that you didn't know, the Gift of Knowledge can be profound.

Looking back, I can see so many of the true Gifts of Knowledge I picked up along the way as I built my coaching business. For example, until I began working with large enterprise company clients, I didn't even know that I didn't know who was responsible for the hiring of coaches. I had (incorrectly) assumed that the executives I was having discovery calls with were both the sponsor and the client. I was wrong. An early Gift of Knowledge that I picked up was that much of the coaching budget was held by the Learning & Development team who are part of Human Resources group inside large companies.

Once I discovered that I didn't even know I didn't know who was the ultimate decision maker for which coaches get hired by a company, that changed the entire approach to how I enrolled executive clients. I began to treat my HR colleagues as the sponsors and saw a clear path to engaging them very differently from the executives I was working with. By separating the client role (the executives) from the sponsor role (the HR team) I was able to satisfy the needs of both audiences and my ability to enroll corporate clients went from slow and difficult to relatively fast and easy. I knew which audience needed which message and how to work with both.

For me, it was like driving a car with the emergency brake on and stuck in first gear. Technically, I was moving, but there was an awful squeaking noise and anytime I attempted to speed up, the engine was whining at me. The minute I took off the emergency brake and discovered how to shift into higher gears, the performance of my car improved dramatically. So get curious. If your coaching business is the car in this example, what proverbial gear are you currently in? What Gift of Knowledge would you need to have in order to shift into higher gears and take off the proverbial emergency brake?

The best part is that the Gift of Knowledge is just the first of three gifts. Rather than treating them separately, we can see how each of these gifts interconnect to substantially impact the power of your coaching business. Knowledge is just the first gift that can illuminate what to explore further, how to innovate differently, navigate clearly or what specific actions to take. With these in mind, let's dig into the next gift: The Gift of Power.

Gift of Power

When examining the gift of power, it's helpful to hold the perspective that life is happening FOR me, not TO me. That simple, yet profound notion changes how you feel about any challenging situation you will inevitably come across while building and scaling your coaching business. Rather than feeling defeated by one of your ideal customer prospects saying, "No", get curious about what muscles are being strengthened by the experience.

Rejection can lead to feeling sorry for yourself– that is, until you are able to hold a deeper understanding of the muscle strength you are building. Allow me to explain using a gym analogy. Imagine that you walk into your gym and see an extremely muscular person lifting hundreds of pounds. When he is done with his reps, you decide to give it a try. You can't even lift them once. Part of you knew that would be the outcome, but another part of you wanted to try anyway. Rather than being bummed out for the rest of the day, you simply remove the weights until you get to an amount you are confident you can lift. And just like that, you're back lifting the appropriate amount of weight for your current muscle strength.

Now let's apply that learning to your coaching business when one of your prospective ideal clients says "No." Notice that their decision not to hire you as their coach is just that – their decision. What muscles do you then need to work on in your mind to become stronger, not weaker, because of this event. Let's take a look at some of the option.

Powering Up Your Empathy Muscles

Rather than feeling the full weight of rejection and allowing it to prevent you from having the coaching business you desire, see the "No" as another weight in your mental gym. You can apply it to yourself, your prospective client and the situation you just experienced. By looking at all three, you begin to see just how valuable and important a prospective client saying "No" to you can be for you, them and the coaching business you desire.

Starting with empathy for yourself. Imagine how powerful will you become when you are committed to preventing a prospect's decision not to hire you from having any impact on you, your day and your feelings about yourself? Strengthening your empathy muscles will help you achieve just that. This is not the same thing as being in denial about the rejection or allowing your Hyper-Rational Saboteur to have you be void of any emotion at all. When you have deep empathy for yourself and your self-empathy muscles are truly strong, you can see that you are, in fact, doing your best given where you are in your journey. Rather than judging yourself, you give yourself empathy knowing that despite this unwelcome decision, you are proud of yourself for playing full out. Self-empathy removes any blinders used by your Saboteurs thereby allowing you to see the progress you're making (even before the first sale is made). You're taking the precise actions you need to take to succeed. Rather than feeling sorry for yourself, you acknowledge yourself for doing the work and get excited for your next call.

You can then turn your attention to strengthening your empathy muscles for your prospective client. Rather than judging them for saying no to you, turn it around. How courageous it must have been for your prospective client to be decisive in their decision *not* to hire you. Sometimes it's harder to say "No" to an offer than it is to receive that no. Feel the depth of that empathy for your prospect. To have had such a powerful coaching session with you and still have the courage to say "No" to your offer, took strength. Honor that decision with deep empathy for the person who made it. See that it was likely difficult for them to come to that decision and grow your empathy muscle towards them for making the best decision for where they are today.

Then you can turn to strengthening your empathy muscle for the entire enrollment process. This is not a situation that most people are excited to be in – on either side. Have empathy for you as the coach making the offer and your ideal customer prospect making the decision. This is a very necessary part of growing any business. And yet, for most people it's not all that enjoyable. Think about the last time you purchased a car. Were you excited about the prospect of going to the dealership and negotiating the deal? Probably not. See that every time you practice enrollment of a client, you are strengthening your empathy for the process of enrollment itself.

As legendary advertising man, David Oglivy used to say, "Nothing happens until the sale is made." It's true. Only after your prospective client says "Yes" can you support them as their coach. It's an important part of the process of building and scaling any coaching business. As you grow your empathy muscles toward the entire end-to-end process of enrollment, any reluctance you previously had about enrolling clients evaporates. What's left is a loving and joyful opportunity to support the people you care most about. When you detach from the decision itself and double down on your commitment to being in the service of your niche, you will feel very differently about enrollment. It truly can be a loving and joyful experience. Until it is, see the gift of power waiting for you here in your own empathy circuitry.

Powering Up Your Explore Powers

A question I often get is, "What's the difference between the gift of knowledge and the gift of power as it applies to Sage Explore powers?" Spending time examining the gift of knowledge naturally activates your Explore power. That said, it's helpful to see them as separate. When you are broadly sifting through all the gifts of knowledge available to you, it tends to be about asking questions and seeing what gifts can be generated. You're in full learning mode.

Powering up your Explore powers is different in that you become a fascinated anthropologist as you examine what took place. You are strengthening your own powers of observation as you look objectively at what happened. Specifically:

- What worked?
- What didn't work?
- What do I get to add / remove / modify for next time?

While the gift of knowledge is about asking probing questions and can often activate your Explore Powers, the gift itself is learning to be an objective observer of what "what is" versus what your Saboteurs would like you to interpret. It's the difference between "fact" and "interpretation" when reviewing your results. Let me illustrate:

> Fact: You had a discovery call and your prospect choose not to hire you.
> Interpretation: Your Judge lies to you and tells you that you're no good at enrollment and you'll never be able to successfully sell your coaching services.

Fact: One of your clients decided to wind down your work together.
Interpretation: Your Judge lies to you and tells you your prices are too high, your abilities as a coach are lacking, and you'll never be able to retain clients for very long.

Fact: Your website isn't producing appointments on your calendar.
Interpretation: Your Judge lies to you and tells you that your website is embarrassing and there's no chance it ever could generate appointments without investing tens of thousands of dollars with the latest marketing "expert."

Rather than allowing these false interpretations as "evidence" that you're terrible at what you do, you can continue strengthening your Explore power by remaining an objective observer who is just interested in the facts – not Saboteur interpretations of these facts. So, to strengthen your powers here, pull on the red thread connecting these facts to reveal what may really be going on. That looks something like the five whys technique.

Fact: A prospective client didn't hire you. *Why is that? (Focusing on facts only)*
Why #1: I don't qualify my calendar appointments to determine if they are my niche.
Why #2: I'm afraid that if I do, I'll push away people who could hire me.
Why #3: I'm just starting out and I really, really want to generate some clients.
Why #4: I'm afraid of failing. I don't want to look foolish for being a coach who is unable to generate enough clients to stay in business.
Why #5: I've failed before and I don't want to repeat that mistake again.

By being honest with yourself, you can reveal some truths that will point you to what's really not working. In this example, the coach's fear of failure was becoming a self-fulfilling prophecy. That wasn't obvious by the surface fact of a client not hiring them. However, as a fascinated anthropologist, you can just keep digging deeper and deeper to find the core of the issue.

For most coaches, our Saboteurs are strong and deeply entrenched. Our fears are not always present, but they impact our work. Until we live in ease and flow with our Sage self, our Saboteurs will find ways to hold us back and have us play small. Growing our Explore powers will help us uncover powerful gifts that we can work on and continuously improve.

How empowering would it be to *know* that deep down you're terrified of failing and so you are risk-adverse all but ensuring your failure? When your Sage discernment realizes that mistakes are inevitable (and not only recoverable, but also incredibly valuable) the fear dissipates. You're willing to take bigger calculated risks knowing that what Nelson Mandela says is true, "I never lose. I either win or I learn."[64]

The gifts of knowledge are powerful. Even more powerful are your mental muscle and resilience that are built when you can learn to use the Sage Power Explore to *objectively* review what happened – just the facts. This muscle development will allow you to learn faster and more accurately and then trust that you can act on what you have discovered. Once your Sage muscles are strong enough to separate facts from interpretations, you will see clearly what action you must take next as you continuously improve.

Powering Up Your Innovate Powers

When it comes to growing and scaling your coaching business, your Sage Innovate powers can be your best friend. Your pure essence Sage-self lives in the quantum realm – the field of all possibilities. You truly can "Yes, and …" yourself out of any problem or challenge you find yourself in. Isn't that wild? When you power up your Sage, you are literally unstoppable. There is nothing – no single problem or circumstance – that you can't innovate a solution to. How freeing is that?

Sure, those Saboteurs may be challenging this and rolling their eyes here, but your Sage knows this is true. You are the 1% – literally:

> "Every human on planet Earth is made up of millions and millions of atoms which all are 99% empty space. If you were to remove all of the empty space contained in every atom in every person on planet earth and compress us all together, then the overall volume of our particles would be smaller than a sugar cube."[65]

So, if you're made up of 99% empty space, then you are the field of all possibilities. That's why your Sage is infinitely creative. You need only allow your subconscious to go to work for you to solve any problem you can identify. Even when you're spouting off ideas that sound far-fetched and crazy, there's always a solid 10% of that idea that's not only possible, but could break through the precise problem you currently face.

It's our limiting beliefs that stop us from having everything we desire in this lifetime. And, as we remove our desires, we find that our beingness is more than enough. That is to say:

---

[64] https://www.quotespedia.org/authors/n/nelson-mandela/i-never-lose-i-either-win-or-learn-nelson-mandela/

[65] https://interestingengineering.com/science/due-to-the-space-inside-atoms-you-are-mostly-made-up-of-empty-space

All I need is within me now!

The moment you live into this truth, you will stop seeking the answers "out there" and trust that everything you need is already inside of you. Sage Power Innovate is there to help you pull it from inside of you onto paper, a whiteboard or computer screen so that you can give birth to the innovation that's always been there waiting for you to discover it.

Think about that for a moment. Every word of this book came from inside of me. What's amazing is that every day when I sit down to write, about a thousand or so words flow from me from "somewhere." As I write, I'm connected to my Sage and allowing him to speak to you. As my thoughts flow, so do my fingers to generate something from nothing.

You do this all the time. Every email you send. Every LinkedIn post, comment and share. Anything you give your energy to receives your power. So why would you willingly give your energy to your problems? Instead, give your energy to generating innovative solutions to any problem you face. Don't dwell on the problem. State it as clearly as you can, then enter the quantum field of all possibilities as you allow the answers to flow from within you.

That's why I love Sage Power Innovate so much. The gift of strengthening your Innovate power is that you tap your own source. For some this is a spiritual experience. For others, it's becoming supernatural. And for others who "don't believe in that woo woo crap" it's the grounded and powerful connection you have inside of you – who cares how it got there?

Remember, we're all on our individual journeys towards self-actualization. Some are just starting and others are already pretty far along. But regardless of where you are in your individual journey, growing your Sage Innovate Power is what will bring you so much joy and happiness in your coaching business. When you internalize that you can handle any problem that comes your way, you feel like a superhero – like your childhood self playing the ultimate game of make believe. Whatever it is for you, it's really fun and enjoyable.

With that as your context, what will you do the next time a prospect says no? Or a client winds down their work with you? Or something else "bad" happens in your coaching business? These are gifts (often well disguised) waiting for you to open them. As you play the "Yes, and ..." game on any of these problems, you soon will see you are so much more powerful than any individual circumstance. It's just like drawing a bum card from a board game. Who cares, right? It's a temporary set-back at worst and at best it's another weight in your mental fitness gym that will strengthen you and shape you so that you can be the amazing coach you are destined to be.

Powering Up Your Navigate Powers

Another way to reframe when things don't go your way in your coaching business is to further strengthen your Sage Navigate Power by recommitting to your vision, mission and purpose. Remember at the beginning of this chapter, I shared, "When you're committed, you find a way. When you're not committed your find an excuse." Finding that way is much easier when you have a clear focus on your ultimate outcome. This is your north star and each time you reconnect with it you strengthen your own Sage Navigate power.

By focusing and channeling negative feelings on your short-term setback, you erode your broader and more vital connection to why you're doing all of this in the first place. One possible gift in the setback is to have you double down on your commitment to your coaching practice by realigning with your vision, mission and purpose.

Imagine that your coaching business is a car and you're driving it towards your desired outcome. When you see, clear as day, what you're up to and why your niche needs you to succeed, the short-term setback is nothing more than a pothole in the otherwise newly paved road to your future. Why allow yourself to hit that pothole so hard that you blow out a tire and need to pull over from the road you were on? Where your focus goes your energy flows, so why focus on the pothole when you can focus on where the road is leading you – towards your ultimate outcome.

I remember hearing the craziest story about this desert road in the middle of nowhere. For miles in every direction, there's nothing but barren desert. But along the side of the road there is a series of telephone poles that cross the same desert. Cars tend to speed through this barren flat land. And occasionally, the road turns. What's astounding is just how many cars are totaled in the middle of nowhere as they crash into a random telephone pole. An inquiry showed that the drivers weren't asleep or intoxicated. It turns out that the thought, "Don't hit that telephone pole" began in the backs of their minds and the more they focused on *not* hitting the telephone pole, sooner or later they actually did. The slightest swerve in either direction no matter how fast the car was going and they'd veer off the road onto the sand with no damage. But time and time again, drivers that smashed into a telephone pole shared a similar story of attempting to avoid hitting it.

The more we focus on something, the more we give energy to it. Where are you placing the bulk of your focus today? Are you reinforcing the vision of being a powerful six or seven-figure coach who supports their niche in achieving their most important outcomes? Or are you obsessed with why your coaching business hasn't taken off or scaled to the level you want?

Sometimes, you can't help it. Inevitably you *will* hit potholes. But the severity of the damage left by that pothole depends on how blindsided you were by it and how much you focus on the damage it caused. When you keep your attention on the road ahead, these potholes are but a minor inconvenience. Even when you must pull over and change a tire, you remain committed to your journey and excited to get back on the road doing your thing.

Each time you experience a setback in your coaching business, there is a gift there of strengthening your Sage Navigate power by using the setback to double down on your commitment to your vision, mission and purpose. Having a clear picture in your mind as to why your coaching business is vital to your niche and delivering a positive impact in the world will see you through any challenge that crops up for you.

At a mastery level, you become grateful for these setbacks. They give you an invitation to pause, reflect and recommit to your goal. Rather than being deterred by them, you welcome these setbacks as opportunities for your own personal growth and development. Each setback reminds you of why you are doing the work you're doing. Instead of being annoyed, angry, frustrated and feeling resentment, you see this as nothing more than a reminder to strengthen your Sage Navigate power and confirm that you're still headed in the direction of your ultimate desired outcome. If you're not headed in the right direction, feel free to course correct so that you are. If so, enjoy the ride!

Powering Up Your Activate Powers

And the final gift of power comes in the form of Activate. Not every setback in your coaching business will require action. But for those that do, this is an opportunity to strengthen your resolve towards action. Setbacks in your coaching business have a way of triggering your amygdala (your fight, flight or freeze response). How many times have you found yourself "frozen" when something "bad" happens? This inability to act can lead toward a downward spiral of inaction. Equally problematic is the flight response where you are taking action in the opposite direction.

Rather than allowing fear, anxiety and other negative emotions to settle in, you have another choice. You can strengthen your Sage Power Activate. Taking immediate action in the areas where you have agency, power and control feels amazing. Rather than going off to a corner and licking your proverbial wounds, you acknowledge the setback and take action where you can.

Action for action's sake isn't what we're going for. In the context of your coaching business, you're looking at what actions you could take that would remedy the setback. For example, when a prospect declines to hire you, identify what actions you could take to generate more discovery calls so that you can increase the number of offers you make to your ideal customer prospects. When a client winds down their work with you, you can take actions that would generate more qualified appointments on your calendar.

The power comes from the act of taking actions – regardless if these individual actions would mitigate the setback itself. The gift is in the actions themselves. They will either bring you closer to the outcomes you want or they will generate incredibly valuable feedback on what's not working so that you can correct course as needed.

Either way, you won't have the time to dwell on the nine "Nos" you received when you're onboarding the next client who chooses to say "Yes!" As soon as you've had your completion session with a client you've had for some time, it's time to channel that new time toward acquiring your next client – perhaps at a higher financial commitment. Again, you won't have time to dwell on a previous client when you're onboarding your new client who has chosen to hire you at an even better rate than the previous client was paying you.

Strengthening your Sage Power Activate ensures you keep momentum going in the right directly despite any circumstances that show up in your space. Remember, only you can stop you from having the coaching business of your dreams. The more focused and strategic action steps you take toward your desired outcome, the faster you speed up your success. More of the right actions taken toward your desired outcome increases your probability of success. If you only have one prospective client on your calendar this week, then their decision to hire you matters a great deal more than when you have 10 bookings. More action tends to lead toward more opportunities while, at the same time, growing and shaping your abilities to succeed.

Said another way, "success begets more success." Early on you may find it difficult to land your first client. It may discourage you and make you want to give up. But with each client win, something inside of you changes. You stop believing the lies of your Saboteurs and you gain the confidence you need to keep going no matter what. This is gift! As you strengthen your Sage Power Activate, you are taking more and more actions that lead to greater and greater success in your coaching business. With each action, you learn, you grow and you expand your practice. Inaction does the opposite. That's the gift of strengthening your Sage Power Activate applied to your coaching business.

Gift of Inspiration

The Sage Perspective that everything can be turned into a gift and opportunity need not be directly correlated to your coaching business. The gift of inspiration means that whatever "bad thing" that happens in your coaching business can be the seed of inspiration – even *outside* your coaching business.

For example, let's say that a client decides to wind down their work with you. Upon deeper reflection, you see that you hadn't built the kind of relationship you truly wanted with this particular client. The gift of inspiration might be to channel that deep desire for having epic relationships in your life towards your spouse or a family member. Your inspiration to improve your relationships need not be siloed into your coaching business. An event in your coaching business can lead to inspiration outside and have a positive impact in all that you do.

And while the gift of inspiration may have been channeled outside your coaching business, see how it always returns back there. Imagine for a moment that you were struggling with your relationship with your spouse. You knew there was another level that would invite deeper love and connection than you were experiencing. You are inspired to make that change and work on bringing your Sage into the relationship more and catch your Saboteur interference. After a few months you are certain that you've accomplished what you were inspired to do. Your relationship with your spouse has never been better. Watch what happens in your coaching business now.

With your heart full of love, joy and happiness, you show up differently in every aspect of your coaching business. You notice that generating appointments has somehow become "easier." When talking to your ideal customer prospects, you observe that you're going deeper into the work than you've gone previously, and when it comes to time to enroll them into your coaching business, you notice more people saying yes than before. What's going on?

You've activated your Sage contagion. With your own heart full and your own emotional batteries all charged up you have become a magnet attracting your niche into your coaching business. They witness you living your life in Sage and they want what you have. Nothing seems to get you down. Everything associated with you appears in alignment with who you are and what you're up to in the world. Who wouldn't want to have that in their life?

That's the power of the gift of inspiration. When you are so inspired to make a powerful shift in your life, it really doesn't matter what you are inspired to shift so much as the shift itself. This can be personal or professional. Any part of you that feels "out of alignment" can be an invitation to deepen your own Sage in some meaningful way. As you inspire yourself to go deeper in this work, everyone around you notices – especially your niche. When they see just how authenticly you are living your life, they are attracted to who you are as a person (not just what you do as a coach).

There truly is nothing more enticing than witnessing another human being living their best life. As you move towards self-actualization and Sage Mastery, your daily actions really do feel easier and in flow with what you are up to in the world, and that shines a bright light on the paradox and lies of your Saboteurs. Your Saboteurs will have you believe that life needs to be hard and difficult. Society honors all the "hard work" and "resilience" that entrepreneurs embody. Yet how many of those same entrepreneurs burn out? The proverbial "grind" is as difficult as it is unnecessary.

When you walk the path of the Sage, you do it in ease and flow. The gift of inspiration is about using any and all perceived obstacles as beautiful gifts to propel you forward rather than set you back. Where I used to fear and avoid obstacles, I now seek them out. I no longer imagine them as hurdles making my journey harder. I visualize them as boosts that empower me to go twice as fast as I was previously going.

This is the paradox of the challenges and obstacles you uncover in your coaching business. At first, they seem like deterrents from what you deeply desire. As you learn to trust yourself and your inner wisdom, they become important strategic lessons that support you in doubling down on your successful outcomes. They weren't put there to stop you. They are an incredible gift waiting to be discovered, understood and applied to your personal growth and, by extension, the growth of your coaching business.

Afterall, what is your coaching business, but a full embodiment and extension of you? As you continue to do your own personal development, your lessons will show up inside your coaching business and reflect your core values and principles applied to your niche.

One Last Gift

You did it! I'd like to take this moment to acknowledge you for completing this book. I have poured a combination of my last 30 years of business expertise with the past four years I've spent with Shirzad Chamine. I trust that you have a deep understanding of what *Sage Business Development* is all about: YOU!

When you are committed to walking the path of the Sage, your journey is one of continued learning, growth and mastery. While we believe we are seeking a final destination, as we walk the path of the Sage we discover it's the journey itself that is the gift. Who we become on this journey is profoundly more important than whatever destinations we visit along the way.

You were born Sage. Walking the path of the Sage is your destiny and your birthright. You need not seek permission from anyone. Along your path you will find extremely helpful guides and false prophets alike. Trust your inner wisdom to know the difference. Inevitably, you'll be misled and veer off your Sage path – either by your own Saboteurs or others you choose to walk besides in your journey. I invite you to see these detours as their own gifts of knowledge, power and inspiration.

We are destined to repeat our "mistakes" as frequently and as often as we need to in order to learn the powerful lessons the universe is committed to having us learn. As you embrace the perfectly imperfect human being you are, may you give yourself grace for where you are at any point in your journey. Your Saboteurs are in a rush to have you "complete" your journey and arrive at specific destinations. Your Sage knows this is your life's work, so enjoy the journey for the sake of the journey itself.

When you find yourself climbing a steep incline or feel stuck and not sure where to go next, allow your Sage to continue to guide you. Sometimes slowing down is the best strategy for speeding up. At all times, continue to check-in with yourself. As you notice your own feelings and emotions, allow your inner wisdom to support you on your way. Remember that all you need is within you now. As you allow your inner wisdom to surface, trust that you'll make the best decisions in the moment. Even when you make the "wrong" decision, seek the gift to turn it into a powerful learning lesson you need not repeat in the future.

Thank you for spending so much time with me. I honor your commitment to finish what you started. I trust our paths will cross again in the future. I love you. I appreciate you. The Sage in me honors and recognizes the Sage in you. Thank you for doing the incredible work that you do in the world. We are all better because of your continued commitment to the niche you serve as well as your commitment to bring mental fitness into the world. I am inspired by what it will be like when most human beings are mentally fit and allow their Sage to lead. What an incredible world we get to create together. Thank you!

ASKBILL.US
https://app.AskBill.us

Perhaps the greatest advancement in technology since the internet is artificial intelligence (AI). And yet, the most popular platforms can surface inaccurate answers simply by the nature of where the AI is trained to source its content.

You are invited to incorporate everything you are learning in this book and *apply it to your business today* **for free**. AskBill.us is my AI engine that only accesses my content (not the internet or other third-party content). The answers you get back will "feel" like you're talking to me because I trained this platform exclusively on my content. Cool, right?

Books are awesome. And they are limited to delivering the 20% insights we all need. To extract the full value of your time investment in this book, you need the 80% muscle building that puts all these tried and proven insights to work for YOU. Otherwise, this book might scratch your curiosity itch, but it will in no way deliver you the financial freedom you desire *unless* you follow up with your plan of action.

And, of course, if you're more interested in hiring the *real* Bill Carmody either as your coach, as part of a specific training, an upcoming keynote or for a business-trajectory-changing VIP Day, the best way to do that is to visit my website which is my name BillCarmody.com (i.e. https://www.BillCarmody.com).

ACKNOWLEDGMENT NOTE

T his book would not be possible without the abundant love of my wife, Elena, and my kids Will and Violet. Thank you for supporting me and giving me the space I needed to write this book. To Tony Robbins, Rich Litwin, Kendal SummerHawk, Peter Cook, Suzanne Evans, Grant Cardone, Peter J. Reding, Chad Cooper, and Shirzad Chamine. Each of you has taken the time to mentor me when I needed it most. I am eternally grateful for your pointing me in the right direction. To Doug James, I would not be here today without your ongoing support as my coach. Thank you for coaching actual rock stars and still making time for me. And to my fellow Firekeepers, Sue Mann and David Fisher – thank you for your daily accountability support and weekly check-ins to ensure I completed what I started. Without you, this book would have remained inside of me rather than available to the coaches who need it most.

ABOUT BILL CARMODY

TEDx Speaker | Bestselling Author | Chief Coaching Officer for Positive Intelligence

Bill Carmody is the Chief Coaching Officer for Positive Intelligence, which in 2023 was named the 567th fastest growing private company in the United States according to Inc Magazine. Together with CEO Shirzad Chamine, Bill has supported more than 100,000 coaches globally in becoming mentally fit through our coaching grant program. (see PositiveIntelligence.com/100x).

Bill Carmody is also responsible for the creation and rollout of the *Sage Business Development* program and has a passion for supporting coaches in eradicating scarcity and tapping into their infinite abundance so that they can elevate the business end of their coaching business.

Bill has had some epic adventures. From becoming a Top 100 sales influencer to standing next to Tony Robbins as he rang the opening bell for NASDAQ to dropping 50 pounds and finishing in the top 50% in his first 140.6 mile Ironman. He was even flown to Brazil to interview Sir Richard Branson. Bill's pronouns are he, him, his and he is a Diversity, Equity, Inclusion + Belonging Ally-in-Training.

Bill Carmody founded and successfully exited two highly profitable and award-winning multimillion-dollar marketing agencies. With 30 years of marketing experience, he has been in the digital marketing industry since its inception in 1994. Bill Carmody built the first commercial websites for AT&T, CBS, MasterCard and Coors Brewing Company.

The purpose of Bill's life is to be an inspirational leader who solves problems and creates breakthroughs for himself and others. His second book, the *Three Rules of Marriage*, is a bestseller, and his TEDx talk on the power of storytelling has been watched by nearly 25,000 people.

Bill Carmody is a former columnist for Inc, Entrepreneur and Forbes Magazines, having written over 350 articles. He has spoken at dozens of industry conferences across the globe and has had the opportunity to interview many high-profile industry professionals such as Tony Robbins, Sir Richard Branson, Malcolm Gladwell, Stephen M. R. Covey, Seth Godin, Rich Litvin, Grant Cardone, Jeffrey Gitomer, Tim Sanders and many others.

Bill is a highly sought after trainer and a well-seasoned Professional Certified Coach (PCC) with the International Coaching Federation (ICF). He works with world-changing visionaries who are brave enough to build a better future. You are in good hands with Bill. He's here to support you in achieving your deeply desired outcomes. For more information, connect with him on LinkedIn (https://www.linkedin.com/in/billcarmody/), BillCarmody.com or ThreeRulesofMarriage.com

The B Corp Movement

Dear reader,

Thank you for reading this book and joining the Publish Your Purpose community! You are joining a special group of people who aim to make the world a better place.

What's Publish Your Purpose About?

Our mission is to elevate the voices o en excluded from traditional publishing. We intentionally seek out authors and storytellers with diverse backgrounds, life experiences, and unique perspectives to publish books that will make an impact in the world.

Beyond our books, we are focused on tangible, action-based change. As a woman- and LGBTQ+-owned company, we are com- mitted to reducing inequality, lowering levels of poverty, creat- ing a healthier environment, building stronger communities, and creating high-quality jobs with dignity and purpose.

Certified

B

Corporation

As a Certified B Corporation, we use business as a force for good. We join a com- munity of mission-driven companies building a more equitable, inclusive, and sustainable global economy. B Corporations must meet high standards of trans- parency, social and environmental performance, and accountability as determined by the nonprofit B Lab. The certification process is rigorous and ongoing (with a recertification requirement every three years).

How Do We Do This?

We intentionally partner with socially and economically disadvantaged businesses that meet our sustainability goals. We embrace and encourage our authors and employee's differences in race, age, color, disability, ethnicity, family or marital status, gender identity or expression, language, national origin, physical and men- tal ability, political affiliation, religion, sexual orientation, socio-economic status, veteran status, and other characteristics that make them unique.

Community is at the heart of everything we do—from our writing and publishing programs to contributing to social enterprise nonprofits like reSET (https://www. resetco.org/) and our work in founding B Local Connecticut.

We are endlessly grateful to our authors, readers, and local community for being the driving force behind the equitable and sustainable world we are building together.

To connect with us online, or publish with us, visit us at www.publishyourpurpose.com.

Elevating Your Voice,

Jenn T. Grace

Jenn T. Grace
Founder, Publish Your Purpose

www.ingramcontent.com/pod-product-compliance
Lightning Source LLC
Chambersburg PA
CBHW040137200326
41458CB00025B/6299